D1288684

FLORIDA STATE
UNIVERSITY LIBRARIES

APR 28 1998

TALLAHASSEE, FLORIDA

Critical Models *Interventions and Catchwords*

European Perspectives

EUROPEAN PERSPECTIVES

A Series in Social Thought and Cultural Criticism
Lawrence D. Kritzman, Editor

European Perspectives presents English translations of books by leading European thinkers. With both classic and outstanding contemporary works, the series aims to shape the major intellectual controversies of our day and to facilitate the tasks of historical understanding.

Julia Kristeva	*Strangers to Ourselves*
Theodor W. Adorno	*Notes to Literature*, vols. 1 and 2
Richard Wolin, editor	*The Heidegger Controversy*
Antonio Gramsci	*Prison Notebooks*, vols. 1 and 2
Jacques LeGoff	*History and Memory*
Alain Finkielkraut	*Remembering in Vain: The Klaus Barbie Trial and Crimes Against Humanity*
Julia Kristeva	*Nations Without Nationalism*
Pierre Bourdieu	*The Field of Cultural Production*
Pierre Vidal-Naquet	*Assassins of Memory: Essays on the Denial of the Holocaust*
Hugo Ball	*Critique of the German Intelligentsia*
Gilles Deleuze and Félix Guattari	*What Is Philosophy?*
Karl Heinz Bohrer	*Suddenness: On the Moment of Aesthetic Appearance*
Alain Finkielkraut	*The Defeat of the Mind*
Julia Kristeva	*New Maladies of the Soul*
Elisabeth Badinter	*XY: On Masculine Identity*
Karl Löwith	*Martin Heidegger and European Nihilism*
Gilles Deleuze	*Negotiations, 1972–1990*
Pierre Vidal-Naquet	*The Jews: History, Memory, and the Present*
Norbert Elias	*The Germans*
Louis Althusser	*Writings on Psychoanalysis: Freud and Lacan*
Elisabeth Roudinesco	*Jacques Lacan: His Life and Work*
Ross Guberman	*Julia Kristeva Interviews*
Kelly Oliver	*The Portable Kristeva*
Pierra Nora	*Realms of Memory: The Construction of the French Past*, vol. 1: *Conflicts and Divisions*, vol. 2: *Traditions*, vol. 3: *Symbols*
Claudine Fabre-Vassas	*The Singular Beast: Jews, Christians, and the Pig*

Critical Models *Interventions and Catchwords*

Theodor W. Adorno

*Translated and with a Preface
by Henry W. Pickford*

Columbia University Press *New York*

HN
16
.A3313
1998

The Press gratefully acknowledges a grant from Inter Nationes toward costs of translating this work.

Columbia University Press
Publishers Since 1893
New York   Chichester, West Sussex
Eingriffe: Neun kritische Modelle copyright © 1963 by Suhrkamp Verlag, Frankfurt am Main
Stichworte: Kritische Modelle 2 copyright © 1969 by Suhrkamp Verlag, Frankfurt am Main
Translation copyright © 1998 Columbia University Press
All rights reserved
Library of Congress Cataloging-in-Publication Data
Adorno, Theodor W., 1903–1969.
    [Eingriffe. English]
    Critical models : interventions and catchwords / Theodor W. Adorno ;
    translated and with a preface by Henry W. Pickford.
        p.   cm. — (European perspectives)
    Includes bibliographical references and index.
    ISBN 0–231–07634–7
        1. Social history—20th century.   2. Social sciences—Philosophy.
    I. Adorno, Theodor W., 1903–1969. Stichworte. English.   II. Title.
    III. Series.
    HN16.A3313   1998
    301'.01—dc21   97–39500

∞

Casebound editions of Columbia University Press books are printed on permanent and durable acid-free paper.
Printed in the United States of America
c 10 9 8 7 6 5 4 3 2 1

Contents

Preface

Translators are the post-horses of
enlightenment.

— *Pushkin*

The present volume is a critical edition of the
two essay collections Adorno subtitled "critical models" and is based on
the texts in the second part of volume 10 of his collected writings
(*Gesammelte Schriften: Kulturkritik und Gesellschaft II*, edited by Rolf
Tiedemann [Frankfurt: Suhrkamp, 1977]). *Eingriffe: Neun kritische
Modelle*, was published in 1963 as volume 10 in the series *edition suhrkamp*; although Adorno had corrected the galleys, the second volume,
Stichworte: Kritische Modelle 2, did not appear until shortly after his
unexpected death in 1969, as volume 347 in *edition suhrkamp*. Also
included here from volume 10 of the collected writings are two very late
essays, "Critique" and "Resignation," which Adorno had set aside for an
eventual third volume of "critical models," and an introduction to the
lecture "The Meaning of Working Through the Past." Finally, this edition provides a translation of the discussion between Adorno and his
audience when he first gave this lecture; the discussion transcript was
included in the essay's initial publication though not in the subsequent
book edition or in the collected writings. This document offers a vivid
portrait of Adorno in the role of public intellectual, explicating himself ad
hoc about what could be considered the practical motive of these essays:
to promote political maturity by bringing reified consciousness to self-
awareness. The purposefulness of that intention transcends the contingency of the occasions for which Adorno wrote many of these texts.

For the context underlying the genesis and development of these essays is Adorno's enormous role as a public philosopher and cultural critic following his return to Germany in 1949. Indeed, with the publication of *Minima Moralia* in 1951 Adorno became virtually a popular author; in a letter to his friend and early mentor, Siegfried Kracauer, he ascribed his surprising success to a fortunate conjunction of a general cultural vacuum and the waning interest in Heideggerian themes and reveled in the freedom his new fame afforded him.[1] And in 1963 he wrote with a mixture of pride and astonishment to his old friend that a paperback edition of *Prisms* (1955) was printed with a run of 25,000 copies, while *Interventions* appeared with an initial run of 18,000 copies; by 1969 the former was in its third edition and the latter had 33,000 copies.[2] This popularity reflects Adorno's resumption of the journalistic activities in mass print and radio he had pursued so robustly before the war.[3] Incomplete documentation indicates that between 1950 and 1969 Adorno participated in more than 160 radio programs. While the medium of course lent itself to Adorno's reflections on music, the overwhelming majority of his contributions was broadly intellectual, just as most of the essays collected here began as radio lectures. The Adorno emerging here is a far cry from the stereotypical mandarin aesthete; as his editor at Hessischer Rundfunk in Frankfurt recounts, Adorno told him:

> "I want to be understood by my listeners" . . . [Adorno] thought that I, as "an expert," knew better how to achieve that. It was, surprisingly, of the utmost importance that he be understood even and especially in a medium of the "culture industry." The sound technicians who were responsible for recording him afterward had to repeat spontaneously and in their own words what he had said, and often there ensued a discussion that was much better and more comprehensible than the lecture he had just read into the microphone. We had to take care that when he came to the radio station, there were appropriate sound technicians who were able to justify their answers to him. It was preferable to postpone a session rather than Adorno having to forego the important discussion afterward with our assistant. Once we recorded one such discussion between Adorno and his sound technician without him or her noticing, and then played it back to them. He found himself "surprisingly good," which meant a great deal in consideration of his demanding conceit, his pronounced skepticism toward the mass media, and his general aversion for organizations and institutions that shape opinion.[4]

Although at times he seemed to dismiss these lectures as modest bagatelles and occasional pieces quickly dispatched,[5] Adorno neverthe-

less conscientiously reworked and published them, primarily in popular
journals, which were read by well-educated citizens and those in positions of cultural and political authority, before finally collecting them in
the new inexpensive paperback book form. His engagement in the mass
media was a logical consequence of his eminently practical intentions to
effect change.[6] The concrete recommendations incorporated into several
of these essays were meant as direct "interventions"; for example, along
with other leading cultural figures Adorno was asked in 1969 for his position on the continued illegality and persecution of homosexuality in
West Germany. The published anthology of responses included these
introductory remarks to an extract from the essay "Sexual Taboos and
Law Today":

> Kindest thanks for your lovely letter. What I have to say on the
> topic of sexual morality, in the most diverse spheres of the harm
> that it wreaks, can be found in the essay "Sexual Taboos and Law
> Today" in *Interventions*, and in "Morals and Criminality" in the
> third volume of *Notes to Literature*. Both works I sent immediately
> to Dr. Heinemann as soon as he took over the Ministry of Justice,
> asking him to read them in the context of plans to reform the penal
> law, and I received an extremely friendly response. At the moment
> I wouldn't know what to add to what I have written there. That I
> most fiercely oppose every kind of sexual repression should in the
> meantime be more or less common knowledge, which I gladly con-
> firm explicitly to you.[7]

In these essays perhaps more than anywhere else in his compendious
oeuvre are the practical and political motivations of Adorno's thought
most visibly at work.

Those motivations in turn shape the structure and style of "critical
models": specific analyses that tactically employ the negative dialectical
strategy he expounded and exemplified with three "thought models" in
Negative Dialectics, by which a phenomenon or concept pretending to
self-sufficient immediacy is discursively unmasked as a societally mediated, historical result. Present conditions are shown to contradict the
reigning ideology, and—rather than being discarded for not representing
reality—the ideology is taken 'at its word', as the as yet unfulfilled
promise of its realization.[8] When Adorno upholds that "the element of
the *homme de lettres*, disparaged by a petty bourgeois scientific ethos, is
indispensable to thought," he is invoking a German tradition in neo-
Marxist essayism that effloresced in the Weimar Republic but that
reaches back via Nietzsche to the figure of the French Enlightenment
moralist and the discursive form of the nonsystematic critique, as in

Voltaire's *Philosophical Dictionary*; in an analogy he repeats in his introduction to *Catchwords*, Adorno says of negative dialectics that "thinking
as an encyclopedia, rationally organized and nonetheless discontinuous,
unsystematic, loose, expresses the self-critical spirit of reason."[9]

As a critical edition, this book provides an apparatus operating in a
number of registers. Adorno's footnotes appear at the bottom of the page,
as in the original. The translator's notes are intended for variable use and
presume the educated general audience Adorno sought to engage. Contemporary cultural, political, and philosophical allusions are glossed, and
particular linguistic ramifications of the translation vis-à-vis the original
are discussed. Cross-references to Adorno's other writings refer to his
collected works (*Gesammelte Schriften* edited by Rolf Tiedemann with
Gretel Adorno, Susan Buck-Morss and Klaus Schultz [Frankfurt: Suhrkamp, 1970–1986]) with the abbreviation *GS* followed by volume number and English translations where available. Variant texts of original
radio broadcasts and earlier published versions are also indicated; while
some of these variants are more substantial and telling than others, the
criterion of completeness was followed. Adorno often reworked an essay
a dozen times, and the notes provide a convenient means to follow the
changes he made in public redactions to suit argument and occasion.[10]
Unless otherwise indicated, translations of German materials in the
notes are mine.

This translation strives to convey as much of the syntactic density and
semantic idiosyncrasy of Adorno's style as English can sustain while still
remaining intelligible. That style follows directly from its author's intentions of doing justice to the object of his analysis. Presentation and exposition are not linear, but cumulative and dialectical, each descriptive
moment standing equidistant from the phenomenon it is trying to
'name' by unfolding its conceptual and historical mediations. "Thought
does not progress in a single direction; instead, the moments are interwoven as in a carpet. The fruitfulness of the thoughts depends on the density of the texture."[11] Hence paragraph caesurae fall not according to the
principle of concision, but that of saturation; paragraphs are the periods
of an essay. The "fear of page-long paragraphs," Adorno called "a fear
created by the marketplace—by the consumer who does not want to tax
himself and to whom first editors and then writers accommodated for the
sake of their incomes." The texture of thought in an essay is equally
expressed by the "physiognomic status" of Adorno's punctuation, about
which he wrote a miniature treatise including the dialectical functions of
two of his preferred hieroglyphs: the semicolon, which as both pause and
continuation is the image of sublation, and the dash, in which "thought
becomes aware of its fragmentary character."[12] Dashes are used instead

of parentheses because they "block off the parenthetical material from the flow of the sentence without shutting it up in a prison, capture both connection and detachment." Likewise dashes set between sentences, a nineteenth-century typographic custom, "have something of the fatefulness of the natural context and something of a prudish hesitancy to make reference to it." Out of the same resistance to the reified segregation of language and judgment Adorno eschews the use of quotation marks to indicate irony; the translation must try to capture the shift in tone, which in the hands of skillful practitioners such as Adorno and Karl Kraus is weapon enough to transfix stupidity. While Adorno could rely on the gender specificity of German to transform relative pronouns into the turning points of dialectical reversals and qualifications, the English translation must tolerate a brute repetition of nouns from which the original modestly refrains.

In his essay "On the Question: 'What is German?'" Adorno himself takes a dim view of the prospects for translating German (idealist) philosophical vocabulary into English successfully. Depending on context, in this volume *Geist* is rendered as "spirit," "mind," or "intellect," accordingly *geistig* as "spiritual" or "intellectual." *Moment*, Hegel's term for an essential element of a composite whole, is usually translated as "moment," "element," or "aspect." *Schein*, appearance that is deceptive, is rendered as "semblance," occasionally as "illusion." *Wissenschaft*, "science," possesses a larger semantic field in German than in English as it extends beyond the natural sciences to encompass all forms of academic and scholarly research. Hegelian *Entäußerung*, translated as "externalization," is the development of consciousness through its immersion in what lies outside it, a process Adorno calls genuine *Erfahrung*, "experience."[13] In a different vein, Adorno's confrontation with the student movement in several late texts draws on vocabulary specific to that time. In particular, "action," "actionism," etc. mean not planned activism but confrontation and agitation as a direct response to any political conflict.

One problem unique to an English language translation of Adorno lies in his frequent use of foreign words, a practice he justified in two essays after readers and radio listeners complained.[14] In those cases, the word has been kept in the original Greek, Latin, French, English, etc., and italicized. Where such words appear within quotation marks in the German text they will be similarly marked. English originals are marked with an asterisk (*) and where Adorno provided his own German equivalent, it is italicized and placed in square brackets immediately following. Otherwise all square brackets include the original German or a short English explication at the discretion of the translator.

The publication information at the end of the book lists the earlier published and radio broadcast versions of each essay, together with any previous English translations. While I have profited from consulting the latter, all essays have been retranslated for this volume.

This book is in many ways a product "made in Germany." Support from a Fulbright Fellowship and the Germanistic Society of America and subsequently a grant from the German Academic Exchange Service (DAAD) sustained the project and the research involved. I would like to thank Rolf Tiedemann and Henri Lonitz of the Theodor W. Adorno Archiv in Frankfurt for permission to examine materials relating to these essays; the archives of Hessischer Rundfunk, Deutschlandfunk, Sender Freies Berlin, Süddeutscher Rundfunk, and Westdeutscher Rundfunk, for allowing me to listen to original radio recordings of Adorno or providing me with copies of the broadcasts; Ingrid Belke and the staff of the Deutsches Literaturarchiv in Marbach am Neckar for their assistance during my idyllic sojourn there to read Adorno's correspondence; Karsten Harries and Geoffrey Hartman of Yale University, and likewise Winfried Menninghaus, Michael Theunissen, Albrecht Wellmer, and especially Christoph Menke of the Freie Universität, Berlin, for their support at key moments during the project; the Institut für Philosophie and the Institut für Hermeneutik of the Freie Universität for providing a congenial and generous intellectual environment; and Lennie Douglass in New Haven and Ina-Maria Gumbel in Berlin for invaluable administrative assistance. Sonja Asal; Gordon Finlayson; Lynne Frame and Rick Hoskins; Brian Jacobs; Martin Jay; Thomas Levin; John MacKay; Eberhard Ortland; Heather, Maureen, and Win Pickford; Colin Sample; Timothy Sergay; Gary Smith; Ruth Sonderegger; Rochelle Tobias; Eric Walczak; and an anonymous reader all helped in different ways to improve the quality of the manuscript. Ann Miller of Columbia University Press dispensed patient understanding and deadline remonstrances with uncanny finesse, and Sabine Seiler's exactitude in copyediting was matched by her indulgence in discussing the metaphysics of punctuation across the internet. While the translation is deeply indebted to the responsiveness of all these people, whatever infelicities remain are the translator's responsibility alone.

Henry W. Pickford

Critical Models *Interventions and Catchwords*

Interventions *Nine Critical Models*

Introduction

Language meets its catastrophe not merely in its individual words and syntactical structure. Many words clump together in the pull of communication, prior and contrary to all meaning. Karl Kraus recognized this phenomenon and persecuted it almost tenderly in such turns of phrase as "fully developed and consolidated."[1]

One such clump is the illegal intervention, which typically ensues when relations turn out not to have been without consequence.[2] Presumably the abuse of language is so much a part of objective spirit's flesh and blood that it could never be made to give it up. But perhaps what has happened to words should be taken at its word. If prohibition was already once associated with interventions, then considerations that propose to intervene should at least metaphorically recall it and transgress taboo and consent.

Thematically, the articles extend from so-called grand philosophical subjects to political topics and on to relatively ephemeral, occasional pieces, from professional-academic experiences to very nonacademic questions. The presentation follows suit: its rigor and density vary according to the subject being presented. An autonomous language that ignores the requirements entailed by successive changes in subject matter is no style. Everywhere, however, where topically relevant material is treated, the adversary is the same malfeasance upon which every particular depends and which nevertheless only appears in the particular.[3]

Thus a catchword that unintentionally recurs in many of the articles suggests itself: reified consciousness, into which the essays seek to intervene, whether it be in the work of the human sciences or in the attitude of teachers toward philosophy, in the cliché of the twenties or the evil survival of sexual taboos, in the prefabricated world of television or in unfettered opinion. This unity at the same time prescribes the limit: consciousness is criticized where it is merely the reflection of the reality that sustains it.

The practical prospects therefore are limited. Whoever puts forward proposals easily makes himself into an accomplice. Talk of a "we" one identifies with already implies complicity with what is wrong and the illusion that goodwill and a readiness to engage in communal action can achieve something where every will is powerless and where the identification with *hommes de bonne volonté* is a disguised form of evil. A purist attitude, however, that refrains from intervening likewise reinforces that from which it timorously recoils. Such a contradiction cannot be settled by reflection; it is the constitution of reality that dictates the contradiction. At a historical moment, however, where a praxis that would refer to the totality appears to be blocked everywhere, even paltry reforms may presume more right than they in fact are due.

December 1962

Why Still Philosophy

To a question such as "why still philosophy?"—for the formulation of which I myself am responsible, although its dilettantish tone does not escape me—most people will already guess the answer. They will expect a train of thought that accumulates all kinds of difficulties and reservations in order to lead ultimately, more or less cautiously, to a "nevertheless" and the affirmation of what at first had been rhetorically cast into doubt. This all too familiar circuit corresponds to a conformist and apologetic attitude that characterizes itself as positive and reckons in advance on consent. And indeed perhaps nothing better can be expected from someone whose job it is to teach philosophy, whose bourgeois existence depends on its continued survival, and who undermines his own immediate interests as soon as he contests it. All that notwithstanding, I have some right to raise the question for the simple reason that I am not at all sure of the answer.

Anyone who defends a cause deemed obsolete and superfluous by the spirit of the age places himself in the most disadvantageous position. His arguments sound halfhearted. "Yes but . . . ," "Consider, however . . . ," he says, as though trying to talk his audience into something they don't want. Anyone who doesn't want to be dissuaded from philosophy must take this misfortune into account. He must know that philosophy is no longer applicable to the techniques for mastering one's life—techniques in both the literal and figurative senses—with which philosophy was once so closely entwined. And philosophy no longer offers a medium of self-cultivation beyond these techniques, as was the case during the era of Hegel, when for a few short decades the very small class of German intellectuals communicated in their collective philosophical language. Roughly since the death of Kant philosophy has made itself suspect because of its disparity with the positive sciences, especially the natural sciences, and it was the first discipline in public awareness to succumb to the crisis of the humanistic concept of culture, about which I need not say a great deal. The Kantian and Hegelian revivals, whose titles alone already reveal the feebleness of their programs, have not changed the situation much. Finally, in the general tendency toward specialization, philosophy too has established itself as a specialized discipline, one purified of all specific content. In so doing, philosophy has denied its own constitutive concept: the intellectual freedom that does not obey the dictates of specialized knowledge. At the same time, by abstaining from all definite content, whether as a formal logic and theory of science or as the legend of Being beyond all beings, philosophy declared its bankruptcy regarding concrete societal goals. To be sure philosophy thereby merely ratified a process that is largely tantamount to its own history. More and more fields were snatched away from it and transformed into science; it scarcely had any other choice but to become either a science itself or a minuscule, tolerated enclave,[1] which as such already conflicts with what it wants to be: a non-particularized pursuit. Newtonian physics was still called philosophy. Modern scientific consciousness would see in this an archaic relic, a vestige of that earlier epoch of Greek speculation when sound explanation of nature and sublime metaphysics were still inseparably interwoven in the name of the essence of things. This is why some resolute beings have proclaimed that such archaic themes constitute the only philosophy and have tried to restore them. But the consciousness suffering from the fissured state of the world and conjuring up a past unity out of its own deprivation contradicts the very contents it aspires to win for itself. Therefore it must autocratically promote its own primordial language.[2] Restoration is as futile in philosophy as it is anywhere else. Philosophy has to protect itself from the chatter of culture and the abracadabra of worldviews. It also should not imagine that specialized work in epistemological theory, or whatever else prides itself on being research, is actually philosophy. Yet a philosophy forswearing all of that must in the end be irreconcilably at odds with the dominant consciousness. Nothing else raises it above the suspicion of apologetics. Philosophy that satisfies its own intention, and does not childishly skip behind its own history and the real one, has its lifeblood in the resistance against the common practices of today and what they serve, against the justification of what happens to be the case.

Even the greatest achievement of philosophical speculation to date, that of Hegel, is no longer binding. Anyone whom public opinion has once categorized as a dialectician—and no one who in any way has a public life can escape being classified—must indicate how he distinguishes himself from Hegel. It is not at all a difference of individual conviction. Rather, the difference is demanded by the movement of the subject matter itself, and it was no one less than Hegel himself who demanded that thought abandon itself to the subject matter without reservation. Traditional philosophy's claim to totality, culminating in the thesis that the real is rational, is indistinguishable from apologetics.[3] But this thesis has become absurd. A philosophy that would still set itself up as total, as a system, would become a delusional system. Yet if philosophy renounces the claim to totality and no longer claims to develop out of itself the whole that should be the truth, then it comes into conflict with its entire tradition. This is the price it must pay for the fact that, once cured of its own delusional system, it denounces the delusional system of reality. No longer is it then a self-sufficient, stringent network of argumentative justification. The state of philosophy in society, which philosophy itself should scrutinize rather than deny, corresponds to its own desperate state: the necessity of formulating what nowadays under the title of 'the absurd' is already being recuperated by the machinery. After everything,[4] the only responsible philosophy is one that no longer imagines it had the Absolute at its command; indeed philosophy must forbid the thought of it in order not to betray that thought, and at the same time it must not bargain away anything of the emphatic concept of truth. This contradiction is philosophy's element. It defines philosophy as negative. Kant's famous dictum that the critical path is the only one still open to us belongs to those propositions constituting a philosophy that proves itself because the propositions, as fragments, survive beyond the system that conceived them. Admittedly, the idea of critique itself hearkens back to the philosophical tradition that today lies in ruins. While in the meantime the domain of every kind of knowledge has been confiscated by the specialized disciplines to such a degree that philosophical thought feels terrorized and fears being refuted as dilettantism whenever it takes on specific content, in reaction to this the concept of primordiality has attained an honorable status it does not merit. The more reified the world becomes, the thicker the veil cast upon nature, the more the thinking weaving that veil in its turn claims ideologically to be nature, primordial experience. On the other hand, ever since the celebrated pre-Socratics, traditional philosophers have practiced critique. Xenophanes, whose school the current anti-conceptual concept of Being dates back to, strove to demythologize the forces of nature. And Aristotle in turn saw through the Platonic hypostatization of the concept of Being into an idea. In modernity, Descartes convicted the scholastic philosophy of turning mere opinion into dogma. Leibniz criticized empiricism, and Kant criticized the philosophies of both Leibniz and Hume at once; Hegel criticized Kant's philosophy, and Marx in turn criticized Hegel's. For all of these thinkers, critique was not a mere adornment accompanying what the jargon of ontology thirty years ago would have called their 'project.' It did not document a point of view that could be adopted according to personal taste. Rather its very existence lay in cogent argumentation. Each of those thinkers found his own truth in critique. Critique alone, as the unity of the problem and its arguments, not the adoption of received theses, has laid the foundation for what may be considered the productive unity of the history of philosophy. In the progressive continuity of such critique even those philosophers whose doctrines insist on the eternal and the timeless acquired their temporal nucleus, their historical status.

Contemporary philosophical critique is confronted with two schools of thought that, by constituting the spirit of the age, *nolens volens* exert an influence beyond the walls of the academic preserve. They diverge and nonetheless complement each other. Especially in the Anglo-Saxon countries logical positivism, originally inaugurated by the Vienna Circle, has gained ground to the point of becoming a virtual monopoly. Many consider it modern in the sense of being the most rigorous faculty of enlightenment, adequate to the so-called technical-scientific age. Whatever does not conform to it is relegated to the status of residual metaphysics, its own unrecognized mythology or, in the terminology of those who know nothing of art, art. Opposed to this movement are the ontological approaches, active above all in the German-speaking countries. The school of Heidegger, who, incidentally, since his publications following the so-called turn has become rather averse to the word "ontology,"[5] pursues the archaic theme farthest, whereas the French version, existentialism, modified the ontological approach with enlightenment motives and political engagement. Positivism and ontology are anathema to one another; Rudolf Carnap, one of positivism's foremost representatives, has attacked Heidegger's theory, indeed quite wrongly, for being meaningless.[6] Conversely, for the ontologists of Heideggerian provenance positivist thinking is forgetful of Being, a profanation of the authentic question. The ontologists are afraid of getting their hands dirty with the merely factually existent, which lies in the positivists' hands alone. Thus it is all the more surprising that the two directions coincide in an essential point. Both have chosen metaphysics as their common enemy. In positivism this goes without saying: because metaphysics essentially transcends that which is the case,[7] it is not tolerated by positivism, whose very name indicates its adherence to the positive, the existent, the given.

But Heidegger as well, schooled as he is in the metaphysical tradition, has tried emphatically to disassociate himself from it. With the name of metaphysics he baptizes the thinking that, at least since Aristotle, if not already in Plato, separates Being [*Sein*] and being [*Seiendes*], the concept and what is conceptualized; one could, in a language Heidegger rejected, say: subject and object. According to Heidegger, a thinking that analyzes and differentiates, destroys through reflection what the words them-selves say; in short, everything Hegel called "the labor and the exertion of the concept" and equated with philosophy[8] is for Heidegger already the apostasy from philosophy and beyond repair because prefigured in the nature of Being itself, "through the historicity of Being." In both pos-itivism and Heidegger—at least in his later work—speculation is the tar-get of attack. In both cases the thought that autonomously raises itself above the facts through interpreting them and that cannot be reclaimed by them without leaving a surplus is condemned for being empty and vain concept-mongering; according to Heidegger, however, thinking, in the sense it has received in occidental history, profoundly misses the truth. For him that truth is an appearing in itself, a self-disclosing; legiti-mate thinking is nothing other than the ability to perceive this. Crypti-cally, philology becomes a philosophical authority. This common aver-sion against metaphysics lessens the immediate sense of paradox when one of Heidegger's students working in Kiel, Walter Bröcker, recently attempted to combine positivism and the philosophy of Being by grant-ing positivism the entire realm of existence and superimposing over it, as on a higher plane, the doctrine of Being, expressly identified as mythol-ogy.[9] Being, in whose name Heidegger's philosophy increasingly concen-trates itself, is for him—as a pure self-presentation to passive conscious-ness—just as immediate, just as independent of the mediations of the subject as the facts and the sensory data are for the positivists. In both philosophical movements thinking becomes a necessary evil and is broadly discredited. Thinking loses its element of independence. The autonomy of reason vanishes: the part of reason that exceeds the subor-dinate reflection upon and adjustment to pre-given data. With it, how-ever, goes the conception of freedom and, potentially, the self-determina-tion of human society. If their humane compunctions did not keep most of the positivists from going so far, they would have to demand that praxis adapt itself to the facts, before which thinking is for them power-less, simply an anticipation or classification, invalid in the face of the only thing that counts: that which simply is the case. For Heidegger, however, thinking would be the reverentially conceptless, passive hearkening to a Being that always only speaks Being, without any right to critique and constrained to capitulate equally before everything that can appeal to the shimmering mightiness of Being. Heidegger's falling in with the *Führerstaat*, Hitler's leader state, was no act of opportunism but rather a consequence of a philosophy that equated Being and *Führer*.

If philosophy is still necessary, it is so only in the way it has been from time immemorial: as critique, as resistance to the expanding heteronomy, even if only as thought's powerless attempt to remain its own master and to convict of untruth, by their own criteria, both a fabricated mythology and a conniving, resigned acquiescence on the other of untruth. It is incumbent upon philosophy, as long as it is not prohibited as it was in the christianized Athens of late antiquity, to provide a refuge for freedom. Not that there is any hope that it could break the political tendencies that are throttling freedom throughout the world both from within and without and whose violence permeates the very fabric of philosophical argumentation. Whatever takes place within the interior of the concept always reflects something of the movement of reality. But if the two heteronomies are the untruth and if this can be convincingly demonstrated, then this not only adds a new link to the dreary chain of philosophical movements but also registers a trace of the hope that unfreedom and oppression—the evil whose malevolence requires as little philosophical proof as does its existence—nonetheless may not have the last word. Such a critique would need to define the two prevailing philosophies as isolated aspects of a truth that historically was forced to diverge. As little as these two aspects can be glued together into a so-called synthesis, nonetheless they should be reflected upon individually. The error in positivism is that it takes as its standard of truth the contingently given division of labor, that between the sciences and social praxis as well as that within science itself, and allows no theory that could reveal the division of labor to be itself derivative and mediated and thus strip it of its false authority. If in the age of emancipation philosophy wanted to provide a foundation for science, and if Fichte and Hegel interpreted philosophy as the one and only science, then the most general structure derived from the sciences, its ingrained and societally rigidified procedure, would constitute the philosophy of positivism, the mechanism for its own self-legitimation, a circle that, surprisingly, seems hardly to disturb the fanatics of logical tidiness. Philosophy resigns by equating itself with what should in fact first be illuminated by philosophy. The existence of science *telle quelle*, just as it occurs within and amid all the insufficiencies and irrationalities of the societal fabric, becomes the criterion of its own truth. With such a reverence for reified reality, positivism is reified consciousness. Despite all its hostility toward mythology it forsakes the anti-mythological impulse of philosophy to smash through human-made constructions and return them to their human measure.

Fundamental ontology, however, blinds itself to the mediation not of the factual but of the concept. It suppresses the knowledge that those essences—or whatever it calls the results of progressive sublimation it opposes to the 'facts' of positivism—are always also results of thinking, subject, spirit. Precisely the existence of the subject and its conditioned-ness indicate a being that has not sprung whole out of Being: societalized individuals. In the hutted sanctuary[10] in which the philosophy of repristination entrenches itself against the profanity of mere fact as well as against concepts—which are related to each other in that facts are separate from and subsumed under conceptual unities—one encounters again the schism the harbingers of the indivisible think themselves immune to. Their words are inevitably concepts, to the extent that they can be thought at all; but the doctrine of Being would like to be a thinking still within the ambit of resolute archaism. However, just as concepts by their very meaning require a content that fulfills them, and just as, in Hegel's unparalleled insight, the mere thought of identity requires non-identity from which alone identity can be asserted, so too even the purest concepts depend on their Other immanently, and not merely from a polar duality. Thinking itself, of which all concepts are a function, cannot be imagined without the activity of someone thinking implied in the word "thinking." This reverse relation already contains the element that, according to the idealist tradition, must first be constituted by the concept and that, according to the mythology of Being, is together with the concept an epiphenomenon of a third element. Without the determination by those two elements this third thing would be wholly indeterminate; just to be able to indicate it at all amounts to defining it by means of the same elements that are being so assiduously denied. Even the Kantian transcendental subject, whose legacy transcendental-subjectless Being would like to inherit, as a unity requires the manifold as much as, inversely, the manifold requires the unity of reason.[11] Independent of the contents that constitute a unity, the concept of unity itself remains unintelligible, and it is just as impossible to conjure away the trace of the factual from those contents as it is to remove the difference between the concept and the contents it requires. No unity, no matter how formal, even if it be pure logical unity, can be conceived even as a possibility without that toward which it gestures; even the formal-logical Something is the remnant of the material that pure logic was so proud of having separated out.[12] However, the reason for what Günther Anders called the 'pseudo-concretion' in the thinking of Being, and consequently for all the fraud it propagates, is that it claims to be inviolably pure of what it ultimately is and from whose concreteness it likewise profits.[13] It celebrates its triumph in a strategic retreat. Its mythical ambiguity merely camouflages the specific imbrication of the constitutive elements of thought from which it can no more easily free itself than conditioned consciousness ever could. Because being and concept remain artfully undifferentiated in the mythology of Being, this ambiguity presents Being as though it were beyond being as well as concept and, as Kant would say, obtains its absolute character surreptitiously.[14] Even the mythology of Being, by suppressing the human participation in the highest concepts and idolizing them, is reified consciousness. But dialectic means nothing other than insisting on the mediation of what appears to be immediate and on the reciprocity of immediacy and mediation as it unfolds at all levels. Dialectic is not a third standpoint but rather the attempt, by means of an immanent critique, to develop philosophical standpoints beyond themselves and beyond the despotism of a thinking based on standpoints. In the face of the naiveté of an autocratic consciousness that considers its own limitation—namely what is 'given' to it—to be unlimited, philosophy should be the binding commitment to non-naiveté. In a world that has been thoroughly permeated by the structures of the social order, a world that so overpowers every individual that scarcely any option remains but to accept it on its own terms, such naiveté reproduces itself incessantly and disastrously. What people have forced upon them by a boundless apparatus, which they themselves constitute and which they are locked into, virtually eliminates all natural elements and becomes 'nature' to them. Reified consciousness is perfectly naive and, as reification, also perfectly unnaive. Philosophy must dissolve the semblance of the obvious as well as the semblance of the obscure.

The integration of philosophy and science, already inscribed *in nuce* in the earliest documents of Western metaphysics, strove to protect thought from dogmatic tutelage, which thought resembles by its autocratic nature and which is the negation of all freedom. But freedom was the goal of the postulate of the direct "involvement" of vital, active mind in all acts of cognition, the indefeasible norm of self-evidence ever since Spinoza.[15] It was, in the realm of mere logic, the anticipatory image of an actual state in which human beings would finally be free, rid of every kind of blind authority. This has reversed itself. The invocation of science, of its ground rules, of the exclusive validity of the methods that science has now completely become, now constitutes a surveillance authority punishing free, uncoddled, undisciplined thought and tolerating nothing of mental activity other than what has been methodologically sanctioned. Science and scholarship, the medium of autonomy, has degenerated into an instrument of heteronomy.[16] The original raison d'être is removed, consigned to the contingency of defamed aperçus, isolated, and in fact degraded into prattle about worldviews. The philosophical critique of scientivism, which conclusively refutes such a system of thought, is therefore not what its well-meaning adversaries accuse it of being but rather the destruction of what is already destructive. The critique of the current philosophies does not plead for the disappearance of philosophy nor for its replacement by separate disciplines such as social science. It intends both formally and materially to promote precisely that manner of intellectual freedom that has no place in the regnant philosophical movements. A thinking that approaches its objects openly, rigorously, and on the basis of progressive knowledge, is also free toward its objects in the sense that it refuses to have rules prescribed to it by organized knowledge. It turns the quintessence of the experience accumulated in it to the objects, rends the veil with which society conceals them, and perceives them anew. Were philosophy to beat back the fear caused by the tyranny of the prevailing philosophical movements—the ontological intimidation not to think anything that is not pure, and the scientistic intimidation not to think anything that is not "connected" to the corpus of findings recognized as scientifically valid—then it would be capable of recognizing what that fear prohibits, what an unmarred consciousness in fact would be intent upon. The "to the things themselves"[17] that philosophical phenomenology had dreamed of like a dreamer who dreams he's waking up[18] can only come true for a philosophy that stops hoping to acquire knowledge with the magical stroke of eidetic intuition,[19] and instead thinks through the subjective and objective mediations without, however, conforming to the latent primacy of organized method, which over and over again offers phenomenological movements only a series of fetishes, homemade concepts instead of their longed-for things. Had not all positivist locutions become deeply suspect, then one could imagine that only a consciousness both free and reflected in itself would be open to what traditional philosophy has obstructed by confusing itself with what it intends to interpret. Within traditional philosophy's exhaustion at the succession of its variations lies the potential for a philosophy that could break the magic spell.

Nonetheless it is completely uncertain whether philosophy, as a conceptual activity of the interpretive mind, is still the order of the day, whether it has fallen behind what it should conceptualize—the state of the world rushing toward catastrophe. It appears to be too late for contemplation. Whatever is manifestly absurd flies in the face of any idea of comprehending it. The abolition of philosophy was forecast more than a hundred years ago.[20] The fact that in the East *Diamat* is proclaimed to be Marxist philosophy, as though it were compatible with Marxist theory just like that, testifies to the inversion of Marxism into a static dogma

deadened to its own contents or, as they themselves say, into an 'ideology.'[21] Anyone who still philosophizes can do so only by denying the
Marxist thesis that reflection has become obsolete. Marx believed that
the possibility of changing the world from top to bottom was immediately present, here and now. But only stubbornness could still maintain
this thesis as Marx formulated it. The proletariat to whom he appealed
was not yet integrated into society: it was rapidly sinking into destitu-
tion, whereas on the other hand societal power did not yet command the
means to assure overwhelming odds for itself in the event of any serious
conflict. Philosophy, as at once both rigorous and free thought, now finds
itself in an entirely different situation. Marx would have been the last
person to tear thought free from the real movement of history. Hegel,
who was aware of the transience of art and prophesied its end, had made
its progress dependent upon the "consciousness of needs."[22] But what is
right for art is just as right for philosophy, whose truth content con-
verges with that of art, by virtue of the technical procedures of art
diverging from those of philosophy. The undiminished persistence of
suffering, fear, and menace necessitates that the thought that cannot be
realized should not be discarded. After having missed its opportunity,
philosophy must come to know, without any mitigation, why the
world—which could be paradise here and now—can become hell itself
tomorrow. Such knowledge would indeed truly be philosophy. It would
be anachronistic to abolish it for the sake of a praxis that at this historical
moment would inevitably eternalize precisely the present state of the
world, the very critique of which is the concern of philosophy. Praxis,
whose purpose is to produce a rational and politically mature humanity,
remains under the spell of disaster unless it has a theory that can think
the totality in its untruth. It goes without saying that this theory should
not be a warmed-over idealism but rather must incorporate societal and
political reality and its dynamic.

   In the last forty or fifty years philosophy has been claiming, most of
the time spuriously, to oppose idealism. What was genuine in this was
the opposition to decorative platitudes; to the intellectual hubris that
makes spirit into an absolute; to the glorification of this world, as though
it already were freedom. The anthropocentrism inherent in all idealistic
conceptions cannot be saved; one need only remember the changes in
cosmology during the last one hundred and fifty years. Surely not the
least of the tasks incumbent upon philosophy is to help spirit[23] appropriate the experiences of the natural sciences without recourse to amateurish analogies and syntheses. An unproductive gulf exists between the
natural sciences and the so-called realm of spirit; so great a gulf that at
times the spirit's engagement with itself and the social world appears to

be a gratuitous conceit. Something would already be achieved if philosophy at least sought to bring people's consciousness of themselves to the same state of knowledge that they have of nature, instead of them living like cavemen in thrall to their own knowledge of a cosmos in which the hardly sapient species *homo* makes a helpless go of it. In the face of this task and the undiminished insight into society's laws of motion, philosophy could hardly presume to affirm that it posits out of itself something like a positive meaning. To this extent it makes common cause with positivism, even more with modern art, before whose phenomena most of what passes today for philosophical thinking fails for lack of any relationship to them. But philosophy's turn against idealism, which has been proclaimed ad nauseam, did not intend militant enlightenment but resignation. Thought has been intimidated and no longer dares raise itself, not even in fundamental ontology's devotional submissiveness to Being. In its opposition to such resignation, there is a moment of truth in idealism. The realization of materialism would mean today the end of materialism, of the blind and degrading dependence of human beings upon material conditions. Spirit is no more the absolute than it is entirely reducible to a concrete entity. It will come to know what it is only when it stops invalidating itself. The force of such resistance is the sole criterion for philosophy today.[24] It is as irreconcilable with reified consciousness as Platonic enthusiasm once was. Only the excess of this consciousness beyond the factual makes it possible to call the universally conditioned by its rightful name. Philosophy desires peace with that Other, being, that the affirmative philosophies degrade by praising it and adapting themselves to it. For those philosophies everything becomes functional; even the conformity to what exists is for them a pretext for subjugating it intellectually. But what exists does not want to be deformed. Anything that has a function is already spellbound within the functional world. Only a thinking that has no mental sanctuary, no illusion of an inner realm, and that acknowledges its lack of function and power can perhaps catch a glimpse of an order of the possible and the nonexistent, where human beings and things each would be in their rightful place. Because philosophy is good for nothing, it is not yet obsolete; philosophy should not even invoke this point, lest it blindly repeat its wrong: self-justification by self-positing.[25]

This wrong was passed down from the idea of *philosophia perennis*—that philosophy is the vested bearer of eternal truth. This idea is exploded by Hegel's astounding proposition that philosophy is its own time comprehended in thought. The requirement seemed so self-evident to him that he did not hesitate to introduce it as a definition.[26] He was the first to gain insight into the temporal nucleus of truth. This was connected for him with the confidence that every significant philosophy, by expressing its own stage of consciousness as a necessary aspect of the totality, at the same time also expressed the totality. The fact that this confidence together with the philosophy of identity met with disappointment lessens not only the pathos of subsequent philosophies but also their standing. What for Hegel was self-evident cannot possibly be claimed by the regnant philosophies today. No longer are they their own time comprehended in thought. Ontology even makes a virtue out of its provincialism.[27] The faithful counterpoint to this attitude is the helpless conceptual poverty of the positivists. They've tailored the rules of the game so that the reified consciousness of uninspired *bright boys** can consider itself to be the cutting edge of the spirit of the age. However, they are merely its symptom, and they disguise their deficiencies as the incorruptible virtue of those who will not have the wool pulled over their eyes. At most both movements belong to the spirit of the age as one of regression, and Nietzsche's backworldsmen once again have literally become backwoodsmen.[28] Against them philosophy must prove itself the most advanced consciousness—permeated with the potential of what could be different—but also a match for the power of regression, which it can transcend only after having incorporated and comprehended it. When today's philosophical archaism evades this requirement, which it surely perceives, by offering ancient truth as an alibi, and abuses progress, which it merely prevents by pretending to have already overcome it, then these are all just so many excuses. No dialectic of progress suffices to legitimate an intellectual condition that believes itself safe and sound only because its corner has not yet been infiltrated by the deployment of objectivity, with which even that spiritual condition itself is intertwined and which ensures that all appeals to what is safe and sound immediately reinforce the calamity.[29] The self-righteous profundity that treats the progressive consciousness *en canaille* is flat. Reflections extending beyond the magical incantations of the ontologists as well as beyond the *vérités de faits* of the positivists are not trendy stupidities, as the ideology of the yellowed lampoons would have it,[30] rather they are motivated by those very facts of the matter that ontologists as well as positivists pretend are the only things worthy of regard. As long as philosophy retains the faintest trace of the title of a book published by an old Kantian more than thirty years ago, *From the Philosophy Corner*, it will remain nothing more than the fun its detractors make of it.[31] Not by avuncular advice will it transcend the academic industry. All wisdom has degenerated into wizened prudence.[32] There is also no avail to philosophy in the behavior of that teacher who in the prefascist era felt prompted to set his age aright and inspected Marlene Dietrich's Blauer Engel so as to see firsthand how bad things really were.[33] Flights of this sort into concrete experience convict philosophy of being the refuse of precisely the history with whose agent philosophy mistakenly confuses itself out of a sense of nostalgia for its erstwhile cultural role. Not to resemble any of this in any way at all would not be the worst criterion for philosophy nowadays. Philosophy should not with foolish arrogance set about collecting information and then take a position; rather it must unrestrictedly, without recourse to some mental refuge, experience: it must do exactly what is avoided by those who refuse to forsake the maxim that every philosophy must finally produce something positive. Rimbaud's *"il faut être absolument moderne"* is neither an aesthetic program nor a program for aesthetes: it is a categorical imperative of philosophy. Whatever wants nothing to do with the trajectory of history belongs all the more truly to it. History promises no salvation and offers the possibility of hope only to the concept whose movement follows history's path to the very extreme.

Philosophy and Teachers

It is my intention to say a few words about the so-called general test in philosophy, which is part of the examination that qualifies candidates for academic posts in secondary schools in the *Land* of Hessen.[1] What I have observed over the last eleven years has made me more and more concerned that the meaning of the test is misunderstood and that the test fails its purpose. Moreover, I have had cause to think about the mentality of those being tested. I believe I sense their own discontent with the test. From the beginning many feel alienated and not really equal to it; some harbor doubts about its significance. I believe I must speak about this matter because the very results of the test often depend on factors I have encountered and that are often not fully recognized by the candidates. An examiner would have the wrong attitude altogether if he did not fundamentally try to help those people whom he is professionally obliged to judge, even when such help has a sting to it. I alone answer for my words here, though my colleagues might share my opinion in many respects. In particular, I know that Horkheimer reached the same conclusions. Obviously there are many candidates for whom my fears are unfounded. They are mainly those who personally have a specific interest in philosophy; as participants in our seminars they have often developed a genuine relationship to philosophy. Beyond this group, there is no lack of students with wide horizons and intellectual sensibilities. Truly cultured individuals, they already bring with them at the outset what the test, fragmentarily and insufficiently enough, is supposed to detect the presence or absence of. But my critique is in no way directed only at those who have not passed the exam: often they are only more careless but certainly no less qualified than the majority who are passed in accordance with formal criteria. Rather it is the sign of the fatal condition—really a condition regardless of any particular faults of those who fail—whose marks are borne even by the students who sail through the exam or who, as an expression that itself is already fundamentally offensive puts it, "receive a solid average." Often one has the feeling that this or that candidate should be passed because he answered most of the concrete and verifiable questions more or less correctly; but this decision, no matter how welcome to the person in question, does not exactly lighten the examiner's heart. If the test were conducted strictly according to the spirit and not the letter of the exam regulations, such students would have to receive a negative evaluation, above all in consideration of the youth who will be entrusted to them once they become teachers and with whom I do not yet feel too old to identify myself. The mere need for teachers should not profit those who by their nature presumably will have the opposite effect of what that need requires. The entire situation is suspect precisely in those aspects for the sake of which the general test was first introduced. I think it better to say this openly and to stimulate discussion than to carry on silently with a practice that inevitably must lead the examiners to routine and resignation and the candidates to disdain for what is expected of them, a disdain that often only thinly veils their disdain for themselves. It is kinder to be unkind than to disregard with an all-too-convenient, friendly indulgence what in the consciousness of the examinees affronts their own better aptitudes, which I am sure every candidate possesses. It goes without saying that humanitarianism embraces goodwill and consideration, and among those in our department of philosophy at the university who must administer examinations none are lacking these qualities. But we wish to be humane not only toward the candidates, whose anxiety we can well understand, but also toward those who will one day sit before them, whom we do not see, and who are threatened with greater injustice at the hands of an immature and uneducated intellect than anyone who might be threatened by our intellectual demands. One does not need what Nietzsche called the "love of strangers" for this: a little imagination is quite sufficient.[2]

When I said that those who are equal to the test are often the ones who participated actively in the philosophy seminars, I did not mean to exercise any institutional pressure. I take the idea of academic freedom extremely seriously and am completely indifferent as to how a student educates himself, whether as a participant in seminars and lectures or merely through private reading. I had absolutely no intention of equating the significance of this examination with professional training in the specific discipline of philosophy. I only meant to say that those who push themselves beyond the activities of a single academic specialty to that consciousness of spirit that is philosophy usually fit the conception of the examination. It would be childish to expect that everyone could or would want to become a professional philosopher. I fundamentally mistrust precisely that category. We do not want to expect from our students that *déformation professionelle* of those who automatically think that their particular field is the center of the world. Philosophy fulfills itself only where it is more than a specialty. The general test, according to paragraph 19 of the exam regulations, to which so many cling scrupulously, "should determine whether the applicant has understood the educational significance and strengths of the disciplines he has studied and understands how to consider them from the vantage point of the vital philosophical, pedagogical, and political questions of the present" (p. 46). There is then added expressly: "yet the philosophically accentuated test should not lose itself in specialized questions, but rather must orient itself according to such questions as are essential for the living culture of today, whereby the particular disciplines of the applicant constitute the point of departure." In other words, the general test intends, to the extent that any test can do it, to give an idea of whether the candidates, in reflecting upon their specialized discipline—that is, in reflecting upon what they are fulfilling—and in reflecting upon themselves transcend the bounds of what they have actually learned. Quite simply one could say: whether they are intellectual, spiritual people if that phrase did not have a distinct tone of arrogance, did not evoke exactly those desires for elitist domination that prevent the academic from self-reflection. The phrase "spiritual person" may be abominable, but its actual significance is brought out only by something more abominable—an encounter with someone who lacks any trace of the spiritual. This test therefore should permit us to see whether those candidates, who as teachers in secondary schools are burdened with a heavy responsibility for the spiritual and material development of Germany, are intellectuals or, as Ibsen said more than eighty years ago, merely specialized technicians.[3] The fact that the term "intellectual" ["*Intellektuelle*"] came into disrepute at the hands of the National Socialists seems to me just one more reason to use it in a positive sense: the first step toward self-reflection would be to stop cultivating vagueness as a higher ethos and stop slandering enlightenment, and instead resist the baiting of intellectuals, no matter what disguise it might take. However, whether someone is an intellectual or not is manifested above all in his relationship to his own work and to the societal totality of which it is a part. This relationship, not the work in specialized domains like epistemology, ethics, or even the history of philosophy, is what constitutes the essence of philosophy in the first place. It was formulated in this way by a philosopher whose qualifications in the particularized philosophical disciplines would be difficult to dispute. In the *Deduced Plan for an Institute of Higher Learning to be Established in Berlin*, that is, the university, Fichte says: "Now that which scientifically comprehends the entire spiritual activity, including all particular and further determinate expressions of it, is philosophy: thanks to the formation given them by the art of philosophy, the specific sciences should receive that which constitutes their proper art; that part of them which up to the present has simply been their natural gift dependent on the mercy of chance should be elevated to the rank of reflected ability and activity; the spirit of philosophy would be that which understood first itself and thereby all other spirits within it; the artist in a particular science must above all else become a philosophical artist, and his particular art would merely be a further determination and a single application of his universal philosophical art." Or, perhaps even more strikingly: "Thus with this developed philosophical spirit, that of the pure form of knowledge, the entire scientific or scholarly material would then need to be comprehended and penetrated in its organic unity, at the institution of higher learning."[4] These propositions are no less valid today than they were one hundred and fifty years ago. The emphatic concept of philosophy intended by the movement of German Idealism in the epoch when it was in accord with the spirit of the age did not add philosophy as a subject to the sciences, but rather sought philosophy in the vital self-reflection of the scientific and scholarly spirit. However, if the process of specialization, which denigrated this idea of philosophy into a platitude to be intoned by officiating orators, were viewed actually as an expression of the reification spirit itself underwent in step with an increasingly reified exchange society, then philosophy would be precisely the force of resistance inherent in each individual's own thought, a force that opposes the narrow-minded acquisition of factual knowledge, even in the so-called philosophical specialties.

Please do not misunderstand me. I am not ignoring the necessity of philosophy's becoming autonomous vis-à-vis the individual scientific and scholarly disciplines. Without that separation the natural sciences at least could hardly have experienced such rapid development. Perhaps even philosophy itself was not able to attain its most profound insights until, like Hegel, it had voluntarily or involuntarily taken its leave from the activities of the individual disciplines. It is futile to hope for a magical reunification of what has been separated; even the *philosophicum*, the philosophy examination, must beware of this illusion. Several highly developed disciplines in the humanities, for instance classical philology, have taken on such a specific gravity and have such a refined methodology and material at their disposal that philosophical self-reflection almost inevitably appears dilettantish in comparison. There is hardly a direct path leading from the practices of those disciplines to philosophical reflection. Conversely, the development of philosophy into a specialized discipline cannot simply be ignored. In the absence of familiarity with the products of specialized philosophy, philosophical self-reflection on the part of individual disciplines easily takes on a chimerical quality. Consciousness that would behave as though in its material it were at once also philosophical not only could all too easily sidestep the density of the material and veer into arbitrariness but would moreover be condemned to regress to stages of philosophical amateurism long ago superseded. I am neither overlooking nor intentionally ignoring this objective difficulty of the exam. But I think that one should not stop with that and, above all, that one should not get carried away. If in fact there is no direct path available between the work of the individual disciplines and that of philosophy, then this does not mean that the pursuits have nothing to do with one another. An expert in German philology would quite rightfully be indignant were he required to toss out historico-philosophical interpretations of the linguistic laws governing sound shifts. But, for instance, a problem such as how the mythical legacy of folk religions in the *Nibelungenlied*, though archaic from a Christian point of view, nonetheless takes on postmedieval Protestant traits in the figure of Hagen, assuming that the episode on the Danube signifies something like this[5]— such a problem would be legitimate in the eyes of the philologists and at the same time would be productive for philosophy. Or: if the great lyric poetry of the Middle Ages in large measure lacks what in the form of nature lyric then became so deeply rooted in the concept of the lyrical since the end of the eighteenth century, then the absence of this element that for such a long period of time is virtually taken for granted as part of later lyrical consciousness would be a theme just as much of interest to philosophers as to philologists. There are countless connections of this kind and the candidates could surely choose themes from their own areas of research. To understand Schiller it is essential to know his relation to Kant, by which I mean not the biographical and intellectual-historical contexts but rather the influence of Kant upon the very contours of Schiller's dramas and poems; and likewise in order to understand Hebbel one must know the historical-philosophical conception that infuses his dramaturgy. I am almost never presented with proposals for themes of the sort I've just improvised here. Of course, I do not mean by this that specifically philosophical themes should be excluded or that they should be considered exceptional. Yet for the moment it is enough to indicate the difference between the usual proposals and those involving some self-reflection, if not upon particular problems within the individual disciplines then at least upon the more extensive questions and areas of research. For my own part I would be content with themes that reveal at least some inclination toward what I have envisioned here.

The complaint is often heard that philosophy burdens future teachers with a supplementary discipline and, moreover, with one many people lack any connection with. I must return the reproach: very often it is the candidates, and not we, who transform the general test into a specialized one. When a candidate is, in the parlance, "allotted" to me, then I try to discuss with him the area he has chosen and try to distill a working theme from which something like the intellectual self-conception of his work can be inferred. However, by no means does this arouse pure joy and enthusiasm. On the contrary. If it were up to the desires of the students, then the written part of the test would always set topics purely about specialized disciplines, the history of philosophy, or summaries of philosophy. Quickly enough one discovers a predilection for certain philosophers and certain writings that enjoy a reputation for being particularly easy; thus the *Meditations* of Descartes, the English empiricists, Shaftesbury, Kant's *Grounding of the Metaphysics of Morals*, an ensemble so limited thematically that by now it has come to arouse all kinds of doubts in us. I am not easily persuaded that a Germanist or historian finds special significance or indeed any particular interest in the *Essay Concerning Human Understanding* of Locke, whom Kant called excellent and who is not exactly light reading for me either; and I am no less convinced when, as occurs more often of late, the candidate quickly produces pat reasons to justify his study of this extremely digressive founding text of *common sense**. By the way, the distinction between easy and difficult philosophers, which I suspect is paralleled by a distinction between easy and difficult examiners, is completely spurious. The abysses Locke smoothly glides over gape wide in his texts and at times make even a coherent presentation of his thought prohibitively difficult, while such an ill-reputed thinker as Hegel reaches a much higher level of rigor precisely because in his work the problems are not obscured by comfortable opinions but are addressed openly and without reservation. The intellectual or reflective person should feel free to entertain such considerations. If, however, heeding the watchword *safety first**, one wants to pass the exam by taking as few risks as possible, then this behavior does not exactly reinforce the intellectual powers and ultimately endangers an already tentative sense of security. For all that, I hope that the examiners will not now be engulfed by a wave of questions on Hegel.

If in fact one insists that the topic chosen be more than superficially connected to the candidate's particular area of interest, then one encounters the most peculiar difficulties. I once had the hardest time simply bringing one person to state his area of interest; everything interested him, he replied, and thereby awakened my suspicion that nothing interested him. Finally he indicated a specific period, and I thought of a work that offers a historico-philosophical interpretation of that era. I proposed that he work on this topic and ended up only terrifying him. He asked me whether the author in question actually was a renowned philosopher important for the disciplines he was studying, as the examination regulations stipulated; the verbatim text of the regulations often becomes the means of escaping their intention. Where the regulations provide points of orientation by which the examiner and the candidate can conduct the exam, some candidates hold fast and cling to them as though they were inviolable norms. One student declared that he was interested in Leibniz and his critique of Locke. When in preparing to take the test for the second time he proposed the same topic and the examiner explained that he thought it inappropriate to discuss the same things again, the student's first reaction was to ask whether he again had to study two philosophers. His behavior echoes a proposition from Hofmannsthal, which indeed he puts in the mouth of Clytemnestra, consumed by fear: "There must be proper rites for everything."[6] The candidates here in question search everywhere for cover, prescriptions, tracks that have already been laid down, both in order to find their way via well-worn paths and also to normalize the procedure of the examination so that precisely those questions for which the entire examination was first instituted are not posed. One encounters, in a word, reified consciousness. But this, the inability to experience and to engage with a topic in a free and autonomous manner, is the flagrant contradiction of everything one can reasonably and without pathos conceive to be the "genuine cultivation of mind" that the exam regulations identify as the purpose of the secondary schools. In negotiating the choice of topics one gets the impression that the candidates have taken as their maxim Brecht's phrase, "But I do not want to be a person at all," even and especially when they have learned the categorical imperative in its various formulations.[7] Those who become indignant at the imposition of philosophy as an academic discipline are the same people for whom philosophy means nothing more than an academic discipline.

For more than one reason we've learned not to overrate the written parts of the test in the overall evaluation of the candidates and to place

more weight upon the oral section. However, what one hears and sees
there is hardly more encouraging. If a candidate expresses his aversion to
the expectation that he should be an intellectual by pointedly sighing
throughout the exam, then undoubtedly that is more a matter of
upbringing than of spirit, although both have more to do with one
another than might occur to such a candidate. But specialized personnel
has—if I may be permitted this *contradictio in adjecto*—its orgy in the
orals.[8] "The candidate," as the exam regulations stipulate, "should
demonstrate that he grasps the fundamental concepts of the philosopher
he has studied and that he understands their historical evolution." A candidate questioned about Descartes was able, as is usually the case, to give
a quite accurate overview of the line of reasoning in the *Meditations*. The
discussion came to the concept of *res extensa*, extended substance, its
merely mathematical-spatial definition, and the lack of dynamic categories in the Cartesian conception of nature. In response to a question
about the consequences of this lack for the history of philosophy, the candidate explained, to his credit quite honestly, that he did not know; he had
never looked beyond Descartes, whom he had down pat, even so far as to
see what insufficiencies in the Cartesian system motivated Leibniz's critique and thereby also led to Kant. The specialized concentration upon a
certified great philosopher had diverted him from what the exam regulations require, the knowledge of the historical evolution of the problem.
Nevertheless he passed the exam. Another candidate presented with
unpleasant loquacity the line of reasoning in the first two *Meditations*. I
interrupted him in order to see how much he understood, and asked him
whether the hypothesis of doubt and the conclusion of an indubitable
ego cogitans completely satisfied him. I was entertaining the less than
abstruse idea that the individual empirical consciousness underpinning
Cartesian theory is itself intertwined with the spatio-temporal world
from which, according to Descartes, it stands apart as an irreducible and
imperishable difference. The candidate looked at me for a moment, during which he was more sizing me up than reflecting about the Cartesian
deduction. The result was apparently that he took me to be a man with an
understanding of higher things. In order to oblige me, he answered: no—
there is indeed a genuine encounter. Let us suppose that he had really
thought of something, for example, that in the recesses of his memory he
had remembered something of the doctrines that accord mind an immediate and intuitive knowledge of reality. In any case if he meant something like this, he did not know how to articulate it, and philosophy is
after all, as our old teacher Cornelius defined it, the art of self-expres-
sion.[9] What is characteristic in the response, however, is that he tossed
me a platitude taken from a run-down and, in the given context, ques-

tionable existentialist philosophy in the belief that he would thereby demonstrate his sophistication and possibly give me a name-brand pleasure. The specialist's credence in facts, for whom every consideration of what is not the case is an annoyance and possibly a sacrilege of the scientific spirit, has its complement in the faith in grandiose expressions and magical turns of phrase from the jargon of authenticity that chokes the air in Germany nowadays.[10] When reflection upon the subject matter itself, the intellectual sensibility of science and scholarship, comes to a stop, then what takes its place are platitudes steeped in worldviews, spellbound by that ill-fated German tradition according to which the noble idealists go to heaven and the base materialists go to hell. More than once I've encountered students who ask me whether they are also allowed to express their own views in their papers, whom all too innocently I have encouraged to go right ahead, and who then strive to demonstrate their independence by means of propositions such as this: Voltaire, who brought about the abolition of torture, lacked genuine religious sentiments. This alliance between the brutishness of *terre à terre* and the stereotype of an officially sanctioned worldview reveals an intellectual constitution akin to the totalitarian mind. National Socialism lives on today less in the doctrines that are still given credence—and it remains questionable whether its doctrines were ever believed—than in certain formal features of thought. These features include the eager adjustment to the reigning values of the moment; a two-tiered classification dividing the sheep from the goats; the lack of immediate, spontaneous relations to people, things, ideas; a compulsive conventionalism; and a faith in the established order no matter what the cost. Structures of thought and syndromes such as these are, strictly speaking, apolitical in their content, but their survival has political implications. This is perhaps the gravest aspect of what I am trying to say.

The patchwork of acquired—which most often means memorized—facts and worldview declamations indicates that the connection between the subject matter and its reflection in thought has been sundered. This is confirmed again and again in the examinations and must be directly due to the absence of what anyone wishing to educate and cultivate others must himself have, namely, culture. Despite warnings from her examiner a student wanted to choose Bergson for the subject of her oral exam. In order to see whether the student had any idea of what is called intellectual context, the examiner asked her about some painters contemporaneous with the philosopher and whose work might have something to do with the spirit of his philosophy. At first she maintained that it was naturalism. When queried for names she first mentioned Manet, then Gauguin, and finally, with a good deal of help from the examiner, Monet. The examiner insisted on asking for the name of this great movement in painting of the late nineteenth century, and the student answered triumphantly: expressionism. Alas, she had not indicated impressionism as her topic but only Bergson; yet living culture would consist precisely in the awareness of such relations between the *Lebensphilosophie* and the impressionistic style in painting. Whoever does not understand that also cannot understand Bergson himself; and indeed the candidate actually was absolutely incapable of explaining the two texts she claimed to have read: *Introduction à la métaphysique* and *Matière et mémoire*.

If we were countered with the question, for instance, of how a culture that would encourage the association of Bergson and impressionism should be acquired, then we examiners in philosophy would feel quite embarrassed. For culture is precisely that for which there are no correct rules; it is acquired only by spontaneous effort and interest and is not guaranteed by courses alone, even if they be those of the type of a *studium generale*, "general studies." In truth, culture is not even about applied effort, but rather about having an open mind and the general ability to engage in intellectual matters, to take them up productively within one's own consciousness instead of merely learning something and, as the unbearable cliché says, "confronting" it.[11] If I did not fear being mistaken for a sentimentalist, then I would say that culture requires love: what is lacking is probably the ability to love. Any suggestions for how this condition might be changed are dangerous; most often it is decided in an early stage of childhood development. But anyone in want of this ability should hardly teach others. Not only do such individuals perpetuate that suffering in the classroom poets were denouncing sixty years ago and that people think, quite falsely, is now long gone, but rather the defect is passed on to the pupils and reproduces ad infinitum that intellectual condition that in my view is not an innocent naiveté but rather was partially responsible for the catastrophe of National Socialism.

This lack shows itself most palpably in the relationship to language. According to paragraph 9 of the examination regulations, particular importance should be accorded to linguistic expression; in the case of severe deficiencies in language, the work must be deemed unsatisfactory. I do not dare to imagine what would happen if the examiners adhered to this rule. I fear that even the most urgent openings for teachers could not be filled, and it would not surprise me if many candidates relied on this state of affairs. Only exceedingly few candidates have any idea of the difference between language as a means of communication and language as the precise expression of the matter under consideration; they believe that knowing how to speak is sufficient to know how to write, although it is true enough that whoever cannot write most often is also incapable of speaking. I hope I'm not one of the *laudatores temporis acti*, but my memories of *Gymnasium* evoke teachers whose linguistic sensibility, or rather whose simple correctness of expression, is distinguished from the sloppiness that reigns today, a sloppiness that probably could be justified by appealing to the overall predominant usage of language and that in fact reflects the objective spirit. Sloppiness usually gets along splendidly with schoolmasterly pedantry. Whenever I meet with a candidate to discuss his theme for the *Staatsexamen*,[12] as soon as I have the impression that he lacks a sense of responsibility toward language—and the reflection upon language is the prototype of all philosophical reflection—I bring this paragraph of the regulations to his attention and try to describe for him in advance what I expect in these examination papers. The fact that such paræneses bear so little fruit seems to indicate that it is a matter of more than just laxness;[13] the candidates have lost all relation to the language they speak. The more mediocre works teem with grammatical and syntactical errors. The basest clichés, such as "somewhat," "the genuine concern," and the famous "encounter," are used without the least embarrassment, indeed with gusto, as though the employment of catchphrases meant that one is absolutely up-to-date.[14] Worst of all is the articulation of propositions. Somewhere in the back of one's mind there is probably the reminder that a philosophical text should possess logical integrity or coherence based on reasoned argument. However, this in no way bears any connection to the relations between the thoughts themselves, or rather the affirmations that so often merely pretend to be thoughts. Pseudo-logical and pseudo-causal relations are produced with the help of particles that paste together the propositions superficially at a linguistic level, but thoughtful reflection reveals them to be irrelevant; thus, for example, of two propositions one is presented as the conclusion of the other at the level of language, whereas at the level of logic neither proposition entails the other.

As for style, most of the candidates, though they may have studied linguistics, have not the slightest idea; instead they awkwardly and affectedly sift out from their customary manner of speaking what they mistakenly think is a scientific or scholarly tone. However, the language in the examination papers is outdone by what is heard in the oral part of the exam. Often it is a stammering interspersed with vague, qualifying phrases, such as "to a certain extent," that in the same instant they are uttered try to evade responsibility for what is said. Words of foreign derivation, even names of foreigners, constitute hurdles that are seldom surmounted without some damage to either hurdle or candidate; for instance, most of the candidates who have chosen for their exam a philosopher who is apparently as easy to classify as Hobbes, speak of him as Hob*bes*, as though the *bes* belonged to the dialect in which *ebbes* means "*etwas*."[15] The very idea of dialect. One may rightly expect from culture that it accustom a regional language's coarseness to more polished manners. This is out of the question. The conflict between High German and dialect ends in a draw, which pleases no one, not even the future teacher, whose disgruntlement clatters in every word. The speaker's closeness to his dialect, that sense in which—in the case of a dialect still quite rustic—he is at least speaking his own language, or as the vernacular has it, "speaking off the top of his head," has been lost.[16] The objective standard language has not been achieved, but remains disfigured by the scars of the dialect; it sounds a bit the way those boys in provincial towns look who are called in to help with the Sunday dinner crowds and are rigged out in a waiter's jacket that does not fit them at all.[a] Certainly I do not want to say anything against the friendly institution of German language courses for foreigners the university organizes, but courses for natives would perhaps be more important, even if they did nothing more than rid the future teacher of that intonation in which the brutality of the rustic indistinctly blends with his future pedagogical dignity. The complement of vulgarity is pomposity, the fondness for using words that lie beyond the speakers' horizon of experience and that therefore in their mouths sound like those foreign words they presumably one day will harass their pupils with. Such expressions are almost always sedimented cultural goods of the privileged class or, in terms less academic, a worn-out gentleman's wardrobe that enters the so-called pedagogical sector only when no one in the realm of free spirits will touch it.[17] Urbanity is part of culture, and its locus is language. No one should be reproached for coming from the country, but no one should make a virtue out of it either and obstinately continue it; whoever does not succeed in emancipating himself from provincialism remains extraterritor-

---

[a] The letters I have received lead me to be more precise. I do not mean that culture signifies that every trace of dialect within a pitiless standard language has been eradicated. It merely suffices, for example, to hear the Viennese intonation in order to learn just how deeply linguistic humanitarianism is realized in such tonalities. But the difference between, on the one hand, a German language that divests dialect of its coarseness by harmoniously absorbing its trace and, on the other hand, an idiom in which both linguistic levels remain hopelessly incompatible and in which pedantic correctness is belied by the remnants of a formless dialect—this difference is decisive; it is nothing less than the difference between culture [*Kultur*] such as it replaces nature, absorbs it within itself, and a mechanism of actual repression that perpetuates itself in spirit. Imprisoned within it, repressed nature, merely disfigured, destructively returns. Whether a person has a sense for language: his culture comes to the fore precisely in that he is able to perceive such nuances.

ial to culture. It would be good for those who intend to teach others if they would become explicitly conscious of their duty to deprovincialize themselves instead of helplessly imitating whatever is considered culture. The persistent divergence between city and country, the cultural amorphousness of the agrarian, whose traditions meanwhile are irrevocably on the ebb, is one of the forms in which barbarism perpetuates itself. It is not a matter of the refinements of intellectual and linguistic elegance. The individual becomes mature only when he frees himself from the immediacy of conditions that are in no way natural but, on the contrary, the vestiges of a historic development that has been surpassed—something that is dead and does not even know it.

If one happens to be cursed with an exact imagination, then one can very well imagine how the choice of career occurs: the family discussion about what the boy should do to get somewhere in life, perhaps after having doubted that he'd pull it off on his own without the protection of a career guaranteed by a diploma; local dignitaries may have lent their encouragement and put their connections to work, and together they would have concocted the most profitable course of study. Here a role is played by that ignominious scorn for the teacher's profession that is widespread not only in Germany and that in turn motivates the candidates to make all too modest demands upon themselves. In truth, many have resigned themselves even before they begin, and consequently have no more esteem for themselves than they have for their intellectual work. In all this I sense a humiliating necessity that paralyzes in advance all resistance to such an attitude. The situation this type of high school graduate finds himself in probably really leaves him scarcely any other choice. It would be too much to presume him capable of perceiving the dubiousness of his enterprise at the moment he decides upon his future. Otherwise he would already be liberated from the constraint that is revealed later in the examination as a lack of intellectual freedom. The people I have in mind are trapped within a vicious circle; their interest compels them to make the wrong decision of which they themselves ultimately become the victims. Nothing would be more unjust than to blame them for this. But if the idea of freedom still has any meaning at all, then it should allow these ill-suited students to come to the obvious conclusion at the point in their development when they become aware of the difficulty—the rupture between their existence and their profession and everything it involves—and this awareness must inevitably develop sometime at university. Either they must in good time renounce the profession with which they are incompatible—during an economic boom the excuse hardly holds that other possibilities are blocked—or with all the energy of self-criticism they must confront the condition, some symptoms of which I have here enumerated, and must attempt to change it. Precisely this attempt, not any determinate result, would be the culture that candidates should acquire and, I would like to add, would also be what the examination requires by way of philosophy: that the future teachers gain some insight into what it is they do, instead of remaining captured within it and understanding nothing. The handicaps that, as I well know, hamper many of them, are not invariants.[18] For that reason self-reflection and critical exertion have real potential. That potential would be the opposite of the blind and dogged diligence that the majority have once and for all decided upon. This diligence contradicts culture and philosophy because from the outset it is by definition the learning of what is already given and valorized, in which the subject, the person who is actually learning, his judgment, his experience, the substrate of freedom, are all absent.

For what actually alarms me about the examinations is the gulf between the philosophical work presented and the students themselves. Whereas their study of philosophy should promote the convergence of their genuine interest with the academic specialty through which they are developing themselves, instead their study merely perpetuates their own self-alienation. This self-alienation even increases to the extent that philosophy is felt to be a ballast preventing them from acquiring useful knowledge: either the candidate's preparations in his major disciplines, and thereby hindering his progress, or his learning material necessary for his profession. The philosophy studied for the exam becomes its own contrary; instead of leading initiates to self-understanding, it serves no other function than to demonstrate to them and to us just how badly culture has failed, not only in the case of the candidates but in general. The surrogate they take in its stead is the concept of science. This concept once used to mean the requirement that nothing be accepted without first being examined and tested: the freedom and emancipation from the tutelage of heteronomous dogmas. Today one shudders at just how pervasively scientificity has become a new form of heteronomy for its disciples. They imagine that their salvation is secured if they follow scientific rules, heed the ritual of science, surround themselves with science. The approbation of science becomes the substitute for the intellectual reflection upon the facts, once the very foundation of science. The armor masks the wound. Reified consciousness installs science as an apparatus between itself and living experience. The more the suspicion grows that the best has been forgotten, the more the operation of the apparatus itself serves as consolation. Again and again I am asked by candidates whether they may, should, must use the secondary literature and what I recommend. Now a familiarity with the secondary literature is always good so that one does not lag behind the current state of research and thus perhaps discover the North Pole all over again. Those who want to acquire academic qualifications must ultimately also demonstrate that they master the ground rules of scientific and scholarly work. But often the concern with secondary literature means something entirely different. First, the expectation that the secondary literature will furnish the thoughts the candidate masochistically believes himself incapable of generating, and then the hope, perhaps not even conscious, of belonging to science's mystical predestined elect through demonstrations of scholarly folderol, citation, extensive bibliographies, and references. The students wish at least to be one of science's chosen few, because otherwise they are nothing. I have no inclination to existentialist philosophy, but in such moments it contains an element of truth. Science as ritual exempts them from thinking and from freedom. They are told that freedom must be saved, that it is threatened from the East, and I do not delude myself about the regimentation of consciousness on the far side of the border. But sometimes it seems to me as though freedom were already undermined among those who formally still have it, as though their spiritual habitude has already aligned itself with the regression, even in those areas where it is not expressly regulated, as though something in the people themselves waits to be relieved of the autonomy that once signified all that was to be respected and preserved in Europe. Within the inability of thought to transcend itself there already lurks the potential for integration, for submission to any kind of authority, which is already evident today in the way people compliantly cling to the status quo. Many go so far as to glorify the captivating spell even to themselves, exalting it into what the jargon of authenticity calls a "genuine bond." But they are deceiving themselves. They have not passed beyond the isolation of autonomous spirit but rather have fallen behind individuation and therefore cannot overcome it as they would like to believe.

The idea of practical progress possesses such an unshakable supremacy for many people that for them nothing else seriously compares with it. Their attitude is one of automatic defensiveness, and for that reason I do not know whether I can reach them at all. One of the characteristics of reified consciousness is that it hunkers down within itself, stubbornly persists in its own weakness, and insists on being right no matter what the cost. I am always astounded by the acumen exhibited by even the most obtuse minds when it comes to defending their mistakes. One could reply, with little risk of being contradicted, that this is all very well known but that nothing can be done about it. In support of this assertion general reflections could be marshaled such as: where could anyone today find the faintest glimmer of a larger meaning that might illuminate his own work? Further, and here I would be the first to agree, one could invoke the fact that social conditions such as where one comes from, which are beyond anyone's control, are responsible for the inability to satisfy the emphatic concept of culture: the majority have been cheated out of the experiences that precede all explicit instruction and that sustain culture. Furthermore, one could refer to the insufficiencies of the university and its own failure: quite often the university itself does not provide what we complain of not finding in the candidates. Finally, one could draw attention to the overload of material to be learned and the awkwardness of the examination situation itself. I will not enter into a dispute about how much of all this is accurate and how much mere pretext: there are insights that in themselves are true but that become false as soon as they are used to serve narrow interests. So much I would concede: that in a situation where the virtual dependence of everyone on the structure as a whole reduces the possibility of freedom to a minimum, the appeal to the freedom of the individual rings rather hollow. Freedom is not an ideal hovering inalienably and immutably above the heads of human beings—not without reason does the image recall the sword of Damocles—but rather its possibility varies as a function of the historical moment. In the present moment the economic pressure upon most people is still so unbearable that it destroys all self-consciousness and critical reflection: it is no longer the material needs of former times but more the feeling of overall impotence within society as a whole, a universal dependence that no longer makes individual self-determination possible.

But can one expect a man to fly? Is enthusiasm something that can be regulated? Plato, who after all knew what philosophy is, considered it to be the most important subjective condition for philosophy.[19] The answer is not as simple as the dismissive gesture might suppose. For this enthusiasm is not a contingent phase simply due to the biological stage of adolescence. It has an objective content, the dissatisfaction with a pure and simple immediacy of the subject matter, the experience of it as semblance. The subject matter itself will require that its semblance be transcended as soon as the person with goodwill immerses himself in it. The transcendence I have in mind is one with the immersion. Every person senses quite well on his own what is missing: I know that I am not saying anything new here but at most what many people prefer not to admit. The most urgent recommendation would be Schelling's *Lectures on the Method of Academic Study*.[20] In his approach from the standpoint of identity philosophy many themes can be found that I reached coming from completely different premises; it is astounding that the situation in 1803, when the German philosophical movement had reached its height, does not differ so much in regard to the issues here under discussion from the present day when philosophy no longer exercises such authority. It is not so much a matter of future teachers pledging allegiance to something they find strange and irrelevant, but that they should follow the needs arising in their work and not let themselves be dissuaded by the supposed constraints of their formal course of study. Intellectual activity may be more questionable today than in Schelling's age, and to preach idealism would be foolish, even if it still had its former philosophical relevance. But spirit itself, to the extent that it does not acquiesce to what is the case, carries within itself that momentum that is a subjective need. Every person who has chosen an intellectual profession has undertaken an obligation to entrust himself to its movement. That obligation should be no less honored than the expectation that the examination regulations will be followed. What I wanted to say, and perhaps have been unable to express with complete clarity, should not be brushed aside with an air of superiority that masks hard-boiled cynicism. It would be better if each person pursued the goals he has set for himself. It is not a question of drawing comfort from the thought that things just are that bad and nothing can be done about it; rather, each must reflect upon this fatality and upon its consequences for one's own work, including one's examination. This would be the beginning of that philosophy that closes itself only to those who blind themselves to the reasons why it remains closed to them.

Note on *Human Science and Culture*

Among the aspects of today's university, in the context of which the expression crisis is more than a mere cliché, I would like to emphasize one in particular that, though I certainly did not discover it, has hardly received sufficient attention in the public discussion. It is related to, but in no way coincides with, that general phenomenon known as the divergence between self-cultivation and specialized training. It is not easy to speak of it, and the vagueness and thesis-like style of this improvised attempt must be excused. It bears on the question of whether in the contemporary university culture still succeeds in those pursuits where its concept is thematically and traditionally maintained, that is, in the so-called human sciences[1]—whether in general the student of the human sciences can still gain in any measure that kind of intellectual and spiritual experience that the concept of culture meant and that inheres in the significance of the very objects he studies. There is much supporting the view that precisely the concept of science, which arose after the decline of grand philosophy and since then has enjoyed a kind of monopoly, undermines the culture to which it lays claim by virtue of its monopoly. Scientific discipline is an intellectual form of what Goethe as well as Hegel called for under the name of 'externalization':[2] the devotion of spirit to something opposed and alien to it and through which alone spirit attains freedom. Anyone who has shirked this discipline through dilettantish, impulsive thinking and practiced gossip will easily fall below the level of what had aroused his legitimate aversion: the method heteronomously imposed upon him. But this discipline and its corresponding conception of science—which in the meantime has become the contrary of what Fichte, Schelling, and Hegel understood by the term—has acquired a fatal preponderance to the detriment of its contrary aspect, a preponderance that cannot be revoked by fiat. Spontaneity, imagination, freedom toward the subject matter, despite all explanations to the contrary, are so restricted by the omnipresent question "but is it science?" that even in its native regions spirit is threatened with being dispirited.[3] The function of the concept of science has become inverted. The often invoked methodological neatness, universal confirmation, the consensus of competent scholars, the verifiability of all assertions, even the logical rigor of the lines of reasoning, is not spirit: the criterion of watertight validity always also works against spirit. Where the conflict against the unregimented understanding is already decided, dialectic and culture, the internal process between subject and object as it was conceived in the age of Humboldt, cannot arise. Organized human science is a stock-taking and a reflective form of spirit rather than its proper life; it wants to come to know spirit as something dissimilar from itself and elevates that dissimilarity into a maxim. But if human science tries to usurp spirit's place, then spirit vanishes, even in science itself. This happens as soon as science is considered the only instrument of culture and the organization of society sanctions no other. The more profoundly science senses that it does not provide what it promises, the more it tends to manifest an intolerance toward the spirit that is unlike it, and the more science insists on its own privilege. The disappointment of many students of the human sciences in the first semesters is due not only to their naiveté but also to the fact that the human sciences have renounced that element of naiveté, of the immediate relation to the object without which spirit cannot live; the human sciences' lack of self-reflection is no less naive. Even when their worldview opposes positivism, they have secretly fallen under the spell of the positivistic way of thinking, that of reified consciousness. Discipline, in accord with an overall tendency of society, becomes the taboo placed on anything that does not stubbornly reproduce what already exists: but precisely that would be the definition of spirit. In a foreign university a student of art history was told: "You are not here to think, but to do research." In Germany, indeed, out of respect for a tradition of which little more remains than that respect, such sentiments are not expressed so bluntly, but here, too, they have not left working habits unaffected.

The reification of consciousness, the deployment of its ingrained conceptual apparatuses often preempts its objects and obstructs culture, which would be one with the resistance to reification. The network in which organized human science has enmeshed its objects tends to become a fetish; anything that is different becomes superfluous, and science has no place for it. The philosophically dubious cult of primordiality practiced by the Heideggerian school would hardly have so fascinated students in the human sciences if it did not address a genuine need. Every day they see that scientific thinking, instead of elucidating the phenomena, readily makes do with the shape into which each phenomenon has already been deformed. Yet because the very societal process that reifies thinking goes unrecognized, they in turn make primordiality itself into a field, into an allegedly radical and therefore specialized question. What reified scientific consciousness desires in place of its subject matter is, however, something societal: to be protected by the institutionalized branch of science that such consciousness invokes as its sole authority as soon as anyone dares to remind it of what it has forgotten. This is the implicit conformism of human science. Whereas it pretends to cultivate intellectual-spiritual people, it is rather precisely these people whom it breaks. They install within themselves a more or less voluntary self-censor. This leads them first of all not to say anything that lies outside the established rules of conduct in their science; gradually they lose the ability even to perceive such things. Even when confronted with spiritual creations, precisely those who are academically involved with them find it genuinely difficult to think of something different than what corresponds to a tacit and hence all the more powerful scientific ideal.

The repressive power of this ideal is in no way restricted simply to pedagogical or technical disciplines. The dictate exercised here by practical utility has also engulfed those disciplines that cannot claim any such utility. For the dispiriting is immanent in the concept of science that has inexorably expanded ever since science and philosophy broke away from one another, due to each and to the detriment of each. Even where academic culture is engaged with spiritual matters it unconsciously falls into step[4] with a science that takes for its standard what already exists, the factually real and its processing—that facticity with which the vital force of spirit should not content itself. Just how profoundly deprivation of spirit and scientification are intertwined at their roots is manifest in the way that ready-made philosophemes are then imported as an antidote. They are leached into interpretations made in the human sciences in order to lend them the luster they otherwise lack, without such philosophemes being the result of coming to know the spiritual creations themselves. With ridiculous solemnity the same thing is read invariably, again and again, out of them.[5]

Between spirit and science a vacuum has developed. Not only specialized education but culture itself no longer cultivates. Culture is polarized between the elements of the methodological and the informational. In the face of this the cultivated spirit would be a form of involuntary reaction as much as its own master. Nothing in cultural and educational institutions, not even the universities, offers any support to spirit. While unreflective scientification increasingly ostracizes spirit as a kind of extraneous nonsense, it also entangles itself ever more deeply in the contradiction between the content of its activity and the task it sets itself. If the universities are to change their orientation, then there is no less reason to intervene in the human sciences than in the disciplines they falsely imagine to be backward in spirit.

Those Twenties

For Daniel-Henry Kahnweiler

Slogans make themselves suspect not just because they serve to degrade thoughts into mere counters; they are also the index of their own untruth. What the public, and particularly the revivalist vogue, nowadays thinks belonged to the nineteen-twenties was in fact already fading at that time, by 1924 at the latest. The heroic age of the new art was actually around 1910: synthetic cubism, early German expressionism, the free atonalism of Schönberg and his school. Adolf Frisé has noted this fact in a recent radio interview with Lotte Lenya.[1] I can clearly remember that after an IGNM festival in Frankfurt in 1927 I published an article entitled "The Stabilized Music."[2] It was not, as is usually assumed, the pressure exerted by the National Socialist terror that brought regression, neutralization, and a funereal silence to the arts, for these phenomena had already taken shape in the Weimar Republic, and in liberal continental European society generally. The dictatorships did not swoop down upon this society from outside in the way Cortez invaded Mexico; rather they were engendered by the social dynamic following the First World War, and they cast their shadows before them.

This is immediately evident in the products of mass culture manipulated by a highly centralized economic power. One has only to listen to the record albums that are now being revived as the hits, songs, and chansons from the twenties to be astonished at how little has changed in this whole sphere. As with fashion, the packaging changes; but the thing itself, a conventional language composed of signals to suit the conditioned reflexes of consumers, essentially remained the same, as jazz, for instance, was a perennial fashion.[3] While it seems that such past fashions have a naive and awkward aspect in comparison with the current trend—that they are what the *slang** of American light music calls *corny**—this is due less to the substance of what is disseminated than to the time factor *in abstracto*, at most to the progressive perfecting of the machinery and of social-psychological control. The quality of being not yet quite so smart, which provokes smiles from the same type of people who in those days acclaimed Mistinguett and Marlene, is of the same nature as the idealizing nostalgia that clings to those same products today. The period's comparative backwardness in the techniques of consumer culture is misinterpreted as though to mean it was closer to the origins, whereas in truth it was just as much organized to grab customers as it is in 1960. In fact, it is a paradox that anything at all changes within the sphere of a culture rationalized to suit industrial ideals; the principle of *ratio* itself, to the extent that it calculates cultural effects economically, remains the eternal invariant. That is why it is somewhat shocking whenever anything from the sector of the culture industry becomes old-fashioned. The shock value of this paradox was already exploited by the surrealists in the twenties when they confronted the world of 1880; in England at that time a book like *Our Fathers* by Allan Bott had caused a similar effect.[4] Today the shock effect is produced by the twenties, similar to the effect the world of images of the 1880s produced around 1920. But the repetition deadens the shock effect. The defamiliarization[5] of the twenties is the ghost of a ghost.

In the German-speaking world the imago of the twenties is probably not so strongly marked by the intellectual movements of the period. Expressionism and the new music at the time probably found far less resonance than do the radical aesthetic tendencies of today. It was rather an imagistic world of erotic fantasy, and was nourished by theatrical works that at the time stood for the spirit of the age and that today still easily pass for the same, even though their composition does not have anything especially avant-garde about it. The *Songspiele* that Brecht and Weill composed together, *The Threepenny Opera* and *Mahagonny*, and Ernst Krenek's *Jonny* are representative of this sphere.[6] The subsequent discontent with civilization's progressive desexualizing of the world, which at the same time paradoxically keeps pace with the lifting of taboos, transfers onto the twenties romantic desires for sexual anarchy, the *red light district** and the *wide open city**. There is something immeasurably mendacious in all this. The enthusiasm for barroom Jennys goes together with the persecution of prostitutes, who catch it from society's crystal-clear order when no more suitable targets are at hand. If life in the twenties had really been so nice, then it would be enough to leave the floozies in peace and stop trying to clean up the streets. Instead, antiseptically erotic films are made about the *naughty twenties**, or better still, about the Toulouse-Lautrec of our grandparents' time. And yet even back then those girls weren't doing it for free. The wretched commercialized sex industry of the Kurfürstendamm, as portrayed by George Grosz and transfixed by the words of Karl Kraus, was no closer to utopia than is the sterilized atmosphere of today.

Nevertheless, the idea that the twenties were a world where, as Brecht puts it in *Mahagonny*, "everything may be permitted,"[7] that is, a utopia, also has its truth. At that time, as again shortly after 1945, there seemed to be a real possibility of a politically liberated society. But it only seemed so: already in the twenties, as a consequence of the events of 1919, the decision had fallen against that political potential that, had things gone otherwise, with great probability would have influenced developments in Russia and prevented Stalinism. It is hard to avoid the conclusion that this twofold aspect—on the one hand, a world that could have taken a turn for the better and, on the other, the extinguishing of that hope by the establishment of powers that later revealed themselves fully in fascism—also expressed itself in an ambivalence in art, which in fact is quite specific to the twenties and has nothing to do with the vague and self-contradictory idea of the modern classics. Precisely those operatic works that earned fame and scandal then seem now, in their ambiguous stance toward anarchy, as though their main function was to furnish National Socialism with the slogans it later used to justify its cultural terrorism, as though that assiduously exaggerated disorder was already lusting for the order Hitler subsequently imposed across Europe. This is not something for the twenties to boast of. The catastrophe that followed the period was engendered by its own societal conflicts, even in what is customarily called the cultural sphere.

The extent to which the nostalgia for the twenties in fact clings to something intellectual, and not merely to a fata morgana of a period supposed to be at once both avant-garde and not yet enwrapped in the cellophane of modernity, is decided less by the level and quality of what was produced at the time than by the true or putative intellectual posture itself. Preconsciously one senses how much the revived culture is being absorbed by the ideology it had never ceased to be. Since one does not dare to acknowledge this, one projects an ideal image[8] of a past condition in which spirit supposedly had not yet been forced to admit its incongruity with the forces of reality. In comparison to what has happened since then, spirit altogether takes on an aspect of triviality. It feels culpable because it could not prevent the horror; but its own tenderness and fragility in turn presuppose a reality that could have escaped barbarism. The imago of the time immediately preceding the catastrophe is invested with everything spirit nowadays is felt to be denied. The absence of intellectual movements that can intervene today—even the existentialism of the first years after the war was nothing more than a resuscitative renaissance—awakens even in the most naive people the sentiment of sterility. It contributes to the legend of the twenties as the time when the very domain of spirit tottered, while still maintaining its earlier relevance to people's lives. The fact that after 1918 cubism lost its appeal is certainly a symptom that can be diagnosed only postmortem. Kahnweiler reports: "Picasso me dit encore bien souvent à l'heure actuelle que toute ce qui a été fait dans les années de 1907 à 1914 n'a pu être fait que par un travail d'équipe. D'être isolé, seul, cela a dû l'inquiéter énormément et c'est alors qu'il y a eu ce changement."[a] The isolation that destroyed the continuity of the painter's work and brought him, and not only him, to start revising, was hardly the fate of a contingent biography. That isolation reflects the loss of the collective energies that had produced the great innovations in European art. The shift in the relationship between the individual spirit and society extended even into the secret-most impulses of those for whom any adaptation to the demands of society was anathema. There was no lack here of what the naive faith in culture calls creative gifts. The very idea of intellectual production had been poisoned. Its self-confidence, the certainty that it is making history, is undermined. This accords with the fact that, precisely to the extent that it is assimilated, intellectual production no longer has any actual effect. Even its most extravagant expressions are no longer safe from being integrated into industrialized culture. Because the world spirit no longer coincides with spirit, the latter's last days shine resplendently as though they had been the golden age that in fact they never were. What remains is more an echo of fascist authority than anything itself living: the cultural respect for received values, even if they are merely touted as being important. Better would be a consciousness that realized its own diminished potential: Beckett has it. It would no longer be a culture of renewed deception, but instead one

---

[a] Daniel-Henry Kahnweiler, *Mes galeries et mes peintres: Entretiens avec Francis Crémieux* (Paris: Gallimard, 1961), 73. [*Translator's note*: English translation of the passage Adorno quotes in the original: "Picasso still tells me quite often today that everything that was done in the years from 1907 to 1917 [*sic*] could only have been done through teamwork. Being isolated, being alone, must have upset him enormously, and it was then that there was this change" (Daniel-Henry Kahnweiler with Francis Crémieux, *My Galleries and Painters*, trans. Helen Weaver [New York: Viking Press, 1971], 54).]

that would express in its structure what denigrates spirit to the level of such deception. The only means by which culture can cure its curse of futility is by submitting that curse to interrogation.

The uncertain relationship between the present day and the twenties is conditioned by a historical discontinuity. Whereas the fascist decade in all its essential aspects was established in the epoch immediately preceding it, with roots deep within expressionism—one of whose spokesmen, Hanns Johst, rose to become a Nazi celebrity, and incidentally was already being parodied in the twenties by Brecht, who had good instincts[9]—the popular Nazi phrase "clean break"[10] sadly turned out to be right. The tradition, including the tradition of anti-traditionalism, was broken off, and half-forgotten tasks remain. And whatever now is artistically engaged with that epoch not only eclectically reaches back to a creative productivity that has died in the meantime, but at the same time also obeys an obligation not to forget those things that remain unfinished. It is necessary to pursue to its own logical consequences what was buried in the explosion of 1933, which itself in an entirely different sense was a consequence of that epoch.

It is quite clear how contemporary art, in view of its own problematic, should behave in regard to the avant-gardism of the past, and the artists of importance know this well. Anti-conventionalism remains indispensable; forms return only within the interior of works, not as something imposed upon them heteronomously. Such works must consciously measure themselves against the historical situation of their material: they must neither abandon themselves blindly and fetishistically to the material nor mold it from outside with subjective intentions. Only what is free from cowardice and ego-weakness and advances without protection, refusing everything indicated in the German language of the post-Hitler epoch by that loathsome expression "guiding image,"[11] has a chance of creating something that is not superfluous. Every consideration of possible effects, even under the pretext of social function or regard for the so-called human being, is untenable, but then so is the high-handed imperiousness of both the subject and its expression from the heroic days of modern art. It is no longer possible to evade the aspect of paradox in all art itself: this paradox, and not any existential philosopheme, is what the label "absurd" means. In every one of its elements contemporary artistic production must bear in mind the crisis of meaning: the meaning subjectively given a work of art as well as the meaningful conception of the world. Otherwise artistic creativity sells its services to legitimation. The only legitimately meaningful artworks today are those opposing the concept of meaning with the utmost recalcitrance.

The impulses must be recovered that in the vaunted twenties were already threatening to petrify or dissipate. From the distance of the present one may observe how many artists whose aura is identified with that of the twenties had in fact already passed their peak in that decade, in any case toward the end of it; Kandinsky, surely Picasso, Schönberg, even Klee. Just as it is beyond question that Schönberg's twelve-tone technique developed completely logically from his own earlier achievement, from the emancipation from tonal language as well as the radicalization of motive-thematic work, so it is equally certain that some of the best was lost in the transition to systematic principles. Despite the material having been revolutionized, the musical language aligned itself with that of the tradition more than in Schönberg's best works before the First World War; the unfettered spontaneity and independence of the compositional subject was restrained by a need for order that revealed itself to be problematical, because the order it produced was born of that need, not of the matter itself. The appearance of stagnation in the music of the last decades, the often and somewhat maliciously observed risk of the avant-garde's becoming a second orthodoxy, is largely the legacy of this need for order. The musical task bequeathed to us from the twenties seems to be precisely the revision of that need for order: the pursuit of a *musique informelle*.[b] This idea of order passed down from the twenties can only be warmed over, not taken up productively. It was nothing other than the abstract negation of the supposed state of chaos that was feared far too much for it to have actually existed.

---

[b] To designate a third entity between serial and post-serial music Adorno "coined the term *musique informelle* as a small token of gratitude towards the nation for whom the tradition of the avant-garde is synonymous with the courage to produce manifestos." Although he dialectically explicates the notion of informal or aserial music through recourse to specific works, Adorno broaches an initial description:

> What is meant is a type of music which has discarded all forms which are external or abstract or which confront it in an inflexible way. At the same time, although such music should be completely free of anything irreducibly alien to itself or superimposed on it, it should nevertheless constitute itself in an objectively compelling way, in the musical substance itself, and not in terms of external laws. Morever, wherever this can be achieved without running the risk of a new form of oppression, such an emancipation should also strive to do away with the system of musical co-ordinates which have crystallized out in the innermost recesses of the musical substance itself.

He adds that, as "an image of freedom," such music, "had been a real possibility once before, around 1910. The date is not irrelevant, since it provides a demarcation line dividing the age from the vastly overrated twenties." Adorno, "Vers une musique informelle," originally in *Quasi una fantasia* (1963), now in GS 16: 493–540; English: *Quasi una fantasia: Essays on Modern Music,* trans. Rodney Livingstone (London: Verso, 1992): 269–322 (cited: pp. 272–73).

What requires reflection is both the necessity of pursuing without compromise the process that was suspended internally and externally and the limits of a possible resumption. It is perfectly self-evident that after thirty or forty years, after the absolute break, one cannot simply pick up where things were left off. The significant works of that epoch owed much of their power to the productive tension with a heterogeneous element: the tradition against which they rebelled. This was still a force confronting them, and it was precisely the most productive artists who had a great deal of that tradition within them. Much of the constraint that inspired those works was lost when the friction with this tradition disappeared. Freedom is complete, but threatens to become freewheeling without its dialectical counterpart, whereas that counterpart cannot be maintained simply by an act of the will. Contemporary art must become conscious not only of its technical problems, but also of the conditions of its own existence, so that it does not become a mere rehash of the twenties, does not degrade into precisely what it refused to be: cultural property. Art's social arena is no longer an advanced or perhaps even decayed liberalism, but rather a fully manipulated, calculated, and integrated society, the "administered world." Whatever protest is made against this in terms of artistic form—and it is no longer possible to conceive of an artistic form that is not a protest—itself becomes integrated into the universal planning it is attacking and bears the marks of this contradiction. Since their material has been emancipated and processed in every dimension nowadays, artworks evolve purely from their own formal laws, without any heterogeneous element, and so they tend to become all too shiny, tidy, and innocuous. In this sense, wallpaper swatches are the writing on the wall. It is precisely the discomfort caused by this that draws attention back to the twenties but without this nostalgic yearning being satisfied. Anybody who is sensitive to such things need only examine the titles of the innumerable books, paintings, and compositions of the past few years to have the sobering feeling of the secondhand. It is so unbearable because every work created nowadays makes its entrance—whether intentionally or not—as though it owed its existence to itself alone. The desire that proved fatal, namely, the absence of a work's necessity to exist, gives way to the abstract consciousness of up-to-dateness. This ultimately reflects the absence of any political relevance. When it is completely transposed into the aesthetic domain, the concept of radicalness becomes an ideological distraction, a consolation for the real powerlessness of political subjects.

However, there is no more compelling evidence of the contemporary cultural aporia than the fact that the critique of this ideological aspect of a sanitized, pure aesthetic progress itself immediately becomes ideology again. In the entire Eastern zone such a critique serves simply to make the conformity total by stifling the last unruly stirrings that have taken refuge in art. This surely means nothing less than that the foundation of art itself has been shaken, that an unrefracted relation to the aesthetic realm is no longer possible. The concept of a cultural resurrection after Auschwitz is illusory and absurd, and every work created since then has to pay the bitter price for this. But because the world has outlived its own downfall, it nevertheless needs art to write its unconscious history. The authentic artists of the present are those in whose works the uttermost horror still quivers.

Prologue to Television

The social, technical, and artistic aspects of television cannot be treated in isolation. They are in large measure inter-dependent: artistic composition, for instance, depends upon an inhibiting consideration of the mass public, which only helpless naiveté dares disregard; the social effect depends upon the technical structure, also upon the novelty of the invention as such, which certainly was decisive during television's beginnings in America, but the social influence also depends upon the explicit and implicit messages television programs convey to their viewers. The medium itself, however, as a combination of film and radio, falls within the comprehensive schema of the culture industry and furthers its tendency to transform and capture the consciousness of the public from all sides. Television is a means for approaching the goal of possessing the entire sensible world once again in a copy satisfying every sensory organ, the dreamless dream; at the same time it holds the possibility of inconspicuously smuggling into this duplicate world whatever is thought to be advantageous for the real one. The gap between private existence and the culture industry, which had remained as long as the lat-

---

The "Prologue to Television," as well as "Television as Ideology," are based on studies the author conducted in 1952–1953 as scientific director of the Hacker Foundation in America. The results can in no way be applied directly to German television. However, they indicate general tendencies of the culture industry.

ter did not omnipresently dominate all dimensions of the visible, is now being plugged. Just as it is hardly possible to take a step outside of working hours without stumbling across some proclamation of the culture industry, so too are the various media it utilizes so seamlessly intermeshed that reflection can no longer catch its breath between them in order to realize that their world is not the world. "In the theater reflection is very much curtailed because of the visual and auditory amusement"—Goethe's presentiment[1] would first find its true object in a total system where the theater has long since become a museum of intellectualization but that in recompense works on its consumers without respite with cinema, radio, magazines, and in America especially with *funnies** and *comic books**. Only the interaction of all the processes, working together though differing from one another in terms of technique and effect, constitutes the climate of the culture industry. That is why it is so difficult for the sociologist to say *what television does to people**. For although the advanced techniques of empirical social research may isolate the "factors" characteristic of television, nonetheless these factors receive their effective force only within the totality of the system. Rather than being changed, people become welded to the unavoidable. Presumably television makes them once again into what they already are, only more so. This would correspond to the economically justified overall tendency of contemporary society not to try to progress beyond its present stage in its forms of consciousness—the status quo—but on the contrary to reinforce it relentlessly and reestablish it wherever it may appear threatened. The pressure under which people live has increased so much that they could not endure it if the precarious achievements of adjustment they had once accomplished were not again and again demonstrated to them and repeated in them internally as well. Freud taught that the repression of the instinctual drives never succeeds entirely or for long and that for this reason the unconscious psychic energy of the individual is ceaselessly squandered in retaining within the unconscious everything that should not enter into consciousness. This Sisyphean labor of every individual's psychic economy of drives appears to be "socialized" today, brought into direct control by the institutions of the culture industry for their benefit as well as that of the powerful interests they conceal. Television, such as it is, makes its own contribution to this. The more completely the world becomes appearance, the more imperviously the appearance becomes ideology. The new technology diverges from film in that, like radio, it brings the product into the home of the consumer. The visual images are much smaller than those in the cinema. The small picture is a source of complaint for the American public: attempts are made to increase the size of the screen, but it seems questionable whether the illusion of life-size the cinema screen affords can be attained in furnished, private apartments. Perhaps the images can be projected onto the wall. Yet the need, in any case, is telling. Earlier, the miniature format of human beings on the television screen was supposed to hinder habitual identification and heroization. Those on the screen speaking with human voices are dwarfs. They are hardly taken seriously in the same way that characters in film are. To abstract from the real size of the phenomenon, to perceive it no longer naturally but aesthetically, requires precisely that ability of sublimation that cannot be assumed to exist in the audience of the culture industry and that is weakened by the culture industry itself. The little men and women who are delivered into one's home become playthings for unconscious perception. There is much in this that may give the viewer pleasure: they are, as it were, his property, at his disposal, and he feels superior to them. In this point television borders on the *funnies**, those half-caricatured adventure series, in which the same figures appear from episode to episode over the years. In terms of content, too, many of the television serializations, especially farces, are related to the *funnies**. Contrary to the *funnies**, however, which do not intend any realism, the discrepancy in television between the more or less naturally rendered voices and the miniaturized figures cannot be ignored. Such discrepancies permeate all products of the culture industry and recall the deceit of the doubled life. It has on occasion been remarked that even sound film is silent, that a contradiction reigns between the two-dimensional images and the very true-to-life speech. Such contradictions are apparently increasing, the more that elements of sensible reality are absorbed into the culture industry. The analogy to the totalitarian states of both varieties suggests itself: the more disparate elements are integrated under a dictatorial will, the more the disintegration progresses, the more those things disperse that do not inherently belong together but are merely combined externally. The seamless world of images turns out to be fragile.[2] On the surface the public is hardly disturbed by this. But it surely recognizes it unconsciously. The suspicion grows that the reality being served up is not what it pretends to be. But the first reaction is not resistance; on the contrary, what is inevitable and what one loathes in one's heart of hearts is loved, with clenched teeth, all the more fanatically.

Observations such as these about the role of the physical dimensions of television programs cannot be isolated from the specific context of television, that of home viewing. It too will reinforce a tendency of the total culture industry: that of lowering the distance between product and spectator, in both the literal and figurative senses. Once again this tendency is economically predetermined. Anything that is served up by the culture industry, simply by virtue of the function of advertising avowed in America, offers itself as a commodity, an art for consumption, probably in direct proportion to how aggressively it is forced upon the consumer through the centralization and standardization of the industry itself. The consumer is encouraged to do what he is already inclined to do anyway: not to experience the work as an entity in itself, to which he owes his attention, concentration, effort, and understanding, but rather as a pleasantry rendered him, which he may then appreciate if he finds it pleasant enough. What has long since happened to the symphony, which the tired office worker tolerates with a distracted ear while sitting in shirt sleeves and slurping his soup, is now overtaking images as well. They are supposed to lend luster to his dreary quotidian life and nevertheless essentially resemble it: in this way they are futile from the start. Anything different would be unbearable because it would remind him of what he is being deprived of. Everything appears as though it belonged to him, because he does not belong to himself.[3] He doesn't even have to rouse himself to go to the cinema anymore, and in America whatever costs no money and requires no effort loses all the more value in his eyes. The world, threateningly devoid of warmth, comes to him like something familiar, as if specially made just for him: the contempt he feels for it is the contempt he feels for himself. The lack of distance, the parody of fraternity and solidarity has surely contributed to the extraordinary popularity of the new medium. Commercial television avoids everything that might recall, no matter how vaguely, the cultic origins of the work of art, its celebration of particular occasions. Under the pretext that watching television in the dark is painful to the eyes, people leave the lights on in the evening and refuse to close the shutters during the day: the viewing environment should deviate as little as possible from the normal situation. It is inconceivable that the experience of the subject matter itself might remain unaffected. The border between reality and the work becomes blurred for consciousness. The artwork is perceived to be a part of reality, a kind of accessory for the apartment, something that came with the purchase of the television set, the very possession of which itself is already a symbol of prestige among children. It is hardly too farfetched to suppose that, inversely, reality is viewed through the filter of the television screen, that the meaning given quotidian life on the screen is reflected back upon everyday life itself.

Commercial television atrophies consciousness, but not because the contents of its programs are any worse than those of film or radio. Admittedly one often hears the claim in Hollywood, especially among film people, that television programs lower the standard still further. But in this case the older sectors of the culture industry, many of which are perceptibly threatened by the competition, are surely using television as a scapegoat. A reading of some television scripts, admittedly hardly reflecting the entire creative production, leads to the conclusion that they are no less worthwhile than film scripts, which by now have become totally normalized and ossified.[4] Moreover, the television material is probably worth more than the *soap opera** so popular in radio, those serializations of family novels in which a mother figure or a seasoned older gentleman always helps the tumultuous young people out of their embarrassing predicaments. Nonetheless there is something to the claim that television makes things worse and not better, similar to how the invention of sound recording lowered the aesthetic and social quality of film, though such a claim should not imply demanding the resurrection of silent film or the abolition of television today. The responsibility lies with the How, not the What. That awkward "intimacy" of television, which allegedly engenders a community through the effect of the television set around which family members and friends sit idiotically who supposedly would otherwise have nothing to say, satisfies not only an avidity that allows no place for anything intellectual unless it is transformed into property but, moreover, obscures the real alienation between people and between people and things. It becomes a substitute for a social immediacy that is being denied to people. They confuse what is mediated through and through—the life deceptively programmed for them—with the solidarity they are so acutely deprived of. This reinforces the regression: the viewing situation itself stultifies, even when what is being viewed is no more stupid than the usual fodder fed to compulsive consumers. The fact that they probably indulge themselves more in television, it being convenient and inexpensive, than in cinema and more than in radio, because they receive the visual on top of the acoustic, contributes further to the regression. Addiction is immediately regression. And the increased dissemination of visual products plays a decisive part in this regression. Whereas certainly the sense of hearing is in many respects more "archaic" than that of sight, which is devoted to the world of things, nonetheless the language of images, which escapes the mediation of the concept, is more primitive than the language of words. Yet because of television, people's familiarity with language is growing even more tenuous than it already is throughout the world. The shadows may speak on the television screen, but their speech—if possible even more than in film—is nothing more than an aural translation of the visual, a mere appendage to the images, not an expression of intention, of thought, but rather a clarification of gestures, a commentary on the directives emanating from the image. In the same vein, occasionally in comic cartoons the words are written in balloons above the characters' heads, so as to insure that what is going on will be understood quickly enough.

Only more differentiated research can conclusively ascertain viewer reactions to television today. Since the material aspires to affect the

unconscious, direct questioning would not help. Preconscious or unconscious effects are inaccessible to direct verbalization by those being questioned. They would produce either rationalizations or abstract statements to the effect that television "entertains" them. What actually
occurs in people could be detected only with difficulty, for instance, if one
used television images without words as projective tests and studied the
associations they evoke in the subjects. Complete information could
probably be obtained only through numerous psychoanalytically
inflected individual case studies of habitual television viewers. First of all,
one would need to determine to what extent the reactions are actually
specific at all and to what extent the habit of watching television simply
serves the need of killing meaningless free time. All the same, a medium
that reaches countless millions and that especially in adolescents and
children often dulls every other interest should be considered, as it were,
a voice of objective spirit, even when it no longer spontaneously results
from the play of societal forces but instead is industrially planned. To a
certain degree industry must still take its consumers into account, if only
in order to find a match for the specific commodities of each program's
patrons, the *sponsors**. However, notions to the effect that television as
the culmination of mass culture is the authentic expression of the collective unconscious falsify the object by putting the emphasis in the wrong
place. Certainly mass culture taps into the conscious and unconscious
schemata, which it rightly assumes to be widespread among its consumers. This source consists primarily of the repressed, or simply unsat-
isfied, instinctual impulses of the masses, which are either directly or
indirectly accommodated by cultural commodities—mainly indirectly:
as the American psychologist G. Legman, for example, has emphatically
shown, sexuality is replaced by the representation of desexualized brutality and acts of violence.[5] In television this can be demonstrated even in
its apparently harmless farces. Nonetheless, by virtue of these and other
modifications the will of those in charge enters that language of images,[a]
which so much wants to pretend it is the language of its consumers. By
awakening and representing in the form of images what slumbers pre-

---

[a] The interpretation of mass culture as a "hieroglyphic writing" is found in the unpublished
part of the chapter "Culture Industry," sketched out in 1943, in *The Dialectic of Enlightenment*
by Max Horkheimer and Theodor W. Adorno. The same concept is used completely independently of this context in the article "First Contribution to the Psycho-Analysis and Aesthetics
of Motion-Picture" [sic] by Angelo Montani and Guilio Pietranera (*Psychoanalytic Review*,
April 1946). The differences between the two treatments cannot be discussed here. The Italian
authors also contrast the status of mass culture with the unconscious of autonomous art but do
not elevate the opposition to the level of theory.

conceptually in people, it also shows them how they should behave. Whereas the images of film and television strive to evoke those that lie buried in the viewer and indeed resemble them, they also, by flashing up and slipping away, approach the effect of writing. They are grasped, but not contemplated. The eye is carried along by the film as it is by the line of a text, and in the gentle jolt of a scene change a page is turned. As image, the image-writing is a medium of regression in which producer and consumer meet; as writing, it makes the archaic images available to modernity. Disenchanted enchantment, they do not convey any mystery; rather they are models of behavior that corresponds to the gravitation of the total system as well as to the will of the controllers. The perplexing thing about the interaction, which promotes the mistaken belief that the moguls' own spirit is the spirit of the age, lies in the fact that the manipulations, which condition the public[6] according to the requirements of behavior well adjusted to the established order, can always appeal to characteristics of the conscious and unconscious life of the consumers themselves and thereby with apparent legitimacy put the blame on them. Censorship and the inculcation of conformist behavior, which are conveyed by even the most anodyne gestures of any television program, not only have to reckon with people who have had drilled into them the schema of mass culture, which dates back to the beginnings of the English novel at the end of the seventeenth century and has in the meantime attained an air of nobility. On the contrary, these types of behavior had established themselves throughout the early modern period long before they were deployed in ideological manipulations, and so are now internalized as second nature. The culture industry grins: become what you are,[7] and its deceit consists precisely in confirming and consolidating by dint of repetition mere existence as such, what human beings have been made into by the way of the world. The culture industry can insist all the more convincingly that it is not the murderer but the victim who is guilty: that it simply helps bring to light what lies within human beings anyway.

Instead of paying tribute to the unconscious by elevating it to consciousness so as to fulfill its urge and simultaneously pacify its destructive force,[8] the culture industry, with television at the vanguard, reduces people to unconscious modes of behavior even more so than do the conditions of an existence that promises suffering to those who see through it and rewards to those who idolize it.[9] The rigidity is not dissolved but hardened even more. The vocabulary of the image-writing is composed of stereotypes. They are defended with technological imperatives, such as the need to produce in a minimal period of time a terrific quantity of material, or the necessity of presenting vividly and unmistakably to the viewer the name and character traits of the protagonists in the sketches, which most often are only a quarter-hour or half-hour long. Criticism of this practice is countered with the rebuttal that art has always operated with stereotypes. But there is a radical difference between the die-cast stereotypes calculated with psychological cunning and those that are clumsy and awkward, between those that intend to model human beings like mass production and those that try to conjure up objective essences out of the spirit of allegory one more time. Above all the highly stylized character types, like those in the *Commedia dell'arte*, were so removed from the everyday life of its public that no one could possibly succumb to the idea of conceiving their own experience in terms of the model of the masked clowns. On the other hand, the stereotypes in television resemble externally, up to and including intonation and dialect, every Tom, Dick, and Harry, and they propagate maxims—such as that all foreigners are suspect[10] or that success is the supreme goal of life—while they also, through the simple behavior of their heroes, present these maxims as though they were divinely sanctioned laws cast in stone once and for all, before one might draw a moral that sometimes even means the inverse. That art supposedly has something to do with the protest of the unconscious at being disfigured by civilization should not serve as an excuse for misusing the unconscious so that civilization may more radically ruin it. If art is to render justice to what is unconscious and pre-individual, then to that end it requires the utmost effort of consciousness and individuation; if instead of making this effort, one gratifies the unconscious by mechanically reproducing it, then the unconscious degenerates into mere ideology in the service of conscious objectives, no matter how stupid the aims may ultimately turn out to be. In an epoch where aesthetic differentiation and individuation have increased with such liberating energy as in the novelistic work of Proust, such individuation is being recanted in favor of a fetishized collectivism that has become an end in itself and a boon for a few profiteers: and this surely sanctions barbarism. During the last forty years there have been enough intellectuals who, whether out of masochism or material interests or both, have joined the heralds of this tendency. They must realize that what is societally effective and what is societally just do not coincide and that today the one is nothing less than the opposite of the other. "Our participation in public affairs is mostly only philistinism"—Goethe's statement from Makarie's archive[11] also holds for those public services the institutions of the culture industry claim to provide.

It is impossible to prophesy what will become of television. What it is today does not depend on the invention, not even on the specific forms of its commercial exploitation, but rather on the totality in which the marvelous wonder is embedded. The cliché about modern technology being the fairy-tale fulfillment of every fantasy ceases to be a cliché only when it is accompanied by the fairy tale's moral: that the fulfillment of the wishes rarely engenders goodness in the one doing the wishing. Wishing for the right things is the most difficult art of all, and since childhood we are weaned from it. Like the husband who is granted three wishes from the fairy and who proceeds to use two of them by making a sausage appear and then disappear from his wife's nose, so too whomever the genius to dominate nature has granted the ability to see far into the distance, sees only what he habitually sees, enriched by the illusion of novelty that gives its existence a false and inflated significance. His dream of omnipotence comes true in the form of perfected impotence. To this day utopias come true only so as to extirpate the idea of utopia from human beings altogether and to make them swear their allegiance all the more deeply to the established order and its fatefulness. In order for television to keep the promise still resonating within the word,[12] it must emancipate itself from everything with which it—reckless wish-fulfillment—refutes its own principle and betrays the idea of Good Fortune for the smaller fortunes of the department store.

Television as Ideology

The treatment of the formal characteristics of television within the system of the culture industry should be supplemented by closer consideration of the specific contents of programs.[1] In any case the contents and the form of presentation are so complicitous with one another that each may vouch for the other. Abstracting from the form would be philistine vis-à-vis any work of art;[2] it would amount to measuring by its own standard a sphere that ignores aesthetic autonomy and replaces form with function and packaging. It is advisable to submit television scripts to content analysis because they can be read and studied repeatedly, whereas the performance itself flits by. The objection that the ephemeral phenomenon hardly produces all the potential effects defined by an analysis of the script may be answered with the observation that since those effects are to a large extent specifically designed for the unconscious, their power over the viewer presumably increases when they are perceived in a mode that just as nimbly eludes the control of his conscious ego. Furthermore, the characteristics under consideration here do not belong to one particular case or another, but rather to a general schema. They recur countless times. And in the meantime the planned effects have formed a sediment.

The material under study comes from thirty-four television shows of various genres and quality.[3] In order to obtain a representative sample with statistical validity for studies of this sort, it would have been necessary to select the material strictly by random survey, whereas in the pilot study we had to settle for the scripts that had been made available to us. Nevertheless, because of the standardization of the entire production process as well as the uniformity of the evaluated scripts, it may be expected that an investigation organized along the lines of an American *content analysis** would add supplementary categories to those already developed but would not produce any fundamentally new results: the investigations by Dallas W. Smythe have made this supposition even more plausible.[4]

The material made available to us in Beverly Hills is probably above average. The study was limited to television dramas. These are similar to films in several respects, and incidentally, films make up a considerable part of the programs.[5] The main difference lies precisely in the brevity of the television dramas: most often they are a quarter-hour, at most a half-hour long. This affects the quality as well. Even the modest development of plot and character permitted in film is impossible: everything must be set up immediately. This supposedly technological necessity, itself dictated by the commercial system, favors the stereotypes and the ideological rigidity the industry in any case justifies on the basis of consideration for a juvenile or infantile public. These television dramas relate to films in a manner similar to the way detective novellas compare to detective novels: in both cases the formal shallowness serves an intellectual one. Aside from that one should not exaggerate the specific character of television productions for fear of contributing to the ideology. Their similarity to films attests to the unity of the culture industry: it hardly makes any difference where it is tackled.

Television dramas occupy a great deal of broadcasting time. The December 1951 edition of *Los Angeles Television* by Dallas W. Smythe and Angus Campbell, published by the National Association of Educational Broadcasters, showed that dramas were the most common type of program. More than a quarter of all programs offered during any given week were reserved for such dramas "for adults." During evening hours, i.e., the prime broadcasting time, the figure grew to 34.5 percent. And this did not include television dramas for children.[6] Meanwhile, in New York the volume of television dramas climbed to 47 percent of the entire production. Since the element of social-psychological manipulation, which, incidentally, other types of programs do not lack, is most clearly manifested in these numerically significant programs, it seems completely legitimate to limit the pilot study to them.

In order to show how these programs affect their viewers, one must recall the all too familiar notion of the multilayered structure of aesthetic works: the fact that no work of art on its own communicates its actual content unambiguously. Rather it is multilayered, cannot be nailed down, and unfolds only within a historical process. Independent of the analyses in Beverly Hills, Hans Weigel in Vienna showed that film, a product of commercial planning, does not have this complexity;[7] it is the same with television. But it would be too optimistic to believe that aesthetic complexity has been replaced by informational univocity. The multilayered structure, or rather, its degraded form, is refunctioned for the benefit of the producers.[8] They accept the legacy of aesthetic complexity by presupposing in the viewer several superimposed psychological layers, while at the same time trying to penetrate those layers in pursuit of a homogeneous and—according to the concepts of those in control—rational goal: the reinforcement of conformism in the viewer and the consolidation of the status quo. They tirelessly assail the spectators with open and hidden "messages." Perhaps the latter have priority in the programming because they are psychotechnically more effective.[9]

The heroine of a serialized television farce, which was awarded a prize by a teachers' association, is a young teacher. Not only does she earn a pitiful salary, she must constantly pay various fines imposed by the ridiculously pompous and authoritarian school principal. So she lacks money and goes hungry. The supposed humor consists in showing how she devises petty ruses to get invited to dinner by all her acquaintances but in the end always without success; by the way, it appears that the culture industry considers the mere mention of food already funny. The ambitions of the farce aim no higher than such humor and the slight sadism of the embarrassing situations in which the young woman finds herself: the sketch sells no idea. The hidden message lies wholly in the script's view of people, which seduces the audience into assuming the same attitude without realizing it. The heroine maintains so much good cheer and intellectual superiority that her pleasant qualities appear to be compensation for her wretched fate: the viewer is encouraged to identify with her. Every word she speaks is a joke. The farce says to the viewer: when you have humor, when you're good-natured, quick on the ball, and charming, then you don't need to get so worked up about your starvation wages; all the same, you remain what you are.

In another farce in the same series an eccentric old woman drafts a will for her cat and names as heirs a pair of schoolteachers from earlier shows in the series. The thought of the will seduces each heir into pretending that he knew the testator. The latter's name is Mr. Casey, consequently the heirs apparent do not know that the affair concerns a cat. No one admits never having seen his benefactor. Later it comes to light that the inheritance is worthless, nothing but cat's toys. But at the end it is discovered that the old lady hid a hundred dollar bill in each toy, and the heirs have to root through the garbage in order to get at their money. The moral of the story, which should make the viewer laugh, is, first, the cheap and skeptical maxim that everyone is ready to cheat a bit if he believes that no one will find out, and at the same time the warning not to yield to such impulses, just as moralistic ideology counts on the fact that its partisans are always ready to go too far the moment no one is looking. However, what remains concealed under this is disdain for the universal daydream of a windfall inheritance from out of the blue. One must be realistic, maintains the ideology; whoever indulges in dreams arouses suspicion of being a lazybones, good-for-nothing, and a swindler. That this message is not "read into" the farce, as the apologetic argument runs, can be shown by the fact that similar themes perpetually recur; in one Wild West show, for instance, a character says: when a large inheritance is at stake, villainy is not far behind.

Such synthetic complexity functions only within a fixed frame of reference. When a television sketch is called "Dante's Inferno," and when the first scene takes place in a nightclub of the same name, where a man with his hat on sits at the bar and at some distance from him a woman with sunken eyes, too much make-up, and her legs crossed high orders herself another double cocktail, then the habitual television viewer knows that he can look forward to a murder. If he knew nothing more than the title "Dante's Inferno," perhaps he could be surprised, but he sees the show in the schema of "crime drama," where care is taken to insure that horrible acts of violence will occur. The woman perched on the barstool presumably will not be the principal criminal, but she will end up paying for her dégagé lifestyle; the hero, who has not even appeared yet, will be rescued from a situation all human reason would conclude is hopeless. Certainly experienced viewers will not translate such shows directly into everyday life, but they are encouraged to construe their experiences just as rigidly and mechanically. They learn that crime is normal. What also contributes to this is the fact that the dime-store romanticism of heinous deeds shrouded in mystery is connected with the pedantic imitation of all the accessories of real life. If one of the characters were merely to dial a telephone number different from the one usually used in the series, then the station would receive indignant letters from the audience, who is ready to complacently entertain the fiction that a murderer is lurking on every corner. The pseudo-realism provided by the schema infuses empirical life with a false meaning, the duplicity of which viewers can scarcely see through because the nightclub looks exactly like the ones they know. Such a pseudo-realism reaches into the smallest detail and corrupts it. Even chance, ostensibly untouched by the schema, bears its mark, for it is conceived under the abstract category "the accidental nature of everyday life"; nothing sounds more false than when television pretends to let people speak the way they usually do.

Let us choose at random some of the stereotypes operating within the schema and deriving their power from its power while at the same time constituting it; they attest to the total structure. A play treats a fascist dictator, half Mussolini, half Perón, at the moment of his downfall. Whether his fall is due to a popular uprising or a military revolt is just as little touched on by the plot as any other social or political aspect of the situation. Everything is private, the dictator nothing but a foolish scoundrel who mistreats his secretary and the crudely idealized figure of his wife; his opponent, a general, is the wife's former lover, although despite everything she remains loyal to her spouse. Finally the dictator's brutality forces her to flee, and the general saves her. The terrible moment of the horror story occurs when the guards protecting the dictator in his palace abandon him as soon as his magnificent wife is no longer at his side. Nothing of the objective dynamics of dictatorships enters the field of vision. One gets the impression that totalitarian states are the result of the character defects of ambitious politicians and that their fall is due to the noblesse of the personalities with whom the public identifies. An infantile personalization of politics is being pursued here. Certainly politics in the theater can only be undertaken at the level of individuals. But in this case it would be necessary to show what totalitarian systems do to the people who live under them, instead of showing the kitsch psychology of celebrated heroes and villains, whose power and greatness the viewer is supposed to respect even when the reward for their deeds is their downfall.

One of the favorite maxims of television humor is that the cute girl is always right. The heroine of a highly popular comic series is what Georg Legman called a *bitch heroine**, and would probably need to be labeled in German as "beast" [*Biest*].[10] She behaves toward her father in an indescribably cruel and inhuman way, and her behavior is of course immediately rationalized as "funny pranks." But nothing ever happens to her, and indeed, according to the operative logic, whatever befalls the principal characters in the shows should be accepted immediately by the viewers as an objective verdict. In another show from a series purporting to warn the public of swindlers, the cute girl is a criminal. Yet after the viewer is so taken by her in the opening scene, he must not be disappointed: sentenced to a long prison term, she is immediately pardoned and has every chance of marrying her victim, especially since she nevertheless found the opportunity to radiantly preserve her sexual purity. Shows of this sort unquestionably serve to reinforce the social acceptance of parasitic behavior; a premium is placed on what psychoanalysis calls orality, the combination of dependency and aggressivity.

By no means is the psychoanalytic interpretation of cultural stereotypes too far-fetched: the short skits themselves flirt with psychoanalysis, in keeping with market trends. Sometimes the latent motives presumed by psychoanalysis come to the surface. Especially widespread is the stereotype of the artist as an abnormal weakling, unsuited for life and somewhat ridiculous, or an emotional cripple. Today's overaccentuated popular art appropriates all this: it glorifies the virile man, its image of the man of action, and insinuates that artists are in fact homosexual. One farce presents a young man who not only has to wear the ever popular mask of the fool, but moreover is supposed to be a poet, shy, and, as the jargon has it, "introverted." He is in love with a boy-crazy girl but is too shy to respond to her advances. In keeping with a favorite principle of the culture industry, the sex roles are reversed, the girl is active, the man on the defensive. The heroine of the piece, of course a different girl than the boy-crazy one, tells her friend of the foolish poet's infatuation. To the question, "Infatuated with whom?" she responds, "With a girl of course," and her friend replies, "What do you mean, of course? The last time he was in love with a turtle, and its name was Sam." The culture industry forgets its moralism as soon as it has the opportunity to make suggestive jokes about the image of the intellectual that it has fabricated itself. Through innumerable opportunities the schema of television cozies up to the international climate of anti-intellectualism.

But the perversion of truth, the ideological manipulation, is in no way limited merely to the realm of the irresponsibly anodyne or the cynically cunning. The sickness lies not in wicked individuals but in the system. That is why it also erodes whatever sets higher goals and aims at being respectable, to the extent that such ambitions are allowed. A script of serious intent contains the portrait of an actress. The plot attempts to show how the famous and successful young woman is cured of her narcissism, becomes a real person, and learns to do what she could not do before: love. She is brought to this conversion by a young and, for once, sympathetically portrayed intellectual—a dramatist who loves her. He writes a drama in which she plays the main role, and her inner confrontation with the role is supposed to act as a kind of psychotherapy, change her personality, and smooth out the difficulties between them. The role allows her to live out her manifest maliciousness as well as ultimately the noble impulses that, as the play assumes, are latently present in her. Whereas she scores a hit in keeping with the model of the *success story**, she has conflicts with the playwright, who functions as an amateur psychoanalyst, somewhat similar to the way amateur detectives intercede. The conflicts are caused by her psychological "resistance." It comes to a severe clash after the premiere, when the actress, intoxicated by her own success, performs a hysterical, exhibitionistic scene before her friends. — She sends her young daughter away to be raised in a boarding school, because her career could be damaged were it known that she has a child of that age. The girl would like to return to her mother, but senses that she is not wanted. The daughter runs away from school and takes a rowboat out onto the stormy ocean. The heroine and the playwright hurry to her rescue. Again the actress behaves egocentrically, without the least consideration for anyone else. The playwright tames her. The girl is saved by valiant sailors, the heroine collapses, renounces her resistance, and decides to love. In the end she accepts her playwright and makes a kind of profession of general religious faith.

The pseudo-realism of the show is not so simple that it would smuggle into the public's consciousness such contraband as the idea that crime is something completely natural. Rather what is pseudo-realistic is the internal construction of the plot. The psychological process that is put on view is fraudulent—in a word, *phony**, for which there is utterly no equivalent in German. Psychoanalysis, or whatever type of psychotherapy involved, is reduced and reified in a way that not only expresses disdain for this type of praxis but changes its meaning into its very opposite. The dramaturgical necessity of concentrating lengthy and elaborate psychodynamic processes into a half-hour episode, a necessity the producers then use as a pretext, harmonizes all too well with the ideological distortion the show diligently cultivates. Supposedly profound changes in the individual and a relationship modeled on that between doctor and patient are reduced to rationalistic clichés and illustrated by simplistic and unambiguous actions. All sorts of character traits are tossed about without the decisive point ever appearing: the unconscious origin of those character traits. The heroine, the "patient," is from the very beginning lucidly self-aware. This displacement to the surface renders the entire ensuing psychological process puerile. The fundamental changes in people appear as though all anyone need do is confront their "problems" and trust the better insight of a confidant, and everything will be fine. Within the psychological routine and the "psychodrama" there still lurks the old pernicious idea of the taming of the shrew: that a sensitive and strong man overcomes the capricious unpredictability of an immature woman. The gesture toward psychological depth serves only to make stale patriarchal conceptions palatable to the spectators, who in the meantime have heard something about "complexes." Rather than the psychology of the heroine expressing itself concretely, the two protagonists chatter with each other about psychology. In flagrant contradiction to the entire modern understanding of the mind, psychology is transposed into the conscious ego. Nothing is indicated of the difficulties that a "phallic character" like that of the actress must seriously confront. Thus the television show presents to the viewer a distorted image of psychology. The viewer will expect exactly the opposite of psychology's intention, and the already widespread hostility toward effective self-reflection will intensify even more.

In particular, Freud's idea of "transference" is perverted. The amateur analyst has to be the lover of the heroine. His practiced distance, pseudo-realistically modeled after the analyst's technique, fuses with the culture industry's vulgar stereotype according to which the man must continually protect himself from the woman's seductive arts and conquers her only by rejecting them. The psychotherapist resembles the hypnotist, and the heroine resembles the cliché of the "split ego." Sometimes she is a noble, loving person, who represses her own feelings only because of certain unhappy experiences, and other times she is a hussy, pretentious and in love with herself but exaggerating her caprices far too much for one not to know from the outset that her inner loveliness will ultimately emerge. No wonder that under such conditions the cure progresses quickly. Hardly does the heroine begin to play the role of the selfless woman, with whom she is supposed to identify so as to find her so-called better ego, and already her friends realize that something is happening to her, that in her relationship to the role she is transforming herself. Any complicated childhood reminiscences are superfluous here. Whereas the show intimates how familiar it is with the latest breakthroughs in the soul's anatomy, it operates with completely rigid and static concepts. The people are what they are, and the changes that they undergo reveal only what was already inside them, their true "nature." Thus the show's hidden message stands in contradiction to its explicit message. On the surface it employs psychodynamic notions; in truth it preaches a conventional black-and-white psychology, according to which personalities are given once and for all; like physical characteristics, they cannot be modified but at most only uncovered.

This is not merely a case of erroneous scientific information, rather it goes to the very substance of the show. For the nature of the heroine, which should emerge when she becomes conscious of herself in the role, is nothing other than her *conscience*. Psychology presents the superego as a reaction formation to repressed impulses of the id, sexuality; yet here the id, the physical urges of the heroine as crudely illustrated in one scene, becomes an epiphenomenon, and it is the superego that is repressed. It may be acknowledged that psychologically such manifestations really exist: ambivalence between the instinctual and compulsive aspects of character. But there is no question of ambivalence in the television show. It clings to the sentimental idea of a human being who is good at heart but hides her inner fragility beneath an armor of egotism. In the *scène à faire*, in which the two egos of the heroine struggle with each other while she gazes into a mirror, her unconscious is crudely equated with conventional morality and the repression of her instincts, rather than that the instincts themselves break free. It is only her conscious self that wants to disturb the peace. Thus what is practiced is "psychoanalysis in reverse" in the literal sense: the play glorifies the very defense mechanisms, the penetration and illumination of which is the goal of those analytical processes the television show claims to demonstrate. This alters the message. The viewer is apparently taught lessons such as that he should love, without having to worry about whether it can be taught—and that he should not think materialistically, whereas since Fontane's *Frau Jenny Treibel* the people who talk of ideals without restraint are the same people who think that money is more important than anything else.[11] But in truth what is drummed into the viewer is something completely different than these surely banal and dubious, but relatively innocuous, opinions. The piece amounts to the slandering of individuality and autonomy. One should "devote" oneself, and moreover less to love than to respect for what society and its ground rules expect. The capital sin the heroine is accused of is that she wants to be herself; she herself says as much. And that is precisely what cannot be allowed: she is taught *mores**, "broken," just as a horse is tamed. In his grand tirade against materialism, the strongest point her educator hurls at her is tellingly enough the concept of *power*. He extols to her the "necessity of spiritual values in a materialist world," yet he finds no more adequate expression for these "values" than that there is a power "greater than us and our petty, conceited ambition." Of all the ideas presented in the piece, power is the only one that is concretized: as brutal, physical force. When the heroine wants to jump into a boat in order to save her child, her spiritual provider slaps her across the face, completely in line with the Eisenbart tradition that claims to cure hysterical women by knocking some sense into them, since it's all just their imagination anyway.[12] In the end the heroine submissively declares that from now on she wants to improve and to believe. This is the proof of her transformation.

Nothing is more odious than the introduction and propagation of religion in the piece in the name of crude authority. The heroine's cure at the same time should convert her from the illusory world of the theater to reality; probably the woman who wrote the piece had picked up something of religious existentialism, of Kierkegaard's distinction between the aesthetic and ethical spheres. But in her hands all this becomes the debased cultural goods of the upper estate.[13] She reduces the controversy between the moralist and the artist to the level where the latter, quite reasonably, refers to her métier and to the fact that she is just playing a role and is not really the person represented, and for this she receives a poor grade. However, the theologian Kierkegaard had demonstrated precisely the contrary in his important essay on the actress: that only a mature woman can interpret the role of a young girl, precisely because she does not resemble what she is personifying.[14] While the show ends with a pious gaze heavenward, it draws religion itself into the circle of conformism and convention. The actress discovers her religious feelings in the moment when her daughter is rescued, a bit like the saying that there are no atheists during artillery barrages. Ultimately the piece subverts its own message. Not only does it coarsely mix psychological dilettantism with the praise of humility but the exhortation to faith at the end transforms this humility into a means used for psychological ends. The viewer is encouraged to practice religion because it is healthy for him: once you have a belief in "something," there is no more need to torture yourself with narcissism and hysteria. In fact, a figure in the show who is positively portrayed as a representative of religion says in a kind of sermon that one becomes "happy" when one ceases searching for happiness in oneself and for oneself. A worldly sentiment of happiness becomes the justification for transcendental faith. It would have been nice to hear Kierkegaard's voice in response to such a theology. Advertising for religion in the name of hygiene is blasphemous.

For all the crassness with which products of this sort display their inferiority and falsity, nonetheless they must be investigated and taken seriously despite their own intentions. For the culture industry is not at all disturbed by the idea that none of its creations are serious, that everything is simply merchandise and entertainment. Long ago it made this a part of its own ideology. Among the scripts analyzed, several consciously play at being kitsch, and they give the less naive viewer a knowing wink as though saying that they do not take themselves seriously, they are not that stupid; they take the viewer, as it were, into their confidence by flattering his intellectual vanity. But a shameful deed is made no better by denouncing itself as such; one must do the offense the honor it refuses itself and take it at its own word—the one that sinks into the viewers. There is here no danger of overloading the chosen examples, for each is a *pars pro toto* and not only allows but requires drawing conclusions about the entire system. In the face of the system's omnipotence detailed proposals for improvement have at once something ingenuous about them. The ideology is so happily fused with the specific gravity of the apparatus that every suggestion can be dismissed with the most reasonable explanations, as naive, technically unproven, and impractical: the idiocy of the whole is built up out of nothing but healthy common sense. The possibility of remedying the situation through goodwill should not be overrated. The culture industry is so fundamentally entangled with powerful interests that even the most honest efforts in its sector could not get very far. With an inexhaustible arsenal of arguments the culture industry can justify or reason away what is obvious to everybody. The falsity and inferiority exert a magnetic attraction upon their defenders, and even the worst of them become far more astute than their intellectual capabilities would warrant when they look for arguments in favor of what they themselves in their heart of hearts know is profoundly untrue. The ideology creates its own ideologues, discussion, and points of view: in this way it has a good chance of staying alive. However, one should resist being driven into defeatism and being terrorized by that well-practiced demand for positive results, which usually only wants to thwart any change in the state of things. It is far more important, first of all, to raise consciousness about phenomena such as the ideological character of television, and that not only among those on the production side but also in the public. Precisely in Germany, where economic interests do not directly control the programming, there is some hope in trying to raise awareness.[15] If the ideology, which avails itself of a truly modest number of endlessly repeated ideas and tricks, were taken down a peg or two, then perhaps the public could develop an aversion to being led around by the nose, no matter how much the ideology gratifies the dispositions—themselves produced by the societal totality—of innumerable viewers. It would then be possible to imagine a kind of inoculation of the public against the ideology propagated by television and its related media. Of course, this idea would require far more extensive investigations, which would have to separate out and isolate social-psychological norms in television production. Instead of tracking down vulgar words and indecency like most organs of self-censorship, the producers would need to be vigilant and remove those provocations and stereotypes that, according to the judgment of a committee of responsible and independent sociologists, psychologists, and educators, result in the stultification, psychological crippling, and ideological disorientation of the public.[16] The investigation of such norms is not as utopian as it appears at first glance, because television as ideology is not the result of evil intentions, perhaps not even of the incompetence of those involved, but rather is imposed by demonic objective spirit. Through countless mechanisms it reaches all those involved in production. A very great number of them recognize, with aesthetic sensibility if not with theoretical conceptuality, just how rotten their product is and continue producing it solely because of economic pressure; in general the aversion is greater the closer one gets to the writers, directors, actors, and only the business and its lackeys proclaim their consideration for the consumers. If a science that does not stultify or content itself with administrative surveys but instead takes up the research of ideology itself would give its support to those artists kept in check, then they would stand a better chance against their bosses and the censors.[17] It is obvious that the social-psychological norms should not dictate what television must do. However, just as everywhere else, the canon of the negative would not be far from that of the positive.

Sexual Taboos and Law Today

In Memory of Fritz Bauer

The theorist who intervenes in practical controversies nowadays discovers on a regular basis and to his shame that whatever ideas he might contribute were expressed long ago—and usually better the first time around. Not only has the mass of writings and publications grown beyond measure: society itself, despite all its tendencies to expand, in many cases seems to be regressing to earlier stages, even in its superstructure, in law and politics. Embarrassingly enough, this means that time-honored arguments must once again be trotted out. Even critical thought risks becoming infected by what it criticizes. Critical thought must let itself be guided by the concrete forms of consciousness it opposes and must go over once again what they have forgotten. Thought is not purely for itself: especially practical thought, so closely tied to the historical moment that in this regressive age it would become abstract and false were it to continue to evolve from its own élan regardless of the regression. This alone is the bitter truth to the talk of "the thinker in indigent times":[1] what he produces depends on the fact that in making it conscious he activates the moment of regression imposed upon him. And especially when it comes to enlightenment about sexual taboos it is difficult to say anything that was not known already and then repressed again, most recently during the era of women's alleged emancipation. Freud's insights into infantile sexuality and the partial instincts,[2] which stripped the last shreds of legitimacy from conventional sexual morality, retain their full validity even in an age that would like to disarm depth psychology, and what Karl Kraus wrote in his incomparable early work *Morals and Criminality*—recently reprinted as the eleventh volume of his *Works* by Langen-Müller[3]—cannot be surpassed in rigor or authority. The situation itself helps perpetuate what has become obsolescent and therefore now truly evil: it is noted that nothing new is being said, as though that alone amounted to a refutation. But the second enlightenment that is nowadays played off against the first merely amounts, in Enzensberger's phrase, to abolishing the original.[4]

Yet sabotage of enlightenment in the name of its obsolescence also derives its pretexts from the object itself. Talk of sexual taboos sounds anachronistic in an era where every young girl who is to any extent materially independent of her parents has a boyfriend; where the mass media, which are now fused with advertising, incessantly provide sexual stimulation, to the fury of their reactionary opponents, and where what in America is called a *healthy sex life** is so to speak a part of physical and psychic hygiene. It includes, to use the nice formulation of the sociologists Wolfenstein and Leites, a sort of morality of pleasure, a *fun morality.**[5] In comparison with all this, proposals for the reform of legislation on sexuality *prima vista* have something venerably suffragette-like about them. And the guardians of absolute order can respond with a cheap irony that rarely misses. People have their freedom, they do what they want to anyway, and only crimes should be checked by the law—so why reforms?

There is no other response to this than that sexual liberation in contemporary society is mere illusion. This illusion arose together with the phenomenon sociology elsewhere describes with its favorite expression, 'integration': the same way in which bourgeois society overcame the proletarian threat by incorporating the proletariat. Rational society, which is founded upon the domination of inner and outer nature and disciplines the diffuse pleasure principle that is harmful to the work ethic and even the principle of domination itself, no longer needs the patriarchal commandment of abstinence, virginity, and chastity. On the contrary, sexuality, turned on and off, channeled and exploited in countless forms by the material and cultural industry, cooperates with this process of manipulation insofar as it is absorbed, institutionalized, and administered by society. As long as sexuality is bridled, it is tolerated. Formerly, society had reluctantly accepted sexuality through the sacrament of marriage; today, it takes sexuality directly under its control without any intermediate authorities like the church, often even without any state legitimation. But, at the same time, sexuality has changed because of this.

If in his attempt to describe what is specifically sexual Freud emphasized the element of indecency—and this means what is offensive to society— then on the one hand, this element has disappeared, and on the other hand only now is it truly loathed, rejected. This reveals nothing less than a desexualization of sexuality itself. Pleasure that is either kept cornered or accepted with smiling complaisance is no longer pleasure at all; psychoanalysts would be able to demonstrate without difficulty that in the entire sex industry—monopolistically controlled and standardized as it is, with its ready-made appliqués of film stars—fore-pleasure and pleasure-substitutes have surpassed pleasure itself.[6] The neutralization of sex, which has been traced in the disappearance of grand passion, blanches sex even where it is believed to be unabashedly satisfied.

However, one can conclude from this—and the contemporary neuroses should confirm this—that in truth the sexual taboos have not fallen away. Only a new, deeper form of repression has been reached, with all its destructive potential. Whereas sexuality has been integrated, that which cannot be integrated, the actual spiciness of sex, continues to be detested by society. If it is true that what is specifically sexual is what is *eo ipso* forbidden, then this prohibition knows how to make itself felt even in the manifestations of sex that are allowed or sanctioned. Surely nowhere more than in the zone of what is still consistently ostracized can so much of the concealed monstrosity be revealed. In an unfree society, sexual freedom is hardly any more conceivable than any other form of freedom. Sexuality is disarmed as *sex**, as though it were a kind of sport, and whatever is different about it still causes allergic reactions.

Thus despite everything it is necessary to take up once again the subject of sexual taboos and the legislation of sexuality, not only because of a presumably powerless solidarity with the victims but also in consideration of all the damage that might be done by the increasing repression accompanying societal integration. This repression may permanently feed into the reservoir of authoritarian personalities, who are ready to run behind totalitarian governments of whatever stripe. One of the most palpable results of the *Authoritarian Personality* was that those people who had the specific character structure that predisposed them to become followers of totalitarianism were especially plagued by persecution fantasies against those whom they considered to be sexual deviants and, in general, by wild sexual notions they rejected in themselves and projected onto other groups. The German sexual taboos fall within the same ideological and psychological syndrome of prejudice that helped National Socialism build its mass support and whose manifest content lives on in a depoliticized form. But it could concretize itself politically at the right moment. Immanent to the system and yet also imperceptible, today it is more dangerous to democracy than are the neofascist groups, which for the time being find far less resonance and have far fewer material and psychic resources at their disposal.[a]

Psychoanalysis investigated sexual taboos and their expression in law, especially in the criminological area—one need only mention Aichhorn's studies[7]—and what it revealed at that time is still valid today. But this work needs to be supplemented if it is to comprehend the state of affairs in its most recent historical phase. In Freud's era everything stood under the sign of precapitalist or high-bourgeois forms of authority: the patriarchalism of the nuclear family, repression by the father and its consequences, the compulsive character together with the anal syndrome ascribed to it. Of course, the thesis that the societal superstructure transforms itself more slowly than the base has also been borne out psychologically in the relative constancy of the unconscious, which Freud emphasized. In the face of the predominance of the real processes of society, the individual psyche is in fact secondary or, if you will, superstructure. Among the collective powers that have replaced the individual authority of the father, the father imago lives on, as Freud had already ascertained in *Group Psychology and the Analysis of the Ego*.[8] However, since that time changes have occurred in the authoritarian structure of society that affect at least the concrete form of sexual taboos. Genital sexuality, against which the traditional threat of castration is directed, is no longer the target. The *Lebensborn* stud farms of the SS, the young girls who were encouraged to enter into temporary liaisons with those who had proclaimed themselves an elite and had organized themselves as such, are, like many pioneering crimes of the Third Reich, merely an anticipation in extremis of the tendencies of society as a whole.[9] The SS state was no more a realm of erotic freedom than is the libertinage of the beaches and camp sites nowadays, which by the way can be revoked at any moment and returned to the state of what the language of taboos calls healthy attitudes. Anthropological traits such as young people's overvaluation of the concrete, the atrophy of the imagination, the passive accommodation to overpoweringly given conditions, represent an aspect that rather precisely corresponds to the new form of sexual taboos.

According to Freudian theory, the prevailing form of sexuality sanctioned by civilization, genital sexuality, is not what it pretends to be— originary—but on the contrary is the result of an integration. Under the

---

[a] Cf. "The Meaning of Working Through the Past."

constraint of social adjustment, the partial instincts of the child are combined through the agency of the family into a unified drive serving the societal purpose of reproduction. The precarious nature of this integration into genital sexuality did not escape Freud's notice and, in a thoroughly patriarchal and bourgeois gesture, he deplored it. A true, instinctually erotic life, the relations that generate pleasure, is by no means that *healthy sex life** that in the most advanced industrial countries today is encouraged by all sectors of the economy, from the cosmetics industry to psychotherapy. Rather the partial libido lives on within the genitality into which it was fused. All happiness is aroused by the tension between the two. Just as the partial instincts remain thwarted to the extent that they are not fulfilled genitally, as though they were part of a stage that did not yet know pleasure, so too the genitality, purged of all the partial drives proscribed as perverse, is impoverished, impassive, as though shrunken to a point. From a psychodynamic point of view, the desexualization of sexuality would surely be considered the form of genital sex in which genital sex itself becomes a powerful generator of taboos and where the partial instincts are inhibited or obliterated. It's a nice bit of sexual utopia not to be yourself, and to love more in the beloved than only her: a negation of the ego-principle. It shakes that invariant of bourgeois society in the widest sense, which since time immemorial has always aimed at integration: the demand for identity. At first it had to be produced, ultimately it would be necessary to abolish it again. What is merely identical with itself is without happiness. Genital sexuality's concentration on the ego and its likewise self-centered Other—and it is not by chance that the designation "partner" has come into fashion—harbors narcissism. Libidinal energy is displaced onto the power that dominates it and thereby deceives it. Nonetheless, the sense of indecency that Freud emphasized clings to the excess of the partial instincts beyond genitality and confers upon genitality its force and its prestige. The traditional social taboos attacked both genitality and the partial drives in one, although they probably were chiefly directed against the latter; Sade's œuvre was a revolt against this attack. In tandem with the increasing social reinforcement of genitality the pressure mounts against the partial drives and against their representatives in genital relations. What remains of the partial drives is cultivated only as socialized voyeurism, as forepleasure. Contemplation by many replaces union with one and thereby expresses the tendency to socialize sexuality that itself constitutes an aspect of sexuality's fatal integration. The desexualization of sexuality is strengthened by the premium patriarchal society places upon the female character, her passive docility, weaned from all personal affect, if possible from all aspiration to her own pleasure. Sexuality is confiscated by an ideal of the natural life and in a culture of healthy outdoor living is reduced as much as possible to pure genitality that rebels against every refinement. The form that taboos assume in the environment of formal freedom should be studied; some importance should be given to such models as this idea of naturalness but also to the standardized, as it were, cellophane-wrapped samples of sex. In a climate that mixes the subterranean force of prohibitions with the lie claiming that those prohibitions have lost their force, the latest style of persecutions is flourishing. Unless appearances are deceptive, more than ever the partial drives are being repressed mentally and materially—complementary to the ego-weakness evident everywhere as a specific psychological inability to deviate from what everyone else is doing—while at the same time the partial drives are also being manipulated by society; the less, apparently, is considered indecent, the worse the vengeance exacted on what for all that is still judged to be so. The hygienic ideal is more rigorous than the ascetic ideal, which never wanted to remain what it was. However, the taboos in the midst of the illusion of freedom cannot be taken lightly, above all because no one completely believes in them anymore, whereas they are still reinforced by both the unconscious of individuals and by institutional powers. In general, the more eroded repressive ideas have become, the more cruelly they are enforced: their application must be exaggerated so that the terror persuades people that what is so powerful must also be legitimate. The witch trials flourished after Thomistic universalism had already waned.[10] The exhibitionist confessions of sin by those who give free reign to their moralism by associating it with the word 'rearmament' are likewise so attractive to the masses because the concept of sin when detached from theological dogma no longer has any substance.[11] This is also what reinforces the specific character of taboo. Whereas primitive taboos were irresistible because they were motivated by the incest prohibition, whose power of psychological repression excluded all rational justification, sexual taboos in the age of at once both total and stymied enlightenment have an augmented power, since they no longer have a raison d'être even for those who obey them. The prohibition as such now absorbs the energies it used to receive from other sources that have become exhausted in the meantime. The lie branded onto the taboo becomes itself an element of sadism that overtakes the chosen victim and with a knowing nod gives him to understand that his fate is due not to the offense but rather to the fact that he happens to be somehow different, that he deviates from the collective, that he belongs to a precisely designated minority. — Nevertheless, the taboos nowadays do not have any new content: they are rather the imitation of more ancient ones.

Lying deeply buried within the cultural imagination, these taboos can be exploited by manipulative powers. They are reawakened from above. Their imitative pallor serves social repression. They allow the accumulated ancient indignation to be redirected at whatever is timely and opportune, regardless of its quality: otherness as such is the chosen enemy. An empirical investigation is needed to explore how taboos, which are half forgotten and from a social standpoint in fact relatively obsolete, are able to be mobilized. At present it is difficult to say whether the rage exploited by the demagogy of morality is primarily and immediately a reaction to erotic privations. It is also conceivable that it is a reaction to the entire constitution of contemporary life. In the context of formal freedom each individual is burdened with an autonomy that, from an anthropological standpoint alone, he cannot bring off, while through the disproportion between the overpowering institutions and the minuscule scope of action granted him the individual also objectively feels overtaxed and threatened; a threat surely containing within itself, concealed and long since become unrecognizable, the ancient threat of castration. The taboos can be reawakened because social suffering—in psychological terms, that of the ego—is repressed and displaced onto sexuality, the age-old ache.[12] In total contradiction to what takes place on the surface, sexuality becomes the nerve center of society; at present the sexual taboos are stronger than all others, even the political taboos, despite the virulence with which the latter are hammered home.

The public sphere resounds with declarations either welcoming or deploring these changes in sexual morals. They are closely related to those current theses about the end of ideology that furnish stifling cynicism with the good conscience of enlightenment while at the same time suspecting every idea that points beyond the present conditions of being anachronistic.[13] That despite all these views the taboos are not eliminated can be discerned in the forms of objective spirit, in the unspoken conventions and mores, and even more in the sphere of law. Everywhere prostitutes are being persecuted, whereas they were more or less left in peace during the era when sexual oppression was allegedly harsher.[14] It is a mendacious and flimsy pretense to claim that there is no need for whores anymore after the success of women's emancipation. It befits the zealots least of all to justify their measures with the same moral freedom they want once again to abolish. The technique of police raids, the closing of bordellos, which itself degrades prostitution into the nuisance it is so often accused of being, the fervor declaring some quarters particularly menaced, only then to wax indignant at the rampant influx of whores in the places where they must seek refuge—like the Jews they should have no shelter—all this indicates an attitude that, while crying murder over the degradation of eros, does all it can to degrade it once again: by condemning it to never know happiness. The prostitute, the image of what inexperience and envy imagine to be vice, is undoubtedly identified largely with the partial instinct. She is supposedly the source of perversity, in the most amazing contradiction to the miserable and miscarried way of making a living that prostitution has become in a society of glasshouses where every hiding place has been smoked out. There is no need to harbor illusions about the *off-limits** sector, and yet the whores, who in the meantime have become as repulsive as society's envy spitefully imagines them and treats them, should be defended against the ignominy of morality as unsuspecting representatives of an alternative sexuality. The arguments brought forward by this ignominious morality, the damages the whores cause, the offense they give, are nugatory; no one need tarry with them unless he wants to see them, even less if bordellos were tolerated. It is doubtful that the appearance of a streetwalker offers much novelty to young people, who are courted with devotion by the magazine kiosks; the harm such sights allegedly cause is fictitious. Ridiculous and annoying is a quid pro quo like the one that occurred when a Protestant pastor in a metropolitan quarter promised in his sermons and meetings to eradicate prostitution instead of restricting his nightlife to the evening concerts that are planned for him and his like and in which he can repress to his heart's content. It is even more unbearable when the pimps, instead of ignoring him as is usual, shot at his apartment. However, the eventual police explanation that those shots had nothing to do with the pastor's moral crusade does indeed represent a grave danger for public morality. In a society even remotely as politically mature as its constitution would suggest, the publicity alone would make such incidents impossible. It is indicative of the overall state of affairs that things like this occur and are flogged to death by the press without anyone perceiving the humor. Certainly it would be illusory to seek consolation in the thought that a backward and fanatical minority noisily imposes its will upon the majority. Unbridled morality could not work the street and give the offense it pretends to take if that morality were not in harmony with the population's structure of instincts. It is undeniably clear that in Germany, where there are a thousand reasons to be wary of persecuting defenseless groups, prostitutes continue to be persecuted relentlessly. Murders of prostitutes go unpunished, and indeed perhaps in each individual case there might be a plausible reason why this is so; nevertheless, the frequency of such unsolved cases, in comparison with the swiftness, for instance, with which justice is meted out in cases of crimes against property, indicates that society's power, however unconsciously, wishes death to those who in its eyes incarnate, erroneously, the pleasure that ought not to be.[b] The hunt is raised against prostitutes not despite the fact that extramarital liaisons have become the rule but rather precisely because of it. Although women won emancipation professionally, they still have to bear their surplus of social burden, and even while being tolerated passively, they sense the taboo that can fall upon them at any moment: for example, they may fall foul of the law on procuration that has been expanded absurdly to cover absolutely anything, or they may become pregnant. This engenders vindictiveness. Part of the hopeless dynamic of what sociology likes to call interpersonal relations is also the fact that those who feel pressure attempt to transfer it onto other, weaker groups, and either rationally or irrationally perpetuate the odium. One of the favorite targets, distinguished by their powerlessness, are prostitutes. Prostitution is made to atone not only for men's rancor at official monogamy, from which it in turn makes its livelihood, but moreover also for the rancor of women who, while often reluctantly enough getting involved in affairs because that's just the way things are, continue to mourn the role for which bourgeois society has been training them for centuries, and secretly cherish the quite understandable desire for the security and reputation that marriage brings. The survival of sexual taboos confirms that persecution makes things no better, neither for those women who have been integrated into bourgeois professions, because in their private life they are denied bourgeois privileges, nor for the women who are made outcasts. Of all the nefarious effects of the shady and unacknowledged sexual oppression this is perhaps the worst. It is especially striking in that type of homosexual whose admiration of virility is coupled with an enthusiasm for order and discipline and who, with the ideology of the noble body, is ready to set upon other minorities—intellectuals, for instance.

The abominable paragraph on the law books against homosexuals managed to find safe passage into postwar liberated Germany. The mitigation that permits at least culprits of minor age to go unpunished can easily become an invitation to blackmail. Actually, there is no need to bring forth arguments against this paragraph: it suffices merely to recall

---

[b] An illustration of how the hostility to pleasure has found expression in juridical language is the definition of the concept of sexual offense, which comes from the *Reichsgericht* [*translator's note*: German Supreme Court until 1945] and which was adopted by the *Bundesgerichtshof* [the postwar Federal Supreme Court]. According to this juridical definition, sexual offense includes all acts that, objectively, following healthy consideration, injure the sense of shame and morality in sexual relations and that, subjectively, are undertaken with lascivious intentions.

its disgraceful character. Let me indicate just one, often overlooked, aspect of the ostracism of homosexuals, who of course are perceived as the portent of a sexuality alienated from its proper purpose.[15] Some people say that so long as they do not abuse minors or dependents, *in praxi* homosexuals are far less harried nowadays than they were earlier. But it is absurd that a law is justified with the explanation that it will be not be applied, or only sparingly so. It is not necessary to spell out what such conceptual schemas imply for protection under the law and the real relation of people to the legal order. Even if homosexuals were finally left more or less in peace, the atmosphere of persistent legal discrimination would necessarily subject them to unremitting anxiety. If one accepts the psychoanalytical theory that claims that homosexuality in many cases is neurotic, a manner of resolving childhood conflicts that prevents the so-called normal resolution of the Oedipal complex, then the social and legal pressure, even if indirectly, will perpetuate and reinforce the neuroses, according to the psychological law of anaclisis.[16] There are said to be many homosexuals who are intellectually gifted, psychogenetically the probable explanation being that the extreme identification with the mother leads them to internalize those traits the mother possesses in contrast to the father, the representative of a practical sense of reality. If my observations do not deceive me, then precisely among the intellectually gifted homosexuals is the psychological shackling of their productivity conspicuous, the inability to realize all that they are surely capable of. The permanent pressure of anxiety, and the social ostracism, which both inspires and in turn is reinforced by the legislation, play a large part here. Through the paragraph against homosexuality, society tends toward the same thing within the legal sphere as in countless other spheres, toward the destruction of intellectual powers. Where at least the social taboo against homosexuality is more modest, for instance in many aristocratic, closed societies, homosexuals appear to be less neurotic, in terms of characterology less deformed than in Germany.

However, the strongest taboo of all at the moment concerns everything that goes by the catchword "minor age," a taboo that was already in full swing when Freud discovered infantile sexuality. The universal and well-founded feeling of guilt experienced by the world of adults cannot do without its inverse image and refuge, what it calls the innocence of children, and will use any and all means to defend it. It is common knowledge that a taboo becomes all the stronger the more its adherents themselves unconsciously desire what is proscribed and punished. The cause of the complex about minors probably lies in the extraordinarily powerful instinctual impulses against which it operates as a defense mechanism.[17] This complex should be considered together with the fact that in the twentieth century, possibly due to an unconscious homosexualiza-tion of society, the erotic ideal has become infantilized; it has become what thirty or forty years ago with a lecherous shudder was called a "girl-child." The success of *Lolita*, which is not a lascivious novel and moreover possesses too much literary quality to be a best-seller, could only be explained by the power of this imago. It is likely that the cen-sured wish-image[18] also has a social aspect, the accumulated animadver-sion to a state of affairs that pulls people's puberty and independence apart temporally. Lolita, Tatjana, and Baby Doll[19] have as their comple-ment the public initiative groups who, if they had their way, would post a morally mature policewoman at every playground behind each child to protect it from the evil that adults are just waiting to perpetrate. Were a descendant of Fontane's Herr von Ribbeck in Havelland to give pears to young girls, then his humanity would immediately be suspect.[20]

The zone touched on here is delicate not only because of the violent affects that are unleashed as soon as one does not echo the dominant opinion, but also because of the undeniable protective function of the law. Of course, children must be protected from becoming victims of violence, and superiors must be prevented from misusing their position to force those who are dependent upon them to do their will. If a man who has committed sexual crimes against children is allowed to roam free because his parents have taken him in and gotten him a job—as though there were the least relation between the one and the other—then that would ultimately justify those purity-crazed organizations that sue the author-ities: in their thoughtlessness the authorities may really bear the respon-sibility if soon afterward the man in question kills a young girl. But this kernel of truth has been encompassed by a mass of opinions that first of all must be examined instead of sanctimonious zealotry preventing any closer reflection. For instance, the allegedly dangerous effects of reading and viewing pornography are hypothetical. It is both foolish and an infringement upon personal liberty to withhold pornography from adults who enjoy it. As for minors, it is first of all necessary to ascertain the existence and nature of the harmful effects: neurotic defects, phobias, conversion hysteria, or whatever else.[21] The awakening of interest in sex-uality, which often is already present, cannot be defamed as harmful, unless one were radical enough to condemn sex altogether—an attitude that would hardly find much sympathy nowadays and that the apostles of morality are careful to avoid. Unmutilated, unrepressed sex in itself does not do any harm to anyone. This not only should be stated without qualification but also should imbue the logic of legislation and its applica-tion. In view of the actual and potential damage that at present can be wreaked upon humankind by its administrators, the need to protect sexuality has something crazy about it. But those who dare to say so openly are even fewer in number than those who protest against such prestigious social institutions as bacteriological and atomic warfare.

Concerning laws protecting minors, we should at least examine whether they really are the victims of violence or cunning ploys, or whether in fact they have not already reached that stage of development the law takes it upon itself to postpone, that is, whether they have not themselves provoked their own abuse for their own pleasure, or perhaps simply for purposes of blackmail. For the time being, a male prostitute who afterward murders and robs his clients, and then declares in court that he acted out of disgust at the things he was expected to do, has good chances of finding lenient judges. In addition, the protection afforded dependent persons is all too summary. Were the praxis to exhaust the letter of the law, there would not be prison space enough for all the offenders; certainly this alone is no argument but nonetheless a symptom. Moreover, it may well be that the regulations in force permit the theater director to have a liaison with his actress but forbid the theater manager from having an affair with one of his office employees. The relevant paragraphs need to be modified sensibly so that they are applied only to such cases where superiors exploit their position of power against subordinates, actually and demonstrably threaten them with dismissal and other disadvantages, but not when the situation itself brings the couple together, as for example Paulo and Francesca during their reading.[22] A cautious version of paragraph 174 of the current penal code that excludes every misapplication is all the more urgent as it is precisely this paragraph—though by no means only this one among the paragraphs devoted to morality—that constitutes an invitation to, as it is called in the modern German jargon so conscious of tradition, knock off [*abschießen*, literally "shoot down"] those who are politically or otherwise undesirable.[23]

On the whole it is not just a matter of moderating the legislation. Much should be strengthened, especially the paragraphs addressing crimes of brutality. As Karl Kraus recognized, prohibited tenderness toward minors is consistently punished more harshly than when the children are beaten half to death by parents or teachers.[24] If someone commits brutal acts of violence while drunk, then his condition will be taken into account and his punishment will be mitigated accordingly, as though in the heart of the *esprit des lois* there lives a code of conduct that not only tolerates drunkenness as an excess but requires it as proof of manly virtue. The fact that it is again and again affirmed to be no mere peccadillo when tipsy drivers—by the way still in full possession of their senses—have run someone down, simply shows how ingrained is the proclivity to see it precisely as a peccadillo, and jurisprudence should also take this into account. German driving practices, in contradistinction to those in the Anglo-Saxon as well as the Romance countries, surely belong to those national characteristics in which something of the spirit of Hitler's Reich visibly survives: the contempt for human life. And indeed, it is an age-old ideology, already thrashed into every *Gymnasium* pupil, that human life is not the highest good. What earlier was an object of scorn for being merely empirical as opposed to the majesty of the moral law has now become, as a result of the evolution of a society proud of having rid itself of ideologies, an object of scorn for the most primitive impulses of self-preservation, the urge to get ahead in the nonmetaphorical sense, the incarnation of a healthy will to succeed. Admittedly this behavior too is not wholly without ideology. Where formerly the moral law held sway, now surveillance insures that the traffic regulations are respected: the precondition for killing someone with a good conscience is the green light. In an analogous fashion social psychology in its investigation of National Socialist mores introduced the concept of legality.[25] Planned murders were covered by some kind of arrangement or other, even *post festum*, as when the "people's representatives" declared them lawful. The brutality manifested in street traffic apparently has just as much need for legal justification as does the persecution of innocent victims and innocent offenses. The endorsement of brutality and twisted instincts wherever they harmonize with institutional social forms faithfully accompanies the litany of hate against the partial drives. In principle and with unavoidable exaggeration, one could surely say that *in law and morals sympathy is accorded to everything that perpetuates the modes of behavior of societal oppression—and ultimately sadistic violence—whereas modes of behavior that are contrary to the violence of the social order itself are dealt with mercilessly.* A reform of penal law worthy of the name, which admittedly is hardly imaginable here and now, would free itself from the spirit of the *Volk*, from those *faits sociaux* Durkheim had already wanted to recognize by the pain they cause.[26]

In cases where actions are the results of conflicts between the ego and the id, the question of whether juridical judgments should be severe or lenient centers on the controversy concerning freedom of the will. Usually the partisans of free will decide in favor of the theory of retribution, which Nietzsche had already seen through, and in favor of severe punishment.[27] The determinists, on the other hand, opt for the theory of education (special prevention) and for the theory of deterrence (general prevention). This alternative is disastrous. The problem of freedom of the will probably cannot be resolved abstractly at all, that is, by using idealized constructions of the individual and its character as something existing purely for itself, but only with the consciousness of the dialectic of individual and society. Freedom, even that of the will, must first be realized and should not be assumed as positively given. On the other hand, the general thesis of determinism is just as abstract as the thesis of *liberum arbitrium*: the totality of the conditions upon which, according to determinism, acts of the will depend is not known and itself constitutes an idea and should not be treated as an available sum. At its height philosophy did not teach one or the other alternative, but rather expressed the antinomy of the situation itself. Kant's theory that all empirical actions are determined by the empirical character that is itself originally posited by the intelligible character in an initial act of freedom, is perhaps the most extraordinary model of this antinomy, no matter how difficult it is to imagine a subject capable of giving himself his character,[28] and whereas in the meantime psychology has revealed the factors in early childhood that determine character formation, factors German philosophy, at least at the end of the eighteenth century, had not the faintest idea of. The more the elements of character must be attributed to the empirical sphere, the more vague and intangible becomes the intelligible character supposedly underlying everything. It probably cannot even be defined as an individual psyche at all, but only as the subjective disposition of an association of objectively free people. All this turns traditional philosophy, the field where jurisprudence locates its foundations in the debate concerning penal law, into a wasteland. This makes it easy for the arbitrariness of a mere worldview to surreptitiously assume supreme authority. Whether one adheres to determinism or the doctrine of free will depends for the time being on the alternative one chooses, for God knows what reasons. Whereas all other domains of the world are being so relentlessly transformed into scientific disciplines that expertise and specialization confiscate every possible knowledge, a discipline that prides itself on its scientific rigor as much as jurisprudence does, at a decisive juncture, takes *common sense** as its central criterion, with all of its inherent murkiness, right down to healthy popular sentiment and the average opinion. This gives the destructive instincts psychology discovered behind the authoritarian need to punish an opportunity to come into play exactly where the demand for reason in jurisprudence becomes emphatic: where reason extends beyond the domain in which it is institutionally reinforced. Nevertheless, the contradiction in which philosophy has entangled itself, that is, that humanity is inconceivable without the idea of freedom while in reality people are neither internally nor externally free, is not a failure of speculative metaphysics but the fault of the society that deprives people even of inner freedom. Society is the true determining factor, while at the same time its organization constitutes the potential for freedom. After the decline of great philosophy, which was completely aware of the objective societal elements inherent in subjective freedom, the antinomy it perceived has been reduced to isolated slogans that are not even antithetical anymore. On the one hand, there is the hollow pathos of freedom evoked in official declamations, which mostly performs a rallying function in favor of unfreedom—that is, in favor of the authoritarian ranks—and on the other hand lies the obtuse and abstract determinism that goes no further than merely affirming determination and in most cases does not get at the true determining factors. At the center of the controversies in moral and legal philosophy once again absolutism and relativism shadowbox each other. The unmediated division between freedom and unfreedom is false, although even this has its element of truth: a distorted expression of the real separation of subjects from one another and from society.

A rigorous determinism, for all the accuracy with which it expresses the unfreedom of people within the established order, would in effect have nothing convincing to oppose the praxis of Auschwitz. Here it encounters the limit that is neither transcended by the substitute philosophy of so-called values[29] nor dissolved in the mere subjectivity of morality. This limit marks the irresolvably differential moment within the relation of theory to praxis. Praxis is not tantamount to autarchic, immobilized thought: the hypostasis of theory as well as that of praxis is itself an element of theoretical untruth. Anyone who helps a victim of persecution is theoretically more in the right than someone who persists in meditating on whether there is an eternal natural law or not although moral praxis requires all one's theoretical consciousness. To this extent Fichte's proposition that the moral law is intuitively self-evident for all its dubiousness still makes a valid point.[30] A philosophy that makes impossible demands on itself in regard to praxis, to the point where it would like to force a complete identification of praxis and theory, is just as false as a decisionistic praxis that eliminates all theoretical reflection. Healthy common sense, which simplifies this in order to have something tangibly useful, threatens the life of truth itself. Today philosophy is not to be transformed smoothly into legislation and juridical procedures. A certain modesty is proper to them, not only because they are not on a par with the complexity of philosophy but also for the sake of the theoretical state of knowledge. Instead of just up and cheerfully thinking away and betraying the question to a false profundity or a radical superficiality, jurisprudence must first of all catch up with the most advanced level of psychological and social knowledge. Science everywhere is occupying the field of naive consciousness, to the very point of paralyzing every unregimented thought; yet in the field jurisprudence takes for its own, the sciences of sociology and psychology indeed have at their disposal more information than do the juridical experts. The latter combine a pedantic-logical systematic with an intellectual attitude that acts as though science had learned nothing about determinant factors and as though each person could choose on his or her own the philosophy that suits him or her best and then substitutes a clattering bustle of homemade concepts for the knowledge currently available. In general one may venture the hypothesis that a philosophy mobilized in an auxiliary role—nowadays most evident in existential ontology—actually has only a reactionary function. On the other hand, the undiluted discoveries of psychoanalysis should be applied to sexual taboos and to legislation concerning sexuality: they should be made productive for questions of criminology. Without any claim to systematicity, several possible investigations may be enumerated.

1. A representative survey should be conducted centering on the relationship between sexual prejudices and fantasies of punishment on the one hand and ideological predispositions and inclinations of an authoritarian nature on the other. The so-called F-scale from *The Authoritarian Personality* could serve as the point of departure.[31] However, it would be necessary to adapt the research instrument in terms of the range and variety of opinions about sexuality. It should be stressed that at that time in America the query statements related to this area were the most powerfully selective and continue to be so in attempts to adapt the American scale to conditions in Germany.

2. For a given limited period, a sample of the judicial opinions handed down in morality trials should be selected, probably at random, and the decisive standpoints as well as the argumentative structure should be identified and analyzed. The prevailing categories as well as the logic of the presentation of evidence should be confronted with the findings of analytical psychology. It is to be expected that the justifications encountered here in many cases resemble the kinds of items recurring regularly in the newspapers: that the body of Mrs. X, a social security pensioner, was recovered from a river, that it is a case of suicide, and that psychological depression is assumed to be the motive of the deed.

3. A representative sample of prisoners incarcerated for having committed sexual offenses or sexual crimes should undergo psychoanalytical study for the duration of their sentence. The analyses should then be compared with the judicial opinions for the purpose of examining their soundness.

4. The categorial structure of the relevant penal laws should be critically analyzed. However, a fixed external standpoint should not be adopted: they must be examined only with a view to their immanent log-

ical consistency. The tendency of what to expect can be discerned, for example, in the notion of a partial compos mentis. It allows for the lunacy where the same person is first consigned to prison or a correctional house when judged responsible for his actions, and then to a mental institution when subsequently judged not responsible.

5. Certain aspects of the code of criminal procedure relevant to sexuality would merit specific study. Thus in all cases where a defendant is accused of offending public decency, particular emphasis should be given to the police reports referring to the often confused situation in which the crime is supposed to have been committed. Much suggests that these reports often arise as a result of pressure exercised upon intimidated defendants caught in the course of a police raid. Certainly many of them are unaware of the significance of the statements they make to the police. — Also the fact that the accused are not permitted a lawyer during the preliminary examination often makes their defense more difficult. This too should be investigated.

6. Individual trials, which need not directly involve sexual offenses, but in which elements relating to sexuality are touched upon, should be studied in detail in order to ascertain in what manner those elements have helped determine the course of the trial and possibly the rendering of the verdict. The recent past offers the case of Vera Brühne. It is conceivable that correlations can be shown between the severe verdict handed down on the basis of hardly conclusive circumstantial evidence and the erotic matters brought up in the trial, although much of it had no plausible connection with the murder. The indefensible belief that a woman who has a libertine sex life is also capable of murder surely played a latent role in the trial.[32]

7. Dogmatic concepts that still haunt legislation today, such as those of healthy popular sentiment, universally valid opinion, natural morality, and the like, should be isolated and analyzed by those trained in philosophy. Particular attention should be devoted to the rationalistic justifications *more iuridico* of actions that in truth follow the laws of psychological irrationality.

8. With full awareness of the unquestionably extreme difficulties confronting such a project, one should undertake empirical studies of the question whether certain actions and behavior tacitly believed to have a harmful influence on adolescents actually do cause verifiable harm. Exhibitionists, often presented as monsters, are in reality mostly innocuous and harmless, if credence can be given to psychoanalysis. They do nothing more than look compulsively for their pathetic satisfaction and surely belong in therapy more than in prison. The psychic damage, however, they supposedly cause the minors who see them is for the time

being merely asserted. Although it has not been proven, it is indeed possible that encounters with exhibitionists cause psychic disturbances in children; yet, it is not too far-fetched that some girls and women, for psychogenic motives, invent terrible experiences with exhibitionists or, as psychoanalysis terms it, that they fantasize their pasts: criminology is well acquainted with the situation thanks to the testimony of witnesses. Likewise the effect that so-called indecent depictions have on youth should be investigated. A group of adolescents who have read some book considered immoral could be questioned about the various dimensions of their intellectual and psychic state, their ideas about morality, eroticism, even about their desires and urges, and another group that has not read the book could be similarly interrogated. Particular care must be taken that the groups are not self-selected, that is, that those people who read the book are not already at the outset sexually more experienced or inquisitive than those who will not read it. It is wholly to be expected that such investigations will prove to be unfeasible practically, or that it will be impossible to develop a method that guarantees sound and unambiguous results. However, even this would be instructive: the simple fact that the presumed damage can be neither proven nor denied would have to result in legislation that would proceed extremely cautiously with the concept of such damage.

9. On the question of the survival of sexual taboos within popular mores: a study should be undertaken of what the prevailing regulations and rules of voluntary self-censorship within the film industry remove from their productions—for instance, caresses, exhibitionism, and alleged obscenity—and, on the other hand, what they permit that is in fact seriously harmful, such as exemplary models of sadistic acts, violent crimes, technically perfect burglaries; certainly it is true that the indignation at cruelty is not seldom coupled with indignation at sex. Yet in America ten years ago attention had already been drawn to this flagrant disproportion between what is forbidden and what is permitted, without anything in the praxis having changed in the meantime: the sexual taboos have just as lasting an effect as does society's complicity with the principle of violence.

The Meaning of Working Through the Past

The question "What does working through the past mean?" requires explication.[1] It follows from a formulation, a modish slogan that has become highly suspect during the last years. In this usage "working through the past" does not mean seriously working upon the past, that is, through a lucid consciousness breaking its power to fascinate. On the contrary, its intention is to close the books on the past and, if possible, even remove it from memory. The attitude that everything should be forgotten and forgiven, which would be proper for those who suffered injustice, is practiced by those party supporters who committed the injustice. I wrote once in a scholarly dispute: in the house of the hangman one should not speak of the noose, otherwise one might seem to harbor resentment.[2] However, the tendency toward the unconscious and not so unconscious defensiveness against guilt is so absurdly associated with the thought of working through the past that there is sufficient reason to reflect upon a domain from which even now there emanates such a horror that one hesitates to call it by name.

One wants to break free of the past: rightly, because nothing at all can live in its shadow, and because there will be no end to the terror as long as guilt and violence are repaid with guilt and violence; wrongly, because the past that one would like to evade is still very much alive. National Socialism lives on, and even today we still do not know whether it is merely the ghost of what was so monstrous that it lingers on after its own death, or whether it has not yet died at all, whether the willingness to commit the unspeakable survives in people as well as in the conditions that enclose them.

I do not wish to go into the question of neo-Nazi organizations.[3] I consider the survival of National Socialism *within* democracy to be potentially more menacing than the survival of fascist tendencies *against* democracy. Infiltration indicates something objective; ambiguous figures make their *comeback** and occupy positions of power for the sole reason that conditions favor them.[4]

Nobody disputes the fact that in Germany it is not merely among the so-called incorrigibles, if that term must be used, that the past has not yet been mastered. Again and again one hears of the so-called guilt complex, often with the association that it was actually first created by the construction of a German collective guilt. Undoubtedly there is much that is neurotic in the relation to the past: defensive postures where one is not attacked, intense affects where they are hardly warranted by the situation, an absence of affect in the face of the gravest matters, not seldom simply a repression of what is known or half-known. Thus we often found in group experiments in the Institute for Social Research that mitigating expressions and euphemistic circumlocutions were chosen in the reminiscences of deportation and mass murder, or that a hollow space formed in the discourse; the universally adopted, almost good-natured expression *Kristallnacht*, designating the pogrom of November 1938, attests to this inclination. A very great number claim not to have known of the events at that time, although Jews disappeared everywhere and although it is hardly believable that those who experienced what happened in the East constantly kept silent about what must have been for them an unbearable burden; surely one may assume that there is a relation between the attitude of "not having known anything about it" and an impassive and apprehensive indifference. In any case the determined enemies of National Socialism knew quite early exactly what was going on.[5]

We[6] all are also familiar with the readiness today to deny or minimize what happened—no matter how difficult it is to comprehend that people feel no shame in arguing that it was at most only five and not six million Jews who were gassed. Furthermore, the quite common move of drawing up a balance sheet of guilt is irrational, as though Dresden compensated for Auschwitz. Drawing up such calculations, the haste to produce counter-arguments in order to exempt oneself from self-reflection, already contain something inhuman, and military actions in the war, the examples of which, moreover, are called "Coventry" and "Rotterdam," are scarcely comparable to the administrative murder of millions of innocent people. Even their innocence, which cannot be more simple and plausible, is contested.[7] The enormity of what was perpetrated works to justify this: a lax consciousness consoles itself with the thought that such a thing surely could not have happened unless the victims had in some way or another furnished some kind of instigation, and this "some kind of" may then be multiplied at will.[8] The blindness disregards the flagrant disproportion between an extremely fictitious guilt and an extremely real punishment. At times the victors are made responsible for what the vanquished did when they themselves were still beyond reach, and responsibility for the atrocities of Hitler is shifted onto those who tolerated his seizure of power and not to the ones who cheered him on. The idiocy of all this is truly a sign of something that psychologically has not been mastered, a wound, although the idea of wounds would be rather more appropriate for the victims.

Despite all this, however, talk of a guilt complex has something untruthful to it. Psychiatry, from which the concept is borrowed with all its attendant associations, maintains that the feeling of guilt is pathological, unsuited to reality, psychogenic, as the analysts call it. The word "complex" is used to give the impression that the guilt, which so many ward off, abreact, and distort through the silliest of rationalizations, is actually no guilt at all but rather exists in them, in their psychological disposition: the terribly real past is trivialized into merely a figment of the imagination of those who are affected by it. Or is guilt itself perhaps merely a complex, and bearing the burden of the past pathological, whereas the healthy and realistic person is fully absorbed in the present and its practical goals? Such a view would draw the moral from the saying: "And it's as good as if it never happened," which comes from Goethe but, at a crucial passage in *Faust*, is uttered by the devil in order to reveal his innermost principle, the destruction of memory.[9] The murdered are to be cheated out of the single remaining thing that our powerlessness can offer them: remembrance. The obstinate conviction of those who do not want to hear anything of it does indeed coincide with a powerful historical tendency. Hermann Heimpel on several occasions has spoken of how the consciousness of historical continuity is atrophying in Germany, a symptom of that societal weakening of the ego Horkheimer and I had already attempted to derive in the *Dialectic of Enlightenment*.[10] Empirical findings, for example, that the younger generation often does not know who Bismarck and Kaiser Wilhelm I were, have confirmed this suspicion of the loss of history.[11]

Thus the forgetting of National Socialism surely should be understood far more in terms of the general situation of society than in terms of psychopathology. Even the psychological mechanisms used to defend against painful and unpleasant memories serve highly realistic ends.

These ends are revealed by the very people maintaining the defense, for instance when in a practical frame of mind they point out that an all too vivid and persistent recollection of what happened can harm the German image abroad. Such zeal does not accord well with the declaration of Richard Wagner, who was nationalistic enough, to the effect that being German means doing something for its own sake—provided that it is not defined a priori as business.[12] The effacement of memory is more the achievement of an all too alert consciousness than its weakness when confronted with the superior strength of unconscious processes. In the forgetting of what has scarcely transpired there resonates the fury of one who must first talk himself out of what everyone knows, before he can then talk others out of it as well.

Surely the impulses and modes of behavior involved here are not immediately rational in so far as they distort the facts they refer to. However, they are rational in the sense that they rely on societal tendencies and that anyone who so reacts knows he is in accord with the spirit of the times. Such a reaction immediately fits in well with the desire to get on with things. Whoever doesn't entertain any idle thoughts doesn't throw any wrenches into the machinery. It is advisable to speak along the lines of what Franz Böhm so aptly called "non-public opinion."[13] Those who conform to a general mood, which to be sure is kept in check by official taboos but which for that reason possesses all the more virulence, simultaneously qualify both as party to it and as independent agents. The German resistance movement after all remained without a popular base, and it's not as if such a base was magically conjured up out of Germany's defeat just like that. One can surely surmise that democracy is more deeply rooted now than it was after the First World War:[14] in a certain sense National Socialism—anti-feudal and thoroughly bourgeois—by politicizing the masses even prepared, against its will, the ground for democratization. The Junker caste as well as the worker's movement have disappeared. For the first time something like a relatively homogeneous bourgeois milieu has developed. But the belated arrival of democracy in Germany, which did not coincide with the peak of economic liberalism and which was introduced by the Allied victors, cannot but have had an effect on the relationship of Germans to democracy. That relationship is only rarely expressed directly, because for the time being things are going so well under democracy and also because it would go against the community of interests institutionalized by political alliances with the West, especially with America.[15] However, the resentment against re-education* is sufficiently explicit. What can be said is that the system of political democracy certainly is accepted in Germany in the form of what in America is called a working proposition*, something that has functioned well up until now and has permitted and even promoted prosperity. But democracy has not become naturalized to the point where people truly experience it as their own and see themselves as subjects of the political process. Democracy is perceived as one system among others, as though one could choose from a menu between communism, democracy, fascism, and monarchy: but democracy is not identified with the people themselves as the expression of their political maturity. It is appraised according to its success or setbacks, whereby special interests also play a role, rather than as a union of the individual and the collective interests, and the parliamentary representation of the popular will in modern mass democracies already makes that difficult enough. In Germany one often hears Germans among themselves making the peculiar remark that they are not yet mature enough for democracy. They make an ideology out of their own immaturity, not unlike those adolescents who, when caught committing some violent act, talk their way out of it with the excuse that they are just teenagers. The grotesque character of this mode of argumentation reveals a flagrant contradiction within consciousness. The people who play up their own naiveté and political immaturity in such a disingenuous manner on the one hand already feel themselves to be political subjects who should set about determining their own destiny and establishing a free society. On the other hand, they come up against the limits strictly imposed upon them by the existing circumstances. Because they are incapable of penetrating these limits with their own thought, they attribute this impossibility, which in truth is inflicted upon them, either to themselves, to the great figures of the world, or to others. It is as though they divide themselves yet once more into subject and object. Moreover, the dominant ideology today dictates that the more individuals are delivered over to objective constellations, over which they have, or believe they have, no power, the more they subjectivize this powerlessness. Starting from the phrase that everything depends on the person, they attribute to people everything that in fact is due to the external conditions, so that in turn the conditions remain undisturbed. Using the language of philosophy, one indeed could say that the people's alienation from democracy reflects the self-alienation of society.

Among these objective constellations, the development of international politics is perhaps the most salient. It appears to justify retrospectively Hitler's attack against the Soviet Union. Since the Western world essentially defines itself as a unity in its defense against the Russian threat, it looks as though the victors in 1945 had foolishly destroyed the tried and tested bulwark against Bolshevism, only to rebuild it a few years later. It is a quick jump from the obvious statement "Hitler always said so" to the extrapolation that he was also right about other things.

Only edifying armchair orators could quickly ease themselves over the historical fatality that in a certain sense the same conception that once motivated the Chamberlains and their followers to tolerate Hitler as a watchdog against the East has survived Hitler's downfall. Truly a fatality. For the threat that the East will engulf the foothills of Western Europe is obvious, and whoever fails to resist it is literally guilty of repeating Chamberlain's *appeasement**.[16] What is forgotten is merely— merely!—the fact that precisely this threat was first produced by Hitler's campaign, who brought upon Europe exactly what his expansionist war was meant to prevent, or so thought the *appeasers**. Even more than the destiny of single individuals, it is the destiny of political entanglements that constitutes the nexus of guilt. The resistance to the East contains its own dynamic that reawakens the German past. Not merely in terms of ideology, because the slogans of struggle against Bolshevism have always served to mask those who harbor no better intentions toward freedom than do the Bolsheviks themselves. But also in terms of reality. According to an observation that had already been made during the era of Hitler, the organizational power of totalitarian systems imposes some of its own nature upon its adversaries. As long as the economic disparity persists between East and West, the fascist variety has better chances of success with the masses than the East's propaganda has, whereas admittedly, on the other hand, one is not yet pushed to the fascist ultima ratio. However, the same character types are susceptible to both forms of totalitarianism. Authoritarian personalities are altogether misunderstood when they are construed from the vantage point of a particular political-economic ide- ology; the well-known oscillations of millions of voters before 1933 between the National Socialist and Communist parties is no accident from the social-psychological perspective either. American studies have shown that this personality structure does not correlate so easily with political-economic criteria. It must be defined in terms of character traits such as a thinking oriented along the dimensions of power and power- lessness, a rigidity and an inability to react, conventionality, the lack of self-reflection, and ultimately an overall inability to experience. Author- itarian personalities identify themselves with real-existing power per se, prior to any particular contents. Basically, they possess weak egos and therefore require the compensation of identifying themselves with, and finding security in, great collectives. The fact that one meets figures everywhere who resemble those in the film *Wir Wunderkinder* is neither due to the depravity of the world as such nor to the supposedly peculiar traits of the German national character.[17] It is due rather to the identity of those conformists—who before the fact already have a connection to the levers of the whole apparatus of political power—as potential followers of totalitarianism. Furthermore, it is an illusion to believe that the National Socialist regime meant nothing but fear and suffering, although it certainly was that even for many of its own supporters. For countless people life was not at all bad under fascism. Terror's sharp edge was aimed only at a few and relatively well defined groups. After the crises of the era preceding Hitler the predominant feeling was that "everything is being taken care of," and that did not just mean an ideology of *KdF* trips and flower boxes in the factories.[18] Compared with the laissez-faire of the past, to a certain degree Hitler's world actually protected its own people from the natural catastrophes of society to which they had been abandoned. A barbaric experiment in state control of industrial society, it violently anticipated the crisis-management policies of today. The often cited "integration," the organizational tightening of the weave in the societal net that encompassed everything, also afforded protection from the universal fear of falling through the mesh and disappearing. For countless people it seemed that the coldness of social alienation had been done away with thanks to the warmth of togetherness, no matter how manipulated and contrived; the *völkisch* community of the unfree and the unequal was a lie and at the same time also the fulfillment of an old, indeed long familiar, evil bourgeois dream. The system that offered such gratification certainly concealed within itself the potential for its own downfall. The economic efflorescence of the Third Reich in large measure was due to its rearmament for the war that brought about the catastrophe. But the weakened memory I mentioned earlier resists accepting these arguments. It tenaciously persists in glorifying the National Socialist era, which fulfilled the collective fantasies of power harbored by those people who, individually, had no power and who indeed could feel any self-worth at all only by virtue of such collective power. No analysis, however illuminating, can afterward remove the reality of this fulfillment or the instinctual energies invested in it. Even Hitler's *va banque* gamble was not as irrational as it seemed to average liberal thought at the time or as its failure seems to historical hindsight today. Hitler's calculation, to exploit the temporary advantage gained over the other nations thanks to a massively accelerated armaments program, was by no means foolish in consideration of what he wanted to achieve. Whoever delves into the history of the Third Reich and especially of the war will feel again and again that the particular moments in which Hitler suffered defeat seem to be accidental and that only the course of the whole appears necessary, the ultimate victory of the superior technical-economic potential of the rest of the world that did not want to be swallowed up: so to speak a statistical necessity, but by no means a discernible step-by-step logic. The surviving sympathy for

National Socialism has no need for laborious sophistry in order to convince itself and others that things could just as well have gone differently, that in fact only some mistakes were made, and that Hitler's downfall was a world-historical accident the world spirit may perhaps yet rectify.

On the subjective side, in the psyche of people, National Socialism increased beyond measure the collective narcissism, simply put: national vanity. The individual's narcissistic instinctual drives, which are promised less and less satisfaction by a callous world and which nonetheless persist undiminished as long as civilization denies them so much, find substitute satisfaction in the identification with the whole.[a] This collective narcissism was severely damaged by the collapse of Hitler's regime, but the damage occurred at the level of mere factuality, without individuals making themselves conscious of it and thereby coping with it. This is the social-psychological relevance of talk about an unmastered past. Also absent is the panic that, according to Freud's theory in *Group Psychology and the Analysis of the Ego*,[19] sets in whenever collective identifications break apart. If the lessons of the great psychologist are not to be cast to the wind, then there remains only one conclusion: that secretly, smoldering unconsciously and therefore all the more powerfully, these identifications and the collective narcissism were not destroyed at all, but continue to exist. Inwardly the defeat has been as little ratified as after 1918. Even in the face of the obvious catastrophe the collective Hitler integrated has held together and clung to chimerical hopes like those secret weapons that in truth the other side possessed. Furthermore, social-psychology adds the expectation that the damaged collective narcissism lies in wait of being repaired and seizes upon anything that brings the past into agreement with the narcissistic desires, first in consciousness, but that it also, whenever possible, construes reality itself as though the damage never occurred. To a certain degree this has been achieved by the economic boom, the feeling of "how industrious we are." But I doubt whether the so-called economic miracle—in which, to be sure, everyone participates even while speaking of it with some disdain—social-psychologically really reaches as deeply as one might suppose in times of relative stability. Precisely because famine continues to reign across entire continents when technically it could be eliminated, no one can really be so delighted at his prosperity. Just as individually, for instance in films, there is resentful laughter when a character sits down to a very good meal and tucks the napkin under his chin, so too humanity begrudges itself the comfort it all too well knows is

---

[a] Cf. "Opinion Delusion Society."

still paid for by want and hardship; resentment strikes every happiness, even one's own. Satiety has become an insult a priori, whereas the sole point of reproach about it would be that there are people who have nothing to eat; the alleged idealism that especially in today's Germany so pharisaically sinks its teeth into an alleged materialism frequently owes its self-proclaimed profundity merely to repressed instincts.[20] Hatred of comfort engenders in Germany discomfort at prosperity, and it transfigures the past into a tragedy. However, this malaise does not at all issue solely from dark and troubled waters but rather once again from far more rational ones. The prosperity is due to an economic upswing, and no one trusts its unlimited duration. If one seeks consolation in the view that events like the Black Friday of 1929 and the resultant economic crisis could hardly repeat themselves, then this already implicitly contains the reliance on a strong state power that, one then expects, will offer protection if economic and political freedom no longer work. Even in the midst of prosperity, even during the temporary labor shortage, the majority of people probably feel secretly that they are potentially unemployed, recipients of charity, and hence really objects, not subjects, of society: this is the fully legitimate and reasonable cause of their discomfort. It is obvious that at any given moment this discomfort can be dammed up, channeled toward the past, and manipulated in order to provoke a renewal of the disaster.

Today the fascist wish-image unquestionably blends with the nationalism of the so-called underdeveloped countries, which now, however, are instead called "developing countries." Already during the war the *slogans** about Western plutocracies and proletarian nations expressed sympathy with those who felt shortchanged in the imperialist competition and also wanted a place at the table. It is difficult to discern whether and to what extent this tendency has already joined the anti-civilization, anti-Western undercurrent of the German tradition and whether in Germany itself there exists a convergence of fascist and communist nationalism. Nationalism today is at once both obsolete and up-to-date. Obsolete, because in the face of the compulsory coalition of nations into great blocs under the supremacy of the most powerful country, which is already dictated by the development in weapons technology alone, the individual sovereign nations, at least in advanced continental Europe, have forfeited their historical substance. The idea of the nation, in which the common economic interests of free and independent citizens once united against the territorial barriers of feudalism, has itself become a barrier to the obvious potential of society as a totality. But nationalism is up-to-date in so far as the traditional and psychologically supremely invested idea of nation, which still expresses the community of interests within the international economy, alone has sufficient force to mobilize hundreds of millions of people for goals they cannot immediately identify as their own. Nationalism does not completely believe in itself anymore, and yet it is a political necessity because it is the most effective means of motivating people to insist on conditions that are, viewed objectively, obsolete. This is why, as something ill at ease with itself, intentionally self-deluded, it has taken on grotesque features nowadays.[21] Admittedly nationalism, the heritage of barbarically primitive tribal attitudes, never lacked such traits altogether, but they were reined in as long as liberalism guaranteed the right of the individual—also concretely as the condition of collective prosperity. Only in an age in which it was already toppling has nationalism become completely sadistic and destructive.[22] The rage of Hitler's world against everything that was different—nationalism as a paranoid delusional system—was already of this caliber. The appeal of precisely these features is hardly any less today. Paranoia, the persecution mania that persecutes those upon whom it projects what it itself desires, is contagious. Collective delusions, like anti-Semitism, confirm the pathology of the individual, who shows that psychologically he is no longer a match for the world and is thrown back upon an illusory inner realm. According to the thesis of the psychoanalyst Ernst Simmel, they may well spare a half-mad person from becoming completely so.[23] To the extent that the delusional mania of nationalism openly manifests itself in the reasonable fear of renewed catastrophes so, too, does it promote its own diffusion. Delusional mania is the substitute for the dream that humanity would organize the world humanely, a dream the actual world of humanity is resolutely eradicating. Everything that took place between 1933 and 1945 goes together with pathological nationalism.

   That fascism lives on, that the oft-invoked working through of the past has to this day been unsuccessful and has degenerated into its own caricature, an empty and cold forgetting, is due to the fact that the objective conditions of society that engendered fascism continue to exist. Fascism essentially cannot be derived from subjective dispositions. The economic order, and to a great extent also the economic organization modeled upon it, now as then renders the majority of people dependent upon conditions beyond their control and thus maintains them in a state of political immaturity. If they want to live, then no other avenue remains but to adapt, submit themselves to the given conditions; they must negate precisely that autonomous subjectivity to which the idea of democracy appeals; they can preserve themselves only if they renounce their self. To see through the nexus of deception, they would need to make precisely that painful intellectual effort that the organization of everyday life, and not least of all a culture industry inflated to the point of totality, prevents. The necessity of such adaptation, of identification with the given, the status quo, with power as such, creates the potential for totalitarianism. This potential is reinforced by the dissatisfaction and the rage that very constraint to adapt produces and reproduces. Because reality does not deliver the autonomy or, ultimately, the potential happiness that the concept of democracy actually promises, people remain indifferent to democracy, if they do not in fact secretly detest it.[24] This form of political organization is experienced as inadequate to the societal and economic reality; just as one must adapt, so would one like the forms of collective life also to adapt, all the more so since one expects from such adaptation the *streamlining** of the state as a gigantic business enterprise within a certainly less than friendly competition of all against all. Those whose real powerlessness shows no sign of ceasing cannot tolerate even the semblance of what would be better; they would prefer to get rid of the obligation of autonomy, which they suspect cannot be a model for their lives, and prefer to throw themselves into the melting pot of the collective ego.[25]

I have exaggerated the somber side, following the maxim that only exaggeration per se today can be the medium of truth.[26] Do not mistake my fragmentary and often rhapsodic remarks for Spenglerism; Spenglerism itself makes common cause with the catastrophe. My intention was to delineate a tendency concealed behind the smooth façade of everyday life before it overflows the institutional dams that, for the time being, are erected against it. The danger is objective, not primarily located in human beings. As I said, there is much that indicates that democracy with all it implies has a more profound hold on people than it did during the Weimar period. By failing to emphasize what is so obvious, I have neglected what circumspect consideration must not ignore: that within the German democracy from 1945 to today the material life of society has reproduced itself more richly than during any other time in living memory, and this is also relevant from a social-psychological perspective. It certainly would not be all too optimistic to affirm that the German democracy is not doing badly these days and that therefore the real reappraisal of the past is also doing fine, provided that it is given enough time and much else besides. Except that the concept of having enough time contains something naive and at the same time contemplative in the bad sense. We are neither simply spectators of world history, free to frolic more or less at will within its grand chambers, nor does world history, whose rhythm increasingly approaches that of the catastrophe, appear to allow its subjects the time in which everything would improve on its own.[27] This bears directly on democratic pedagogy. Above all enlightenment about what has happened must work against a forgetfulness that all

too easily turns up together with the justification of what has been forgotten—for instance,[28] parents who must endure embarrassing questions from children about Hitler and in response, indeed to whitewash
their own guilt, speak of the good aspects and say that in fact it was not so
awful. In Germany it is fashionable to complain about civic education,
and certainly it could be better, but sociology already has data indicating
that civic education, when it is practiced earnestly and not as a burdensome duty, does more good than is generally believed. However, if one
takes the objective potential for the survival of National Socialism as
seriously as I believe it must be taken, then this sets limits even for a pedagogy that promotes enlightenment. Whether it be sociological or psychological, such a pedagogy in practice will probably reach in general
only those people who are open to it anyway and who therefore are
hardly susceptible to fascism.[29] On the other hand, it is certainly not at all
superfluous to fortify this group with enlightened instruction against the
non-public opinion. On the contrary, one could easily imagine that from
this group something like cadres could develop, whose influence in the
most diverse contexts would then finally reach the whole of society, and
the chances for this are all the more favorable, the more conscious the
cadres become. Obviously, the work of enlightenment will not be limited
to these groups. Here I will refrain from a question that is very difficult
and laden with the greatest responsibility: namely, of how far it is advisable to go into the past when attempting to raise public awareness, and
whether precisely the insistence on it does not provoke a defiant resistance and produce the opposite of what it intends. It seems to me rather
that what is conscious could never prove so fateful as what remains
unconscious, half-conscious, or preconscious. Essentially it is a matter of
the way in which the past is made present; whether one remains at the
level of reproach or whether one withstands the horror by having the
strength to comprehend even the incomprehensible. For this, however, it
would be necessary to educate the educators themselves. But such education is gravely impaired by the fact that what in America are called the
*behavioral sciences** are either not represented at all or woefully under-
represented in Germany at present. It is absolutely imperative that universities strengthen a sociology that would work together with the historical research about our own era. Instead of holding forth with secondhand profundities about the Being of man,[30] pedagogy should set itself
the task *re-education** is so vehemently accused of having superficially
handled. Criminology in Germany is not yet up to modern standards at
all. But above all one should think of psychoanalysis, which is still being
repressed today as much as ever. Either it is altogether absent, or it is
replaced by tendencies that while boasting of overcoming the much-

maligned nineteenth century, in truth fall back behind Freudian theory, even turning it into its very opposite. A precise and undiluted knowledge of Freudian theory is more necessary and relevant today than ever. The hatred of it is directly of a piece with anti-Semitism, by no means simply because Freud was a Jew but rather because psychoanalysis consists precisely of that critical self-reflection that makes anti-Semites livid with rage. Although it is so difficult to carry out something like a mass analysis because of the time factor alone, nonetheless if rigorous psychoanalysis found its institutional place, its influence upon the intellectual climate in Germany would be a salutary one, even if that meant nothing more than taking it for granted that one should not lash outward but should reflect about oneself and one's relation to whatever obdurate consciousness habitually rages against. In any case, however, attempts to work subjectively against the objective potential for disaster should not content themselves with corrections that would hardly approach the severity of what must be confronted.[31] Likewise, attention to the great achievements of Jews in the past, however true they may be, are hardly of use and smack of propaganda. And propaganda, the rational manipulation of what is irrational, is the prerogative of the totalitarians. Those who resist totalitarians should not imitate them in a way that would only do themselves a disservice. Panegyrics to the Jews that isolate them as a group already give anti-Semitism a running start. Anti-Semitism is so difficult to refute because the psychic economy of innumerable people needed it and, in an attenuated form, presumably still needs it today. Whatever happens by way of propaganda remains ambiguous. I was told the story of a woman who, upset after seeing a dramatization of *The Diary of Anne Frank*, said: "Yes, but *that* girl at least should have been allowed to live." To be sure even that was good as a first step toward understanding. But the individual case, which should stand for, and raise awareness about, the terrifying totality, by its very individuation became an alibi for the totality the woman forgot.[32] The perplexing thing about such observations remains that even on their account one cannot advise against productions of the Anne Frank play and the like, because their effect nonetheless feeds into the potential for improvement, however repugnant they also are and however much they seem to be a profanation of the dignity of the dead. I also do not believe that too much will be accomplished by community meetings, encounters between young Germans and young Israelis, and other organized promotions of friendship. All too often the presupposition is that anti-Semitism in some essential way involves the Jews and could be countered through concrete experiences with Jews, whereas the genuine anti-Semite is defined far more by his incapacity for any experience whatsoever, by his unresponsiveness. If anti-Semitism primarily has its foundation in objective society, and only derivatively in anti-Semites, then—as the National Socialist joke has it—if the Jews had not already existed, the anti-Semites would have had to invent them. As far as wanting to combat anti-Semitism in individual subjects is concerned, one should not expect too much from the recourse to facts, which anti-Semites most often will either not admit or will neutralize by treating them as exceptions. Instead one should apply the argumentation directly to the subjects whom one is addressing. They should be made aware of the mechanisms that cause racial prejudice within them. A working through of the past understood as enlightenment is essentially such a turn toward the subject, the reinforcement of a person's self-consciousness and hence also of his self. This should be combined with the knowledge of the few durable propaganda tricks that are attuned exactly to those psychological dispositions we must assume are present in human beings. Since these tricks are fixed and limited in number, there is no overwhelming difficulty in isolating them, making them known, and using them as a kind of vaccine. The problem of how to carry out practically such a subjective enlightenment probably could only be resolved by the collective effort of teachers and psychologists, who would not use the pretext of scholarly objectivity to shy away from the most urgent task confronting their disciplines today. Yet in view of the objective power behind the continuing potential of anti-Semitism, subjective enlightenment will not suffice, even if it is undertaken with a radically different energy and in radically deeper psychological dimensions than it has been up to now. If one wishes to oppose the objective danger objectively, then no mere idea will do, not even the idea of freedom and humanitarianism, which indeed—as we have learned in the meantime—in its abstract form does not mean very much to people. If the fascist potential links up with their interests, however limited those interests may be, then the most effective antidote is still a persuasive, because true, demonstration of their own interests and, moreover, their most immediate ones. One would really be guilty of speculative psychologizing in these matters if one disregarded the fact that the war and the suffering it brought upon the German population, although indeed being insufficient to remove the fascist potential, nonetheless offers some counterweight against it. If people are reminded of the simplest things: that open or disguised fascist revivals will cause war, suffering, and privation under a coercive system, and in the end probably the Russian domination of Europe, in short, that they lead to a politics of catastrophe, then this will impress people more deeply than invoking ideals or even the suffering of others, which is always relatively easy to get over, as La Rochefoucauld already knew.[33] Compared with this prospect, the present *malaise** signifies little more than the luxury of a certain mood. Despite all the psychological repression, Stalingrad and the night bombings are not so forgotten that everyone cannot be made to understand the connection between the revival of a politics that led to them and the prospect of a third Punic war. Even if this succeeds, the danger will still exist. The past will have been worked through only when the causes of what happened then have been eliminated. Only because the causes continue to exist does the captivating spell of the past remain to this day unbroken.[34]

Opinion Delusion Society

Despite its several meanings, the concept of *public* opinion is widely accepted in a positive sense. Derived from the philosophical tradition since Plato, the concept of opinion *in general* is neutral, value-free, in so far as opinions can be either right or wrong. Opposed to both these concepts of opinion is the notion of pathogenic, deviant, delusional opinions, often associated with the concept of prejudice. According to this simple dichotomy there is, on the one hand, something like healthy, normal opinion and, on the other, opinion of an extreme, eccentric, bizarre nature. In the United States, for instance, the views of fascistic splinter groups are said to belong to the *lunatic fringe**, an insane periphery of society. Their pamphlets, whose body of ideas also includes ritual murders and *The Protocols of the Elders of Zion* despite their having been conclusively disproved, are considered "farcical." Indeed, in such products one can scarcely overlook an element of madness, which nevertheless is quite likely the very ferment of their effect. Yet precisely that should make one suspicious of an inference habitually drawn from the widely held idea: namely, that in the majority the normal opinion necessarily prevails over the delusional one. The naive liberal reader of the *Berliner Tageblatt* between the wars thought no differently when he imagined the world to be one of *common sense** that, although troubled by rabid extremists on the right and the left, nonetheless must be right in the end. So great was the trust in normal opinion versus the idée fixe that many elderly gentlemen continued to believe their favorite paper long after it had been forced into line by the National Socialists who, cleverly enough, retained only the paper's original masthead.[1] What those subscribers experienced when their prudence toppled overnight into helpless folly as soon as things no longer followed the approved rules of the game should have made them critically examine the naive view of opinion as such, which depicts a peaceful and separate juxtaposition of normal and abnormal opinion. Not only is the assumption that the normal is true and the deviant is false itself extremely dubious but so is the very glorification of mere opinion, namely, of the prevailing one that cannot conceive of the true as being anything other than what everyone thinks. Rather, so-called pathological opinion, the deformations due to prejudice, superstition, rumor, and collective delusion that permeate history, particularly the history of mass movements, cannot at all be separated from the concept of opinion per se. It would be difficult to decide a priori what to ascribe to one kind of opinion and what to the other; history also admits the possibility that in the course of time hopelessly isolated and impotent views may gain predominance, either by being verified as reasonable or in spite of their absurdity. Above and beyond that, however, pathological opinion, the deformed and lunatic aspects within collective ideas, arises within the dynamic of the concept of opinion itself, in which inheres the real dynamic of society, a dynamic that produces such opinions, false consciousness, necessarily. If resistance to that dynamic is not to be condemned at the outset to harmlessness and helplessness, then the tendency toward pathological opinion must be derived from normal opinion.

Opinion is the positing, no matter how qualified, of a subjective consciousness restricted in its truth content. The form of such an opinion may actually be innocuous. If someone says that in his opinion the new faculty building is seven stories high, then that can mean that he heard it from someone else but does not know exactly. Yet the sense is completely different when someone says that at all events in his opinion the Jews are an inferior race of vermin, as in Sartre's instructive example of Uncle Armand, who feels special because he detests the English.[2] Here the "in my opinion" does not qualify the hypothetical judgment, but underscores it. By proclaiming his opinion—unsound, unsubstantiated by experience, conclusive without any deliberation—to be his own, though he may appear to qualify it, simply by relating the opinion to himself as subject he in fact lends it an authority: that of a profession of faith. What comes across is that he stands behind his statement with heart and soul; he supposedly has the courage to say what is unpopular but in truth all too popular. Conversely, when confronted with a convincing and well-grounded judgment that nevertheless is discomfiting and cannot be refuted, there is an all too prevalent tendency to disqualify it by declaring it to be mere opinion. A lecture on the hundredth anniversary of Schopenhauer's death[a] presented evidence that the difference between Schopenhauer and Hegel is not so absolute as Schopenhauer's own invectives would indicate and that both thinkers unwittingly converge in the emphatic concept of the negativity of existence. A newspaper reporter, who may have known nothing about Hegel other than that Schopenhauer reviled him, qualified his account of the lecturer's thesis with the addendum "in his view," thus giving himself an air of superiority over thoughts he in fact could hardly follow, let alone evaluate. The opinion was the reporter's, not the lecturer's: the latter had recognized something. Yet, whereas he suspected the lecturer of mere opinion, the reporter himself had for his own benefit already obeyed a mechanism that foists opinion—namely, his own unauthoritative one—on his readers as a criterion of truth and thereby virtually abolishes the latter.

Things rarely remain at the level of such innocuous opinions as how many floors a new building might have. Of course, the individual can reflect upon his opinion and guard against hypostatizing it. Yet the very category of opinion, as an objective state of mind, is shielded against such reflection. This is first of all due to simple facts of individual psychology. Whoever has an opinion about a question that is still relatively open and undecided, and likewise the answer to which cannot be as easily verified as the number of floors in a building, tends to cling to that opinion or, in the language of psychoanalysis, to invest it with affect. It would be foolish for anyone to claim to be innocent of this tendency. The tendency is based on *narcissism*, that is, on the fact that human beings to this day are obliged to withhold a measure of their ability to love from, for instance, other loved ones, and instead to love themselves in a repressed, unacknowledged, and therefore insidious manner. Personal opinion becomes, as one's possession, an integral component of one's person, and anything that weakens that opinion is registered by one's unconscious and preconscious as though it were a personal injury. Self-righteousness, the propensity to insist on defending ridiculous opinions even when their falsity has become obvious to reason, attests to the prevalence of this sit-

---

[a] Cf. Max Horkheimer, "Die Aktualität Schopenhauers," in Max Horkheimer and Theodor W. Adorno, *Sociologica II: Reden und Vorträge*, 2d ed. (Frankfurt: Europäische Verlagsanstalt, 1967), 124ff. [*Translator's note:* English: "Schopenhauer Today," in *The Critical Spirit: Essays in Honor of Herbert Marcuse*, eds. Kurt H. Wolff and Barrington Moore, Jr. (Boston: Beacon Press, 1967), 55–71.]

uation. Solely in order to ward off the narcissistic injury he undergoes in exposing his opinion, the self-opinionated person develops an acumen that often far surpasses his intellectual means. The cleverness that is expended in the world for the purpose of defending narcissistic nonsense would probably be sufficient to change what is being defended. Reason in the service of unreason—in Freud's language, "rationalization"—rushes to the aid of opinion and so hardens it that nothing more can affect it or reveal its absurdity.[3] Sublime theoretical systems have been built upon the most insane opinions. With regard to the genesis of such a hardened opinion—and its genesis is also its pathogenesis—one may go beyond psychology. The positing of an opinion, the mere statement that something is such and such, already implies the potential for fixation, reification, even before the psychological mechanisms come into play that bewitch the opinion into a fetish. The logical form of a judgment, regardless of whether it is right or wrong, has in it something lordly, proprietary, that is then reflected in the insistence upon opinions as though they were property. Having an opinion at all, judging, already to a certain extent seals itself off from experience and tends toward delusion, while on the other hand only the person capable of judging possesses reason. This is perhaps the most profound and irredeemable contradiction inherent in holding an opinion.

Without a firmly held opinion, without hypostatizing something that is not fully known—that is, without accepting something as the truth while it is impossible to be completely certain that it is the truth—experience, indeed the very preservation of life, is hardly possible. The timid pedestrian who hesitates at the yellow light, judging that if he now crosses the street he will be hit by a car, is not completely sure that this will actually occur. The next automobile could be driven by a humane driver for once, who will not immediately step on the gas.[4] But the moment the pedestrian were to rely on that and cross the street on the light he would, simply because he is no prophet, most probably be killed. In order to behave as the common sense of self-preservation dictates, the pedestrian must, as it were, exaggerate. All thinking is exaggeration, in so far as every thought that is one at all goes beyond its confirmation by the given facts. Yet this difference between thought and its factual confirmation harbors the potential for delusion as well as for truth. Delusion can then really appeal to the fact that, in general, no thought can ever be given the guaranty that the expectation it contains will not be disappointed. There are no discretely conclusive, absolutely reliable, independent criteria; the decision is taken only through a structure of complex mediations. Husserl once pointed out that the individual must presume the validity of innumerable propositions he can neither reduce to their conditions nor completely verify. The daily interaction with technology, which is no longer the privilege of a specialized training, incessantly gives rise to such situations. The difference between opinion and reasoned insight, namely that insight should be verified opinion, as the usual epistemological theory holds, was mostly an empty promise only rarely fulfilled by empirical acts of knowledge; individually and collectively, human beings are also obliged to operate with opinions that are in principle beyond examination. Yet as the difference between opinion and insight itself thereby slips away from lived experience and hovers on the horizon as an abstract assertion, it forfeits its substance subjectively, in the consciousness of people. People have no means available to defend themselves readily against the suspicion that their opinions are in fact reasoned insights and their reasoned insights mere opinions. If philosophers since Heraclitus have carped at the many for remaining captive to mere opinion instead of knowing the true essence of things, then their elitist thinking only put the blame on the *underlying population** for what properly lies with the institution of society. For the authority that relieves people of the decision between opinion and truth, deferred *ad kalendas Graecas*, is society. The *communis opinio* replaces truth, factually, ultimately indirectly even in many positivistic theories of epistemology. What is deemed true and what mere opinion—that is, chance and caprice—is not decided according to the evidence, as the ideology would have it, but rather by societal power, which denounces as mere caprice whatever does not agree with its own caprice. The border between healthy and pathogenic opinion is drawn *in praxi* by the prevailing authority, not by informed judgment.

The more blurred this border becomes, the more unrestrained and rampant opinion grows. Its corrective, that is, the means by which opinion can become knowledge, is the relation of thought to its object. By satiating itself with its object, thought transforms and divests itself of the element of arbitrariness. Thinking is no mere subjective activity but, as philosophy at its height recognized, essentially the dialectical process between subject and object in which both poles first mutually determine each other. The very organ of thinking, prudence, consists not only in the formal strength of the subjective faculty to form concepts, judgments, and conclusions correctly but at the same time in the ability to apply this faculty to what is unlike it. The moment called cathexis in psychology, thought's affective investment in the object, is not extrinsic to thought, not merely psychological, but rather the condition of its truth. Where cathexis atrophies, intelligence becomes stultified. A first indication of this is blindness to the difference between the essential and inessential. Something of this stupidity triumphs whenever the mechanisms of thought run of their own accord, like an engine idling, when they substitute their own formalisms and systemic definitions in place of the matter itself. Traces of this are contained in the opinion that, entrenched solely within itself, continues without meeting any resistance. Opinion is above all consciousness that does not yet have its object. Should such consciousness progress merely by dint of its own motor, without contact with what it intends and what it actually must begin by grasping, then it has an all too easy time of it. Opinion, as *ratio* still separated from its object, obeys a kind of economy of forces, following the path of least resistance, when it abandons itself completely to simple logical consistency. Opinion sees logical consistency as a merit, whereas in many ways such consistency is the lack of what Hegel called "freedom toward the object," that is, the freedom of thought to lose and transform itself in its encounter with the subject matter.[5] Brecht very graphically contrasted such thought with the principle that he who says A must not say B.[6] Mere opinion tends toward that inability to stop that may be called 'pathological projection.'[b]

However, the constant proliferation of opinions is likewise grounded in the object itself. For naive consciousness the opacity of the world is obviously increasing, whereas in so many aspects it is becoming more and more transparent. The predominance of this opacity, which prevents the thin façade from being penetrated, reinforces such naiveté rather than diminishing it, as the innocent faith in education would believe.[7] Yet whatever eludes the grasp of sufficient knowledge is usurped by its imitation: opinion. Opinion deceptively removes the otherness between the epistemological subject and the reality that slips away from him, but that very alienation betrays itself in the inadequacy of mere opinion. Because the world is not our world, because it is heteronomous, it can express itself only distortedly in stubborn and inflexible opinions, and such delusion within opinions in turn ultimately tends to increase the predominance of alienation in totalitarian systems. Therefore, it is not enough for knowledge or for a transformative praxis to reveal the nonsense of immensely popular views, according to which people submit themselves to character typologies and predictions that a commercially revived and

---

[b] Cf. Max Horkheimer and Theodor W. Adorno, *Dialektik der Aufklärung* (Amsterdam: Querido, 1947), 220ff. [*Translator's note:* Reference is to the chapter "Elements of Anti-Semitism: Limits of Enlightenment" in *Dialectic of Enlightenment* by Max Horkheimer and Theodor W. Adorno, trans. John Cumming (New York: Continuum, 1989), 168–208.]

standardized astrology ascribes to the signs of the zodiac.^c People turn themselves into a Taurus or a Virgo not only because they are stupid enough to heed the suggestions of newspaper columns implying that there obviously is something to the whole exercise but also because those clichés and that idiotic practical advice, which merely reiterates what has to be done anyway, give them, no matter how spuriously, some orientation and momentarily soothe their feelings of alienation from life, even from their own lives. Mere opinion's vigorous powers of resistance can be explained by its psychological function. It proffers explanations through which contradictory reality can without great exertion be rendered free of contradiction. And there is the narcissistic satisfaction that the facile opinion affords by reinforcing its adherents' belief that they themselves have always known it, and that consequently they belong to the ones in the know. The self-confidence of the unflinchingly opinionated feels immune to every divergent, contrary judgment. This psychological function, however, is much more readily fulfilled by pathological opinions than by the supposedly healthy ones. Karl Mannheim once pointed out how ingeniously racial mania satisfies a mass-psychological need by allowing the majority to think of itself as an elite and to avenge its own intimations of weakness and inferiority upon a potentially defenseless minority.[8] The weakness of the ego nowadays, which beyond its psychological dimension also registers the effects of each individual's real powerlessness in the face of the societalized apparatus, would be exposed to an unbearable degree of narcissistic injury if it did not seek a compensatory identification with the power and the glory of the collective. This is why pathological opinions are particularly useful, since they ceaselessly issue from the infantile narcissistic prejudice that only "I" am good and all else is inferior and bad.

The development of opinion into its pathological variant is reminiscent of the evolution of dinosaurs that, as the increasing specialization of their organs adapted them ever more closely to the struggle for existence, in the final phase brought forth deformities and excrescences. Such a development is trivialized if it is seen to derive only from people, their

---

^c Cf. Theodor W. Adorno, "Aberglaube aus zweiter Hand," in *Sociologica II*, 142ff. [now in *GS* 8:147ff.]. [*Translator's note:* Original English version "The Stars Down to Earth: The *Los Angeles Times* Astrology Column—a Study in Secondary Superstition," *Jahrbuch für Amerikastudien*, 2 (1957): 19–88; reprinted in *Telos* 19 (Spring 1974): 13–90; the complete original study is now in *GS* 9.2:7–142 and was reprinted in Theodor W. Adorno, *The Stars Down to Earth and Other Essays on the Irrational in Culture*, ed. Stephen Crook (London/New York: Routledge, 1994).]

psychology, or at most from a tendency within thought itself. The undermining of truth by opinion, with all the disaster it entails, is a result of what happened—irresistibly, not as an aberration that might be corrected—to the idea of truth itself. This idea of truth as an objective, unchanging, self-identical, unified being in itself, was the standard from which Plato derived the opposing concept of mere opinion, which he then criticized for being dubiously subjective. The history of spirit, however, has not left unchallenged this rigid opposition separating ideas as the true essence from the mere existence to which feeble opinions are enthralled. Very early on Aristotle objected that idea and existence are not separated by an abyss but are interdependent. The idea of autonomous truth in itself, which in Plato is opposed to opinion, *doxa*, has itself been increasingly criticized as mere opinion, and the question of objective truth has been turned back upon the subject who recognizes it—indeed who perhaps even produces such truth out of himself. At its height in Kant and Hegel, modern Western metaphysics tried to save the objectivity of truth by means of its subjectivization, finally equating truth's objectivity with the epitome of subjectivity, namely, mind. But this conception did not gain any acceptance with people, let alone in science. The natural sciences owe their most fascinating successes to their having abandoned the doctrine of the independence of truth, of pure forms, in favor of the unqualified reduction of what is true first and foremost to subjectively observed, and then processed, facts. Thus the doctrine of truth in itself was repaid with some of its own untruth by the arrogance of the subject that finally sets itself up as objectivity and truth and asserts an equality or reconciliation of subject and object that the contradictory nature of the world readily belies.

Of late the aporia of the concept of objective reason is suffering obscurantist exploitation. Since what is true and what is opinion cannot be ascertained immediately, absolutely, as though per administrative decree, their difference is simply denied, to the greater glory of opinion. The fusion of skepticism and dogmatism, of which Kant was already aware and whose tradition could be traced back to the origins of bourgeois thinking, to Montaigne's defense of Sebond,[9] returns with a vengeance in a society that must tremble in fear before its own reason because it is not yet reason. There is an established term for it: faith in reason. It holds that because every judgment first of all requires that the subject assume whatever is being judged to be the case, that is, that he believe in it, the difference between mere opinion or belief and well-grounded judgment is therefore rendered untenable in principle. Anyone who behaves rationally believes in *ratio* just as the irrational person believes in his dogma. For that reason, the profession of a dogmatic belief in a putatively revealed verity presumably has the same truth content as rational insight emancipated from dogma. The abstractness of the thesis conceals its duplicity. Belief is completely different in the one case and in the other: in dogma, belief attaches itself to statements that are contrary to or incompatible with reason, whereas for reason, belief constitutes nothing other than the commitment to an intellectual posture that neither arrests nor effaces itself but advances determinately in the negation of false opinion.[10] Reason cannot be subsumed under any more general concept of belief or opinion. Reason finds its specific content in the critique of what falls within and aligns itself with these categories. The individual act of holding something to be true—which, by the way, a refined theology itself rejects as insufficient—is inessential to reason. What interests reason is knowledge, not whatever knowledge considers itself to be. Reason's orientation leads the subject away from himself rather than reinforcing him in his ephemeral convictions. Only by a high-handed abstraction can opinion and reasoned insight be reduced to the commonality of a subjective appropriation of the contents of consciousness; rather this commonality, the subjective confiscation of the object, already is the transition to the false. In the kind of motivation underlying each individual proposition, no matter how erroneous it might be, the difference between opinion and reasoned insight emerges concretely. With admirable impartiality, unmarred even by his heavy-handed psychological tone, Arthur Schnitzler outlined this phenomenon a generation ago: "It is for the most part deliberate insincerity to equate the dogmas of the church with the dogmas of science, even where the latter are apparently dubious. What counts, already unjustly, as 'scientific dogma' in every case owes its stature to the honesty and exertion of thinkers and researchers and to confirmation by a thousand observations. The church dogma is in the best of cases the naive assertion of a visionary, the belief in which is often imposed upon thousands of people only through terrorism."[d] One could add that reason, if in fact it does not want to subscribe to a second dogmatism, must also reflect critically upon the concept of science that Schnitzler still somewhat naively assumes. Philosophy has its place in such reflection; while philosophy still relied on itself, its science was nothing other than the achievement of such self-reflection, and the renunciation of this self-reflection is itself a symptom of the regression to mere opinions.[11]

For in the meantime consciousness, weakened and ever more sub-

---

[d] Arthur Schnitzler, "Bemerkungen: Aus dem Nachlaß," in *Die neue Rundschau* 73 (1962): 350.

servient to reality, is losing the ability to make the exertion of reflection required by a concept of truth that does not stand in abstract and reified contraposition to mere subjectivity but rather develops itself through critique, by means of the reciprocal mediation of subject and object. And so in the name of a truth that liquidates the concept of truth as a chimera, a vestige of mythology, the distinction between truth and opinion itself becomes ever more precarious. Of course, these considerations are not entertained by societal consciousness, which long ago took its leave from philosophical consciousness as though from a specialized department. Nevertheless, they are reflected in the procedures of scientific research, which have become the general model of knowledge in contradistinction to mere opinion. Hence their power. Processes that, if one may speak this way, take place within the philosophical concept, have their consequences for everyday consciousness, and especially in its social dimensions. Societal consciousness tacitly renounces a distinction between truth and opinion, a renunciation that does not leave the movement of spirit unaffected.[12] Frequently truth becomes opinion to the consciousness that is wise to the world, as with that journalist. But opinion replaces truth with itself. In place of the both problematical and binding idea of truth in itself there appears the more comfortable idea of truth for us, whether it be for everyone, or at least for many. *"Thirteen million Americans can't be wrong,"** goes a popular advertising slogan, a more faithful echo of the spirit of the age than the isolated pride of those who consider themselves the cultural elite would care to admit. The average opinion—along with the societal power concentrated in it—becomes a fetish, and the attributes of truth are displaced onto it. It is incomparably easier to detect its meagerness, to become outraged or amused by it, than to confront it cogently. Even the strange, presumptuous claims made by the latest form of the dissolution of the concept of truth in many—not all—directions of logical positivism spring to mind; at the same time they can be refuted on their own terrain only with great difficulty. For any refutation presupposes precisely the very relationships of thought to the subject matter, the very experience that is thrown on the scrap heap in the name of the transformation of thought into a method that should be as independent as possible from the subject matter. More in keeping with the times is good old *common sense** that, while priding itself on its own reasonableness, at the same time spitefully repudiates reason, knowing that what matters in the world is not thought so much as property and power, a hierarchy it would have no other way. What parades as the incorruptible skepsis of someone who will have no dust thrown in his eyes is the citizen shrugging his shoulders, "What in God's name could there be on the horizon," as is said at one place in Beckett's *Endgame,* the complacent announcement of the subjective relativity of all knowledge.[13] It amounts to the view that stubborn and blind subjective self-interest is and should remain the measure of all things.

This may be studied, as though in a test tube, in the history of one of the most important concepts of social theory, that of ideology. In its full theoretical elaboration, the concept of ideology was related to a doctrine of society that claimed to be objective, inquired into the objective rules of societal change, and conceived a correct society, one in which objective reason would be realized and the illogicality of history, its blind contradictions, would be resolved. According to this theory, ideology signified a societally necessary false consciousness, that is, the antithesis to a true one, and was determinable only in this antithesis, but at the same time ideology could itself be derived from the objective societal laws, especially from the structure of the commodity form. Even in its untruth, as the expression of such necessity, ideology was also a fragment of truth. The later sociology of knowledge, particularly that of Pareto and Mannheim,[14] took some pride in its scientifically purified concepts and its enlightened, dogma-free viewpoint, when it replaced the older concept of ideology with one that—not by coincidence—was called 'total ideology' and that fit in only all too well with blind, total domination.[e] The theory holds that any consciousness is conditioned from the beginning by interests, that it is mere opinion. The idea of truth itself is attenuated into a perspective that is a composite of these opinions, vulnerable to the objection that it too is nothing but opinion: that of the free-floating intelligentsia. Such universal expansion empties the critical concept of ideology of its significance. Since, in honor of beloved truth, all truths are supposedly mere opinions, the idea of truth gives way to opinion. Society is no longer critically analyzed by theory, rather it is confirmed as that which it in fact is increasingly becoming: a chaos of undirected, accidental ideas and forces, the blindness of which drives the social totality toward its downfall. — The difficulty of accepting Nietzsche's grandiose anticipation of the self-destruction of truth resulting from a process of enlightenment unreflectedly set loose can be observed in just such eccentricities as the attitude toward the pathological opinion par excellence: superstition. Kant, the Enlightenment philosopher of subjectivity in the name of objective truth, had unmasked superstition in his treatise against Swedenborg, "Dreams of a Spirit-Seer."[15] Some empiricists, who indeed—in contrast to Kant—do not want to know anything about con-

---

[e] Cf. "Ideologie," in Institut für Sozialforschung, *Soziologische Exkurse: Nach Vorträgen und Diskussionen* (Frankfurt: Europäische Verlagsanstalt, 1956), 162ff.

stitutive subjectivity yet in their reduction of the concept of truth embrace a very unconscious and therefore all the more uninhibited subjectivism, no longer stand so decidedly opposed to superstition. They would be inclined, even regarding superstition, to retreat to the neutrality of a scientific enterprise based on pure conceptless observation: even "occult facts" could be approached patiently, through observation, without prejudice. They relinquish the prerogative of rejecting the swindle out of hand—that what by its own definition exceeds the limits of the possibility of sensuous experience could then be made the object of such experience. They are still receptive to delusion. There is also a false impartiality, where thought is cut short and entrusts itself without reflection to the isolated materials under examination. Partiality and impartiality cannot be defined in the abstract at all; rather the distinction is drawn solely in the context of knowledge as well as of reality, the context in which the question itself is posed. In a science disposed to apologia indeed there are also those who calmly record even the pathological prejudices and dismiss their theoretical examination, their reduction to social and psychological defects, as itself biased, whereas in their opinion an impartial science can just as well develop a coordinate system in which— as with the late Marburg psychologist Jaensch—the *Authoritarian Personality* would be the positive character type and the potentially free people who resist it would be decadent weaklings.[16] From here it is but a short step to a scientific attitude that is indifferent to the concept of truth and contents itself with the production of more or less harmonious classificatory systems that elegantly ensnare whatever is observed.

The immanence of pathological opinion within so-called normal opinion is demonstrated graphically by the fact that, in crass contradiction to the official misrepresentation of a reasonable society of reasonable people, groundless and absurd ideas of every stripe are by no means the exception and are by no means on the wane. More than half the population of the Federal Republic of Germany believes that there is something to the astrology that in the early days of the bourgeois age, when the methods of scientific critique were less developed than they are today, Leibniz already characterized as the only science for which he felt nothing but contempt. Exactly how many people still believe racial theories that have been refuted innumerable times—for instance, the conviction that certain distinctive marks on the skull coincide with character traits—probably cannot be ascertained, if only because of the prevailing fear in the Federal Republic of the outcome of such surveys, which leads to the result that they are not even undertaken. The conviction that rationality is normality is false. Under the spell of the tenacious irrationality of the whole, the very irrationality of people is normal.[17] This irrationality and the instrumental reason of their practical activity diverge widely, yet irrationality is constantly poised, ready in political attitudes to overflow even this instrumental reason. This touches upon one of the most serious of all difficulties encountered by the concept of public opinion in relation to private opinion. If public opinion legitimately exercises that control function that the theory of democratic society since Locke has attributed to it, then public opinion itself must be controllable in its truth. At present it is considered controllable only as the statistical mean value of the opinions of all individuals. In this mean value the irrationality of that opinion, its arbitrary and objectively gratuitous element, necessarily returns; therefore, it is precisely not that objective authority it claims to be according to its own concept, namely, a corrective to the fallible political actions of individuals. However, if instead of this one wanted to equate public opinion with what are called its organs, which are supposed to know and understand more, then the criterion of public opinion would be the very same control over the means of mass communication, the criticism of which is not the least important task of public opinion. To equate public opinion with the very stratum of society that considers itself the elite would be irresponsible, because in such a group the actual expertise, and hence the possibility of a judgment that is worth more than mere opinion, is indissolubly entangled within particular interests that elite perceives as though they were universal. The moment when an elite knows and declares itself as such, it already makes itself into the opposite of what it claims to be and draws irrational domination from circumstances that could grant it a good deal of rational insight. One may be an elite, for heaven's sake, but one should never feel like one. However, in view of such aporias, simply to delete the concept of public opinion, completely to renounce it, on the other hand would mean losing an element that can still avert the worst in an antagonistic society as long as it stays this side of totalitarian. The revision of the Dreyfus trial, even the fall of the minister of culture in Lower Saxony because of the opposition by Göttingen students, would have been impossible without public opinion.[18] Especially in the Western countries, even in the age of the administered world, public opinion has preserved some of the function it had in the struggle against absolutism. Indeed in Germany, where public opinion never really developed into the voice, however problematical, of an independent bourgeoisie, even now, when for the first time public opinion seems to be stirring more forcefully, it retains something of its old impotence.[19]

The characteristic form of absurd opinion today is nationalism.[f] With new virulence it infects the entire world, in a historical period where,

---

[f] Cf. "The Meaning of Working Through the Past."

because of the state of the technical forces of production and the potential definition of the earth as a single planet, at least in the non-underdeveloped countries nationalism has lost its real basis and has become the full-blown ideology it always has been. In private life, self-praise and anything resembling it is suspect, because such expressions reveal all too much the predominance of narcissism. The more individuals are caught up in themselves and the more fatally they pursue particular interests—interests that are reflected in that narcissistic attitude, which in turn reinforces the rigid power of the interests—the more carefully this very principle must be concealed and misrepresented, so that, as the National Socialist slogan has it, "service before self."[20] However, it is precisely this force of taboo on individual narcissism, its repression, that gives nationalism its pernicious power. The life of the collective has different ground rules than those at work in the relations between individuals. In every soccer match the local fans, flouting the rules of hospitality, shamelessly cheer on their own team; Anatole France, today so prone to being treated *en canaille*—and not without some justification—remarked in *Penguin Island* that each fatherland stands above all others in the world.[21] People would only need take the norms of bourgeois private life to heart and raise them to the level of society. But well-meaning recommendations in this vein overlook the fact that any transition of this kind is impossible under conditions that impose such privations on individuals, so constantly disappoint their individual narcissism, in reality damn them to such helplessness, that they are condemned to collective narcissism. As a compensation, collective narcissism then restores to them as individuals some of the self-esteem the same collective strips from them and that they hope to fully recover through their delusive identification with it. More than any other pathological prejudice, the belief in the nation is opinion as dire fate: the hypostasis of the group to which one just happens to belong, the place where one just happens to be, into an absolute good and superiority. It inflates into a moral maxim that abominable wisdom born of emergency situations, that we are all in the same boat. It is just as ideological to distinguish healthy national sentiment from pathological nationalism as it is to believe in normal opinion in contrast to pathogenic opinion. The dynamic that leads from the supposedly healthy national sentiment into its overvalued excess is unstoppable, because its untruth is rooted in the person's act of identifying himself with the irrational nexus of nature and society in which he by chance finds himself.

In view of all this we are left with the dictum of Hegel, who already perceived the contradiction at the heart of the concept of public opinion before it could fully unfold in reality: according to him, public opinion is to be both respected and disdained. This paradox stems not from the wavering indecisiveness of those who must reflect on opinion but rather is immediately at one with the contradiction of reality toward which opinion is intended and from which opinion is produced. There is no freedom without opinions that diverge from reality, but such divergence endangers freedom. The idea of the free expression of opinion, which indeed cannot be separated from the idea of a free society, necessarily becomes the right to propose, defend, and if possible successfully champion one's own opinion, even when it is false, mad, disastrous. Yet if for that reason one wanted to curb the right of free expression, then one would be heading explicitly for the kind of tyranny that lies implicitly within the logic of opinion itself. The antagonism within the concept of free expression boils down to the fact that the concept posits society as composed of free, equal, and emancipated people, whereas society's actual organization hinders all of that and produces and reproduces a condition of permanent regression among its subjects. The right to freely express one's opinion presumes an identity of the individual and his consciousness with the rational general interest, an identity that is hindered in the very world in which it is formally viewed as a given.

Nowadays it is altogether problematical to oppose mere opinion in the name of truth, because a fatal elective affinity has been established between the former and reality, which in turn proves useful to the stubborn rigidity of opinion. Certainly the opinion of the fool who moves her bed around her bedroom in order to shield herself from the danger of evil rays is pathogenic. But the risk of exposure in a radioactively contaminated world has grown so great that the anxiety is belatedly honored by the same faculty of reason that eschews its psychotic character. The objective world is approaching the image persecution mania renders of it. The concept of persecution mania and pathological opinion as a whole are not spared the same tendency. Anyone who nowadays hopes to comprehend the pathogenic element of reality with the traditional categories of human understanding falls into the same irrationality he imagines himself to be protected from by his loyal adherence to healthy common sense.

One may risk the general definition that pathological opinion is hardened opinion, reified consciousness, the damaged capacity for full experience.[22] The identification of *doxa* with mere subjective reason, repeated many times since the Platonic critique of the Sophists, identifies only one aspect. Opinion, and certainly the pathological kind, is always also a lack of subjectivity and allies itself with this weakness. This is clearly inscribed in the Platonic caricatures of the swaggering adversaries of Socrates. When the subject no longer has the strength of rational synthesis, or desperately denies it in the face of overwhelming power, then opinion settles in. And usually subjectivism does not count for much here; rather subjectivism is used almost automatically as an excuse by a consciousness that is precisely not the self-consciousness knowledge needs in order to become objective. What the subject, in the name of opinion, takes for his personal prerogative is in every respect merely the reproduction of the objective relations in which he is entangled. The supposed opinion of the individual repeats the congealed opinion of everyone. To the subject, who has no genuine relation to the matter at hand, who recoils from its otherness and coldness, everything he says about it, both for the subject and in itself, becomes mere opinion, something that is reproduced and registered and could just as easily be otherwise. The subjectivistic reduction to the contingency of individual consciousness submits itself perfectly to a servile respect for an objectivity that lets such a consciousness stand unchallenged and to which that consciousness still shows reverence in the assurance that whatever it thinks is not binding in view of the force of this objectivity: by its standard, reason is nothing at all. The contingent nature of opinion reflects the rift between the object and reason. The subject honors the elemental powers by degrading himself into his own contingency. For this reason the condition of pathological opinion can hardly be changed by mere consciousness. The reification of the consciousness that deserts and defects to the world of things, capitulates before that world and makes itself resemble it, the desperate conformity of the person who is unable to withstand the coldness and predominance of the world, except by outdoing it if possible, is grounded in the world that is reified, divested of the immediacy of human relations, dominated by the abstract principle of exchange. If there really is no correct life in the false life, then actually there can be no correct consciousness in it either.[23] False opinion cannot be transcended through intellectual rectification alone but only concretely. A consciousness that here and now would completely renounce this hardening of opinion, which constitutes the pathological principle, would be just as problematic as the hardening itself. It would fall victim to the fleeting and unstructured alternation of ideas, that mollusk-like monstrosity that can be observed in many so-called sensitive people and that has not even attained the synthesis of rational insight that then freezes solid in reified consciousness. Such a, so to speak, paradisiacal consciousness would be a priori unequal to the reality it must come to know and which is the hardness itself. Every instruction for attaining correct consciousness would be in vain. In reality consciousness consists solely in the exertion of reflecting unceasingly upon itself and its aporias.

The *Anglo-Saxon* form of the problem of opinion is the watering down of truth by skepticism. The objective knowledge of reality, and hence the question of how it is fashioned, is reduced to the epistemological subjects, and thus to the way in which their interests, not being reconciled in any objective general concept, should according to the doctrine of liberalism blindly reproduce the whole that at the same time they nonetheless continually threaten to tear apart. The latent, self-concealed subjectivism within the objective-scientific mentality of the Anglo-Saxon cultural milieu coincides with the distrust of unbridled subjectivity and with the constant, already automatic, tendency to relativize knowledge by referring to its conditionedness in the epistemological subject. Strong affects defend consciousness from being reminded of its own subjectivism, from the fact that the position that one takes has no other source of legitimacy than what in the final analysis is immediately given to mere individuals, and hence ultimately, merely opinion. — The *German* temptation, if not that of all peoples who live east of the Mediterranean cultural sphere and were never fully Latinized, is the inviolate hardening of the idea of objective truth, which is thereby made into something that is no less subjective than opinion. The capitulation before facts not permeated by thought and the adaptation of thought to given reality in the West corresponds in Germany to the lack of self-reflection, the inexorability of megalomania. Both forms of consciousness, the one that bows before the facts and the other that mistakes itself for an overlord or creator of facts, are like the shattered halves of the truth that was not fulfilled in the world and the failure of which also affects thought. The truth cannot be patched together from its pieces. In effect those pieces get along with each other fairly well:[24] anyone who, in seeking out his spot in the world along with everyone else, leaves the world as it is, confirms it as the true reality, precisely as the law the world is and the imperious mind imagines itself to be. Traditional German metaphysics, and the spirit that produced it and in which it lives on, latches onto the truth and tendentiously counterfeits it into an arbitrary opinion, an eternal *pars pro toto*. Positivism sabotages truth by reducing it to so-called mere opinion and, because nothing remains for it but opinion, sides with it. In both cases nothing helps but the unwavering exertion of critique. Truth has no place other than the will to resist the lie of opinion.[25]

Thought, and probably not just contemporary thought, proves itself in the liquidation of opinion: literally the dominant opinion. This opinion is not due simply to people's inadequate knowledge but rather is imposed upon them by the overall structure of society and hence by relations of domination. How widespread these relations are provides an initial index of falsity: it shows how far the control of thought through domination extends. Its signature is banality. The belief that the banal is something

self-evident and hence unproblematic and that levels of more sophisticated differentiation rise above it is itself a part of opinion that must be
liquidated. The banal cannot be true. Whatever is universally accepted by
people living under false social conditions already contains ideological
monstrosity prior to any particular content, because it reinforces the
belief that these conditions are supposedly their own. A crust of reified
opinions, banality shields the status quo and its law. To defend oneself
against it is not yet the truth and may easily enough deteriorate into
abstract negation, but it is the agent of the process without which there is
no truth. The force of thought, however, is measured by the extent to
which, in its effort to liquidate opinion, thought does not gratify itself all
too easily by sharpening only its outward edge. It should resist as well
the opinion within itself: namely, the momentarily prevailing position or
tendency, and that, in the stage of total societalization, also includes anyone who passionately struggles against it. Societalization constitutes
within thought this element of opinion thought must reflect about,
whose limitedness it must explode. Everything within thought that
repeats a position without reflecting upon it, like those who from the
very beginning share an author's opinion, is bad. In this attitude thought
is brought to a standstill, degraded into the mere recital of what is
accepted, and becomes untrue. For the thought expresses something it
has not permeated yet as though it had reached its own conclusion. There
is no thought in which the remnants of opinion do not inhere. They are
at once both necessary and extrinsic to it. It is the nature of thought to
remain loyal to itself by negating itself in these moments. That is the
critical form of thought. Critical thought alone, not thought's complacent
agreement with itself, may help bring about change.

Catchwords   *Critical Models 2*

Introduction

       Catchwords may be considered the second part of *Interventions*. If possible, there is here an even greater tension between so-called philosophical and currently topical subjects, if that traditional distinction still has any meaning at all.

       The "Notes on Philosophical Thinking" offer reflection upon the procedure that can provide an introduction to the content of thought.[1] "Reason and Revelation" formed the basis for a discussion with Eugen Kogon in Münster; its theses help to protect the author's critique of positivism from reactionary misunderstanding. "Progress," with all the deficiencies of a preliminary study, belongs within the complex of *Negative Dialectics*.[2] The "Gloss on Personality" sketches a concise model of the relationship of traditional categories to their downfall; it is connected with the text on progress. "Free Time" is a résumé, comparable to that on the culture industry in *Ohne Leitbild*.[3]

       The two essays on pedagogy were freely improvised and do not try to deny it. What was said about the teaching vocation in 1965 has only now gained its full relevance. The author was unable to revise the essay on Auschwitz and had to content himself with removing the crudest deficiencies of expression. Where the text speaks of the most extreme things, of harrowing death, the form arouses shame, as though it were sinning against the suffering by unavoidably reducing it to so much available material. Many phenomena of neobarbarism could be understood under

this aspect: the invasion of inhumanity into sequestered culture transforms culture itself—which must defend its sublimations—into something brutish as soon as it takes up the defense: by remaining gentle, culture denies the real brutality. With a logic immanent to spirit, the terror
that temporarily culminated in Auschwitz brings about the regression of
spirit. It is impossible to write stylistically well about Auschwitz; one
must renounce subtle nuances in order to remain faithful to the emotional impulses underlying them, and yet with this renunciation one in
turn falls in with the universal regression.

It must be strongly emphasized that education after Auschwitz can
succeed only in a global situation that no longer produces the conditions
and the people that bear the responsibility for Auschwitz. This global situation has not yet changed, and it is unfortunate that those who desire
the transformation obstinately refuse this idea.

In "On the Question: 'What Is German?'" the author attempted, to use
the currently all-too-popular Brechtian expression, to refunction a question that was put to him.[4] This work should be considered together with
the essay on "Scientific Experiences in America." The latter concerns the
subjective side of the author's controversy with positivism as well.

The "Dialectical Epilegomena," which directly pertain to *Negative
Dialectics*, were intended for a lecture course in the summer semester of
1969, which was disrupted and had to be discontinued.[5] What is said
about theory and praxis brings together, intentionally, philosophical
speculation and drastic experience.

The title *Catchwords* alludes to the encyclopedic form that, unsystem-
atically, discontinuously, presents what the unity of experience crystallizes into a constellation. Thus the technique of a small volume with
somewhat arbitrarily chosen catchwords perhaps might make conceivable a new *Dictionnaire philosophique*. The association with polemics
that the title conveys is a welcome one to the author.

June 1969

Notes on Philosophical Thinking

Dedicated to Herbert Marcuse on his
Seventieth Birthday[1]

If one is obliged to say something about philosophical thinking, stopping in midstride as it were, and not wanting to slip into the arbitrary, then one should confine oneself to just a single aspect. Therefore I want only to recount a few things I believe I have observed in my own thinking, without going into the question of what thinking is in general or into the psychology of thought. In this regard it is useful to separate philosophical thinking from what is thought, from its contents. This brings me into conflict with Hegel's unsurpassed insight into philosophical thinking. According to him, the fissure between what is thought and how it is thought constitutes precisely the error, that bad abstraction it is the task of philosophy to correct by its own means.[2] It is ironic that philosophy so easily arouses the fury of *common sense** by being mistaken for the very abstractness it struggles against. It is certainly better—as in prephilosophical knowledge so in philosophy—not to proceed without a measure of autonomy of thought in relation to its subject matter. The logical apparatus owes its immeasurable improvement beyond primitive consciousness to this autonomy. It contains, intensified, at the level of content, the force of enlightenment that marks the historical development of philosophy.[3] Yet as it became autonomous and developed into an apparatus, thinking also became the prey of reification and congealed into a high-handed method.[4] Cybernetic machines are a crude example of this. They graphically demonstrate to people the nullity of formalized thinking abstracted from its contents insofar as such machines perform better than thinking subjects much of what used to be the proud achievement of the method of subjective reason. Should thinking subjects passionately transform themselves into the instruments of such formalization, then they virtually cease being subjects. They approach the machine in the guise of its imperfect replica. Philosophical thinking begins as soon as it ceases to content itself with cognitions that are predictable and from which nothing more emerges than what had been placed there beforehand. The humane significance of computers would be to unburden the thinking of living beings to the extent that thought would gain the freedom to attain a knowledge that is not already implicit.

In Kant thinking according to its narrow, subjective concept—that is, divorced from the objective rules of logical thought—appears under the name of spontaneity.[5] According to him, thinking is first of all an activity, such as registered by naive consciousness when it distinguishes sensory intuitions—the impressions that seem to be granted to the individual without any exertion on his part—from the experience of the strenuous activity that is involved in thinking. However, Kant's greatness, his ability to subject even his own so-called fundamental positions to a tenacious critique, proved true not least of all when, completely befitting the actual nature of thinking, he did not simply equate spontaneity, which for him is thinking, with conscious activity. The definitive, constitutive achievements of thinking were for him not the same as acts of thought within the already constituted world. Their fulfillment is hardly present to self-consciousness. The illusion of naive realism, the view that in experience one is dealing with things-in-themselves, is based, as one could read in Kant, also on the following: the acts through which consciousness in anticipation forms the sensible material are not yet conscious to it as acts: that is their "depth," thoroughly passive.[6] This idea is characterized system-immanently by the fact that the "I think, which must be able to accompany all of my representations," the formula for defining spontaneity, signifies nothing more than that there exists a unity of subjective, indeed personal, consciousness; and thus that, with all the difficulties involved, it is "my" representation, which can be replaced by that of no other. No one can reproduce the pain of another in one's own imagination. The transcendental apperception comes down to the same thing.[7] Defined by its mere affiliation, the "I think" itself becomes a passive entity, completely distinct from the active reflection upon a "my." Kant thus captured the passive moment in the activity of thinking faithfully, just as even in his most precarious propositions his impressive honesty constantly attends to what presents itself in the phenomena; the *Critique of Pure Reason* is already, in the sense in which Hegel later entitled his analysis of consciousness, a *Phenomenology of Spirit*. Thinking in the conventional sense of this activity is only one aspect of spontaneity and hardly the central one and in fact is localized solely within the region of what is already constituted, correlative to the world of things. At the level Kant calls the transcendental, activity and passivity are by no means administratively separated from each other in the way suggested by the external architecture of the philosophical work. This passive moment conceals the fact, which Kant did not mention, that what is apparently independent—the originary apperception—is actually dependent upon the objective realm, however undetermined it may be, and which in the Kantian system took refuge in the doctrine of the thing-in-itself situated beyond experience. No objectivity of thinking as an act would be possible at all if thinking in itself, according to its own form, were not bound to what is not itself properly thinking: this is where one must seek and work out what is enigmatic in thinking.[8]

Where thinking is truly productive, where it creates, it is also always a reacting. Passivity lies at the heart of the active moment, the ego models itself on the non-ego. Something of this still affects the empirical form of philosophical thinking. In order to be productive, thinking must always be determined from its subject matter. This is thinking's passivity. Its efforts coincide with its capacity for such passivity. Psychology calls this 'object-relation' or 'object-cathexis.'[9] However, it extends far beyond the psychological dimension of the thought process. Objectivity, the truth of thoughts, depends on their relation to the subject matter. From the subjective point of view, philosophical thinking is incessantly confronted with the necessity of proceeding via its own internal logical consistency and nevertheless also of accepting what is different from it and what is not a priori subject to its own lawfulness. Thinking as a subjective act must initially surrender itself to the subject matter, even when, as Kant and the Idealists taught, thinking constitutes or indeed even produces its subject matter. Thinking still depends on the subject matter even when the concept of a subject matter is problematic and thinking alleges that it first establishes it.[10] There is hardly a stronger argument for the fragile primacy of the object and for its being conceivable only in the reciprocal mediation of subject and object than that thinking must snuggle up to an object, even when it does not yet have such an object, even intends to produce it.[11] In Kant, such factuality of method finds its expression in the content. It is true that his thought is indeed directed toward the forms of the subject, yet it seeks its goal in the definition of objectivity. Despite the Copernican turn, and thanks to it, Kant inadvertently confirms the primacy of the object.[12]

The act of thinking can no more be reduced to a psychological process than to a timelessly pure, formal logic. Thinking is a mode of comportment, and its relation to the subject matter with which it comports itself is indispensable. The active moment of the thinking process is concentration. It struggles against whatever might distract it from the matter at hand. Concentration mediates the exertions of the ego through what is opposed to it. Hostile to thought is avidity, the distracted gaze out past the window that wants nothing to escape it; theological traditions such as that of the *Talmud* have warned of it. The concentration of thought bestows upon productive thinking a quality the cliché denies it. Not unlike so-called artistic inspiration, it lets itself be directed, to the extent that nothing distracts it from the matter at hand. The subject matter opens up to patience, the virtue of thinking. The saying, "genius is diligence,"[13] has its truth not in a slavish drudgery but rather in this patience toward the subject matter. The passive connotation of the word "patience" expresses well the nature of this behavior: neither zealous bustling about nor stubborn obsession but rather the long and uncoercive gaze upon the object. The current scientific and scholarly discipline requires that the subject disengage itself for the sake of a naively imputed primacy of the subject matter.[14] Philosophy contradicts this. Thinking should not reduce itself to method; truth is not the residue that remains after the subject has been eradicated. Rather, it must incorporate all innervation and experience into the contemplation of the subject matter in order, according to its ideal, to vanish within it. Mistrust of this is the current avatar of hostility toward thinking. It fastens upon reflective thinking in the narrower sense, which reveals itself to be useful not through zeal but by dint of its dimension of passivity and concentration. Its calmness retains something of that happiness the conventional notion of thinking finds unbearable.[15] The Americans have their own pejorative expression for this: *armchair thinking**, the behavior of one who comfortably sits in an easy chair like a friendly and superfluous grandfather enjoying his retirement.

Yet the malicious resentment against the person who sits and thinks has its detestable justification. Frequently such thinking behaves as if it had no material. It plunges into itself as though into a sphere of alleged purity. Hegel denounces this sphere as empty profundity.[16] The chimera of a Being that is not commandeered or defiled by anything concrete is finally nothing other than the mirror reflection of a thinking in itself, completely indeterminate and formal. It condemns thinking to the parody of the wise man gazing at his navel; it falls prey to an archaism that by undertaking to save for philosophical thinking its specific object— which should not at any price be an object—forfeits the moment of the subject matter itself, the nonidentical. Wisdom today simulates a historically irretrievable agrarian form of spirit, cast from the same mold as those sculptures that mime originality by practicing a protohistorical naiveté and by this ceremony hope to attain an ancient verity that never existed and that nowadays the late industrial world supplies only all too faithfully.[17] The synthetic archaism of philosophizing will fare no better than the plaster of Paris classicism of Canova and Thorwaldsen compared to the Attic classics.[18] But there is just as little ground for transforming reflective thinking into a form of indirect practical activity; that would only foster, from a societal perspective, the repression of thinking. It is characteristic that independent academic institutions were established, reactively, to offer those appointed to them the opportunity to meditate. Without a contemplative moment praxis degenerates into conceptless activity, but meditation as a carefully tended special sphere, severed from possible praxis, would hardly be better.

Certainly reflective thinking has not been described accurately enough. Most likely it should be called expansive concentration. By gauging its subject matter, and it alone, thinking becomes aware of what within the matter extends beyond what was previously thought and thereby breaks open the fixed purview of the subject matter. For its part the subject matter can also be extremely abstract and mediated; its nature should not be prejudged by a surreptitiously introduced concept of concretion. The cliché that thinking is a purely logical and rigorous development from a single proposition fully warrants every reservation. Philosophical reflection must fracture the so-called train of thought that is unrefractedly expected from thinking. Thoughts that are true must incessantly renew themselves in the experience of the subject matter, which nonetheless first determines itself in those thoughts. The strength to do that, and not the measuring-out and marking-off of conclusions, is the essence of philosophical rigor. Truth is a constantly evolving constellation, not something running continuously and automatically in which the subject's role would be rendered not only easier but, indeed, dispensable. The fact that no philosophical thinking of quality allows of concise summary, that it does not accept the usual scientific distinction between process and result—Hegel, as is known, conceived truth as process and result in one[19]—renders this experience palpably clear.[20] Philosophical thoughts that can be reduced to their skeleton or their net profit are of no worth. That countless philosophical treatises are philistine and could not care less about being so is more than just an aesthetic shortcoming: it is the index of their own falsity. Where philosophical thought, even in important texts, falls behind the ideal of its constant renewal through the subject matter itself, it is defeated. To think philosophically means as much as to think intermittences, to be interrupted by that which is not the thought itself. In emphatic thinking the analytic judgments it unavoidably must use become false. The force of thinking, not to swim with its own current, is the strength of resistance to what has been previously thought. Emphatic thinking requires the courage to stand by one's convictions. The individual who thinks must take a risk, not exchange or buy anything on faith—that is the fundamental experience of the doctrine of autonomy. Without risk, without the imminent possibility of error, there is objectively no truth.[21] Most stupidity in thinking takes shape where that courage, which is immanent to thinking and which perpetually stirs within it, is suppressed. Stupidity is nothing privative, not the simple absence of mental ability, but rather the scar of its mutilation. Nietzsche's pathos knew that. His imperialistically adventurous slogan about the dangerous life basically meant instead: to think dangerously, to spur on thought, to shrink back from nothing in the experience of the matter, not to be intimidated by any convention of received thought.[22] Autarkic logical consistency, however, from its societal perspective has not least of all the function of hindering this idea. Wherever thinking today exercises an emphatic and not an agitating influence, this is probably not to be ascribed to individual qualities like talent or intelligence. The reasons are objective: one of them, for instance, is that the thinking person, favored by biographical circumstances, did not allow his vulnerable thinking to be completely extirpated by the control mechanisms. Science needs the person who has not obeyed it; what satisfies his spirit is what defames science: the memento of obtuseness, to which science inevitably condemns itself and for which it feels a preconscious sense of shame.

The mode of philosophical thinking is affected by the fact that in it the relationship between process and subject matter qualitatively diverges from that in the positive sciences. In a certain sense, philosophical thinking continually attempts to express experiences; indeed, they are in no way adequately covered by the empirical concept of experience. Understanding philosophy means assuring oneself of this experience by reflecting on a problem autonomously and yet always remaining in the closest contact with the problem in its given configuration. With every expectation of cheap ridicule one could say that philosophical thought is so constituted that it tends to have its results before it has thought them.[23] One may radically distrust the Heideggerian hyphen-philology and yet not disavow that reflective thinking, as opposed to thinking, linguistically refers to the idea of philosophical construction as one of reconstruction.[24] In this lies at once also the worst temptation, that of apologetics, of rationalization, of the justification of blindly professed convictions and opinions. The *thema probandum* is just as much the truth and untruth of thinking. It relinquishes its untruth insofar as it attempts, through negation, to follow its experience. An adequate philosophical thinking is not only critical of the status quo and its reified replica in consciousness but is equally critical of itself. It does justice to the experience animating it not through compliant codification, but rather by means of objectification. Whoever thinks philosophically hardens intellectual experience by the same logical consistency whose antithesis he wields. Otherwise intellectual experience would remain rhapsodic. Only in this way does reflective thought become more than a repetitive presentation of what is experienced. Its rationality, as a critical one, transcends rationalization. Nonetheless, to him who observes it in itself, philosophical thinking seems to make possible the knowledge of what he wants to learn and only to the extent that he really knows what he wants to learn.[25] This self-experience of thinking contradicts the Kantian limitation, his intention of using thought to lessen thought's power. It also answers the sinister question, how one could think what one thinks and yet live: precisely by thinking it. *Cogito, ergo sum*.

Because the discipline of philosophical thinking manifests itself at first in the formulation of the problem, presentation in philosophy constitutes an indispensable aspect of the subject matter.[26] Probably this is also why cogent solutions that occur to the thinker do not emerge like the sums from a difficult addition, after the line has been drawn and the figures tallied. That much is legitimate in idealism, but it distorts the characteristic nature of philosophical thought into hubris by claiming that, because truth does not join thought externally, the latter is identical with this very truth itself. Philosophy's power of attraction, its happiness, is the fact that even the desperate thought conveys something of this certainty about the product of thinking, a final trace of the ontological proof of God, possibly its ineradicable core.[27] The notion of someone who sits down and "reflects about something" in order to ascertain something he did not know beforehand is as distorted as the inverse idea of winged intuition. Thinking begins in the labor upon a subject matter and its verbal formulation: they ensure its passive element. Put extremely: I do not think, and yet that itself is surely thinking.[28] A not wholly inappropriate material sign for it would be the pencil or fountain pen one holds in the hand while thinking, as is said of Simmel or of Husserl, who apparently couldn't think at all except while writing, similar to how the best thoughts come to many writers while they are writing. Such instruments, which one doesn't even need to use practically, are an admonishment that one should not just up and start thinking, but rather think of something. For this reason texts to be interpreted and criticized are an invaluable support for the objectivity of thought. Benjamin once alluded to this with the dictum that to every respectable thought belongs a respectable portion of stupidity as well.[29] If thought avoids this dictum for the sake of the chimera of its primordiality, if it scents in every concrete object at once the danger of concretization,[30] then the thought is not only lost to the future—which would be no objection, almost the contrary—but in itself it will be unconvincing. Yet it is therefore all the more decisive that those very tasks, the fecundity of which determines in turn the fecundity of thought, are autonomous; that they not be imposed but pose themselves: this is the threshold separating thinking from intellectual technique. Thinking must desperately navigate between such intellectual technique and amateurish dilettantism. Amateurish is the thinking that completely ignores the intellectual division of labor, instead of respecting and transcending it. A naive, fresh beginning stultifies thought no less than does a fervid conformity to the division of labor. Philosophy that, to speak with Kant, would do justice to its cosmical concept, would raise itself above its conception as a specialized science— according to Kant its scholastic concept that a priori is incompatible with its proper concept[31]—no less than above the prattle about worldviews that derives the illusion of its superiority from the pitiful meagerness of the leftovers from specialized knowledge out of which it makes its own specialty. Resistance to the decline of reason would mean for philosophical thinking, without regard for established authority and especially that of the human sciences, that it immerse itself in the material contents in order to perceive in them, not beyond them, their truth content. That would be, today, the freedom of thinking. It would become true where it is freed from the curse of labor and comes to rest in its object.

Reason and Revelation

1

The dispute regarding revelation was fought out in the eighteenth century. It ended in a negative resolution and during the nineteenth century actually fell into oblivion. Its revival today owes more than a little to that oblivion. Because of this revival, however, the critic of revelation at the outset finds himself in a difficult position, and he would do well to describe it lest he become its victim. If one repeats the rather comprehensive catalog of arguments made during the Enlightenment, then one opens oneself up to the reproach of being eclectic, of relying on old truisms that no longer interest anyone. If one finds reassurance in the thought that the religion of revelation at that time could not withstand critique, then one is suspected of old-fashioned rationalism. There is a widely accepted habit of thinking these days that, instead of objectively reflecting about truth and falsity, shifts the decision onto the age as such and even plays a more remote historical past against a more recent one. If one does not want either to fall under the sway of the notion that whatever has long been well known is for that reason false, or to accommodate oneself to the current religious mood that—as peculiar as it is understandable—coincides with the prevailing positivism, then one would do best to remember Benjamin's infinitely ironic description of theology, "which today, as we know, is wizened and has to keep out of sight."[a] Nothing of theological content will persist without being transformed; every content will have to put itself to the test of migrating into the realm of the secular, the profane. In contrast to the richly and concretely developed religious imagination of old, the currently prevailing opinion, which claims that the life and experience of people, their immanence, is a kind of glass case, through whose walls one can gaze upon the eternally immutable ontological stock of a *philosophia* or *religio perennis*, is itself an expression of a state of affairs in which the belief in revelation is no longer substantially present in people and in the organization of their relationships and can be maintained only through a desperate abstraction. What counts in the endeavors of ontology today, its attempt to leap without mediation out of the ongoing nominalistic situation into realism, the world of ideas in themselves, which then for its part is rendered into a product of mere subjectivity, of so-called decision, namely an arbitrary act—all this is also in large measure valid for the closely related turn toward positive religion.

2

Those in the eighteenth century who defended faith in revelation maintained a fundamentally different position than do those who defend it today, just as in general the same ideas can acquire extremely divergent meanings according to their respective historical moments. At that time a scholastic concept, which was inherited from the tradition and more or less supported by the authority of society, was being defended against the attack by an autonomous *ratio* that refuses to accept anything other than what stands up to examination on its own terms. Such a defense against *ratio* had to be carried out with rational means and was in this respect, as Hegel pronounced in the *Phenomenology*, hopeless from the very start: with the means of argumentation it used, the very defense already assumed the principle that belonged to its adversary.[1] Today the turn toward faith in revelation is a desperate reaction to just these very means, to *ratio*. The irresistible progress of *ratio* is seen solely in negative terms, and revelation is invoked so as to halt what Hegel calls the "fury of

[a] Walter Benjamin, *Schriften*, ed. Theodor W. Adorno and Gretel Adorno with the assistance of Friedrich Podszus (Frankfurt: Suhrkamp, 1955), 1:494. [*Translator's note:* "Theses on the Philosophy of History," in *Illuminations*, trans. Harry Zohn, ed. Hannah Arendt (New York: Schocken Books, 1968), 253.]

destruction":[2] because supposedly it would be a good thing to have revelation. Doubts about the possibility of such a restoration are muffled by appealing to the consensus of all the others who also would like it. "Today it is no longer at all unmodern to believe in God," a lady once told me whose family had returned to the religion of her childhood after a stormy enlightenment intermezzo. In the best case, that is, where it is not just a question of imitation and conformity, it is desire that produces such an attitude: it is not the truth and authenticity of the revelation that are decisive but rather the need for guidance, the confirmation of what is already firmly established, and also the hope that by means of a resolute decision alone one could breathe back that meaning into the disenchanted world under whose absence we have been suffering so long, as though we were mere spectators staring at something meaningless. It seems to me that the religious renaissances of today are philosophy of religion, not religion. In any case, here they concur with the apologetics of the eighteenth and early nineteenth centuries in that they strive through rational reflection to conjure up its opposite, but now they apply rational reflection to *ratio* itself with a mounting willingness to strike out at it and with a tendency toward obscurantism that is far more vicious than all the restrained orthodoxy of the earlier period, because it does not completely believe in itself.[3] The new religious attitude is that of the convert, even among those who do not formally convert or who simply support emphatically whatever seems sanctioned as the "religion of the fathers" as well as what with fatherly authority since time immemorial—and even in Kierkegaard's understanding of the individual—helped to suppress through intimidation the rising doubt.[4]

3

The sacrifice of the intellect that once, in Pascal or Kierkegaard, was made by the most progressive consciousness and at no less a cost than one's entire life has since then become socialized, and whoever makes this sacrifice no longer feels any burden of fear or trembling; no one would have reacted to it with more indignation than Kierkegaard himself. Because too much thinking, an unwavering autonomy, hinders the conformity to the administered world and causes suffering, countless people project this suffering imposed on them by society onto reason as such. According to them, it is reason that has brought suffering and disaster into the world. The dialectic of enlightenment, which in fact must also name the price of progress—all the ruin wrought by rationality in the form of the increasing domination of nature—is, as it were, broken off too early, following the model of a condition that is blindly self-enclosed and hence appears to block the exit. Convulsively, deliberately, one ignores the fact that the excess of rationality, about which the educated class especially complains and which it registers in concepts like mechanization, atomization, indeed even de-individualization, is a lack of rationality, namely, the increase of all apparatuses and means of quantifiable domination at the cost of the goal, the rational organization of mankind, which is left abandoned to the unreason of mere constellations of power, an unreason that consciousness, dulled by constantly having to consider the existing positive relations and conditions, no longer dares rise to engage at all. Certainly a *ratio* that does not wantonly absolutize itself as a rigid means of domination requires self-reflection, some of which is expressed in the need for religion today.[5] But this self-reflection cannot stop at the mere negation of thought by thought itself, a kind of mythical sacrifice, and cannot realize itself through a "leap": that would all too closely resemble the politics of catastrophe. On the contrary, reason must attempt to define rationality itself, not as an absolute, regardless of whether it is then posited or negated, but rather as a moment within the totality, though admittedly even this moment has become independent in relation to the totality.[6] Rationality must become cognizant of its own natural essence. Although not unknown to the great religions, precisely this theme requires "secularization" today if, isolated and inflated, it is not to further that very darkening of the world it wants to exorcise.

4

The renaissance of revealed religion particularly enjoys appealing to the concept of bonds that it claims are necessary: as it were, one relies on a precarious autonomy only then to choose the heteronomous. But these days, despite all the world's profanity, there are too many bonds rather than too few. The massive concentration of economic powers, and consequently of political and administrative ones as well, to a large extent reduces every individual into a mere functionary of the machinery. Individuals are probably much more connected today than in the era of high liberalism, when they had not yet called for bonds. Their need for bonds is therefore increasingly a need for a spiritual and intellectual reduplication and justification of an authority that is nonetheless already present. The talk of transcendental homelessness,[7] which once expressed the distress of the individual within individualistic society, has become ideology, has become a pretext for bad collectivism that, as long as no authoritarian state is available, relies on other institutions with supra-individualist pretensions. The disparity between societal power and societal impotence, increasing beyond measure, extends into the weakening of the inner composition of the ego, so that finally the ego cannot endure without identifying itself with the very thing that condemns it to impotence. Only weakness seeks bonds; the urge for bonds, which exalts itself as though it had relinquished the restrictions of egoism, of mere individual interest, in truth is not oriented toward the humane; on the contrary, it capitulates before the inhumane. Certainly underlying this is the illusion society needs and reinforces with all its conceivable means: that the subject, that people are incapable of humanity—the desperate fetishization of presently existing relations. The religious theme of the corruption of the human species since Adam's fall appears in a new guise, radically secularized already in Hobbes, distorted in the service of evil itself. Because it is supposedly impossible for people to establish a just order, the existing unjust order is commended to them. What Thomas Mann in speaking against Spengler called the "defeatism of humanity" has expanded universally.[8] The turn toward transcendence functions as a screen-image for immanent, societal hopelessness. Intrinsic to it is the willingness to leave the world as it is, because the world could not possibly be different. The real determining model of this behavior is the division of the world into two colossal blocs that rigidly oppose and reciprocally threaten one another, and every individual, with destruction.[9] The extreme innerworldly fear of this situation, because there is nothing discernible that might lead beyond it, is hypostatized as an existential or indeed a transcendental anxiety. The victories that revealed religion gains in the name of such anxiety are Pyrrhic. If religion is accepted for the sake of something other than its own truth content, then it undermines itself. The fact that recently the positive religions have so willingly engaged in this and at times compete with other public institutions testifies only to the desperation that latently inheres in their own positivity.

5

The irrationalism of revealed religion today is expressed in the central status of the concept of religious paradox. It is enough here merely to recall dialectical theology. Even it is not a theological invariant but has its historical status. What the apostle in the age of the Hellenistic enlightenment called a folly for the Greeks and what now demands the abdication of reason was not always so. At its medieval height Christian revealed religion defended itself powerfully against the doctrine of the two types of truth by claiming that the doctrine was self-destructive. High Scholasticism, and especially the *Summa* of St. Thomas, have their force and dignity in the fact that, without absolutizing the concept of reason, they never condemned it: theology went so far only in the age of nominalism, particularly with Luther. The Thomistic doctrine reflected not merely the feudal order of its epoch, which indeed had already become problematical, but also accorded with the most advanced developments in science at the time. But once faith no longer accords with knowledge, or at least no longer exists in productive tension with it, it forfeits the quality of binding power, that character of "necessitation" Kant subsequently set out to save in the moral law as a secularization of the authority of faith.[10] Why one should adopt *that* particular faith and not another: nowadays consciousness can find no other justification than simply its own need, which does not warrant truth. In order that I be able to adopt the revealed faith, it must acquire an authority in relation to my reason that would already presuppose that I have adopted the faith—an inescapable circle. If, as high Scholastic doctrine maintains, my will is added as an express condition of faith, then one does not escape the circle. Will itself would be possible only where the conviction about the contents of belief already exists, that is, precisely that which can be gained only by an act of will. If religion at last is no longer folk religion, no longer substantial in the Hegelian sense[11]—if it ever was that at all—then it becomes something taken up contingently, an authoritarian view of the world, in which compulsion and caprice intertwine. It was insight into this situation that probably induced the theology of Judaism to stipulate virtually no dogmas and to demand nothing but that people live according to the law; what is called Tolstoy's primitive Christianity is presumably something very similar. Even if this allows the antinomy of knowledge and faith to be circumvented and the very alienation between the religious precept and the subject to be bridged, the contradiction continues to operate implicitly. For the question of where the authority of doctrine comes from was not resolved but rather removed as soon as the Haggadah element had dissociated itself completely from the halachah element. The excision of the objective element from religion is no less harmful to it than the reification that aims to impose dogma—the objectivity of faith—inflexibly and antirationally upon the subject. The objective element, however, no longer can be asserted because it would have to submit itself to the criterion of objectivity, of knowledge, whose claim it arrogantly rejects.

6

In the wake of the general reductive neutralization of everything intellectual and spiritual to the level of mere culture during the last hundred and fifty years, the contradiction is hardly felt any more between traditional revealed religion and knowledge—rather both simply exist side by side as branches of the culture industry, something like the rubrics "Medicine," "Radio," "Television," "Religion" come one after another in magazines.[12] However, the exorbitant demand that revealed religion has made upon consciousness since the Enlightenment has not diminished but, on the contrary, has increased immeasurably. The reason why no one speaks of it anymore can be explained by the fact that it is no longer possible to bring the two together at all. Attempts to transfer the critical results of modern science into religion, which, for example, particularly flourish on the borders of quantum physics, are rash. Here one should consider not only the geocentric and anthropocentric character of the great traditional religions—which stands in the starkest opposition to the present status of cosmology—whereby this crass incongruity, namely, the ridiculousness of a confrontation of religious doctrine with the findings of the natural sciences in general, is often used in order to ridicule the confrontation itself for being primitive and crude. There once was a time when religion, with good reason, was not so discriminating. It insisted upon its truth even in the cosmological sense, because it knew that its claim to that truth could not be separated from its material and concrete contents without incurring damage. As soon as religion abandons its factual content, it threatens to vanish into mere symbolism and that imperils the very existence of its truth claim.[13] Perhaps more decisive, however, is the rupture between the social model of the great religions and the society of today. The great religions were modeled upon the transparent relations of the *"primary community,"** or at most the simple economy of goods.[14] A Jewish poet once wrote quite rightly that a village air suffuses Judaism and Christianity.[15] This cannot be overlooked without violently reinterpreting the religious doctrinal content: Christianity is not equally close to all ages, and human beings are not affected timelessly by what they once perceived as good tidings. The concept of daily bread, born from the experience of deprivation under the conditions of uncertain and insufficient material production, cannot simply be translated into the world of bread factories and surplus production, in which famines are natural catastrophes wrought by society and precisely not by nature. Or, the concept of the neighbor refers to communities where people know each other face to face. Helping one's neighbors, no matter how urgent this remains in a world devastated by those natural catastrophes produced by society, is insignificant in comparison with a praxis that extends beyond every mere immediacy of human relationships, in comparison with a transformation of the world that one day would put an end to the natural catastrophes of society. Were one to remove phrases such as these from the Gospel as irrelevant, while presuming to preserve the revealed doctrines and yet express them as they supposedly should be understood *hic et nunc,* then one would fall into a dichotomy of bad alternatives. Either revealed doctrines must be adapted to contemporary circumstances: that would be incompatible with the authority of revelation. Or contemporary reality would be confronted with demands that are unrealizable or that fall short of their most essential concern, the real suffering of people. Yet if one were simply to disregard all these concrete socio-historically mediated conditions and to heed literally the Kierkegaardian dictum that holds that Christianity is nothing other than a nota bene—namely, the nota bene that God once became man without that moment entering consciousness as such, that is, as a concretely historical moment—then in the name of a paradoxical purity revealed religion would dissolve into something completely indeterminate, a nothingness that could hardly be distinguished from religion's liquidation.[16] Anything more than this nothingness would lead immediately to the insoluble, and it would be a mere ruse of imprisoned consciousness to transfigure into a religious category this very insolubility itself, the failure of finite man, whereas it instead attests to the present impotence of religious categories. Therefore, I see no other possibility than an extreme ascesis toward any type of revealed faith, an extreme loyalty to the prohibition of images, far beyond what this once originally meant.

Progress

For Josef König

For a theoretical account of the category of progress it is necessary to scrutinize the category so closely that it loses its semblance of obviousness, both in its positive and its negative usage. And yet such proximity also makes the account more difficult. Even more than other concepts, the concept of progress dissolves upon attempts to specify its exact meaning, for instance what progresses and what does not. Whoever wants to define the concept precisely easily destroys what he is aiming at. The subaltern prudence that refuses to speak of progress before it can distinguish progress in what, of what, and in relation to what, displaces the unity of the moments, which within the concept reciprocally elaborate each other, into a mere juxtaposition. By insisting on exactitude where the impossibility of the unambiguous appertains to the subject matter itself, dogmatic epistemology misses its object, sabotages insight and helps to perpetuate the bad by zealously forbidding reflection upon what, in the age of both utopian and absolutely destructive possibilities, the consciousness of those entangled would like to discover: whether there is progress. Like every philosophical term, 'progress' has its equivocations; and as in any such term, these equivocations also register a commonality. What at this time should be understood by the term 'progress' one knows vaguely, but precisely: for just this reason one cannot employ the concept roughly enough. To use the term pedantically merely cheats it out of what it promises: an answer to the doubt and the hope that things will finally get better, that people will at last be able to breathe a sigh of relief. For this reason alone one cannot say precisely what progress should mean to people, because the crisis of the situation is precisely that while everyone feels the crisis, the words bringing resolution are missing. Only those reflections about progress have truth that immerse themselves in progress and yet maintain distance, withdrawing from paralyzing facts and specialized meanings. Today reflections of this kind come to a point in the contemplation of whether humanity[1] is capable of preventing catastrophe. The forms of humanity's own global societal constitution threaten its life, if a self-conscious global subject does not develop and intervene. The possibility of progress, of averting the most extreme, total disaster, has migrated to this global subject alone. Everything else involving progress must crystallize around it. Material needs, which long seemed to mock progress, have been potentially eliminated; thanks to the present state of the technical forces of production no one on the planet need suffer deprivation anymore. Whether there will be further want and oppression—which are the same thing—will be decided solely by the avoidance of catastrophe through the rational establishment of the whole society as humanity. Kant's sketch of a doctrine of progress, indeed, was anchored to the "idea of the human being":[a] "The highest purpose of nature—i.e. the development of all natural capacities—can be fulfilled for mankind only in society, and nature intends that man should accomplish this, and indeed all his appointed ends, by his own efforts. This purpose can be fulfilled only in a society which has not only the greatest freedom, and therefore a continual antagonism among its members, but also the most precise specification and preservation of the limits of this freedom in order that it can co-exist with the freedom of others. The highest task which nature has set for mankind must therefore be that of establishing a society in which *freedom under external laws* would be combined to the greatest possible extent with irresistible force, in other words of establishing a perfectly *just civil constitution*. For only through the solution and fulfillment of this task can nature accomplish its other intentions with our species."[b]

---

[a] Immanuel Kant, *Sämtliche Werke*, vol. 1, *Vermischte Schriften*, ed. Felix Gross (Leipzig 1921), 225 ("Idee zu einer allgemeinen Geschichte in weltbürgerlicher Absicht"). [*Translator's note*: English: "Idea for a Universal History with a Cosmopolitan Purpose," trans. H. B. Nisbet, in *Political Writings*, ed. Hans Reiss, 2d. ed. (Cambridge: Cambridge University Press, 1991), here "Second Proposition," p. 43 (translated as "an idea in [man's] mind [*sic!*]").]

[b] Ibid., 229. [*Translator's note*: English: ibid., 45–46.]

The concept of history, in which progress would have its place, is emphatic, the Kantian universal or cosmopolitan concept, not one of any particular sphere of life. But the dependence of progress on the totality comes back to bite progress. An awareness of this problem animates Benjamin's polemic against the coupling of progress and humanity in the "Theses on the Concept of History," perhaps the most weighty critique of the idea of progress held by those who are reckoned in a crudely political fashion as progressives: "Progress as pictured in the minds of Social Democrats was, first of all, the progress of humanity itself (and not just advances in people's skills and knowledge)."[c] As little as humanity *tel quel* progresses by the advertising slogan of the ever new and improved, so little can there be an idea of progress without the idea of humanity; the sense of the Benjamin passage should then also be more a reproach that the Social Democrats confused progress of skills and knowledge with that of humanity, rather than that he wanted to eradicate progress from philosophical reflection. In Benjamin progress obtains legitimation in the doctrine that the idea of the happiness of unborn generations—without which one cannot speak of progress—inalienably includes the idea of redemption.[d] This confirms the concentration of progress on the survival of the species: no progress is to be assumed that would imply that humanity in general already existed and therefore could progress. Rather progress would be the very establishment of humanity in the first place, whose prospect opens up in the face of its extinction. This entails, as Benjamin further teaches, that the concept of universal history cannot be saved; it is plausible only as long as one can believe in the illusion of an already existing humanity, coherent in itself and moving upward as a unity. If humanity remains entrapped by the totality it itself fashions, then, as Kafka said, no progress has taken place at all,[2] while mere totality nevertheless allows progress to be entertained in thought. This can be elucidated most simply by the definition of humanity as that which excludes absolutely nothing. If humanity were a totality that no longer held within it any limiting principle, then it would also be free of the coercion that subjects all its members to such a principle and thereby would no longer be a totality: no forced unity. The passage from Schiller's "Ode to Joy": "And who never could, let him steal away / weeping from

[c] Walter Benjamin, *Schriften*, ed. Theodor W. Adorno and Gretel Adorno, with Friedrich Podszus (Frankfurt: Suhrkamp 1955), 1:502. [*Translator's note*: Walter Benjamin, "Theses on the Philosophy of History," in *Illuminations: Essays and Reflections*, trans. Harry Zohn, ed. Hannah Arendt (New York: Schocken, 1968), 260 (thesis 13) (translation modified).]

[d] Cf. ibid., 494. [*Translator's note*: English: ibid., 253–4 (thesis 2).]

this league,"[3] which in the name of all-encompassing love banishes whoever has not been granted it, unintentionally admits the truth about the bourgeois, at once totalitarian and particular, concept of humanity. In the verse, what the one who is unloved or incapable of love undergoes in the name of the idea of humanity unmasks this idea, no differently than the affirmative violence with which Beethoven's music hammers it home; it is hardly a coincidence that the poem with the word "steal" in the humiliation of the one who is joyless, and to whom therefore joy is once again denied, evokes associations from the spheres of property and criminology. Perpetual antagonism is integral to the concept of totality, as in the politically totalitarian systems; thus the evil mythical festivals in fairy tales are defined by those who are not invited. Only with the decomposition of the principle of totality that establishes limits, even if that principle were merely the commandment to resemble totality, would there be humanity and not its deceptive image.

Historically the conception of humanity was already implicit in the middle Stoa's theorem of the universal state, which objectively at least amounted to progress, no matter how strange its idea otherwise might have been to pre-Christian antiquity. The fact that this Stoic theorem immediately reconciled itself with the founding of Rome's imperial claims betrays something of what the concept of progress underwent through its identification with increasing "skills and knowledge." Existing humanity is substituted for the unborn generations, and history immediately becomes salvation history. That was the prototype for the idea of progress until Hegel and Marx. In the Augustinian *civitas dei* this idea is connected to the redemption by Christ, as the historically successful redemption; only an already redeemed humanity can be seen as though, after it had been chosen and by dint of the grace it had been vouchsafed, it were moving in the continuum of time toward the heavenly kingdom. Perhaps it was the unfortunate fate of later thinking about progress that it inherited from Augustine the immanent teleology and the conception of humanity as the subject of all progress, while the Christian soteriology faded into speculations about the philosophy of history. In this way the idea of progress was taken up into the *civitas terrena*, its Augustinian counterpart. Even in the dualistic Kant, the *civitas terrena* should progress according to its own principle, its "nature." Within such enlightenment, however, which first of all puts progress toward humanity in people's own hands and thereby concretizes the idea of progress as one to be realized, lurks the conformist confirmation of what merely exists. It receives the aura of redemption after redemption has failed to appear and evil has persisted undiminished. This incalculably far-ranging modification of the concept of progress could not have been avoided. Just as the emphatic claim of successful redemption became a protest in the face of the post-Christian history, so, inversely, in the Augustinian *theologumenon* of an immanent movement of the species toward the blessed state there already lay the motive of irresistible secularization. The temporality of progress itself, its simple concept, links it to the empirical world; yet without such a temporality the heinous aspects of the way of the world would first truly be immortalized in thought, the Creation itself would become the work of a Gnostic demon. In Augustine one can recognize the inner constellation of the ideas of progress, redemption, and the immanent course of history, which should not dissolve into one another, lest they reciprocally destroy each other. If progress is equated with redemption as transcendental intervention per se, then it forfeits, along with the temporal dimension, its intelligible meaning and evaporates into ahistorical theology. But if progress is mediatized into history, then the idolization of history threatens and with it, both in the reflection of the concept as in the reality, the absurdity that it is progress itself that inhibits progress. Expedient expositions of an immanent-transcendent concept of progress pass sentence on themselves by their very nomenclature.

The greatness of the Augustinian doctrine was its for-the-first-time. It contains all the abysses of the idea of progress and strives to master them theoretically. The structure of his doctrine unabatedly expresses the antinomian character of progress. Already in Augustine, as then again at the height of secular philosophy of history since Kant, there is an antagonism at the center of this historical movement that would be progress since it is directed toward the kingdom of heaven; the movement is the struggle between the earthly and the heavenly. All thought about progress since then has received its draft from the weight of the historically mounting disaster. While redemption in Augustine forms the *telos* of history, the latter neither leads directly into the former, nor is the former completely unmediated by the latter. Redemption is embedded in history by the divine world plan but is opposed to it after the Fall. Augustine realized that redemption and history can exist neither without each other nor within each other but only in tension, the accumulated energy of which finally desires nothing less than the sublation of the historical world itself. For the sake of nothing less than this, however, can the idea of progress still be thought in the age of catastrophe. Progress should be no more ontologized, unreflectedly ascribed to Being, than should decline, though indeed the latter seems to be the preference of recent philosophy. Too little of what is good has power in the world for progress to be expressed in a predicative judgment about the world, but there can be no good, not a trace of it, without progress. If, according to a mystical doctrine, all inner-worldly events down to the most insignificant happenstance are of momentous consequence for the life of the absolute itself, then certainly something similar is true for progress. Every individual trait in the nexus of deception is nonetheless relevant to its possible end. Good is what wrenches itself free, finds a language, opens its eyes. In its condition of wrestling free, it is interwoven in history that, without being organized unequivocally toward reconciliation, in the course of its movement allows the possibility of redemption to flash up.

According to conventional thought, the moments in which the concept of progress has its life are partly philosophical and partly societal. Without society the notion of progress would be completely empty; all its elements are abstracted from society. If society had not passed from a hunting and gathering horde to agriculture, from slavery to the formal freedom of subjects, from the fear of demons to reason, from deprivation to provisions against epidemics and famine and to the overall improvement of living conditions, if one thus sought *more philosophico* to keep the idea of progress pure, say, to spin it out of the essence of time, then it would not have any content at all. But once the meaning of a concept necessitates moving to facticity, this movement cannot be stopped arbitrarily. The idea of reconciliation itself—the transcendent *telos* of all progress, measured by finite criteria—cannot be broken loose from the immanent process of enlightenment that removes fear and, by erecting the human being as an answer to human beings' questions, wins the concept of humanitarianism that alone rises above the immanence of the world. Nonetheless, progress is not tantamount to society, is not identical with it; indeed, like society, progress is at times its own opposite. Philosophy in general, as long as it was at all useful, was also a doctrine of society, except that ever since it consigned itself without demur to societal power, philosophy must professedly isolate itself from society; the purity into which philosophy regressed is the bad conscience of its impurity, its complicity with the world. The concept of progress is philosophical in that it articulates the movement of society while at the same time contradicting it. Having arisen societally, the concept of progress requires critical confrontation with real society. The aspect of redemption, no matter how secularized, cannot be removed from the concept of progress. The fact that it can be reduced neither to facticity nor to the idea indicates its own contradiction. For the element of enlightenment within it, which terminates in the reconciliation with nature by soothing nature's terror, is kindred to the aspect of the domination of nature.[4] The model of progress, even if displaced onto the godhead, is the control of external and internal, or human, nature. The oppression exercised by such control, which has its highest form of intellectual reflection in the identity principle of reason, reproduces this antagonism. The more identity is posited by imperious spirit, the more injustice is done to the nonidentical. The injustice is passed on through the resistance of the nonidentical. The resistance in turn reinforces the oppressing principle, while at the same time what is oppressed, poisoned, limps along further. Everything within the whole progresses: only the whole itself to this day does not progress. Goethe's "And all pressing, all struggling / Is eternal calm in God the Master,"[5] codifies this experience, and the Hegelian doctrine of the process of world spirit, the absolute dynamic, as a returning into itself or even its game with itself comes very close to the Goethean aphorism. Only one nota bene could be added to the sum of its intuition: that this whole stands still in its movement, that it knows nothing beyond itself, for it is not the divine absolute, but rather its opposite rendered unfamiliar by thought. Kant neither bowed to this deception nor absolutized the rupture. When, in the most sublime passage of his philosophy of history, he teaches that the antagonism, the entanglement of progress in myth, in nature's hold upon the domination of nature, in short, in the realm of unfreedom, tends by means of its own law toward the realm of freedom—Hegel's "cunning of reason" later came out of this[6]—then this says nothing less than that the conditions for the possibility of reconciliation are its contradiction and that the conditions for the possibility of freedom are unfreedom.[7] Kant's doctrine stands at a watershed. It conceptualizes the idea of this reconciliation as immanent in the antagonistic "development" by deriving it from a design nature harbors for human beings. On the other hand, the dogmatic-rationalistic rigidity with which such a design is presumed in nature—as though nature itself were not included in the development and its own concept thereby altered—is the impress of the violence the identity-positing spirit inflicts upon nature. The static quality of the concept of nature is a function of the dynamic concept of reason; the more this concept usurps from the realm of the nonidentical, the more nature becomes a residual *caput mortuum*, and precisely this makes it easier to equip nature with the qualities of eternity that sanctify its ends. The idea of "design" cannot be conceived of at all except with the provision that reason is attributed to nature itself. Still following metaphysical custom, which Kant in this passage uses when speaking of the concept of nature, bringing it close to the transcendent thing-in-itself, nature remains as much a product of spirit as it is in the *Critique of Pure Reason*. If spirit conquered nature, by making itself at every stage equal to nature according to Bacon's program, then at the Kantian stage spirit has projected itself back onto nature, as far as nature is absolute and not merely constituted, for the sake of a possibility of reconciliation in which, however, the primacy of the subject is not in the least diminished. In the passage where Kant comes closest to the concept of reconciliation, in the thought that the antagonism terminates in its abolition, appears the catchword of a society in which freedom is "bound up with irresistible power."[8] Yet even the talk of power recalls the dialectic of progress itself. While the perpetual oppression that unleashed progress at the same time always arrested it, this oppression—as the emancipation of consciousness—first made the antagonism and the whole extent of the deception recognizable at all, the prerequisite for settling the antagonism. The progress, which the eternal invariant brought forth, is that finally progress can begin, at any moment. Should the image of progressing humanity remind one of a giant who, after sleeping from time immemorial, slowly stirs himself awake and then storms forth and tramples everything that gets in his way, nonetheless his unwieldy awakening is the sole potential for attaining political maturity—that nature's tenacity, into which even progress integrates itself, will not have the final word. For aeons the question of progress made no sense. The question only arose after the dynamic became free, from which the idea of freedom could then be extrapolated. If progress—since Augustine the translation of the natural course of life between birth and death of the individual onto the species as a whole—may be as mythical as the notion of the course the command of fate prescribes to the constellations, then the idea of progress is just as much inherently anti-mythological, exploding the circulation to which it belongs. Progress means: to step out of the magic spell, even out of the spell of progress that is itself nature, in that humanity becomes aware of its own inbred nature and brings to a halt the domination it exacts upon nature and through which domination by nature continues. In this way it could be said that progress occurs where it ends.

This imago of progress is encoded in a concept that all camps today unanimously defame, that of decadence. The artists of *Jugendstil* declared their adherence to it. Certainly the reason for this is not only that they wished to express their own historical situation, which in many ways seemed to them biological morbidity. Their urgency to immortalize their condition in an image was animated by the impulse—and in this they agreed profoundly with the *Lebensphilosophen*—that truth was only preserved in that part of them that appeared to prophesy their own and the world's downfall. Hardly anyone could have expressed this more concisely than Peter Altenberg: "Mistreatment of horses. It will stop only when passersby become so irritable and decadent that they, no longer in control of themselves, mad and desperate in such cases, commit crimes and shoot down the cringing and cowardly coachman————. Inability to tolerate the mistreatment of horses is the deed of the decadent neurasthenic man of the future! Until now people have had only enough wretched strength not to have to bother with *other peoples'* affairs of this sort————."[e] Thus Nietzsche, who condemned pity, collapsed in Turin when he saw a coachman beating his horse. Decadence was the fata morgana of this progress that has not yet begun. The ideal, even if it be narrow-minded and willfully obstinate, of a complete, life-renouncing distance from any type of purpose was the reverse image of the false purposefulness of industry, in which everything exists for something else. The irrationalism of *décadence* denounced the unreason of the dominant reason. A separated, arbitrary, privileged happiness is sacred to irrationalism because it alone vouches for what has escaped, while that immediate notion of happiness of the whole—according to the current liberalist formula, the greatest possible happiness for the greatest possible number of people—barters happiness away to the apparatus, the sworn enemy of happiness, whose only goal is self-preservation, even where happiness is proclaimed to be the goal. In just such a spirit the sentiment dawns on Altenberg that extreme individuation is the placeholder for humanity: "For in so far as an individuality tending in some direction or other has a justification . . . , it should be nothing other than a first, a forerunner in some organic development of the human in general that yet *lies in the natural course of possible development for all human beings!* It is worthless to be *"the only one,"* a miserable trifling of fate with the individual. To be *"the first"* is everything! . . . He knows that the whole of mankind comes behind him! He is merely sent in advance by God! . . . *All* people will one day be wholly fine, wholly delicate, wholly loving. . . . *True* individuality means being alone and *in advance* that which later *everyone, everyone* must become!"[f] Humanity can be thought only through this extreme form of differentiation, individuation, not as a comprehensive generic concept.

The prohibition against any brushed-in portrait of utopia that the dialectical theories of both Hegel and Marx issued keenly sniffs out any betrayal of utopia. Decadence is the nerve center where the dialectic of progress becomes, as it were, bodily appropriated by consciousness. Whoever rails and rages against decadence inevitably takes up the standpoint of sexual taboo, the violation of which constitutes the antinomian ritual of decadence. In the insistence upon this taboo, for the sake of the unity of nature-dominating ego, there rumbles the voice of deceived, unreflec-

---

[e] Peter Altenberg, *Auswahl aus seinen Büchern,* ed. Karl Kraus (Vienna: Anton Scholl, 1932), 122f.

[f] Ibid., 135f.

tive progress. Yet for that reason progress can be convicted of its own irrationality because it always bewitches the means it uses into the ends it truncates. Of course, the opposing position of decadence remains abstract, and not least of all because of this it incurred the curse of being ridiculous. Decadence mistakes the particularity of happiness, which it must insist upon, for immediate utopia, for realized humanity, whereas decadence itself is disfigured by unfreedom, privilege, and class domination; it indeed owns up to all of these, but also glorifies them. Its wish-image, unfettered erotic availability, would also be perpetual slavery, as in Wilde's *Salomé*.

The explosive tendency of progress is not merely the Other to the movement of a progressing domination of nature, not just its abstract negation; rather it requires the unfolding of reason through the very domination of nature. Only reason, the principle of societal domination inverted into the subject, would be capable of abolishing this domination. The possibility of wrestling free is effectuated by the pressure of negativity. On the other hand reason, which wants to escape nature, first of all shapes nature into what it must fear. The concept of progress is dialectical in a strictly unmetaphorical sense, in that its organon, reason, is one; a nature-dominating level and a reconciling level do not exist separate and disjunct within reason, rather both share all its determinations. The one moment inverts into its other only in that it literally reflects itself, in that reason applies reason to itself and in its self-restriction emancipates itself from the demon of identity. Kant's incomparable greatness proved itself not least in that he incorruptibly maintained the unity of reason even in its contradictory uses—the nature-dominating, what he called theoretical, causal-mechanical, and the power of judgment snuggling up to nature in reconciliation—and displaced reason's difference strictly into the self-limitation of nature-dominating reason. A metaphysical interpretation of Kant should not impute a latent ontology to him[9] but instead read the structure of his entire thought as a dialectic of enlightenment, which the dialectician par excellence, Hegel, does not notice, because in the consciousness of Unitary Reason he erases its limits and thereby falls into the mythical totality he considers to be "reconciled" in the absolute idea. Progress comprehends not merely, as in the Hegelian philosophy of history, the compass of what belongs to dialectic; rather it is dialectical in its own concept like the categories of the *Science of Logic*. Absolute domination of nature is absolute submission to nature and yet arches beyond this in self-reflection, myth that demythologizes myth. But the claim of the subject would then no longer be theoretical and also not contemplative. The notion of the domination of pure reason as a being-in-itself, separated from praxis, subjugates even the subject, deforms it into an instrument to be used toward an end. The beneficial self-reflection of reason, however, would be its transition to praxis: reason would see through itself as a moment of praxis and would recognize, instead of mistaking itself for the absolute, that it is a mode of behavior. The anti-mythological element in progress cannot be conceived without the practical act that reins in the delusion of spirit's autarky. Hence progress can hardly be ascertained by disinterested contemplation.

Those who from time immemorial and with perpetually new phrases want the same thing—that there be no progress—have the most pernicious pretense of all. It is sustained by the false inference that because there has been no progress up until now, there never will be any. It presents the inconsolable return of the same as the message of Being, which must be hearkened to and respected, although Being itself, which has had this message put into its mouth, is a cryptogram of myth, the liberation from which would be a moment of freedom. In the translation of historical desperation into a norm that must be adhered to there echoes that abominable construal of the theological doctrine of original sin, the idea that the corruption of human nature legitimates domination, that radical evil legitimates evil. This conviction wields a catchphrase with which it obscurantistically condemns progress in modern times: the belief in progress. The attitude of those who defame the concept of progress as insipid and positivistic is usually positivistic itself. They explain the way of the world, which repeatedly thwarted progress and which also always was progress, as evidence that the world plan does not tolerate progress and that whoever does not renounce it commits sacrilege. In self-righteous profundity one takes the side of the terrible, slandering the idea of progress according to the schema that whatever human beings fail at is ontologically refused them, and that in the name of their finitude and mortality they have the duty to wholeheartedly appropriate both of these qualities. A sober response to this false reverence would be that while indeed progress from the slingshot to the megaton bomb may well amount to satanic laughter, in the age of the bomb a condition can be envisaged for the first time in which violence might vanish altogether. Nonetheless a theory of progress must absorb whatever is cogent in the invectives against belief in progress as an antidote to the mythology from which such a theory suffers. Least of all would it befit a doctrine of progress that has been brought to self-consciousness to deny that a shallow doctrine exists simply because derision of the latter belongs to the treasure chamber of ideology. Despite Condorcet the much-maligned idea of progress of the eighteenth century is less shallow than that of the nineteenth: in Rousseau the doctrine of radical perfectibility is combined with that of the radical corruptness of human nature. As long as the bourgeois class was oppressed, at least in terms of political forms, it took 'progress' as its slogan to oppose the prevailing stationary condition: the slogan's pathos was the echo of this situation. Not until the bourgeois class had occupied the decisive positions of power did the concept of progress degenerate into the ideology that ideological profundity then accused the eighteenth century of harboring. The nineteenth century came up against the limit of bourgeois society, which could not fulfill its own reason, its own ideals of freedom, justice, and humane immediacy, without running the risk of its order being abolished. This made it necessary for society to credit itself, untruthfully, with having achieved what it had failed. This falsity, with which the educated citizens then reproached the belief in progress held by the uneducated or reformist labor leaders, was an expression of bourgeois apologetics. Of course, when the shadows of imperialism descended, the bourgeoisie quickly abandoned that ideology and resorted to the desperate one of counterfeiting the negativity, which the belief in progress had disputed away, into a metaphysical substance.

Whoever rubs his hands with humility and satisfaction while remembering the sinking of the Titanic, because the iceberg supposedly dealt the first blow to the idea of progress, forgets or suppresses the fact that this accident, which incidentally was by no means fateful, occasioned measures that in the following half century protected sea voyages from unplanned natural catastrophes. Part of the dialectic of progress is that historical setbacks, which themselves are instigated by the principle of progress—what could be more progressive than the race for the blue ribbon?—also provide the condition needed for humanity to find the means to avert them in the future. The nexus of deception surrounding progress reaches beyond itself. It is mediated to that order in which the category of progress would first gain its justification, in that the devastation wrought by progress can be made good again, if at all, only by its own forces, never by the restoration of the preceding conditions that were its victim. The progress of the domination of nature that, in Benjamin's simile, proceeds in the reverse direction of that true progress that would have its *telos* in redemption, nevertheless is not entirely without hope.[10] Both concepts of progress communicate with each other not only in averting the ultimate disaster, but rather in every actual form of easing the persistent suffering.

The belief in interiority is felt to be a corrective to the belief in progress. But not this interiority, not the ability of human beings to improve guarantees progress. Already in Augustine the notion of progress—he could not yet use the word—is as ambivalent as the dogma of a successful redemption in the face of an unredeemed world demands it to be. On the one hand, progress is historical according to the six epochs of the world that correspond to the periodization of human life; on the other hand, progress is not of this world but internal, in Augustine's language, mystical. *Civitas terrena* and *civitas dei* are held to be invisible realms, and no one can say who among the living belongs to the one or the other; that decision is made by the secret election to grace, the same divine will that moves history in accordance with its plan. Yet already in Augustine, according to the insight of Karl Heinz Haag, the interiorization of progress allows the world to be assigned to the powers that be and therefore, as with Luther later, Christianity is to be commended because it preserves the political state.[11] Platonic transcendence, which in Augustine is fused with the Christian idea of salvation history, makes it possible to cede the this-worldly to the principle against which progress is conceived and to allow, only on the Day of Judgment and in spite of all philosophy of history, the abrupt restoration of undisturbed creation. This ideological mark has remained to this day engraved on the interiorization of progress. As opposed to this mark, interiority itself, as a historical product, is a function of progress or of its contrary. The constitutive qualities of human beings make up merely one aspect in inner-worldly progress and nowadays certainly not the primary one. The argument claiming that there is no progress because none occurs within interiority is false, because it feigns an immediately humane society, in its historical process, whose law is based on what human beings themselves are. But it is the essence of historical objectivity that whatever is made by human beings, their institutions in the broadest sense, evolve independently of their creators and become second nature. That false conclusion then permits the thesis of the constancy of human nature, whether it be extolled or deplored. Inner-worldly progress has its mythical aspect, as Hegel and Marx recognized, in that it occurs above the heads of subjects and forms them in its own image; it is foolish to deny progress just because it cannot completely manage its objects, the subjects. In order to halt what Schopenhauer called the wheel that unrolls itself, surely that human potential is needed that is not entirely absorbed by the necessity of historical movement.[12] The idea that progress offers a way out is blocked today because the subjective aspects of spontaneity are beginning to atrophy in the historical process. To desperately posit an isolated, allegedly ontological concept of the subjectively spontaneous against the societal omnipotence, as the French existentialists do, is too optimistic, even as an expression of despair; one cannot conceive of a versatile spontaneity outside of its entwinement with society. It would be illusory and idealistic to hope that spontaneity would be enough here and now. One cherishes such hope solely in a historical hour in which no support for hope is in sight. Existentialist decisionism is merely the reflex reaction to the seamless totality of the world spirit. Nevertheless this totality itself is also semblance. The rigidified institutions, the relations of production, are not Being as such, but even in their omnipotence they are man-made and revocable. In their relationship to the subjects from which they originate and which they enclose, they remain thoroughly antagonistic. Not only does the whole demand its own modification in order not to perish, but by virtue of its antagonistic essence it is also impossible for it to extort that complete identity with human beings that is relished in negative utopias. For this reason inner-worldly progress, adversary of the other progress, at the same time remains open to the possibility of this other, no matter how little it is able to incorporate this possibility within its own law.

On the other hand, it can be plausibly asserted that things do not proceed with as much vim and vigor in the intellectual spheres, art, especially law, politics, anthropology, as in the material forces of production. Hegel himself, and Jochmann more extremely, expressed this about art; the idea of nonsynchrony in the movement of superstructure and substructure was then formulated as a principle by Marx in the proposition that the superstructure revolutionizes itself more slowly than the substructure.[13] Apparently no one was astonished that spirit, fleeting and mobile, should be thought stationary in contrast to the *rudis indigestaque moles* of what, even in the context of society, is not named 'material' for nothing. Analogously, psychoanalysis teaches that the unconscious, from which even consciousness and the objective forms of spirit are fed, supposedly is ahistorical. Certainly that which itself is subsumed in a brutal classification under the concept of culture and which contains within itself even subjective consciousness raises a perennial objection to the ever-sameness of what merely exists. But it perennially finds its objection futile. The ever-sameness of the whole, human beings' dependence upon vital necessities, the material conditions of their self-preservation, hides as it were behind its own dynamic, the growing increase of alleged societal wealth, and ideology benefits from this. However, it can easily be proved to spirit, which would like to transcend this situation and which is the actual dynamic principle, that it has failed, and this pleases ideology no less. Reality produces the semblance of developing upward and remains *au fond* what it was. Spirit that, to the extent that it is not a part of the apparatus, seeks innovation, in its hopelessly repeated attempts only knocks its head in, as when an insect flying toward the light collides with a windowpane. Spirit is not what it enthrones itself as, the Other, the transcendent in its purity, but rather is also a piece of natural history. Because natural history appears in society as a dynamic since the time of the Eleatics and Plato, spirit imagines that it has the

Other, that which is removed from the *civitas terrena* in the immutable self-same, and its forms—logic, above all, which is latently inherent in all that is spiritual—are tailored accordingly. In these forms spirit is seized by something stationary, against which spirit struggles while yet remaining a part of it. Reality's spell over spirit prevents spirit from doing what its own concept wants to do when faced with the merely existent: to fly. Because more tender and fleeting, spirit is all the more susceptible to oppression and mutilation. As the placeholder of what progress could be above and beyond all progress, spirit stands askew to the progress that takes place, and this in turn bestows honor upon the placeholder. Through less than complete complicity with progress, spirit reveals what progress is really up to. However, wherever it can be judged with reason that spirit as being-for-itself progresses, there spirit itself participates in the domination of nature simply because it is not, as it fancies itself to be, χωρίς, but rather is entwined with that life process from which it separated itself in conformity with the law of this process. All progress in the cultural spheres is that of the domination of material, of technique. The truth content of spirit, on the contrary, is not indifferent to this. A quartet by Mozart is not simply better made than a symphony of the Mannheim school, but by being better constructed and more consistent it ranks higher also in an emphatic sense. On the other hand, it is problematic to determine whether thanks to the development of perspectival technique the painting of the high Renaissance truly surpassed so-called primitive painting; whether the best of artworks occur in the incomplete mastery of the material, as a for-the-first-time, something emerging abruptly that vanishes as soon as it becomes a readily available technique. Progress in the mastery of material in art is in no way immediately identical with the progress of art itself. If the gold background had been defended against the use of perspective in the early Renaissance, that would have been not only reactionary but also objectively untrue because contrary to what its own logic demanded; even the complexity of progress unfolds itself only in the course of history. *À la longue* what should persevere and prevail in the afterlife of spiritual creations beyond their momentary progressiveness is their quality, ultimately their truth content, but this only by virtue of a process of progressing consciousness. The notion of the canonical essence of Greek antiquity, which still survived in the dialecticians Hegel and Marx, is not simply an undissolved rudiment of the cultural tradition but in all its dubiousness also the precipitate of a dialectical insight. In order to express its contents art, and in the spiritual sphere not only art, must inevitably absorb the increasing domination of nature. However, it thereby also works surreptitiously against what it wants to say and distances itself from what it nonverbally, nonconceptually opposes to the increasing domination of nature. This might help explain why the apparent continuity of so-called intellectual developments often breaks off, indeed often with an appeal—no matter how motivated by misunderstanding—for a return to nature. The blame for this lies with, among other, especially social, aspects, the fact that spirit is terrified by the contradiction in its own development and that it tries—vainly, of course—to rectify this contradiction through recourse to what it had estranged itself from and what it therefore mistakenly believes to be invariant.

The paradox that there is some progress and yet there is none is perhaps nowhere so graphic as in philosophy, where the very idea of progress has its home. No matter how compelling might be the transitions, mediated by critique, from one authentic philosophy to another, nonetheless the assertion that there was progress between them—Plato and Aristotle, Kant and Hegel, or even in a philosophical universal history as a whole—remains dubious. But the cause for this is not the invariance of the alleged philosophical object, that of true Being, whose concept has dissolved irrevocably in the history of philosophy; nor would a merely aesthetic view of philosophy be defensible that places an imposing architecture of thought or even the ominous great thinkers higher than the truth, which in no way coincides with the immanent closure and rigor of these philosophies. It is a completely pharisaical and false verdict to conclude that progress in philosophy leads it away from what the jargon of bad philosophy baptizes as its concern: in this way need would become the guarantor of truth content. On the contrary, the unavoidable and dubious progress of that which receives its limit from its theme—the limit—is posited by the principle of reason, without which philosophy cannot be thought, because without this principle there can be no thought. One concept after another plunges into the Orcus of the mythical.[14] Philosophy lives in symbiosis with science and cannot break from it without turning into dogmatism and ultimately relapsing into mythology. Yet the content of philosophy should be to express what is neglected or excised by science, by the division of labor, by the forms of reflection entailed by the bustle of self-preservation. For this reason philosophy's progress simultaneously recedes from the necessary goal of its progress; the force of experience that philosophy registers is weakened the more it is honed down by the scientistic apparatus. The movement philosophy as a whole performs is the pure self-sameness of its principle. Every time it pays the price of what it would need to conceptually grasp and can grasp only by virtue of self-reflection, through which it relinquishes the standpoint of stubborn immediacy or, in Hegelian terminology, the philosophy of reflection. Philosophical progress is deceitful because, the tighter it connects arguments, the more airtight and unassailable its propositions become, the more it becomes identity-thinking. Philosophical progress weaves a net over its objects that, by plugging up the holes of what it is not, impudently thrusts itself in place of its object of inquiry. Indeed, finally it seems, in harmony with the actual retrogressive tendencies of society, that vengeance is exacted on the progress of philosophy for having hardly been progress at all. To assume that there has been progress from Hegel to the logical positivists, who dismiss him as obscure or meaningless, is nothing but funny. Even philosophy is not immune to falling prey to that kind of regression, whether into narrow-minded scientification or into the denial of reason, which certainly is no better than the maliciously derided belief in progress.

In bourgeois society, which created the concept of total progress, the convergence of this concept with the negation of progress originates in this society's principle: exchange. Exchange is the rational form of mythical ever-sameness. In the like-for-like of every act of exchange, the one act revokes the other; the balance of accounts is null. If the exchange was just, then nothing should really have happened, and everything stays the same. At the same time the assertion of progress, which conflicts with this principle, is true to the extent that the doctrine of like-for-like is a lie. Since time immemorial, not just since the capitalist appropriation of surplus value in the commodity exchange of labor power for the cost of its reproduction, the societally more powerful contracting party receives more than the other. By means of this injustice something new occurs in the exchange: the process, which proclaims its own stasis, becomes dynamic. The truth of the expansion feeds on the lie of the equality. Societal acts are supposed to reciprocally sublate themselves in the overall system and yet do not. Wherever bourgeois society satisfies the concept it cherishes as its own, it knows no progress; wherever it knows progress, it violates its own law in which this offense already lies, and by means of the inequality immortalizes the injustice progress is supposed to transcend. But this injustice is at once also the condition for possible justice. The fulfillment of the repeatedly broken exchange contract would converge with its abolition; exchange would disappear if truly equal things were exchanged; true progress would not be merely an Other in relation to exchange, but rather exchange that has been brought to itself. Thus thought both Marx and Nietzsche, antipodes of each other; Zarathustra postulates that man will be redeemed from revenge.[15] For revenge is the mythical prototype of exchange; as long as domination persists through exchange, myth will dominate as well. — The interlocking of the ever-same and the new in the exchange relation manifests itself in the imagines of progress under bourgeois industrialism. What seems paradoxical about these imagines is that something different ever appears at all, that the imagines grow old, since the ever-sameness of the exchange principle intensifies by virtue of technology into the domination by repetition within the sphere of production. The life process itself ossifies in the expression of the ever-same: hence the shock of photographs from the nineteenth century and even the early twentieth century. The absurdity explodes: that something happens where the phenomenon says that nothing more could happen; its attitude becomes terrifying.[16] In this experience of terror, the terror of the system forcibly coalesces into appearance; the more the system expands, the more it hardens into what it has always been. What Benjamin called "dialectics at a standstill" is surely less a Platonizing residue than the attempt to raise such paradoxes to philosophical consciousness. Dialectical images: these are the historically-objective archetypes of that antagonistic unity of standstill and movement that defines the most universal bourgeois concept of progress.[17]

Hegel as well as Marx bore witness to the fact that even the dialectical view of progress needs correction. The dynamic they taught is conceived not as a simple dynamic per se, but on the contrary as one unified with its opposite, with something steadfast, in which alone a dynamic first becomes legible at all. Marx, who criticized all notions of the natural growth of society as fetishistic, likewise rejected, against Lasalle's Gotha Program, the absolutization of the dynamic in the doctrine of labor as the single source of societal wealth, and he conceded the possibility of a relapse into barbarism.[18] It may be more than mere coincidence that Hegel, despite his famous definition of history, has no detailed theory of progress and that Marx himself seems to have avoided the word, even in the constantly cited programmatic passage from the preface to the *Critique of Political Economy*. The dialectical taboo on concept fetishes, the legacy of the old anti-mythological Enlightenment in its self-reflective phase, extends even to the category that used to soften up reification: progress, which deceives as soon as it—as a single aspect—usurps the whole. The fetishization of progress reinforces its particularity, its restrictedness to techniques.[19] If progress were truly master of the whole, the concept of which bears the marks of its violence, then progress would no longer be totalitarian. Progress is not a conclusive category. It wants to cut short the triumph of radical evil, not to triumph as such itself. A situation is conceivable in which the category would lose its meaning, and yet which is not the situation of universal regression that allies itself with progress today. In this case, progress would transform itself into the resistance to the perpetual danger of relapse. Progress is this resistance at all stages, not the surrender to their steady ascent.

Gloss on Personality

In reflecting upon personality it is perhaps best to begin with an idiosyncrasy I've felt since my youth and would like to suppose was widely shared by the generation of intellectuals to which I belong. The pen, the tongue itself, would hesitate before a word one would hardly wish to use except to ape it parodically. The aversion was directed toward a sphere of officialdom that was condensed in the concept of 'personality.' Personalities were people decked out with orders and ribbons, deputies of the type that was derided in a Munich song before the First World War. The word suggested putting on airs, being pretentious and self-important. Personalities were people who lived in anticipation of what would be said about them at their gravesides, and they fostered the impression of doing great things. They succeeded in transferring their external, social position onto their person, as if what a man had managed to do in the world justified him, as if success and the individual necessarily coincided harmoniously, although the former at once arouses suspicion about the latter. Karl Kraus exposed such atrocities in the practice of journalists who wrote that a public as such doesn't exist, that it is nothing but an assembly of personalities.[1] After all this, one would like to crawl under the table for shame when one hears of personality, for instance, of a personality in public life.

If there existed a philosophical history of words, then it would have a worthy object in the expression 'personality' and in the changes its meaning has undergone. It would hardly be a mistake to trace the rise of the word, which was simultaneously its decline, back to Kant. In the third chapter of the *Critique of Practical Reason*, which deals with the drives of pure practical reason, the question of personality is discussed with an emphasis the word has never since shaken off. According to Kant, personality is nothing other than "the freedom and independence from the mechanism of nature regarded as a capacity of a being subject to special laws, namely those pure practical laws given by its own reason, so that the person belonging to the world of sense is subject to his own personality so far as he belongs to the intelligible world; for it is then not to be wondered at that man, as belonging to both worlds, must regard his own being in relation to his second and higher vocation with reverence, and the laws of this vocation with the deepest respect."[2] Person and personality are not identical. Yet that respect and esteem personalities later arrogated to themselves was by no means intended for those people who are either really or supposedly prominent in the depraved sense of the term but for the general principle embodied in real existing persons. Kant faithfully respects the grammatical form of the word "personality." The suffix "-ity" indicates an abstraction, an idea, not particular individuals.[3]

Yet, because this universality, moral freedom, indeed belongs to the intelligible, spiritual world and not to the sensible world of empirical individuals though manifesting itself only in them, this Kantian concept of personality declined with the rise of bourgeois individualism and attached itself to individual persons who, according to Kant's own distinction, define themselves more by their price than by their dignity.[4] Gradually the individual, in the interest of some arbitrary external and internal qualities, was to become directly what in Kant's theory he was only indirectly by virtue of the principle of humanity within him. The honor accorded by Kant to the principle of humanity is smugly recuperated by the individual. Instead of having personality in Kant's sense, one is a personality; instead of the intelligible character—the better potential in each person—the empirical person, just as he happens to be, is posited and transformed into a fetish. A high point in this development is found in the famous verses from the "Book of Suleika" in the *West-östlicher Divan*: "Supreme happiness of earth's children / may be only the personality" says the beloved.[5] She equates the selfhood one should not be "missing," the demand "to continue as one is," with manliness and with the beloved. But Goethe doesn't stop there. Hatem responds to her that he found this supreme happiness not in the personality, but in his beloved Suleika. Her name blesses him more than the abstract identity principle of personality. Goethe reaffirms his epoch's ideal of personality, for which his own life largely served as the model, in order to take it back again in remembrance of suppressed nature.

The criterion of personality in general is power and might: rule over people, whether possessing it in virtue of position or gaining it perhaps because of an especial lust for power, through one's behavior and one's so-called presence. The catchword "personality" tacitly implies a strong person, but strength understood as the ability to make others tractable should not at all be confused with the quality of a person. Because it is insinuated that strength is something ethical, language use and collective consciousness capitulate to the bourgeois religion of success. At the same time the illusion is maintained that this quality, by being part of a person's pure essence, is still the moral quality that Kant's doctrine aimed at. This transition is already intimated in the concept of character, the securely integrated unity of an individual in itself, that has a great and not completely unambiguous function in Kant's ethics. Those who are glorified as personalities do not have to be important, rich in themselves, refined, productive, especially clever, or truly good. Those who are really something often lack the relationship to the domination of people that the concept of personality connotes. Often strong personalities are just those who know how to take a hint; they are people with elbows who appropriate everything they possibly can, brutally and manipulatively. In the ideal of personality nineteenth-century society praises its own false principle: a "real" person is someone who is society's equal, internally organized according to the same law that holds society together at its very core.

This ideal of personality, in its traditional, high-liberal form, has become obsolete, and the idiosyncrasy against using the word has become somewhat socialized; certainly it occurs much less frequently now than it did in speeches around 1910. Such genuine personalities are called to mind only by gentlemen of the approved type, who are attractive, with chiseled features, and are observed in the halls of grand hotels. It's hard to say whether they belong to the company board of directors or the hotel reception staff. Those among them who have any real practical power are anyway happily fused with their own *publicity**. They travel as advertisements for themselves or their companies in harmony with the economic development that integrates the formerly separate spheres of production, circulation, and what nowadays is called propaganda and reduces them to their common denominator. From all others besides those who are more cut-out patterns of personalities than what personality used to mean, and from film and photo idols, personality is not even required anymore, is virtually an interference. In Anglo-Saxon countries if it is said of someone that he is *quite a character**, then nothing friendly is intended. He is not cut smooth enough, is an old bird, a bizarre relic. Those who resist the omnipresent mechanisms of conformity are no longer considered to be the more capable persons. Because they do not fully accomplish their self-preservation through conformity, they are looked at askance: as deformed, crippled, weaklings.

Under the present conditions it has become nearly impossible to expect anyone to become a personality in the sense meant by the older ideology of education. A demand of that kind was always impudent when levied at a cleaning woman. The social space that allowed the development of a personality even in the questionable sense of its autocratic sovereignty no longer exists, probably not even at the commanding heights of business and administration. Vengeance is exacted upon the concept of personality for its having leveled the idea of a person's humanity to his being particularly so and not otherwise. Personality is now only a mask of itself. Beckett exemplified this in the figure of Hamm in *Endgame*: personality as clown.

Consequently, the critique of the ideal of personality gradually extends much like the ideal itself did earlier. Thus the iron rations of pedagogical theories wanting to be up-to-date include dismissing the Humboldtian cultural goal of a rounded, developed, and educated person, precisely the personality. The impossibility of realizing this goal—if in fact it ever was supposed to have been realized—imperceptibly becomes a norm. What cannot be also should not be. The aversion to the hollow pathos of personality serves, in the name of a supposedly ideology-free understanding of reality, to justify the universal conformity, as though it is not already triumphing everywhere without any need for justification. But Humboldt's concept of personality was by no means simply the cult of the individual, who like a plant must be watered in order to flourish. Thus in holding fast to the Kantian idea "of the humanity in our person,"[6] at least he did not deny what his contemporaries Goethe and Hegel considered central to the doctrine of the individual. For all these thinkers the subject does not come to itself through the narcissistically self-related cultivation of its being-for-itself but rather through externalization, by devotedly abandoning itself to what is not itself. In the fragment, "Theory of the Self-Cultivation of Man," Humboldt writes: "Merely because both his thought and his action are possible only by virtue of a third thing, only by virtue of the representation and elaboration of something, of which the authentic distinguishing trait is that it is not-man, i.e., is world, man tries to grasp as much world as possible and to join it with himself as closely as he can."[7] It was possible to force this great and humane writer into the role of pedagogical whipping boy only by forgetting his sophisticated theory.

In view of the spiteful gesture of "if something is falling, then give it a shove"[8] that greets the concept of personality nowadays and that potentially awaits every concept not surrendering itself body and soul to society's demand for specialized personnel, the waning notion of personality and its imago finds reconciliation in a reflected shimmer.[9] There is reason to suspect that what should no longer exist, because it did not evolve and supposedly cannot exist, conceals within itself the potential of something better. Devaluating personality by considering it obsolete promotes psychological regression. The hindered formation of the ego, which more and more clearly represents the tendency of the fully forming society, is deemed a higher value, something worth promoting.[10] What is sacrificed is the moment of autonomy, freedom, and resistance that once, no matter how adulterated by ideology, resonated in the ideal of personality. The concept of personality cannot be saved. In the age of its liquidation, however, something in it should be preserved: the strength of the individual not to entrust himself to what blindly sweeps down upon him, likewise not to blindly make himself resemble it. Yet what is to be preserved should not be understood as some reserve of unformed nature in the midst of a society that has been thoroughly permeated with the structures of social order. Precisely society's excessive pressure brings forth unformed nature ever anew. The force of the 'I', which formerly was contained in the ideal of personality and was caricatured into autocratism and now threatens to vanish, is the force of consciousness, of rationality. It is essentially responsible for reality-testing. Within the individual it represents reality, the 'not-I', just as well as it represents the individual himself. Only if the individual incorporates objectivity within himself and in a certain sense, namely consciously, adjusts to it, can he develop the resistance to it. The organ of what was once unashamedly called personality has become critical consciousness. It permeates even that selfhood that had become congealed and rigidified in the concept of personality.

At least something negative can be said about the concept of the real person. He would be neither a mere function of a whole, which is inflicted upon him so thoroughly that he cannot distinguish himself from it anymore, nor would he simply retrench himself in his pure selfhood:[11] precisely that is the form of a bad rootedness in nature that even now still lives on. Were he a real person, then he would no longer be a personality but also not less than one, no mere bundle of reflexes, but rather a third entity. It flashes up in Hölderlin's vision of the poet: "Therefore, go thus unarmed / forward into life, and fear nothing!"[12]

Free Time

The question of free time—what people are to do with it, what possibilities its development offers—cannot be posed in abstract universality. The expression "free time," incidentally of recent origin—formerly one said "leisure" [*Muße*], and it was a privilege of an unconstrained life and hence surely also something qualitatively different, more auspicious—refers to a specific difference, that of unfree time, time occupied by labor and, one should add, time that is determined heteronomously. Free time is shackled to its contrary. This opposition, the relationship within which free time appears, even shapes some of its essential characteristics. Moreover, and far more importantly, free time depends on the totality of societal conditions. That totality now as much as ever holds people under a spell. In reality, neither in their work nor in their consciousness are people freely in charge of themselves. Even those conciliatory sociologies that apply the concept of 'role' like a master key acknowledge this fact to the extent that the concept, borrowed from the theater, hints that the existence imposed on people by society is not identical with what they are in themselves or what they could be.[1] Certainly no simple division should be attempted between human beings as they are in themselves and their so-called social roles. The roles extend deep into the characteristics of people themselves, into their innermost composition. In the age of truly unprecedented social integration it is difficult to discern anything at all in people that might be other than functionally

determined. This has important consequences for the question of free
time. It means nothing less than that, even where the spell loosens its
hold and people are at least subjectively convinced that they are acting of
their own will, this will itself is fashioned by precisely what they want to
shake off during their time outside of work. The question that would do
justice to the phenomenon of free time today would surely be: What will
become of free time in the context of the increasing productivity of labor,
yet under persisting conditions of unfreedom, that is, under relations of
production that people are born into and that prescribe for them the rules
of their existence nowadays just as much as they ever did? Free time has
already expanded exorbitantly, and thanks to the inventions in the
spheres of atomic energy and automation, which by no means have yet
been fully exploited economically, free time should increase enormously.
Should one try to answer the question without ideological asseverations,
then the suspicion is unavoidable that free time is tending toward the
opposite of its own concept and is becoming a parody of itself. Unfreedom
is expanding within free time, and most of the unfree people are as
unconscious of the process as they are of their own unfreedom.

To elucidate the problem I would like to use a trivial personal experience. Time and again in interviews and questionnaires one is asked what
one has for a *hobby**. Whenever the illustrated newspapers report about
one of those matadors of the culture industry—whereby talking about
such people in turn constitutes one of the chief activities of the culture
industry—then only seldom do the papers miss the opportunity to tell
something more or less homely about the *hobbies** of the people in question. I am startled by the question whenever I meet with it. I have no
*hobby**. Not that I'm a workaholic who wouldn't know how to do anything else but get down to business and do what has to be done. But rather
I take the activities with which I occupy myself beyond the bounds of my
official profession, without exception, so seriously that I would be
shocked by the idea that they had anything to do with *hobbies**—that is,
activities I'm mindlessly infatuated with only in order to kill time—if my
experience had not toughened me against manifestations of barbarism
that have become self-evident and acceptable. Making music, listening to
music, reading with concentration constitute an integral element of my
existence; the word *hobby** would be a mockery of them. And conversely,
my work, the production of philosophical and sociological studies and
university teaching so far has been so pleasant to me that I am unable to
express it within that opposition to free time that the current razor-sharp
classification demands from people. Certainly I am well aware that I speak
as someone privileged, with the requisite measure of both fortune and

guilt, as one who had the rare opportunity to seek out and arrange his work according to his own intentions. That is not the least important reason why there is no strict opposition between my activities within and outside of circumscribed working hours. If free time would really finally become that state of affairs in which everyone would enjoy what once was the prerogative of a few—and compared to feudal society bourgeois society indeed has had some success in this direction—then I would imagine the situation along the lines of the model I observe in myself, although under altered conditions this model would change as well.

If we assume with Marx that in bourgeois society labor has become a commodity and that labor consequently has become reified, then the expression *hobby** amounts to the paradox that this condition, which understands itself to be the opposite of reification, a sanctuary of immediate life within a completely mediated total system, is itself reified like the rigid demarcation between labor and free time. This border perpetuates the forms of societal life organized according to the system of profit.

Today the irony in the expression "leisure industry" is as thoroughly forgotten as the expression *show business** is taken seriously. It is widely known, but therefore no less true, that specific phenomena of free time, like tourism and camping, are established and organized for the sake of profit. At the same time the difference between work and free time has been branded as a norm into people's consciousness and unconscious.[2] Because, according to the reigning work ethic, the time free from labor is supposed to regenerate labor power, the time bereft of labor—precisely because it is merely an appendage to labor—is separated from the latter with puritanical fervor. Here one comes up against a behavioral pattern of the bourgeois character. On the one hand, one should concentrate when at work, not be distracted, not fool about; this used to form the basis for wage labor, the precepts of which have been internalized. On the other hand, free time should in no way whatsoever suggest work, presumably so that one can work that much more effectively afterward. This is the reason for the idiocy of many leisure time activities. And yet, surreptitiously the contraband of behavioral mores from work, which never lets go of people, is being smuggled in. In the past school reports used to contain grades for the child's attentiveness. This corresponded to the subjective, perhaps even well-meant, concern of the adults that the children might overstrain themselves in their free time: that they not read too much, or stay up too late in the evening. Secretly parents sense an unruliness of mind or even an insistence upon pleasure that is incompatible with the efficient organization and division of existence. Besides, any sort of mixture, anything not unambiguously and cleanly differentiated, is suspicious to the prevailing spirit. The strict bifurcation of life extols the very reification that meanwhile has almost completely subjugated free time.

This can be seen readily in the ideology of hobbies. The casualness of the question of what *hobby** you have also has the undertone that you must have one, if possible even a selection of *hobbies** that matches the supply offered by the leisure industry. Organized free time is compulsory:[3] woe unto you, if you have no hobby, no leisure time activity; then you are a drudge or an old-timer, an eccentric, and you become the laughingstock of society, which imposes upon you its idea of what your free time should be. Such compulsion is by no means only external. It is linked to the needs of human beings living under the functional system. Camping, which was a favorite activity in the older Youth Movement, was a protest against the tedium and conventionalism of bourgeois life.[4] One wanted to get out, in both senses of the word. Sleeping under the open sky meant having escaped house and family. After the death of the Youth Movement this need was taken up and institutionalized by the camping industry. It could not compel people to buy its tents and trailers, along with innumerable accessories, were there not some longing for such items in people already, but business functionalizes, extends, and reproduces their need for freedom; what they want is being imposed upon them once again. That is why the integration of leisure time succeeds so smoothly; people do not notice in what ways they are unfree even in the areas where they feel the most free, because the rule of such unfreedom has been abstracted from them.

If the concept of free time, in contradistinction to labor, is taken in as strict a sense as it had in an older and today perhaps obsolete ideology, then it acquires a vacuous, or as Hegel would have said, abstract aspect. An exemplary instance is the behavior of those who let themselves roast brown in the sun merely for the sake of a tan, even though dozing in the blazing sun is by no means enjoyable, even possibly physically unpleasant, and certainly makes people intellectually inactive. With the brown hue of the skin, which of course in other respects can be quite pretty, the fetish character of commodities seizes people themselves; they become fetishes to themselves. The thought that a girl is especially attractive erotically because of her brown skin is probably only a rationalization. The tan has become an end in itself, more important than the flirtation it perhaps once was supposed to entice.[5] If employees return from vacation without having acquired the obligatory skin tone, then they can be sure that their colleagues will ask pointedly, "But didn't you go on vacation?" The fetishism that flourishes in free time is subject to additional social control. The fact that the cosmetics industry contributes its share through its overwhelming and inescapable advertising is just as obvious as is the ability of complaisant people to repress it.

The state of dozing in the sun represents the culmination of a decisive element of free time under the present conditions: boredom. Thus insatiable too is the spiteful ridicule about the marvels people promise themselves from vacation trips and other exceptional situations in their free time, whereas even here they do not escape the repetition of the ever-same; no longer are things different in the distant horizon, as they were still at the time of Baudelaire's *ennui*.[6] Ridicule of the victims is automatically associated with the mechanisms that make them victims. Schopenhauer early on formulated a theory of boredom. Faithful to his metaphysical pessimism, he held that either people suffer from the unfulfilled desire of their blind will or become bored as soon as that desire is satisfied.[7] The theory describes quite well what becomes of people's free time under the conditions Kant would have called 'heteronomy' and that are customarily called 'external determination' in the modern jargon; even Schopenhauer's arrogant remark that people are the factory wares of nature expresses in its cynicism something of what people are actually made into by the totality of the commodity character.[8] The angry cynicism, however, still metes out to human beings more honor than the solemn asseverations of man's imperishable essence. Nonetheless Schopenhauer's doctrine should not be hypostatized as something universally valid or even perhaps as the original constitution of the human species. Boredom is a function of life under the compulsion to work and under the rigorous division of labor. Boredom need not necessarily exist. Whenever behavior in free time is truly autonomous, determined by free people for themselves, then boredom rarely sets in; boredom is just as unlikely when people successfully follow their own desire for happiness as when their free time activities are reasonable and meaningful in themselves. Even fooling about need not be inane and can be enjoyed blissfully as a dispensation from the mechanisms of self-control. If people were able to make their own decisions about themselves and their lives, if they were not harnessed to the eternal sameness, then they would not have to be bored. Boredom is the reflex reaction to objective dullness.[9] The situation is similar in the case of political apathy. Its most compelling cause is the by no means unjustified sentiment of the masses that their participation in politics, for which society grants them some latitude, can change little in their actual lives, and moreover in each and every political system of the world today. The connection between politics and people's own interests remains opaque to them, and therefore they shrink back from political activity. The justified or neurotic feeling of powerlessness is closely bound up with boredom: boredom is objective desperation. At the same time it is the expression of deformations meted out to people by the constitution of society as a whole. The most important of these surely is the defamation and atrophy of the imagination. Imagination is as much suspected of being mere sexual curiosity and the desire for what is forbidden as it is suspect in the eyes of the spirit of science that has nothing more to do with spirit. Those who want to adapt must increasingly renounce their imagination. Yet most often the imagination cannot be developed at all because it is mutilated by the experience of early childhood. The lack of imagination that is instilled and inculcated by society renders people helpless in their free time. The impudent question of what the people are supposed to do with the abundant free time they now supposedly have—as though free time were a charity and not a human right—is based on this helplessness. The reason that people actually do not know what to do with their free time is that they have been deprived beforehand of what would make the state of freedom pleasant to them. That state of freedom has been refused them and disparaged for so long that they no longer even like it. People need superficial distraction, for which they are either patronized or reviled by cultural conservatism, in order to summon up the energy for work that is demanded from them by the organization of society defended by cultural conservatism. This is not the least important reason why people remain chained to labor and to the system that trains them for labor, although the system itself to a large extent no longer requires labor.

Under the prevailing conditions it would be absurd and foolish to expect or to demand of people that they accomplish something productive in their free time; for it is precisely productivity, the ability to make something novel, that has been eradicated from them. What they then produce in their free time is at best hardly better than the ominous *hobby**: the imitation of poems or pictures that, under the all but irrevocable division of labor, others can produce better than the leisure time enthusiasts. What they create has something superfluous about it. This superfluousness is imparted to the inferior quality of the product, which in turn spoils any pleasure it might give.

Even the superfluous and senseless activity undertaken in free time is integrated into society. Once more a societal need plays a part. Certain forms of service, especially of domestic service, are dying out, demand is disproportionate to supply. In America only the truly wealthy can maintain domestics, and Europe is following closely behind. This causes many people to practice subaltern activities that formerly were delegated to others. The slogan *"Do it yourself"** [*tue es selbst*] takes this up as practical advice, though it also takes up the weary exasperation people feel toward mechanization, which unburdens them—and this fact cannot be disputed, rather only its usual interpretation—without their knowing how to utilize their newly acquired time. Thus, once again in the interests of specialized industries, people are encouraged to do themselves what others could do better and more effectively for them and what, for this reason, they must in turn despise deep down. Moreover, the belief that one might save the money spent for services in a society defined by the division of labor belongs to a very old stratum of bourgeois consciousness; the belief is founded on stubborn self-interest blind to the fact that the whole mechanism maintains itself solely by the exchange of specialized skills. Wilhelm Tell, the heinous prototype of rugged individuality, proclaims that an axe at home spares the carpenter, and one could compile from the maxims of Schiller an entire ontology of bourgeois consciousness.[10]

The *Do it yourself**, a contemporary type of leisure time behavior, occurs within a much more extensive context. More than thirty years ago, I described such behavior as 'pseudo-activity.'[11] Since then pseudo-activity has expanded to an alarming degree, even, and especially, among those people who believe that they are protesting against society. In general one may suppose that this pseudo-activity corresponds to a pent-up need to transform the petrified relations of society. Pseudo-activity is misguided spontaneity. Misguided, but not by chance; rather people dimly sense how difficult it would be for them to change the burden that weighs upon them. They prefer to let themselves be distracted by spurious, illusory activities, by institutionalized vicarious satisfactions rather than to face the realization of just how much the possibilities for change are blocked today. The pseudo-activities are fictions and parodies of the productivity society on the one hand incessantly demands and on the other hand confines and in fact does not really desire in individuals at all. Only people who have become responsible for themselves would be capable of utilizing their free time productively, not those who, under the sway of heteronomy, have become heteronomous to themselves.

Free time does not, however, stand in opposition only to labor. In a system where full employment in itself has become the ideal, free time is the unmediated continuation of labor as its shadow. We still lack an incisive sociology of sport and especially of the sports spectator. Some insight nevertheless is furnished by the hypothesis that the physical exertion required by sports, the functionalization of the body within the *team**, that occurs precisely in the most popular sports, trains people, in ways unknown to them, in the behavioral techniques that, sublimated to a greater or lesser degree, are expected from them in the labor process. The old argument that one does sports in order to stay *fit** is untrue only because it pretends that *fitness** is an independent goal; *fitness** for labor, however, is one of the clandestine purposes of sport. In sport frequently people first inflict on themselves, and savor as a triumph of their own freedom, exactly what they then must both inflict on and make palatable to themselves under societal pressure.

Let me say a few words about the relationship between free time and the culture industry. Since Horkheimer and I introduced the concept more than twenty years ago, so much has been written about the culture industry as the means of domination and integration that I would like to single out a specific problem we could not get an overall view of at the time. The critic of ideology who turns his attention to the culture industry, if he assumes that the standards of the culture industry are the encrusted ones of old-time entertainment and low art, will tend toward the view that the culture industry concretely and utterly dominates and controls both the conscious and the unconscious of the people at whom it is directed and whose taste during the liberal era first gave rise to the culture industry. And there is reason to speculate that production regulates consumption in the process of mental life just as much as it does in the process of material life, especially where the former has so closely approximated the latter as it has in the culture industry. Thus one might want to claim that the culture industry and its consumers are perfectly matched to each other. But since in the meantime the culture industry has become total, a phenomenon of the eternal sameness from which it promises to distract people temporarily, it is doubtful that the culture industry and the consciousness of its consumers make an absolutely symmetric equation. A few years ago at the Frankfurt Institute for Social Research we conducted a study devoted to this problem. Unfortunately, because of more pressing tasks it was necessary to postpone a full evaluation of the material. Even so, a provisional examination of it reveals some things that might be relevant to the so-called problem of free time. The study followed the wedding of Princess Beatrix of Holland and the junior German diplomat, Claus von Amsberg. The study's aim was to determine how the German population reacted to the wedding, which was broadcast by all the mass media and endlessly recounted in the illustrated papers.[12] Since the mode of presentation as well as the articles written about the event lent it an unusual importance, we expected that viewers and readers would likewise take it seriously. In particular, we expected to see the current characteristic ideology of personalization come into play, through which—apparently as compensation for the functionalization of reality—individuals and private relations are endlessly overvalued in contrast to their actual societal determinants. With all caution, I would like to say that those sorts of expectations were too simplistic. The study offers a virtual textbook case of what critical-theoretical thinking can still learn from and how it can be corrected by empirical social research. It was possible to perceive symptoms of a double consciousness. On the one hand, the event was enjoyed as a *hic et nunc,* what life otherwise withholds from people; it was supposed to be, to use one of the favorite clichés of modern German, "unique." To this extent the reaction of the spectators conformed to the well-known pattern that transforms even the topical and possibly political novelty into a consumer good by the way the information is conveyed. But our interview format was such that the questions seeking to elicit immediate reactions were supplemented, as a control, with questions focusing on the political *significance* the respondents gave to this highly touted event. The results revealed that many of those interviewed—we shall leave aside the question as to how representative they were—suddenly behaved completely realistically and criticized the political and social importance of the same event that in its much-publicized uniqueness they had gazed at in breathless wonder on their television screens. Thus, if my conclusions are not premature, whatever the culture industry sets before people in their free time is indeed consumed and accepted but with a kind of reservation, similar to how even ingenuous people do not simply take events in theater or cinema to be real. Perhaps even more: such things are not completely believed. Apparently the integration of consciousness and free time has not yet wholly succeeded. The real interests of individuals are still strong enough to resist, up to a point, their total appropriation. This would accord with the societal prognosis that a society whose fundamental contradictions persist undiminished also cannot be totally integrated into consciousness. It doesn't happen smoothly, especially not in free time, which surely appropriates people but, according to its own concept, cannot do so completely without overwhelming them. I'll forego a description of the consequences, but I think that there is a chance here for political maturity that ultimately could do its part to help free time turn into freedom.

Taboos on the Teaching Vocation

My lecture today merely frames the problem: it is neither a fully elaborated theory, which as a nonspecialist I could not legitimately offer, nor is it a presentation of definitive results of empirical research. What I have to say should be complemented by investigations, particularly individual case studies, also and especially from a psychoanalytical perspective. My remarks serve at best to bring to light several dimensions of the aversion to the teaching vocation[1] that play a not so evident, but possibly precisely therefore quite considerable, role in the well-known recruitment crisis. In so doing, I will also at least touch upon a series of problems involved in the profession of teaching itself and its problematic; in fact it is difficult to separate the two.

As a point of departure let me first recount an experience. It is precisely among the most gifted of the graduates who have passed their *Staatsexamen*[2] that I observe the strongest resistance to what those exams have qualified them for and what they are actually expected to take up afterward. They sense a sort of coercive force to become teachers, to which they submit only as an ultima ratio. I have after all the opportunity to see a significant cross section of such graduates and therefore am inclined to believe that it does not represent a negative selection.

Many of the motives for this aversion are rational and so familiar to you that they need not be treated here.[3] Thus above all there is antipathy toward the regimentation that is imposed by the development into what my friend Hellmut Becker described as the administered school.[4] Material motivations also play a role here: the notion that teachers hardly earn a bare subsistence is evidently more tenacious than the reality. This disproportion seems to me, if I may anticipate, to be characteristic of the entire complex I wish to discuss: the subjective, and moreover essentially unconscious, motivations for the aversion to the teaching profession. This is what I mean by taboos: the unconscious or preconscious ideas of those considering this vocation but also of other people, above all the children themselves, who as it were place this profession under a psychic ban that exposes teaching to difficulties only rarely perceived at all clearly. I use the concept of taboo thus fairly rigorously, in the sense of a collective manifestation of ideas—like those surrounding the teacher's financial remuneration discussed above—that to a large extent have lost their real basis even earlier than those financial preconceptions and that nonetheless tenaciously persist as psychological and social prejudices and in turn influence reality, become real forces.

Permit me to give you a few trivial examples. If one reads the personal advertisements in the papers—and they really are quite instructive— then these people, if they are teachers, emphasize that they are not typical teachers, not schoolmasters. You will hardly find a personal ad by a teacher without this accompanying reassuring declaration. — Or, not only in German but in other languages as well there exist a series of pejorative expressions for the teacher's vocation. In German certainly the most familiar is *"Pauker"* ["drummer," originally referring to a teacher taking a student over his knee], more vulgar, and likewise taken from the sphere of drumming, *"Steißtrommler"* ["butt-drummer"], the English *"schoolmarm"** for spinsterish, withered, unhappy, dried up schoolteachers. Compared with other academic vocations such as law or medicine, the teacher's profession unmistakably smacks of something society does not take completely seriously. Indeed, the sociology of university education has hardly dealt with the fact that in the general population a distinction is made between elegant and inelegant disciplines; law and medicine belong to the elegant, without a doubt philology does not. In the philosophical faculties the highly prestigious history of art apparently constitutes an exception. If I am correctly informed—I cannot check this because I have no direct contact with the relevant circles—then in a very exclusive *Korps*, supposedly the most exclusive today, philologists are tacitly denied membership.[5] Thus, according to the current view, the teacher is indeed an academician but is not really socially acceptable. One could almost say, a teacher is not considered a *"Herr"* [gentleman], with the particular ring the word *"Herr"* has in modern German jargon, apparently related to the alleged equality of educational opportunities.

Strangely complementary to this is the prestige of the university professor, which until recently remained undiminished and even statistically
documented. Such an ambivalence—on the one hand, the university professor as a profession enjoying the highest prestige, on the other hand,
the faint odium attached to the teacher's vocation—indicates a more fundamental issue. That in Germany the university professors have barred
the title of professor from applying to *Gymnasium* teachers belongs to
this same problem.[6] In other countries like France, this strict boundary is
not drawn because of a system that allows continual ascent. I cannot
judge whether this also has an influence on the respect accorded the
teaching profession and on the psychological aspects I spoke of.[7]

Those who are involved with the problem directly surely could add
other and more compelling symptoms to the ones I have mentioned. But
these may initially form a sufficient basis for several speculations. I said
that the idea of the impoverished teacher is outdated; without a doubt
what persists is the discrepancy between the claim of the intellect to status and power, which the teacher at least ideologically represents, and his
material position. This discrepancy is not without effect on the intellect
and spirit. Schopenhauer indicated this precisely in the context of university teachers. He felt that the subservience he observed in them more
than a hundred years ago was essentially related to their poor salary.[8] It
must be added that in Germany the claim of intellect to status and power,
in itself problematic, was never satisfied. This is supposed to be due to the
belated emergence of the bourgeoisie, the long survival of the rather less
than intellectual institution of German feudalism, which produced the
class of house tutor as a form of servant. Allow me to relate an anecdote
on this topic that I think is characteristic. In a patrician and elegant social
gathering the discussion turned to Hölderlin and his relationship to Diotima. Among those present was a direct descendant of the Gontard family, far along in years and moreover stone-deaf. No one there believed she
could follow the conversation. Suddenly she began to speak and said one
solitary sentence, in good Frankfurt German, "Ah yes, I always had such
a bother with the house tutors." Even in our time, a few decades ago, she
saw these love affairs from the point of view of the patrician who considers a house tutor little better than a lackey, just as back then Herr von
Gontard literally expressed himself to Hölderlin.[9]

In the sense of this *imagerie* the teacher is the heir of the *scriba*, the
scribe.[10] The low regard accorded the scribe has, as I have indicated, feudal
roots and can be documented in the Middle Ages and the early Renaissance. Thus, for example, in the *Nibelungenlied* Hagen's disdain for the
chaplain, the weakling who is then the only one to escape with his life.[11]
Knights who are learned enough to read are the exception—otherwise

Hartmann von der Aue would not have praised his own ability to read.[12] Allusions in antiquity to the teacher as a slave may also have contributed here.[13] Intellect is separated from physical strength. Intellect indeed always maintained a certain function in the management of society but became suspect every time the old primacy of physical strength survived the division of labor. This primeval moment resurfaces again and again. The low esteem for the teacher, at least in Germany, perhaps also in the Anglo-Saxon countries and certainly in England, could be characterized as the resentment of the warrior that subsequently established itself in the general population by means of a mechanism of endless identification. Children, of course, have a strong inclination to identify themselves with the soldierly, as one says so cheerfully today; recall how much they like to dress up as cowboys, what joy they have in running around with their toy rifles. Apparently they are ontogenetically repeating the phylogenetic process that gradually liberated man from physical power; the entire, extremely ambivalent and affect-laden complex of physical power in a world where it is exercised without mediation only in the sufficiently familiar 'limit situations', plays a decisive role here.[14] There is the famous anecdote of the condottiere Georg von Frundsberg, who at the Diet of Worms slapped Luther on the shoulder and said: "My little monk, you are treading a dangerous path," behavior in which the respect for the independence of spirit is mixed with a slight disdain for someone who carries no weapons and in the next moment can be hauled away by the *sbirri*. Out of resentment illiterates consider educated people to be insignificant as soon as the latter confront them with any kind of authority but without, like the high clergy, assuming an elevated social status and exercising social power. The teacher is heir to the monk: the odium or the ambiguity associated with the monk's vocation was transferred to the teacher after monks had largely lost their function.

The ambivalence toward the knowledgeable person is archaic. The great story by Kafka of the country doctor who, after following the false alarm of the night chimes, becomes a victim, is truly mythical; ethnology tells us that a medicine man or tribal chief enjoys his honorable status, just as in certain situations he may be killed or sacrificed.[15] You might ask why archaic taboo and archaic ambivalence were transferred onto the teacher while other intellectual professions were spared. To explain why something is *not* the case always entails great epistemological difficulties. I would like to offer only a *common-sense** remark. Lawyers and doctors, equally intellectual vocations, are not subject to this taboo. However, today they are *independent* professions. They are subject to the mechanism of competition; indeed, they enjoy better material opportunities, but they are not walled within an administrative hierarchy that affords them security, and because they are not so constrained they are more highly esteemed. This suggests a social opposition that quite possibly reaches much further: a rupture in the bourgeois stratum itself, at least in the petit bourgeoisie, between the independent professionals who earn more but whose income is not guaranteed and who may enjoy a certain air of boldness, of knightly gallantry, on the one hand, and the functionaries with assured employment and assured pensions on the other, who are envied because of their security but are surreptitiously seen as office pen pushers with fixed work schedules and a life of bureaucratic toil. Judges and administrative functionaries by contrast are delegated real power, whereas public awareness probably does not take seriously the power a teacher has, since that power is wielded over people who are not considered legal subjects having fully equal rights, that is, children. The teacher's power is resented because it only parodies the real power that is so admired. Expressions such as "classroom tyrant" remind us that the kind of teacher they stereotype is only as irrationally despotic as the caricature of despotism, for a teacher in fact can do no more than imprison his victims, a handful of piteous pupils, in study hall for an afternoon.

The reverse image of this ambivalence is the magical veneration in which teachers are held in many countries, as once in China, and in many groups, for example, among devout Jews. The magical aspect of this attitude toward teachers seems to be stronger wherever the vocation of teacher is bound up with religious authority, whereas the negative association grows with the decline of such authority. It is significant that the teachers who enjoy the highest esteem in Germany, namely the academicians, *in praxi* only extremely rarely exercise disciplinary functions, and that they, at least according to the general and public understanding, productively pursue research. In other words, they are not bound fast to the pedagogical sphere, which is considered to be secondary and, as I said, suspect. The problem of the immanent untruth of pedagogy lies probably in the fact that the pursuit is tailored to its recipients, that it is not purely objective work for the sake of the subject matter itself. Rather the subject matter is subsumed under pedagogical interests. For this reason alone the children are entitled unconsciously to feel deceived. Not only do the teachers recite for their recipients something already established, but also their function of mediator as such—which is like all circulatory activities in society already a priori a bit suspect—incurs some of the general aversion. Max Scheler once said that only because he never treated his students pedagogically did he have any pedagogical effect. If I may be permitted a personal remark, I can confirm this from my own experience. Success as an academic teacher apparently is due to the absence of every kind of calculated influence, to the renunciation of persuasion.

Recently the self-proclaimed introduction of objectivity into the teaching vocation has brought with it a certain change in this respect. One can also detect a structural modification in the relationship to the university professor. Just as in America, where such developments occur much more crassly than here, the professor is becoming gradually, though I would think, inexorably, a peddler of knowledge, who is slightly pitied because he cannot better exploit that knowledge for his own material interests. This is undoubtedly a step in the progress of enlightenment in comparison with the earlier idea that the teacher is like the Good Lord as he is still portrayed in *Buddenbrooks*.[16] At the same time, however, through such instrumental rationality spirit is reduced to a commodity value, and that is as problematical as all progress in the midst of the status quo.

I spoke of the disciplinary function. With this I come, if I am not mistaken, to the central point, but I must repeat that these are hypothetical remarks and not the results of research. Behind the negative imago of the teacher is that of the flogger [*Prügler*], a word, incidentally, that appears in Kafka's *The Trial*.[17] I consider this complex, even after the abolition of corporal punishment, to be decisive for the taboos on the teacher's vocation. This imago presents the teacher as the physically stronger who beats the weaker. In this function still ascribed to him even after the official function was abolished, while indeed in many parts of the country such a function is sustained as an eternal value and genuine bond, the teacher transgresses an old code of honor that is inherited unconsciously and that bourgeois children surely preserve. The teacher is so to say not *fair**, not a good sport. Such *unfairness**—and every teacher, even the university teacher senses this—somewhat taints the advantage of the teacher's knowledge over that of his pupils, an advantage the teacher asserts without having the right, because indeed the advantage is indivisible from his function, whereas he continually bestows upon that advantage an authority he can disregard only with great difficulty. *Unfairness** lies as it were in the ontology of the teacher, if I may make an exception for once and use the expression 'ontology' in this context. Anyone who is capable of self-reflection comes up against it as soon as he considers that he, in the guise of a teacher, perhaps of an academic, at the lectern has the opportunity to speak at great length without being interrupted. The irony of this situation is that when a teacher gives the students the chance to ask questions and thereby tries to make the lecture routine more like a seminar, usually the attempt meets with little approval even today; on the contrary, students in the large courses seem to prefer the dogmatic lecture format. However, not only his vocation compels the teacher to be *unfair** to a certain degree: he knows more, has an advantage, and cannot deny it. Rather, he is forced to be so by society, and this I consider much more significant. Likewise society even now continues to be essentially based on physical power and can impose its regulations when the stakes are real only with physical force; even if this eventuality is so remote in so-called normal life, even now and under the reigning conditions only with the potential of physical violence can it achieve the so-called integration within civilization that should be the task of universal pedagogical doctrine. This physical power is delegated by society and at the same time is disowned by its delegates. Those who exert it are scapegoats for those who issue the orders. The negatively affected archetype—and I am speaking of an *imagerie*, of notions operating unconsciously and not, or only rudimentarily, of reality—the archetype of this *imagerie* is the jailer, more so perhaps the drill sergeant or corporal in the military. I do not know to what extent the facts confirm that in the seventeenth and eighteenth centuries veterans were appointed as elementary school teachers. In any case this popular belief is wholly characteristic of the imago of the teacher. The expression *"Steißtrommler"* sounds soldierly. Perhaps teachers like those veterans are unconsciously imagined as a kind of cripple, as people who have no function within their actual lives, within the real reproductive process of society, but only in an obscure fashion and by the means grace has given them they do their part so that the whole and their own lives somehow keep going. Therefore those who are against corporal punishment represent, for the sake of this *imagerie*, the interests of the teacher at least as much as those of the pupil. A transformation of the entire complex of which I speak can be expected only when the last memory trace of corporal punishment has vanished from the schools, as appears largely to be the case in America.

It seems to me that it is essential for the inner structure of this complex that the physical violence any society based on domination requires must at all costs not be acknowledged, insofar as the society takes itself to be bourgeois-liberal. This also affects the delegation of violence—a gentleman does not deal blows[18]—and thus the disdain for the teacher who does what is necessary and what we know deep down to be evil and what we doubly deplore because we ourselves are complicit, although we are too good to commit such violence directly. My hypothesis is that the unconscious imago of the flogger is decisive for the conceptions of the teacher far beyond the practice of corporal punishment. Had I to suggest empirical investigations into the complex of the teacher, then this would be the first to interest me. The image of the teacher repeats, no matter how dimly, the extremely affect-laden image of the executioner.

The fact that this *imagerie* succeeds in reinforcing the belief that the teacher is not a gentleman but rather a brutal weakling or a monk without a *numinosum* is demonstrated graphically in the erotic dimension. On the one hand, the teacher has no proper erotic function; on the other hand, he plays a great libidinal role, say for the adoring *teenager**.[19] But mostly only as an unattainable object; detecting in him slight stirrings of sympathy is already enough to defame him for being unfair. The unattainability accompanies the notion of a being excluded from the erotic sphere. Psychoanalytically this *imagerie* of the teacher comes down to the idea of castration. A teacher who dresses elegantly, as one very humane teacher did during my childhood, because he has the means or simply because due to an academic's vanity he wishes to stand out a little, immediately falls prey to ridicule. It is difficult to distinguish to what extent such specific taboos are really just psychological, or whether the praxis, the idea of the teacher with the irreproachable life as an exemplary model for adolescents, still necessitates an erotic ascesis greater than in other professions, for example that of traveling salesman, to name just one. In the novels and plays dating from around 1900 that criticize school, the teacher is often portrayed as erotically repressed, as in Wedekind, and crippled, especially as a sexual being. This image of the quasi-castrated, at least erotically neutralized, of the developmentally hampered, or the image of men who do not count in the erotic competition, coincides with the real or putative infantilism of the teacher. I would like to refer to the very important novel of Heinrich Mann, *Professor Unrat*, which is probably known to most people only through its kitsch film version, *The Blue Angel*.[20] The classroom tyrant, whose downfall forms the story of the novel, is not transfigured by the ominous irrepressible sense of humor he has in the film. He behaves toward Fröhlich, the wench whom he calls an artiste, in exactly the same way his pupils do. He resembles them, as Heinrich Mann at one point writes explicitly, in terms of his entire psychic horizon and his reactions; in fact, he himself is a child. The disdain for the teacher also has this aspect; because he is inserted into a child's world that either is his world straight off or is the world to which he has adapted himself, he is not considered to be a full adult, whereas he is an adult and his demands are those of an adult. His awkward dignity is perceived as insufficient compensation for this discrepancy.

All this is only one form—that specific to the teacher—of a phenomenon known to sociology in its generality under the name of *déformation professionelle*. Yet in the imago of the teacher the *déformation professionelle* becomes nothing other than the very definition of the profession itself. In my youth I was told the anecdote about a teacher in a *Gymna-*

sium in Prague, who had said, "Thus, to take an example from everyday life: the commander conquers the city." Everyday life here means the life of the school, where this type of model sentence is presented in Latin class, in the grammatical paradigms. Schooling and the school, which now once again is constantly being invoked and fetishized as though it were a value, a thing in itself, replaces reality, which it carefully holds at a distance by means of organizational structures. The infantile character of the teacher is revealed in the fact that he confuses the microcosm of the school, which is more or less insulated from adult society—parents' associations and the like are desperate attempts to break through this insulation—that he mistakes this walled-in illusory world for reality. Not least for this reason does the school defend its walls so stubbornly.[21]

Often teachers are viewed in the same categories as the unlucky hero of a naturalist tragicomedy; in this respect one could speak of teachers having a *Traumulus* complex.[22] They live under the permanent suspicion of being what is called unworldly. Supposedly they are no more so than those judges whom Karl Kraus proved were out of touch with reality in his analyses of morals trials.[23] The infantile traits of several teachers and those of many pupils swirl together in the cliché "unworldly." What is infantile is the overvalued realism of these pupils. By having adapted themselves to the reality principle more successfully than can the teacher, who must constantly proclaim and embody superego ideals, they intend to compensate for what they sense to be their own deficiency, namely, that they are not yet independent subjects. Probably for this reason teachers who play soccer or drink hardily are so popular with their pupils, for they fulfill their pupils' wish-image of worldliness. During my time in *Gymnasium* those teachers who were thought, rightly or wrongly, to have been members of student *Korporationen* were especially liked. A kind of antinomy holds sway: teacher and pupil do reciprocal injustice to each other when the teacher drones on about eternal values that in general do not exist and the pupils respond by deciding to stupidly venerate the Beatles.

In contexts of this kind one must see the role of teachers' idiosyncrasies, which in large measure constitute targets for the resentment of the pupils. The process of civilization, whose agents are the teachers, aims not least of all at leveling everything. It tries to eradicate from the pupils that uncultivated nature that returns in suppressed form in the idiosyncrasies, speech mannerisms, symptoms of rigidity, tenseness, and awkwardness of the teachers. Those pupils rejoice who perceive in the teacher that against which they instinctively feel the entire painful process of education is waged. This indeed comprises a critique of the educational process itself, which in our culture to this day has generally failed. This failure is attested in the double hierarchy that can be observed within the school: the official hierarchy founded on intellect, achievement, and grades, and a latent hierarchy, in which physical strength, "being a guy," and certain practical abilities that are not honored by the official hierarchy play their role. This double hierarchy was exploited by National Socialism—and incidentally not only in the schools—by inciting the second hierarchy against the first, just as it was in politics by inciting the party against the state. This latent hierarchy in the school should be accorded particular attention in pedagogical research.

These strains of resistance exhibited by children and adolescents, as it were institutionalized in the second hierarchy, were certainly in part bequeathed to them by their parents. Many are based on inherited stereotypes, but some, as I've tried to explicate, lie in the objective situation of the teacher. Here arises something essential and very familiar to psychoanalysis. In overcoming the Oedipus complex, withdrawing from the father and internalizing the father image, children notice that their parents themselves do not live up to the ego ideal they instill in their children. In the teacher they confront for a second time the ego ideal, here possibly more distinctly, and they hope to be able to identify themselves with it. But this is impossible for many reasons, above all because the teachers themselves are to an exceptional degree the product of just that coercive force against which the ego ideal of the child, who is not yet ready to compromise, struggles. Even teaching is a bourgeois profession: only a mendacious idealism will deny it. The teacher is not the unmarred person the children, however dimly, anticipate but rather someone who among all other possible occupations and professions inevitably limited himself to this as his own, who concentrated upon it as his expertise—in fact, he is a priori the opposite of what the child's unconscious hopes of him: that he alone does not belong to the specialized personnel, whereas now more than ever he must.[24] The peculiar sensitivity of children to the idiosyncrasies of teachers, which probably extends beyond everything an adult can imagine of it,[25] comes from the fact that the idiosyncrasy disavows the ideal of a real human being, normal in the emphatic sense of the word, with which the children at first approach the teacher, even when they have already become wiser from experience and hardened by clichés.

There is also a social aspect to this that produces almost irreducible tensions. Already in kindergarten the child is wrested out of the *primary community**, from the immediate, nourishing, warm relations, and in school with a brutal shock experiences alienation for the first time; in the development of the individual the school is virtually the prototype of societal alienation per se. The old bourgeois custom of the teacher offering pretzels to his new pupils on the first day betrays that foreboding: the pretzel is to lessen the shock. The instrument of this alienation is the teacher's authority, and the negatively affected imago of the teacher is the response to it. The civilization he inflicts upon them and the renunciations he demands of them automatically mobilize in the children the imagines of the teacher that have accumulated in the course of history and that, like all the refuse that persists in the unconscious, can be reawakened according to the needs of the psychic economy. For this reason it is so maddeningly difficult for teachers to do things right, because their vocation prevents them from doing what most other professions readily allow, separating their objective work—and their work upon living human beings is exactly as objective as, by analogy, a doctor's—from their personal affect. For their work takes the form of a direct relationship, a give-and-take that, however, they can never fully realize under the spell of their extremely indirect goals. In principle what occurs in school remains far below the pupils' passionate expectations. From this perspective the vocation of teacher is an archaic relic that has long been overtaken by the civilization it represents; perhaps teaching machines will release the teacher from a human demand he is prevented from fulfilling. This archaism belonging to the vocation of teacher as such promotes not only the archaism of the symbols associated with teaching, but also arouses these archaisms in the behavior of the teacher himself, in bickering, grousing, scolding, and the like and in reactions that are always close to physical violence and betray a certain weakness and lack of self-confidence. If, however, the teacher did not react subjectively at all, if he were really so objectified as to allow no false reactions, then he would appear to the children even more inhuman and cold and would be, if possible, even more strongly rejected by them. You thus see that I was not exaggerating when I spoke of antinomy. This can be helped, if I may say so, only by a change in the behavior of the teachers. They should not repress their emotions only then to vent them in rationalized guise; instead they must acknowledge the emotions to themselves and others and thereby disarm their pupils. Most likely a teacher who says, "Yes, I am unjust; I am just as human as you are; some things please me, and some things don't," is more convincing than one who strictly upholds the ideology of justice but then inevitably commits unavowed injustice. It goes without saying that from such reflections it follows directly that psychoanalytic training and self-reflection are necessary to the teaching profession.

In concluding I come to the unavoidable question: What is to be done? I feel, in general, and so too here, quite incompetent to respond. Frequently this question sabotages the logical progress of knowledge that alone allows for change. The gesture of "You talk real good, but you're not in our shoes" is almost automatic in the discussions concerning the problems I have touched upon today. Nevertheless, I would like to enumerate a few motives, without any pretense that they form a system or that they could lead very far in actual practice. First of all, what is necessary is enlightenment about the overall complex I have sketched out here and moreover enlightenment of the teachers, parents, and, as far as possible, also of the pupils, with whom the teachers should discuss the tabooed questions. I do not eschew the hypothesis that in general children may be addressed with far more maturity and seriousness than adults, to insure their own sense of maturity, want to believe. However, the possibility of such enlightenment should not be overestimated. As I've indicated, the motives under discussion here are frequently unconscious, and as one knows, simply indicating unconscious conditions is fruitless unless those who are implicated in these conditions can illuminate them spontaneously with recourse to their own experience, unless the illumination occurs within their own consciousness. By reason of this observation, a psychoanalytical commonplace, one should not expect too much from pure intellectual enlightenment alone, though one should begin with it; a less than adequate, only partially effective enlightenment is nevertheless still better than none at all. — Furthermore, it is imperative to eliminate the real inhibitions and restrictions that still exist and that support the taboos with which the teacher's vocation is invested. Above all the sensitive areas must be addressed early on in the training of teachers, instead of orienting the training around taboos that are already in force. Under no condition is the private life of the teacher to be submitted to any kind of supervision or control that exceeds that of criminal law. — The target of attack should be the ideology of schooling, which is theoretically difficult to get hold of, and also would be denied, and yet nevertheless tenaciously permeates school praxis, as far as I can observe. The school has an immanent tendency to establish itself as a sphere with its own existence and with its own law.[26] It is difficult to decide how necessary this is in order for the school to perform its task; certainly it is not *only* ideology. A school that was completely, freely open to the outside probably would also lose its fostering, formative qualities. I am not embarrassed to confess being reactionary to the extent of thinking it more important that children learn good Latin and if possible Latin stylistics at school than that they make silly class trips to Rome that probably most often end in general indigestion, without them having experienced anything really important about the city. In any case, just because school people once would not let anyone meddle in their affairs, the isolation of the school still has the tendency to inure itself, especially against criticism. Tucholsky provided as an example of this the malicious principal of a village school who, when a friendly couple came to protest the horrors she had made her pupils undergo, justified herself with the explanation: "This is how it is done here."[27] I do not want to know how much "This is how it is done here" still dominates school praxis. This attitude becomes tradition. It must be made clear that school is no end in itself, that its isolation is a necessity and not the virtue certain varieties of the Youth Movement made of it, for instance Gustav Wyneken's ridiculous slogan that youth has its own proper culture, which today has come back with a vengeance in the ideology of youth as a subculture.[28]

If my observations of the *Staatsexamen* do not deceive me, then the psychological deformation of many teachers will probably continue for the time being, although the societal basis for it has largely been removed. Apart from the liquidation of the controls that still exist, rectification should be sought above all through training. With older colleagues, one should simply assert that authoritarian behavior endangers the goal of education even they themselves rationally endorse, though the chances of this working are slim. — One hears again and again—and this I wish only to register, without presuming to pass judgment—that student teachers during their training period are broken, cast in the same mold, that their *élan*, all that is best in them, is destroyed. Radical changes are possible only once research has been done on the course of training teachers undergo. Particular attention should be paid to how far the concept of necessity in schooling suppresses intellectual freedom and intellectual development. This comes to light in the anti-intellectualism of some school administrations, who systematically hinder the scholarly and scientific work of teachers, bring them *down to earth** again and again, and are distrustful of those who, as they like to say, want to go higher or elsewhere. Such anti-intellectualism inflicted upon teachers is in turn propagated all too easily in their behavior toward their pupils.

I have spoken of taboos against the teaching vocation, not of the reality of this vocation, and also not of the current real condition of teachers, but the two are not completely independent of one another. Nevertheless symptoms are evident that permit the hope that, if democracy in Germany realizes its opportunity and seriously develops further, all this will change. This is one of those very limited corners of reality to which the reflective and active individual can make a contribution. It is hardly a coincidence that what I consider to be the most politically important book published in Germany during the last twenty years was written by a teacher: *Über Deutschland*, by Richard Matthias Müller.[29] Certainly it must not be forgotten that the key to radical change lies in society and in its relationship to the school. In this, however, the school is not only an object. My generation experienced the relapse of humanity into barbarism, in the literal, indescribable, and true sense.[30] Barbarism is a condition where all the formative, cultivating influence, for which the school is responsible, is shown to have failed. It is certain that as long as society itself engenders barbarism, the school can offer only minimal resistance to it. But if barbarism, the horrible shadow over our existence, is in fact the contrary to culture, then it is also essential that individuals become debarbarized.[31] Debarbarization of humanity is the immediate prerequisite for survival. School, its limited domain and possibilities notwithstanding, must serve this end, and therefore it needs to be liberated from the taboos, under whose pressure barbarism reproduces itself.[32] The pathos of the school today, its moral import, is that in the midst of the status quo it alone has the ability, if it is conscious of it, to work directly toward the debarbarization of humanity. By barbarism I do not mean the Beatles, although their cult is related to it, but the utmost extreme: delusional prejudice, oppression, genocide, and torture; there should be no doubt about this. As the world appears at the moment, where no possibilities for more extensive change can be discerned, at least for the time being, it is up to the school more than anything else to work against barbarism. For this reason and despite all the theoretical-societal counterarguments, it is so eminently important for society that the school fulfills its task and helps society to become conscious of the fateful ideological heritage weighing heavily upon it.

Education After Auschwitz

The premier demand upon all education is that Auschwitz not happen again. Its priority before any other requirement is such that I believe I need not and should not justify it. I cannot understand why it has been given so little concern until now. To justify it would be monstrous in the face of the monstrosity that took place. Yet the fact that one is so barely conscious of this demand and the questions it raises shows that the monstrosity has not penetrated people's minds deeply, itself a symptom of the continuing potential for its recurrence as far as peoples' conscious and unconscious is concerned. Every debate about the ideals of education is trivial and inconsequential compared to this single ideal: never again Auschwitz. It was the barbarism all education strives against. One speaks of the threat of a relapse into barbarism. But it is not a threat—Auschwitz *was* this relapse, and barbarism continues as long as the fundamental conditions that favored that relapse continue largely unchanged. That is the whole horror. The societal pressure still bears down, although the danger remains invisible nowadays. It drives people toward the unspeakable, which culminated on a world-historical scale in Auschwitz. Among the insights of Freud that truly extend even into culture and sociology, one of the most profound seems to me to be that civilization itself produces anti-civilization and increasingly reinforces it. His writings *Civilization and its Discontents* and *Group Psychology and the Analysis of the Ego* deserve the widest possible diffu-

sion, especially in connection with Auschwitz.[1] If barbarism itself is
inscribed within the principle of civilization, then there is something desperate in the attempt to rise up against it.

Any reflection on the means to prevent the recurrence of Auschwitz is
darkened by the thought that this desperation must be made conscious to
people, lest they give way to idealistic platitudes.[2] Nevertheless the
attempt must be made, even in the face of the fact that the fundamental
structure of society, and thereby its members who have made it so, are
the same today as twenty-five years ago. Millions of innocent people—to
quote or haggle over the numbers is already inhumane—were systematically murdered. That cannot be dismissed by any living person as a
superficial phenomenon, as an aberration of the course of history to be
disregarded when compared to the great dynamic of progress, of enlightenment, of the supposed growth of humanitarianism. The fact that it
happened is itself the expression of an extremely powerful societal tendency. Here I would like to refer to a fact that, very characteristically,
seems to be hardly known in Germany, although it furnished the material for a best-seller like *The Forty Days of Musa Dagh* by Werfel.[3]
Already in the First World War the Turks—the so-called "Young Turk
Movement" under the leadership of Enver Pascha and Talaat Pascha—
murdered well over a million Armenians. The highest German military
and government authorities apparently were aware of this but kept it
strictly secret. Genocide has its roots in this resurrection of aggressive
nationalism that has developed in many countries since the end of the
nineteenth century.

Furthermore, one cannot dismiss the thought that the invention of the
atomic bomb, which can obliterate hundreds of thousands of people literally in one blow, belongs in the same historical context as genocide. The
rapid population growth of today is called a population explosion; it
seems as though historical destiny responded by readying counter-
explosions, the killing of whole populations. This only to intimate how
much the forces against which one must act are those of the course of
world history.

Since the possibility of changing the objective—namely societal and
political—conditions is extremely limited today, attempts to work
against the repetition of Auschwitz are necessarily restricted to the subjective dimension. By this I also mean essentially the psychology of people who do such things. I do not believe it would help much to appeal to
eternal values, at which the very people who are prone to commit such
atrocities would merely shrug their shoulders. I also do not believe that
enlightenment about the positive qualities possessed by persecuted
minorities would be of much use. The roots must be sought in the perse-

cutors, not in the victims who are murdered under the paltriest of pre-
tenses. What is necessary is what I once in this respect called the turn to
the subject.[4] One must come to know the mechanisms that render people
capable of such deeds, must reveal these mechanisms to them, and strive,
by awakening a general awareness of those mechanisms, to prevent people from becoming so again. It is not the victims who are guilty, not even
in the sophistic and caricatured sense in which still today many like to
construe it. Only those who unreflectingly vented their hate and aggression upon them are guilty. One must labor against this lack of reflection,
must dissuade people from striking outward without reflecting upon
themselves. The only education that has any sense at all is an education
toward critical self-reflection. But since according to the findings of depth
psychology, all personalities, even those who commit atrocities in later
life, are formed in early childhood, education seeking to prevent the repetition must concentrate upon early childhood. I mentioned Freud's thesis on discontent in culture. Yet the phenomenon extends even further
than he understood it, above all, because the pressure of civilization he
had observed has in the meantime multiplied to an unbearable degree. At
the same time the explosive tendencies he first drew attention to have
assumed a violence he could hardly have foreseen. The discontent in culture, however, also has its social dimension, which Freud did not overlook
though he did not explore it concretely. One can speak of the claustro-
phobia of humanity in the administered world, of a feeling of being
incarcerated in a thoroughly societalized, closely woven, netlike environment. The denser the weave, the more one wants to escape it, whereas it
is precisely its close weave that prevents any escape. This intensifies the
fury against civilization. The revolt against it is violent and irrational.

A pattern that has been confirmed throughout the entire history of
persecutions is that the fury against the weak chooses for its target especially those who are perceived as societally weak and at the same time—
either rightly or wrongly—as happy. Sociologically, I would even venture to add that our society, while it integrates itself ever more, at the
same time incubates tendencies toward disintegration. Lying just
beneath the surface of an ordered, civilized life, these tendencies have
progressed to an extreme degree. The pressure exerted by the prevailing
universal upon everything particular, upon the individual people and the
individual institutions, has a tendency to destroy the particular and the
individual together with their power of resistance. With the loss of their
identity and power of resistance, people also forfeit those qualities by
virtue of which they are able to pit themselves against what at some
moment might lure them again to commit atrocity. Perhaps they are
hardly able to offer resistance when the established authorities once

again give them the order, so long as it is in the name of some ideal in which they half or not at all believe.

When I speak of education after Auschwitz, then, I mean two areas: first children's education, especially in early childhood; then general enlightenment that provides an intellectual, cultural, and social climate in which a recurrence would no longer be possible, a climate, therefore, in which the motives that led to the horror would become relatively conscious. Naturally, I cannot presume to sketch out the plan of such an education even in rough outline. Yet I would like at least to indicate some of its nerve centers. Often, for instance, in America, the characteristic German trust in authority has been made responsible for National Socialism and even for Auschwitz. I consider this explanation too superficial, although here, as in many other European countries, authoritarian behavior and blind authority persist much more tenaciously than one would gladly admit under the conditions of a formal democracy. Rather, one must accept that fascism and the terror it caused are connected with the fact that the old established authorities of the *Kaiserreich* decayed and were toppled, while the people psychologically were not yet ready for self-determination. They proved to be unequal to the freedom that fell into their laps. For this reason the authoritarian structures then adopted that destructive and, if I may put it so, insane dimension they did not have earlier, or at any rate had not revealed. If one considers how visits of potentates who no longer have any real political function induce outbreaks of ecstasy in entire populations, then one has good reason to suspect that the authoritarian potential even now is much stronger than one thinks. I wish, however, to emphasize especially that the recurrence or nonrecurrence of fascism in its decisive aspect is not a question of psychology, but of society. I speak so much of the psychological only because the other, more essential aspects lie so far out of reach of the influence of education, if not of the intervention of individuals altogether.

Very often well-meaning people, who don't want it to happen again, invoke the concept of bonds. According to them, the fact that people no longer had any bonds is responsible for what took place. In fact, the loss of authority, one of the conditions of the sadistic-authoritarian horror, is connected with this state of affairs. To normal common sense it is plausible to appeal to bonds that check the sadistic, destructive, and ruinous impulse with an emphatic "You must not." Nevertheless I consider it an illusion to think that the appeal to bonds—let alone the demand that everyone should again embrace social ties so that things will look up for the world and for people—would help in any serious way. One senses very quickly the untruth of bonds that are required only so that they produce a result—even if it be good—without the bonds being experienced by people as something substantial in themselves. It is surprising how swiftly even the most foolish and naive people react when it comes to detecting the weaknesses of their betters. The so-called bonds easily become either a ready badge of shared convictions—one enters into them to prove oneself a good citizen—or they produce spiteful resentment, psychologically the opposite of the purpose for which they were drummed up.[5] They amount to heteronomy, a dependence on rules, on norms that cannot be justified by the individual's own reason. What psychology calls the superego, the conscience, is replaced in the name of bonds by external, unbinding, and interchangeable authorities, as one could observe quite clearly in Germany after the collapse of the Third Reich. Yet the very willingness to connive with power and to submit outwardly to what is stronger, under the guise of a norm, is the attitude of the tormentors that should not arise again. It is for this reason that the advocacy of bonds is so fatal. People who adopt them more or less voluntarily are placed under a kind of permanent compulsion to obey orders. The single genuine power standing against the principle of Auschwitz is autonomy, if I might use the Kantian expression: the power of reflection, of self-determination, of not cooperating.

I once had a very shocking experience: while on a cruise on Lake Constance I was reading a Baden newspaper, which carried a story about Sartre's play *Morts sans sépulchre*, a play that depicts the most terrifying things.[6] Apparently the play made the critic uneasy. But he did not explain this discontent as being caused by the horror of the subject matter, which is the horror of our world. Instead he twisted it so that, in comparison with a position like that of Sartre, who engages himself with the horror, we could maintain—almost maintain, I should say—an appreciation of the higher things: so that we could not acknowledge the senselessness of the horror. To the point: by means of noble existential cant the critic wanted to avoid confronting the horror. Herein lies, not least of all, the danger that the horror might recur, that people refuse to let it draw near and indeed even rebuke anyone who merely speaks of it, as though the speaker, if he does not temper things, were the guilty one, and not the perpetrators.

With the problem of authority and barbarism I cannot help thinking of an idea that for the most part is hardly taken into account. It comes up in an observation in the book *The SS State* by Eugen Kogon, which contains central insights into the whole complex and which hasn't come near to being absorbed by science and educational theory the way it deserves to be.[7] Kogon says that the tormentors of the concentration camp where he spent years were for the most part young sons of farmers. The cultural difference between city and country, which still persists, is one of the conditions of the horror, though certainly neither the sole nor the most important one. Any arrogance toward the rural populace is far from my intentions. I know that one cannot help having grown up in a city or a village. I note only that probably debarbarization has been less successful in the open country than anywhere else.[8] Even television and the other mass media probably have not much changed the state of those who have not completely kept up with the culture. It seems to me more correct to say this and to work against it than to praise sentimentally some special qualities of rural life that are threatening to disappear. I will go so far as to claim that one of the most important goals of education is the debarbarization of the countryside. This presupposes, however, a study of the conscious and unconscious of the population there. Above all, one must also consider the impact of modern mass media on a state of consciousness that has not yet come anywhere close to the state of bourgeois liberal culture of the nineteenth century.

In order to change this state of consciousness, the normal primary school system, which has several problems in the rural environment, cannot suffice. I can envision a series of possibilities. One would be—I am improvising here—that television programs be planned with consideration of the nerve centers of this particular state of consciousness. Then I could imagine that something like mobile educational groups and convoys of volunteers could be formed, who would drive into the countryside and in discussions, courses, and supplementary instruction attempt to fill the most menacing gaps. I am not ignoring the fact that such people would make themselves liked only with great difficulty. But then a small circle of followers would form around them, and from there the educational program could perhaps spread further.

However, there should arise no misunderstanding that the archaic tendency toward violence is also found in urban centers, especially in the larger ones. Regressive tendencies, that is, people with repressed sadistic traits, are produced everywhere today by the global evolution of society. Here I'd like to recall the twisted and pathological relation to the body that Horkheimer and I described in *The Dialectic of Enlightenment*.[9] Everywhere where it is mutilated, consciousness is reflected back upon the body and the sphere of the corporeal in an unfree form that tends toward violence. One need only observe how, with a certain type of uneducated person, his language—above all when he feels faulted or reproached—becomes threatening, as if the linguistic gestures bespoke a physical violence barely kept under control. Here one must surely also study the role of sport, which has been insufficiently investigated by a critical social psychology. Sport is ambiguous. On the one hand, it can have an anti-barbaric and anti-sadistic effect by means of *fair play**, a spirit of chivalry, and consideration for the weak. On the other hand, in many of its varieties and practices it can promote aggression, brutality, and sadism, above all in people who do not expose themselves to the exertion and discipline required by sports but instead merely watch: that is, those who regularly shout from the sidelines. Such an ambiguity should be analyzed systematically. To the extent that education can exert an influence, the results should be applied to the life of sport.

All this is more or less connected with the old authoritarian structure, with modes of behavior, I could almost say, of the good old authoritarian personality. But what Auschwitz produced, the characteristic personality types of the world of Auschwitz, presumably represents something new. On the one hand, those personality types epitomize the blind identification with the collective. On the other hand, they are fashioned in order to manipulate masses, collectives, as Himmler, Höss, and Eichmann did. I think the most important way to confront the danger of a recurrence is to work against the brute predominance of all collectives, to intensify the resistance to it by concentrating on the problem of collectivization. That is not as abstract as it sounds in view of the passion with which especially young and progressively minded people desire to integrate themselves into something or other. One could start with the suffering the collective first inflicts upon all the individuals it accepts. One has only to think of one's own first experiences in school. One must fight against the type of *folkways** [*Volkssitten*], initiation rites of all shapes, that inflict physical pain—often unbearable pain—upon a person as the price that must be paid in order to consider oneself a member, one of the collective.[10] The evil of customs such as the *Rauhnächte* and the *Haberfeldtreiben* and whatever else such long-rooted practices might be called is a direct antic-ipation of National Socialist acts of violence.[11] It is no coincidence that the Nazis glorified and cultivated such monstrosities in the name of "cus-toms." Science here has one of its most relevant tasks. It could vigorously redirect the tendencies of folk-studies [*Volkskunde*] that were enthusias-tically appropriated by the Nazis in order to prevent the survival, at once brutal and ghostly, of these folk-pleasures.

This entire sphere is animated by an alleged ideal that also plays a con-siderable role in the traditional education: the ideal of being hard. This ideal can also, ignominiously enough, invoke a remark of Nietzsche, although he truly meant something else.[12] I remember how the dreadful Boger during the Auschwitz trial had an outburst that culminated in a panegyric to education instilling discipline through hardness. He thought hardness necessary to produce what he considered to be the cor-rect type of person.[13] This educational ideal of hardness, in which many may believe without reflecting about it, is utterly wrong. The idea that virility consists in the maximum degree of endurance long ago became a screen-image for masochism that, as psychology has demonstrated, aligns itself all too easily with sadism. Being hard, the vaunted quality education should inculcate, means absolute indifference toward pain as such. In this the distinction between one's own pain and that of another is not so stringently maintained. Whoever is hard with himself earns the right to be hard with others as well and avenges himself for the pain whose manifestations he was not allowed to show and had to repress. This mechanism must be made conscious, just as an education must be promoted that no longer sets a premium on pain and the ability to endure pain. In other words: education must take seriously an idea in no wise unfamiliar to philosophy: that anxiety must not be repressed. When anxiety is not repressed, when one permits oneself to have, in fact, all the anxiety that this reality warrants, then precisely by doing that, much of the destructive effect of unconscious and displaced anxiety will probably disappear.

People who blindly slot themselves into the collective already make themselves into something like inert material, extinguish themselves as self-determined beings.[14] With this comes the willingness to treat others as an amorphous mass. I called those who behave in this way "the manipulative character" in the *Authoritarian Personality*, indeed at a time when the diary of Höss or the recordings of Eichmann were not yet known.[15] My descriptions of the manipulative character date back to the last years of the Second World War. Sometimes social psychology and sociology are able to construct concepts that only later are empirically verified. The manipulative character—as anyone can confirm in the sources available about those Nazi leaders—is distinguished by a rage for organization, by the inability to have any immediate human experiences at all, by a certain lack of emotion, by an overvalued realism. At any cost he wants to conduct supposed, even if delusional, *Realpolitik*. He does not for one second think or wish that the world were any different than it is, he is obsessed by the desire *of doing things** [*Dinge zu tun*], indifferent to the content of such action. He makes a cult of action, activity, of so-called *efficiency** as such, which reappears in the advertising image of the active person. If my observations do not deceive me and if several sociological investigations permit generalization, then this type has become much more prevalent today than one would think. What at that time was exemplified in only a few Nazi monsters could be confirmed today in numerous people, for instance, in juvenile criminals, gang leaders, and the like, about whom one reads in the newspapers every day. If I had to reduce this type of manipulative character to a formula—perhaps one should not do it, but it could also contribute to understanding—then I would call it the type of *reified consciousness*. People of such a nature have, as it were, assimilated themselves to things. And then, when possible, they assimilate others to things. This is conveyed very precisely in the expression "to finish off" ["*fertigmachen*"], just as popular in the world of juvenile rowdies as in the world of the Nazis. This expression defines people as finished or prepared things in a doubled sense. According to the insight of Max Horkheimer, torture is a manipulated and somewhat accelerated adaptation of people to collectives.[16] There is something of this in the spirit of the age, though it has little to do with spirit. I merely cite the saying of Paul Valéry before the last war, that inhumanity has a great future.[17] It is especially difficult to fight against it because those manipulative people, who actually are incapable of true experience, for that very reason manifest an unresponsiveness that associates them with certain mentally ill or psychotic characters, namely schizoids.

In the attempt to prevent the repetition of Auschwitz it seems essential to me first of all to gain some clarity about the conditions under which the manipulative character arises, and then, by altering those conditions, to prevent as far as possible its emergence. I would like to make a concrete proposal: to study the guilty of Auschwitz with all the methods available to science, in particular with long-term psychoanalysis, in order, if possible, to discover how such a person develops. Those people would be able yet to do some good, in contradiction to their own personality structure, by making a contribution so that such things do not happen again. This could be done only if they would want to collaborate in the investigation of their own genesis. Certainly it will be difficult to induce them to speak; by no means should anything related to their own methods be employed in order to learn how they became what they are. In the meantime, however, in their collective—precisely in the feeling that they are all old Nazis together—they feel so secure that hardly any of them has shown the least sentiment of guilt. Yet presumably there exist even in them, or at least in many, psychologically sensitive points conducive to changing this attitude, for instance, their narcissism, baldly put: their vanity. They might have a sense of importance if they could speak of themselves freely, like Eichmann, who apparently recorded whole libraries of tape. Finally, one can assume that even in these persons, if one digs deep enough, one will find vestiges of the old authority of conscience, which today frequently is in a state of dissolution. Once we learn the external and internal conditions that make them what they are—if I may assume hypothetically that these conditions can in fact be brought forth—then it will be possible to draw practical consequences so that the horror will not happen again. Whether the attempt helps somewhat or not cannot be known before it is undertaken; I don't want to overestimate it. One must remember that individuals cannot be explained automatically by such conditions. Under similar conditions some people develop in one way and other people completely differently. Nevertheless it would be worth the effort. Simply posing such questions already contains a potential for enlightenment. For this disastrous state of conscious and unconscious thought includes the erroneous idea that one's own particular way of being—that one is just so and not otherwise—is nature, an unalterable given, and not a historical evolution. I mentioned the concept of reified consciousness. Above all this is a consciousness blinded to all historical past, all insight into one's own conditionedness, and posits as absolute what exists contingently. If this coercive mechanism were once ruptured, then, I think, something would indeed be gained.

Furthermore, in connection with reified consciousness one should also observe closely the relationship to technology, and certainly not only within small groups. The relationship here is just as ambiguous as in sports, to which it is related, incidentally. On the one hand, each epoch produces those personalities—types varying according to their distribution of psychic energy—it needs societally. A world where technology occupies such a key position as it does nowadays produces technological people, who are attuned to technology. This has its good reason: in their own narrow field they will be less likely to be fooled and that can also affect the overall situation. On the other hand, there is something exaggerated, irrational, pathogenic in the present-day relationship to technology. This is connected with the "veil of technology." People are inclined to take technology to be the thing itself, as an end in itself, a force of its own, and they forget that it is an extension of human dexterity. The means—and technology is the epitome of the means of self-preservation of the human species—are fetishized, because the ends—a life of human dignity—are concealed and removed from the consciousness of people.[18] As long as one formulates this as generally as I just did, it should provide insight. But such a hypothesis is still much too abstract. It is by no means clear precisely how the fetishization of technology establishes itself within the individual psychology of particular people, or where the threshold lies between a rational relationship to technology and the overvaluation that finally leads to the point where one who cleverly devises a train system that brings the victims to Auschwitz as quickly and smoothly as possible forgets about what happens to them there. With this type, who tends to fetishize technology, we are concerned—baldly put, with people who cannot love. This is not meant to be sentimental or moralistic but rather describes a deficient libidinal relationship to other persons. Those people are thoroughly cold; deep within themselves they must deny the possibility of love, must withdraw their love from other people initially, before it can even unfold. And whatever of the ability to love somehow survives in them they must expend on devices.[19] Those prejudiced, authoritarian characters whom we examined at Berkeley in the *Authoritarian Personality*, provided us with much proof of this. A test subject—the expression itself already comes from reified consciousness—said of himself: *"I like nice equipment"** [*Ich habe hübsche Ausstattungen, hübsche Apparaturen gern*],[20] completely indifferent about what equipment it was. His love was absorbed by things, machines as such. The alarming thing about this—alarming, because it can seem so hopeless to combat it—is that this trend goes hand in hand with that of the entire civilization. To struggle against it means as much as to stand against the world spirit; but with this I am only repeating what I mentioned at the outset as the darkest aspect of an education opposed to Auschwitz.

As I said, those people are cold in a specific way. Surely a few words about coldness in general are permitted. If coldness were not a fundamental trait of anthropology, that is, the constitution of people as they in fact exist in our society, if people were not profoundly indifferent toward whatever happens to everyone else except for a few to whom they are closely bound and, if possible, by tangible interests, then Auschwitz would not have been possible, people would not have accepted it. Society in its present form—and no doubt as it has been for centuries already—is based not, as was ideologically assumed since Aristotle, on appeal, on attraction, but rather on the pursuit of one's own interests against the interests of everyone else.[21] This has settled into the character of people to their innermost center. What contradicts my observation, the herd drive of the so-called *lonely crowd** [*die einsame Menge*],[22] is a reaction to this process, a banding together of people completely cold who cannot endure their own coldness and yet cannot change it. Every person today, without exception, feels too little loved, because every person cannot love enough. The inability to identify with others was unquestionably the most important psychological condition for the fact that something like Auschwitz could have occurred in the midst of more or less civilized and innocent people. What is called fellow traveling was primarily business interest: one pursues one's own advantage before all else and, simply not to endanger oneself, does not talk too much. That is a general law of the status quo. The silence under the terror was only its consequence.[23] The coldness of the societal monad, the isolated competitor, was the precondition, as indifference to the fate of others, for the fact that only very few people reacted. The torturers know this, and they put it to the test ever anew.

Understand me correctly. I do not want to preach love. I consider it futile to preach it; no one has the right to preach it since the lack of love, as I have already said, is a lack belonging to *all* people without exception as they exist today. To preach love already presupposes in those to whom one appeals a character structure different from the one that needs to be changed. For the people whom one should love are themselves such that they cannot love, and therefore in turn are not at all that lovable. One of the greatest impulses of Christianity, not immediately identical with its dogma, was to eradicate the coldness that permeates everything. But this attempt failed; surely because it did not reach into the societal order that produces and reproduces that coldness. Probably that warmth among people, which everyone longs for, has never been present at all, except during short periods and in very small groups, perhaps even among peaceful savages. The much maligned utopians saw this. Thus Charles Fourier defined attraction as something that first must be produced through a humane societal order; he also recognized that this condition would be possible only when the drives of people are no longer repressed, but fulfilled and released.[24] If anything can help against coldness as the condition for disaster, then it is the insight into the conditions that determine it and the attempt to combat those conditions, initially in the domain of the individual. One might think that the less is denied to children, the better they are treated, the greater would be the chance of success. But here too illusions threaten. Children who have no idea of the cruelty and hardness of life are then truly exposed to barbarism when they must leave their protected environment. Above all, however, it is impossible to awaken warmth in the parents, who are themselves products of this society and who bear its marks. The exhortation to give more warmth to children amounts to pumping out warmth artificially, thereby negating it. Moreover, love cannot be summoned in professionally mediated relations like that of teacher and student, doctor and patient, lawyer and client. Love is something immediate and in essence contradicts mediated relationships. The exhortation to love—even in its imperative form, that one *should* do it—is itself part of the ideology coldness perpetuates. It bears the compulsive, oppressive quality that counteracts the ability to love. The first thing therefore is to bring coldness to the consciousness of itself, of the reasons why it arose.

In conclusion, permit me to say a few words about some possibilities for making conscious the general subjective mechanisms without which Auschwitz would hardly have been possible. Knowledge of these mechanisms is necessary, as is knowledge of the stereotypical defense mechanisms that block such a consciousness.[25] Whoever still says today that it did not happen or was not all that bad already defends what took place and unquestionably would be prepared to look on or join in if it happens again. Even if rational enlightenment, as psychology well knows, does not straightaway eliminate the unconscious mechanisms, then it reinforces, at least in the preconscious, certain counter-impulses and helps prepare a climate that does not favor the uttermost extreme. If the entire cultural consciousness really became permeated with the idea of the pathogenic character of the tendencies that came into their own at Auschwitz, then perhaps people would better control those tendencies.[26]

Furthermore, one should work to raise awareness about the possible displacement of what broke out in Auschwitz. Tomorrow a group other than the Jews may come along, say the elderly, who indeed were still spared in the Third Reich, or the intellectuals, or simply deviant groups. As I indicated, the climate that most promotes such a resurrection is the revival of nationalism. It is so evil because, in the age of international communication and supranational blocs, nationalism cannot really believe in itself anymore and must exaggerate itself to the extreme in order to persuade itself and others that it is still substantial.

Concrete possibilities of resistance nonetheless must be shown. For instance, one should investigate the history of euthanasia murders, which in Germany, thanks to the resistance the program met, was not perpetrated to the full extent planned by the National Socialists. The resistance was limited to the group concerned: precisely this is a particularly conspicuous, very common symptom of the universal coldness. The coldness, however, on top of everything else is narrow-minded in view of the insatiability that lies within the principle of the persecutions. Virtually anyone who does not belong directly to the persecuting group can be overtaken; there is thus a drastic egoistic interest that can be appealed to. — Finally, inquiry must be made into the specific, historically objective conditions of the persecutions. So-called national revival movements in an age in which nationalism is obsolete are obviously especially susceptible to sadistic practices.

All political instruction finally should be centered upon the idea that Auschwitz should never happen again. This would be possible only when it devotes itself openly, without fear of offending any authorities, to this most important of problems. To do this education must transform itself into sociology, that is, it must teach about the societal play of forces that operates beneath the surface of political forms. One must submit to critical treatment—to provide just one model—such a respectable concept as that of "reason of state"; in placing the right of the state over that of its members, the horror is potentially already posited.

Walter Benjamin asked me once in Paris during his emigration, when I was still returning to Germany sporadically, whether there were really enough torturers back there to carry out the orders of the Nazis. There were enough. Nevertheless the question has its profound legitimacy. Benjamin sensed that the people who *do* it, as opposed to the bureaucratic desktop murderers and ideologues, operate contrary to their own immediate interests, are murderers of themselves while they murder others. I fear that the measures of even such an elaborate education will hardly hinder the renewed growth of desktop murderers. But that there are people who do it down below, indeed as servants, through which they perpetuate their own servitude and degrade themselves, that there are more Bogers and Kaduks: against this, however, education and enlightenment can still manage a little something.

On the Question: "What is German?"

"What is German?"—I cannot answer this question directly. First it is necessary to reflect upon the question itself. It is encumbered with those complacent definitions that presume that the specifically German is not what really is German, but what one would like it to be. The ideal must defer to the idealization. In its sheer form the question already profanes the irrevocable experiences of the last decades. It creates an autonomous collective entity, 'German', whose characteristics are then to be determined. The formation of national collectives, however, common in the detestable jargon of war that speaks of the Russian, the American, surely also of the German, obeys a reifying consciousness that is no longer really capable of experience. It confines itself within precisely those stereotypes that thinking should dissolve. It is uncertain whether something like the German as a person or German as a quality, or anything similar in other nations, exists at all. The True and the Better in every people is surely that which does *not* integrate itself into the collective subject and if possible resists it. The formation of stereotypes, on the other hand, promotes collective narcissism. Those qualities with which one identifies oneself, the essence of one's own group, imperceptibly become the good itself and the foreign group, the others, bad. The same thing then takes place, in reverse, with the image the others have of the German. Yet after the most abominable atrocities perpetrated under National Socialism by an ideology of the primacy of

the collective subject at the cost of any and all individuality, there is doubled reason in Germany to guard against relapsing into the cultivation of
self-idolatrous stereotypes.

Tendencies of just this sort have emerged in recent years. They are
conjured up by the political questions of reunification, of the Oder-
Neiße Line, also by several claims raised by the refugees; a further pretext is offered by a completely imagined international ostracism of the
German, or a no less fictive lack of that national self-esteem that so
many would like to incite again. Imperceptibly an atmosphere is slowly
taking shape that disapproves of the one thing most necessary: critical
self-reflection. Once again one hears the ill-fated proverb of the bird
that dirties its own nest, whereas those who grouse about the bird themselves tend to be birds of a feather who flock together.[1] There are more
than a few questions to which almost everybody refrains from voicing
his or her true opinion in consideration of the consequences. Such consideration swiftly becomes autonomous and assumes the authority of
an internal censor that ultimately prevents not only the expression of
uncomfortable thoughts but the thoughts themselves. Because historically German unification was belated, precarious, and unstable, one
tends, simply so as to feel like a nation at all, to overplay the national
consciousness and irritably avenge every deviation from it. In this situation it is easy to regress to archaic conditions of a pre-individualistic
disposition, a tribal consciousness, to which one can appeal with all the
greater psychological effectiveness the less such consciousness actually
exists. To escape these regressive tendencies, to come of age, to look one's
own historical and societal situation and the international situation
straight in the eye, is incumbent upon precisely those people who
invoke the German tradition, that of Kant. His thought is centered
upon the concept of autonomy, the self-responsibility of the reasoning
individual instead of upon those blind dependencies, which include the
unreflected supremacy of the national. According to Kant, the universal
of reason realizes itself only in the individual. If one wanted to give Kant
his rightful due as the star-witness of the German tradition, then this
would mean the obligation to renounce collective obedience and self-
idolatry. Indeed those who most loudly proclaim Kant, Goethe, or
Beethoven to be German property are regularly those who have the least
to do with the contents of these authors' works. They register them as
possessions, whereas what these writers taught and produced prevents
them from being transformed into something that can be possessed. The
German tradition is violated by those who neutralize it into cultural
property that is at once both admired and of no pertinence. Meanwhile
people who know nothing of the obligation inherent in these ideas are

quickly seized with indignation whenever even one critical word falls upon a great name they want to confiscate and exploit as a German brand-name product.[2]

This is not to say that the stereotypes are devoid of any and all truth. Recall the most famous formulation of German collective narcissism, Wagner's: to be German means to do something for its own sake.[3] The self-righteousness of the sentence is undeniable, as is its imperial over-tone contrasting the pure will of the Germans with an allegedly petty mercantile spirit, that of the Anglo-Saxons in particular. However, it remains correct that the exchange relation, the permeation of all spheres, even that of spirit by the commodity form—what is popularly called commercialization—in Germany in the later eighteenth and in the nine-teenth century had not flourished as widely as in the advanced capitalist countries. This lent some power of resistance at least to intellectual pro-duction. It understood itself to be a being in-itself, not merely a being for-something-else or for-others, nor as an object of exchange.[4] Its model was not the entrepreneur operating according to the laws of the market but rather the civil servant fulfilling his duty to the authorities; this has often been emphasized in Kant. In Fichte's doctrine of action as an end-in-itself it found its most rigorous theoretical expression. One might learn what is true in this stereotype by studying the case of Houston Stewart Cham-berlain, whose name and development are linked to the most disastrous aspects of modern German history, the *völkisch* and anti-Semitic. It would be rewarding to understand how the sinister political function of this Germanized Englishman came about. His correspondence with his mother-in-law, Cosima Wagner, offers the richest material for such an inquiry. Chamberlain originally was a sophisticated, delicate man, extremely sensitive to the insidiousness of commercialized culture. He was attracted to Germany in general and to Bayreuth in particular by the proclaimed rejection of commercialism there. That he became a racial demagogue is neither the fault of a natural maliciousness or even of a weakness before the paranoid, power-hungry Cosima but rather of naiveté. What Chamberlain loved in German culture in comparison with the fully developed capitalism of his homeland, he took to be absolute. In it he saw an immutable, natural constitution, not the result of nonsyn-chronous developments in society. This led him smoothly to those *völkisch* notions, which then had incomparably more barbaric conse-quences than the unartistic existence he wanted to escape.

While it is true that without that "for its own sake" at least the great German philosophy and the great German music would have been impossible—significant artists of the Western countries have no less resisted the world disfigured by the exchange principle—it is not the whole truth. Even German society was, and is, an exchange society, and the doing-something-for-its-own-sake is not so pure as it affects to be. Rather behind this was hidden also a for-something-else, also an interest, that was by no means exhausted by the thing itself. But this interest was less the individual than the state, to which thoughts and actions were subordinated and whose expansion was supposed to afford satisfaction to the temporarily restrained egoism of individuals. The great German conceptions in which autonomy and the pure for-its-own-sake are so exuberantly glorified were without exception also available for the deification of the state; the criticism of the Western countries, equally one-sided, had repeatedly insisted on this point. The primacy of the interest of the collective over the individual self-interest was coupled with the aggressive political potential of an offensive war. The urge toward boundless domination accompanied the boundlessness of the 'idea'—the one did not exist without the other. To this day, history proves its nexus of complicity in that the highest forces of production, the supreme manifestations of spirit are in league with the worst.[5] Even the for-its-own-sake, in its relentlessly principled lack of consideration for the other, is no stranger to inhumanity. This inhumanity reveals itself precisely in a certain overbearing, all-encompassing violence of the greatest spiritual creations, in their will to domination. Almost without exception they confirm the existing because it exists. If one is permitted to speculate that something is specifically German, then it is this interpenetration of what is magnificent, not contenting itself with any conventional boundaries, with what is monstrous. In transgressing the boundaries, it at the same time wants to subjugate, just as idealist philosophies and artworks did not tolerate anything that could not be wholly subsumed within the domineering sphere of influence of their identity. Even the tension between these moments is no originary given, no so-called national character. The turn inward, the Hölderlinian "poor in deed yet full of thought,"[6] as it prevails in the authentic works around the turn from the eighteenth to the nineteenth century, had dammed up and overheated forces to the point of explosion, forces that then attempted, too late, to realize themselves. The absolute underwent reversal into the absolute horror. If in fact for long periods of time in the early bourgeois history the meshes of civilization's net—of bourgeoisification—were not so tightly woven in Germany as in the Western countries, this allowed a reserve of untapped natural forces to accumulate. This engendered the unwavering radicalism of spirit just as well as the permanent possibility of relapse.[7] Thus while Hitler can hardly be ascribed to the German national character as its fate, it was nonetheless hardly a coincidence that he rose to power in Germany. Even merely without the German seriousness, which stems from the pathos of the absolute and without which the best could not exist, Hitler could not have flourished. In the Western countries, where the rules of society are more deeply ingrained in the masses, he would have been laughed at. Holy seriousness can turn into deadly seriousness, which with hubris sets itself up literally as the absolute and rages against everything that does not bow to its claim.

Such complexity—the insight that in whatever is German the one cannot be had without the other—discourages every unequivocal answer to the question. The demand for such unequivocality is made at the expense of what eludes it. One then prefers to make the all too complicated thinking of the intellectual responsible for the state of affairs that prevents the intellectual, if he does not want to lie, from making simple determinations according to an either-or schema. Therefore, it is perhaps better if I somewhat reduce the question of what is German and formulate it more modestly: what motivated me, as an emigrant, someone who had been driven out in disgrace, and after what had been perpetrated by the Germans on millions of innocent people, nonetheless to come back. By trying to convey some of the things I myself have experienced and observed, I believe I can best work against the formation of stereotypes. It is an ancient tradition that such people who were capriciously and blindly banished from their homeland by tyranny come back after its fall. Someone who hates the thought of starting a new life will follow this tradition almost naturally, without long deliberation. Moreover, to someone who thinks in terms of society, and who understands fascism socioeconomically, the thesis that blames the German people [*Volk*] is really quite foreign. At no moment during my emigration did I relinquish the hope of coming back. And although the identification with the familiar is undeniably an aspect of this hope, it should not be misconstrued into a theoretical justification for something that probably is legitimate only so long as it obeys the impulse without appealing to elaborate theoretical supports. That in my voluntary decision I harbored the feeling of being able to do some good in Germany, to work against the obduration, the repetition of the disaster, is only another aspect of that spontaneous identification.

Experience has taught me something remarkable. People who conform, who feel generally at one with the given environment and its relations of domination, always adapt themselves much more easily in new countries. Here a nationalist, there a nationalist. Whoever as a matter of principle is never unrefractedly at one with the given conditions, whoever is not predisposed to play along, also remains oppositional in the new country. A sense of continuity and loyalty to one's own past is not the same as arrogance and obstinacy with regard to the person one happens to be, no matter how easily the former degenerates into the latter. Such loyalty demands that rather than relinquishing oneself for the sake of adapting to another milieu, one strive instead to change something in the domain where one is secure and competent in one's experience, where one is able to discriminate, above all really is able to understand people. I simply wanted to go back to the place where I spent my childhood, where what is specifically mine was imparted to the very core. Perhaps I sensed that whatever one accomplishes in life is little other than the attempt to regain childhood. For that reason I feel justified in speaking of the strength of the motives that drew me home, without arousing the suspicion of weakness or sentimentality, not to mention exposing myself to the misunderstanding that I subscribe to the fatal antithesis of *Kultur* and *Culture**.[8] Following a tradition of hostility to civilization that is older than Spengler, one feels superior to the other continent because it has produced nothing but refrigerators and automobiles while Germany produced the culture of spirit. But when this culture becomes entrenched, becomes an end in itself, it also has the tendency of detaching itself from real humanitarianism and becoming self-sufficient. In America, however, in the omnipresent for-other all the way to *keep smiling**, there also flourishes sympathy, compassion, and commiseration with the lot of the weaker. The energetic will to establish a free society—rather than only apprehensively thinking of freedom and, even in thought, degrading it into voluntary submission—does not forfeit its goodness because the societal system imposes limits to its realization. In Germany, arrogance toward America is inappropriate. By misusing a higher good, it serves only the mustiest of instincts. One need not deny the distinction between a so-called culture of spirit and a technological culture in order to rise above a stubborn contraposition of the two. A utilitarian view of life that, impervious to the incessantly increasing contradictions, believes that everything is for the best just as long as it merely functions, is just as blind as the faith in a culture of spirit that, by virtue of its ideal of self-sufficient purity, renounces the realization of its contents and abandons reality to power and its blindness.[9]

Having said this, I will risk speaking about what facilitated my decision to return. A publisher, incidentally a European emigrant, who was familiar with the German manuscript of *Philosophy of New Music*, expressed the wish to publish the main section of it in English. He asked me for a rough translation. When he read it, he found that the book, with which he was already familiar, was *"badly organized"** [*schlecht organisiert*]. I said to myself that, at least in Germany, despite all that has happened there, I would be spared this. A few years later the same thing happened again, only this time grotesquely intensified. I had presented a lecture in the Psychoanalytical Society in San Francisco and given it to their affiliated professional journal for publication. In the galleys I discovered that they had not been satisfied with improving the stylistic deficiencies of an emigrant writer. The entire text had been disfigured beyond recognition, the fundamental intentions could not be recovered. To my polite protest I received the no less polite and regretful explanation, that the journal owes its reputation precisely to its practice of submitting all contributions to such *editing** [*Redaktion*]. The editing provided the journal with its uniformity; I would only be standing in my own way were I to forego its advantages. Nonetheless I did forego them; today the article can be found in the volume *Sociologica II* under the title *"Die revidierte Psychoanalyse"* ["Psychoanalysis Revised"] in a quite faithful German translation.[10] In it one can check whether the text needed to be filtered through a machine, obedient to that almost universal technique of adaptation, reworking, and arranging, to which powerless authors have to submit in America. I give these examples not to complain about the country where I found refuge but to explain clearly why I did not stay. In comparison with the horror of National Socialism my literary experiences were insignificant bagatelles. But once I had survived, it was certainly excusable that I sought working conditions that would impair my work as little as possible. I was perfectly aware that the autonomy I championed as the unconditional right of the author to determine the integral form of his production had, at the same time, something regressive about it in relation to the highly rationalized commercial exploitation even of spiritual creations. What was being demanded of me was nothing other than the logically consistent application of the laws of highly advanced economic concentration to scholarly and literary products. However, what represents progress according to the standards of adaptation inevitably meant regression according to the standards of the subject matter itself. Conformity deprives spiritual creations of whatever is perhaps new and productive in them and by which they raise themselves above the already regulated consumer needs. In this country the demand that spirit also conform is not yet total. The distinction is still drawn, though often enough with problematic justification, between the autonomous creations of spirit and the products for the marketplace. Such economic backwardness, the future toleration of which remains uncertain, is the refuge of everything progressive that does not take the prevailing societal rules to be the ultimate truth. Once spirit, as admittedly countless people would like, is brought up to speed, made to order for the customer who is dominated by the market that takes his inferiority as a pretext for its own ideology, then spirit is just as thoroughly done for as it was under the clubs of the fascists. Intentions that are not content with the status quo—I would say qualitatively modern intentions—live from their backwardness within the process of economic exploitation. This backwardness is also no particularity of German nationality but rather attests to contradictions within the societal totality. History up until now has not known any linear progress. So long as progress runs in a single strand, on the rails of the mere domination of nature, then whatever spiritually extends beyond that will much more likely embody itself in what has not kept up completely with the main trend than in what is *up-to-date**. In a political phase that to a large extent relegates Germany as a nation to a function of world politics, this may yet be the chance for the German spirit—with all the dangers of a reawakening nationalism that implies.[11]

The decision to return to Germany was hardly motivated simply by a subjective need, or homesickness, as little as I deny having had such sentiments. An objective factor also made itself felt. It is the language. Not only because one can never express one's intention so exactly, with all the nuances and the rhythm of the train of thought in the newly acquired language as in one's own. Rather, the German language also apparently has a special elective affinity with philosophy and particularly with its speculative element that in the West is so easily suspected of being dangerously unclear, and by no means completely without justification. Historically, in a process that finally needs to be seriously analyzed, the German language has become capable of expressing something in the phenomena that is not exhausted in their mere thus-ness, their positivity, and givenness. This specific quality of the German language can be most graphically demonstrated in the nearly prohibitive difficulty of translating into another language philosophical texts of supreme difficulty such as Hegel's *Phenomenology of Spirit* or his *Science of Logic*.[12] German is not merely the signification of fixed meanings; rather, it has retained more of the power of expression—more in any case than would be perceived in the Western languages by someone who had not grown up in them and for whom they are not second nature. However, whoever remains convinced that, in contrast to the individual disciplines, the mode of presentation is essential to philosophy—as Ulrich Sonnemann recently put it very succinctly, there has never been a great philosopher who was not also a great writer[13]—will be disposed to the German language. At least the native German will feel that he cannot fully acquire the essential aspect of presentation or of expression in the foreign language. If one writes in a truly foreign language, then whether it is acknowledged or not, one falls under the captivating spell to communicate, to say it in a way such that others can understand. In one's own language, however, if one says the matter as exactly and uncompromisingly as possible, one may hope through such unyielding efforts to become understandable as well. In the domain of one's own language, it is this very language itself that stands as a guarantee for one's fellow human beings. I will not venture to decide whether this circumstance is specific to German or whether it affects far more generally the relationship between each person's native language and a foreign language. Yet the impossibility of conveying without violence not only high-reaching speculative thoughts but even particular, quite precise concepts such as those of *Geist* [spirit, mind, intellect], *Moment* [moment, element, aspect], and *Erfahrung* [experience], including everything with which they resonate in German, speaks for a specific, objective quality of the German language. Unquestionably the German language also has a price to pay for this quality in the omnipresent temptation that the writer will imagine that the immanent tendency of German words to say more than they actually say makes things easier and releases him from the obligation of thinking and, where possible, of critically qualifying this 'more', instead of playfully indulging in it. The returning émigré, who has lost the naive relationship to what is his own, must unite the most intimate relationship to his native language with unflagging vigilance against any fraud it promotes; against the belief that what I should like to call the metaphysical excess of the German language in itself already guarantees the truth of the metaphysics it suggests, or of metaphysics in general. I should perhaps admit in this context that I also for this reason wrote the *Jargon of Authenticity*.[14] Because I attribute just as much weight to language as a constituent of thought as Wilhelm von Humboldt did in the German tradition, I insist upon a discipline in my language, as also in my own thought, that hackneyed discourse only all too happily avoids. The metaphysical character of language is no privilege. One must not borrow from it the idea of a profundity that becomes suspect the moment it stoops to self-praise. This is similar to the concept of the German soul that, whatever it once may have meant, was mortally damaged when an ultraconservative composer gave that as a title to his romantic retrospective work.[15] The concept of profundity itself must not be affirmed without reflection, must not be, as philosophy calls it, hypostatized. No one who writes in German and who knows how much his thoughts are saturated with the German language should forget Nietzsche's critique of this sphere.[16] In the tradition, self-righteous German profundity was ominously in accord with suffering and its justification. For this reason the Enlightenment was denounced as superficial. If there is still anything profound, that is, not content with the blindly inculcated notions, then it

is the denunciation of every clandestine agreement with the uncondi-
tionality of suffering. Solidarity prohibits its justification. It is in the
faithfulness to the idea that the way things are should not be the final
word—rather than in the hopeless attempt to determine finally what is
German—that the sense this concept may still assert is to be surmised: in
the transition to humanity.

Scientific Experiences of a European Scholar in America

An American invitation motivated me to note down some of my intellectual experiences during my time there. Perhaps in this way, from an extreme perspective, a little light may be shed also on what is seldom given exposure. I have never denied that I have considered myself a European from the first to the last.[1] That I would maintain this intellectual continuity seemed self-evident to me, as I fully realized quickly enough in America.[2] I still recall the shock I received during our first days in New York from an emigrant, a young lady from a so-called good family, when she explained: "People used to go to the philharmonic, now they go to Radio City." In no respect did I want to be like her.[3] Both my natural disposition and my past made me inconceivably unsuited for adjusting in matters of intellect and spirit. As much as I recognize that intellectual individuality itself can only develop through processes of adjustment and socialization, I also consider it the obligation and the proof of individuation that it transcends adjustment.[4] By means of the mechanisms of identification with ego ideals, individuation must emancipate itself from this very identification. This relation between autonomy and adjustment was recognized early on by Freud and in the meantime has become familiar to American scholarship. When one came there thirty years ago, however, this was not the case. *Adjustment** was still a magic word, especially to someone fleeing persecution in Europe and from whom it was expected that he would prove himself in the new country and that he would not arrogantly insist on remaining the way he was.

The direction marked out for me through my first thirty-four years was thoroughly speculative, in the simple, prephilosophical sense of the word, though in my case inseparable from philosophical intentions. I thought it suited me personally and was objectively necessary to *interpret* phenomena, not to ascertain, organize, and classify facts, let alone to make them available as information, not only in philosophy but also in sociology. To the present day I have never rigorously separated the two disciplines, though I well know that here as well as over there specialization cannot be reversed by a mere act of will. The treatise "On the Societal Situation of Music," for example, which I published as a *Privatdozent* at Frankfurt in 1932 in the *Zeitschrift für Sozialforschung*,[5] and to which all my later musicological studies relate, already had a thoroughly theoretical orientation, founded on the idea of an inherently antagonistic totality that also "appears" in art and by which art is to be interpreted.[6] A type of sociology for which such a kind of thought had at best the value of hypotheses but not of knowledge was quite contrary to me.[7] On the other hand, I came to America—at least I hope so—as someone completely free of nationalism and cultural arrogance. The problematic of the traditional, especially German, intellectual-historical concept of culture had become far too evident for me to entrust myself to such conceptions. The element of enlightenment even in its relationship to culture, a matter of course in the American intellectual climate, necessarily had affected me in the strongest possible way.[8] Moreover, I was full of gratitude for being delivered from the catastrophe that was already looming in 1937: as willing to do my part as I was determined not to give up being who I was. The tension between these two attitudes should to some extent describe the manner in which I related to my American experience.

In the autumn of 1937 while in London I received a telegram from my friend Max Horkheimer, who before Hitler's ascension had been director of the Institute for Social Research at the University of Frankfurt, which he now was continuing in connection with Columbia University in New York. My speedy emigration to America would be possible if I'd be willing to collaborate on a radio project. After brief deliberation I telegraphed my agreement. I did not even really know what a radio project was; the American use of the word *"project"**, which nowadays in Germany is translated by something like *"Forschungsvorhaben,"*[9] was unknown to me. I was only certain that my friend would not have made the proposal unless he was convinced that I, a philosopher by training, could handle the job. I was only slightly prepared for it. In three years in Oxford I had learned English autodidactically but decently enough. In June of 1937 on invitation from Horkheimer I was in New York for a couple of weeks and nevertheless gained a first impression. In 1936 in the *Zeitschrift für Sozialforschung* I had published a sociological interpretation of jazz, which although suffering painfully from a lack of knowledge about America specifically, at least worked with material that could be considered characteristically American. I thought I would quickly and concentratedly acquire a certain knowledge of American life, in particular of the musical conditions over there; that presented few difficulties.

The theoretical core of that work on jazz was essentially related to the social-psychological investigations I undertook later. I found several of my theorems confirmed by American experts such as Winthrop Sargeant.[10] Nevertheless that work, though intricately involved with the pertinent musical facts, had the defect of being unproven according to American concepts of sociology. It remained in the domain of the "stimulus," the materials that have an effect upon the listener, without my moving or being able to move to the *other side of the fence** through using methods of statistical data collection. I thereby provoked the objection I was to hear many times: *"Where is the evidence?"**

A certain naiveté about the American situation proved to be of greater consequence. I surely knew what monopoly capitalism and the great trusts were; however, I did not know to what extent rational planning and standardization had permeated the so-called mass media, and consequently jazz, whose derivatives contribute so importantly to that media production. In fact, I still accepted jazz as immediate expression, as indeed jazz itself was wont to proclaim, and was not aware of the problem of a fabricated and manipulated pseudo-spontaneity, the problem of the "secondhand" that dawned on me in my American experience and that I later, *tant bien que mal,* tried to formulate. When I had the work "On Jazz" published again, after nearly thirty years, I was very distanced from it.[11] For that reason I could note, besides its weaknesses, whatever merits it might have. Precisely because it does not perceive an American phenomenon with the obviousness it has for Americans, but rather, as nowadays is said à la Brecht somewhat too glibly in Germany, "alienates" it, the study ascertained characteristics that were all too easily hidden by the familiarity of the jazz-idiom and that might be essential to the phenomenon.[12] In a certain sense such a conjunction of the outsider's perspective and unbiased insight is likely characteristic of all my studies on American material.

When I moved from London to New York in February of 1938, I worked half-time for the Institute for Social Research and half-time for the Princeton Radio Project. The latter was directed by Paul F. Lazarsfeld, with Hadley Cantril[13] and Frank Stanton, at that time still Research Director of the Columbia Broadcasting System,[14] as codirectors. I myself was supposed to direct the so-called music study of the project. Because I belonged to the Institute for Social Research I was not as exposed to the immediate competitive struggle and the pressure of externally imposed demands as was otherwise customary; I had the opportunity to pursue my own goals. I tried to do justice to my doubled employment by a certain combination of activities, occupying myself with research at both places. In the theoretical texts I wrote for the institute at that time, I formulated the standpoints and experiences I then wanted to evaluate in the radio project.[15] In the first instance, this work concerned the essay "On the Fetish-Character in Music and the Regression of Listening," which had already appeared in 1938 in the Zeitschrift für Sozialforschung and can be read today in the volume Dissonanzen,[16] and it also concerned the end of the book begun in London in 1937 on Richard Wagner, several chapters of which we placed in the Zeitschrift für Sozialforschung, whereas the entire book was published by Suhrkamp publishers in 1952. The distance between this book and the empirical-musicological publications was considerable. Nevertheless, it belongs to the overall complex of my work at that time. In Search of Wagner[17] endeavored to combine sociological, technical-musical, and aesthetic analyses in such a manner that, on the one hand, societal analyses of Wagner's "social character" and the function of his work would shed light upon its internal composition. On the other hand—and what seemed to me more essential—the internal-technical findings in turn should be brought to societal expression and be read as ciphers of societal conditions. The text on the fetish character was intended to conceptualize the recent musical-sociological observations I had made in America and to sketch out something like a "frame of reference"* [ein Bezugssystem] within which individual investigations could be designed and carried out. At the same time the treatise also represented a sort of critical reply to the work of Walter Benjamin on the "Work of Art in the Age of its Technical Reproducibility" that had recently been published in our journal.[18] I underscored the problematic of production in the culture-industry and the related behavioral responses, whereas it seemed to me that Benjamin strove all too directly to "rescue" precisely this problematic sphere.[19]

The Princeton Radio Project had its headquarters neither in Princeton nor in New York, but in Newark, New Jersey, and indeed, in a somewhat improvised manner, in a disused brewery. Whenever I traveled there, through the tunnel under the Hudson, I felt a little as if I were in Kafka's Nature Theater in Oklahoma.[20] Indeed, I was attracted by the lack of inhibition in the choice of a locality that would have been hardly imaginable in European academic practices. My initial impression of the studies currently underway, however, was not characterized by a great deal of understanding. At Lazarsfeld's suggestion, I went from room to room and talked with colleagues, heard words such as *"Likes and Dislikes Study"**, *"Success or Failure of a Programme"**, and so on, of which at first I could understand little. But I understood enough to realize that it concerned the collecting of data to benefit planning departments in the field of mass media, whether directly in industry or cultural advisory boards and similar bodies. For the first time I saw *administrative research** before me; I do not know today whether Lazarsfeld coined this phrase or I in my astonishment at such a type of science, focused directly on praxis, so utterly unfamiliar to me.

In any case, later Lazarsfeld outlined the distinction between such administrative research and the critical social research that our institute pursued in an article introducing the special volume of our *Studies in Philosophy and Social Science* in 1941 dedicated to "communications research."[21] Admittedly in the framework of the Princeton project there was little room for critical social research. The project's charter, which came from the Rockefeller Foundation, explicitly stipulated that the investigations had to be carried out within the framework of the commercial radio system established in the USA. This implied that the system itself, its social and economic presuppositions and its cultural and sociological consequences, should not be analyzed. I cannot say that I strictly followed that charter. In no way was I drawn by the desire to criticize at all costs, which would have been unbecoming in someone who first of all had to familiarize himself with the so-called cultural climate. Rather what troubled me was a fundamental methodological problem— method understood more in its European, epistemological sense than in the American usage, in which *methodology** indeed virtually signifies practical techniques of data collection. I was completely willing to set out for that famous *other side of the fence**, that is, to study the reactions of listeners, and I still recall how much I enjoyed and how much I learned when I personally, for my own orientation, carried out a series of admittedly quite overgrown and unsystematic interviews. Since earliest childhood I had always felt uneasy with impulsive, undisciplined thinking. On the other hand it seemed to me, and I am still convinced of it today, that in cultural activity what perceptual psychology regards as mere stimulus is itself qualitatively determinate, belonging to spirit, and knowable in terms of its objective contents. I resist having to register and measure effects without placing them in relation to those "stimuli," namely the objectivity of that to which the consumers of the culture industry, here, radio listeners, react. What was axiomatic in the rules of orthodox *social*

research*, that is, to proceed in an experiment from the reactions of the
subjects as if they were something primary, the ultimate legitimate
source of sociological knowledge, seemed to me to be thoroughly mediated and derivative. Or, put more cautiously: it would be incumbent upon
research first of all to investigate to what extent such subjective reactions
of the experiment's subjects are in fact as spontaneous and immediate as
these subjects suppose, or rather to what extent are actually involved not
only the mechanisms of dissemination and the apparatus's power of suggestion, but also the objective implications of the media and the material
with which the listeners are confronted—and ultimately the comprehensive societal structures all the way up to the societal totality. But simply
because I proceeded from objective implications of art instead of statistically measurable listener reactions I collided with the positivistic habits
of thought that reign virtually unchallenged in American science.

Furthermore, I was also hindered in my transition from theoretical
reflection to the empiria by something specifically musical: the difficulty
in verbalizing what music subjectively awakens in the listener, the utter
obscurity of what is so blithely called "the lived experience of music."[22] A
small machine, the so-called *program analyzer**,[23] which enabled a listener to indicate, among other things, what he did and did not like by
pushing a button during the playing of a piece of music, seemed to me
extremely inadequate to the complexity of what needed to be discovered,
despite the apparent objectivity of the data the machine provided.[24] In
any case I considered it necessary first of all to pursue in depth what
could perhaps be called musical *content analysis**,[25] that of the subject
matter itself—without the music being misunderstood as program
music—before going into the field, as they say. I recall how bewildered I
was when my late colleague Franz Neumann of the Institute for Social
Research, the author of *Behemoth*,[26] asked me whether the questionnaires of the music study had already been sent out, whereas I still hardly
knew whether questionnaires could do justice to the questions I considered essential. I still do not know: it has still not been attempted vigorously enough. To be sure—and herein lay my misunderstanding—I was
not expected to provide central insights into the relation between music
and society but only usable information. I felt a strong unwillingness to
switch over to this requirement;[27] as Horkheimer remarked in offering
me encouragement, being as I am, I probably would not have been able to
do it even had I wanted to.

All this was surely also determined in no small measure by the fact
that I approached the specific field of the sociology of music more as a
musician than as a sociologist. Nonetheless a genuine sociological element came into play that I could not account for until years later.[28]

Through recourse to subjective behavioral responses to music I came up against the question of *mediation*. The question arose precisely because the apparently primary, immediate reactions seemed to me to be an insufficient basis for sociological knowledge since they were themselves in fact mediated. One could point out that in the so-called motivation analysis of the social research oriented toward subjective reactions and their generalization a means was available for correcting that semblance of immediacy and for penetrating into the prior conditions of the subjective reactions, for example through supplementary detailed, qualitative *case studies**. However, aside from the fact that thirty years ago empirical social research was not so intensively involved with techniques of motivation research as it has been later, I felt and still feel that such a procedure is not fully adequate, however much it appeals to *common sense**. Even it remains imprisoned in the subjective realm: motivations are located in the consciousness and unconscious of individuals. Motivation analysis alone could not establish whether and how reactions to music are conditioned by the so-called cultural climate and beyond this by structural elements of society. Of course, social objectivities also manifest themselves indirectly in subjective opinions and behavior. The opinions and behavior of subjects are themselves always something objective. They are crucial for the developmental tendencies of the entire society, although not to the degree presumed by a sociological model that simply equates the rules of parliamentary democracy with the reality of living society. Moreover, social objectivities flash up within the subjective reactions, all the way down to concrete details. The subjective material allows conclusions to be drawn about its objective determinants. The claim to exclusivity made by empirical methods rests on the fact that subjective reactions are more ascertainable and quantifiable than the structures, especially those that are of the "total society," which cannot be so easily probed in an empirical manner. It is plausible that one could just as well proceed from the data collected from subjects to the societal objectivity as vice versa, except that sociology stands on more solid ground when it begins with the determination of these data. In spite of all this, however, it remains unproven whether one can actually proceed from the opinions and reactions of individuals to the structure and the essence of society. Even the statistical average of these opinions, as Durkheim already realized, is still an epitome of subjectivity.[29]

It is hardly a coincidence that the representatives of a rigorous empiricism[30] design their theory with such limitations that the construction of societal totality and its laws of motion is impeded. Above all, however, the choice of frames of reference, of categories and procedures employed by science, is not as neutral and indifferent with respect to the contents of the object to be studied as a thinking whose essential ingredients include the strict division between method and object would like to believe. Whether one proceeds from a theory of society and interprets the allegedly reliably observed phenomena as the theory's epiphenomena, or, alternatively, regards these phenomena as the stuff of science and the theory of society merely as an abstraction resulting from the classification—all this has far-reaching, substantive consequences for the conception of society. Prior to every particular bias and every "value judgment," the choice of one or the other "frame of reference" determines whether one conceives of the *abstractum* society as the reality on which everything individual depends, or whether because of its abstraction one deems it, in the tradition of nominalism, a mere *flatus vocis*, an empty word. This alternative extends into all societal judgments, ultimately also to the political. Motivation analysis does not go much beyond particular individual influences that are brought into relation with the reactions of the subjects under study but that, especially within the total system of the culture industry, are only more or less arbitrarily isolated from the totality that not only externally influences people but also has long ago become internalized.

Behind this lie issues far more relevant for "communications research." The phenomena that concern the sociology of mass media, especially in America, cannot be separated from standardization, the transformation of artistic creations into consumer goods, calculated pseudo-individualization, and similar manifestations of what German philosophy calls 'reification.' Corresponding to it is a reified, largely manipulable consciousness, hardly capable any longer of spontaneous experience. I can illustrate what I mean by reified consciousness most easily, without recourse to cumbersome philosophical deliberation, by noting an actual experience I had in America. Among the frequently changing colleagues whom I saw pass through the Princeton project was a young lady. After a few days she had developed some trust in me and asked in a completely charming manner, "Dr. Adorno, would you mind a personal question?" I said, "It depends on the question, but just go ahead," and she continued, "Please tell me: are you an extrovert or an introvert?"[31] It was as though she, a living being, was already thinking according to the model of the cafeteria-style questions from questionnaires. She could subsume herself under such rigid and prescribed categories, as one can also often observe in Germany, such as when people characterize themselves by the zodiac signs under which they were born: "female Sagittarius, male Aries." Reified consciousness is certainly at home not only in America but rather is fostered by the overall tendency of society. It's just that I first became aware of it while I was over there.

And Europe, too, in harmony with the economic-technological development, is following close behind in the formation of this spirit. In the meantime the complex has penetrated the general consciousness in America. However, around 1938 it was anathema to employ the concept of reification at all, which by now has become largely worn out through overuse.

I was particularly irritated by a methodological circle: in order to get a grasp on the phenomenon of cultural reification according to the prevailing norms of empirical sociology, one would have to use methods that are themselves reified, as they stood so menacingly before my eyes in the form of that *program analyzer**. When I was confronted with the requirement, as it was literally stated, "to measure culture," I on the contrary reflected that culture is precisely the very condition that excludes a mentality that would wish to measure it. In general I was hostile to the undifferentiated application of the principle *science is measurement**, which at that time was little criticized even in the social sciences. The primacy granted to quantitative methods of data collection, in relation to which theory as well as individual qualitative studies were to be at best supplementary, implied that one had to undertake just this paradox. The task of translating my deliberations into *research terms** resembled squaring the circle. I am certainly not the right person to judge how much of this is due to my personal equation; however, the difficulties are certainly *also* of an objective nature. They are based in the inhomogeneity of the scientific conception of sociology. No continuum exists between critical theory and the empirical procedures of the natural sciences. They have divergent historical origins and can be integrated only with the most extreme violence.[32]

Doubts of this kind towered up before me such that while I indeed immersed myself in observations about American musical life, in particular the radio system, and managed to set down theorems and theories, nonetheless I was unable to devise questionnaires and interview schemas that at least addressed the essential points. To be sure I was a bit isolated in my activities. The unfamiliarity of the things I had in mind had the effect that I incurred more skepticism than cooperation from my colleagues. Only the so-called secretarial help responded right away positively to my ideas. I still remember with gratitude Rose Kohn and Eunice Cooper, who not only transcribed and corrected my innumerable drafts but also encouraged me greatly. But the higher up in the scientific hierarchy things went, the more precarious became the situation. Thus once I had an assistant of distant German, Mennonite descent, who was supposed to support me particularly in my investigations of light music. He was a jazz musician, and I learned a great deal from him about the technique of jazz as well as about the phenomenon of *song hits** in America. But instead of helping me to translate my formulations of the problem into research strategies, however limited they might be, he wrote a kind of protest memorandum in which he contrasted, not without pathos, his scientific perspective with my arid speculations, as he viewed them. He had not really understood what I was after. A certain resentment was unmistakable in him: the kind of culture I happened to bring with me and about which my critical attitude toward society left me genuinely uncon-ceited, appeared to him to be unjustified arrogance. He harbored a mis-trust of Europeans, such as the bourgeois classes in the eighteenth cen-tury must have cultivated toward émigré French aristocrats. To him I appeared to be a sort of princely pretender, however little I, deprived of all influence, had to do with societal privilege.[33]

Without in the least wanting to gloss over my own psychological dif-ficulties with the project, above all the lack of flexibility of a man who was essentially already set in his goals, I should yet like to add several recollections of this assistant that show that the problems were not alone due to my shortcomings. A colleague who was highly qualified in his own field, which had nothing to do with musicology, and had long achieved high office and esteem, asked me to make several predictions for a study on jazz: whether this form of musical entertainment was more popular in the country or the city, with younger or older people, with churchgoing people or "agnostics," and the like. I answered these ques-tions, which lay well this side of the problems that occupied me in the sociology of jazz, with simple common sense, as an innocent person, unintimidated by science, presumably would answer them. My less than profound prophecies were confirmed. The effect was surprising. My young colleague did not attribute the result, say, to my simple reasoning, but rather to a kind of magical capacity for intuition. I thus earned an authority with him I had in no way deserved for having anticipated that jazz fans more likely live in large cities than in the country. The effect of his academic training obviously left no room for deliberations that were not already secured by strictly observed and registered facts. I actually encountered the argument that developing too many thoughts as hypotheses before empirical research possibly could induce a *"bias"** [*ein Vorurteil*] that would endanger the objectivity of the findings. My exceedingly friendly colleague preferred deeming me a medicine man to conceding validity to something that lay under the taboo of "specula-tion." Taboos of this kind have the tendency to extend beyond their orig-inal intention. Skepticism about what is unproven can easily turn into a prohibition upon thinking. Another scholar, also highly qualified and already recognized in the field, considered my analyses of light music to be "*expert opinion*"*. He logged these under the rubric of effects rather than that of analysis of the object, which, as mere stimulus, he wanted to exclude from the analysis, in his view nothing but a projection. I have encountered this argument time and again. Apparently, outside the special sphere of the humanities it was very difficult to comprehend the idea that anything of spirit could have an objectivity. Spirit is effortlessly equated with the human subject that sustains it, without any recognition of spirit's independence and autonomy. Above all else organized science hardly realizes to what small degree artworks coincide with those who produce them. I once observed this carried to a grotesque extreme. In a group of radio listeners I was given the task—God knows why—of presenting a musical analysis in the sense of structural aspects of listening. In order to connect with something generally familiar and the prevailing consciousness, I chose the famous melody that forms the second main theme of the first movement of Schubert's B-minor symphony and demonstrated the chainlike, imbricated character of this theme that lends it its particular insistence. One of the participants of the *meeting**, a very young man, whom I had noticed on account of his extravagantly colorful clothes, asked to speak and said roughly the following: what I had said was all very well and convincing. But it would have been more effective if I had donned the makeup and costume of Schubert, as if the composer himself was issuing information about his intentions and unfolding these thoughts. Something emerged in experiences of this stamp that Max Weber in his essays on the sociology of culture almost fifty years ago had diagnosed in his doctrine of bureaucracy, something that had already fully developed in the nineteen-thirties in America: the decline of the cultivated person in the European sense, which indeed as a social type never could have become fully established in America. That was particularly clear to me in the difference between an intellectual and a research technician.

I received my first real assistance in connection with the Princeton Radio Research Project when Dr. George Simpson was assigned to be my assistant. I gladly take the opportunity to reiterate my gratitude to him publicly in Germany. He was thoroughly informed in regard to theory; born and raised in America, he was familiar with the sociological criteria acknowledged in the USA, and as the translator of Durkheim's *Division du travail* he was equally familiar with the European tradition.[34] Again and again I could observe how native Americans proved to be more open-minded, above all more willing to help than emigrant Europeans who under the pressure of prejudice and rivalry often showed the proclivity to become more American than the Americans, and also quickly considered every newly arrived fellow European as a kind of disturbance to their own *adjustment**. Officially Simpson functioned as an *"editorial assistant"**; in reality he contributed a great deal more: the first attempts of an integration of my specific endeavors with American methods. The collaboration was accomplished in what was for me an extremely surprising and instructive manner. Like a child who once burnt shuns fire, I had developed an exaggerated caution; I hardly dared any more to formulate my ideas in American English as undisguisedly and vividly as was necessary to give them dimension. Such caution is unsuited to a thinking, however, that corresponded as little to a schema of *trial and error** as mine. But Simpson not only encouraged me to write as robustly and uncompromisingly as possible, he also did everything he could to make it succeed.

Thus between the years 1938 and 1940 in the music study of the Princeton Radio Research Project I completed four longer studies with Simpson's collaboration; without him they would likely not exist. The first was called: "A Social Critique of Radio Music." It appeared in the *Kenyon Review* in Spring 1945 and was a lecture I had presented to my colleagues at the Radio Project in 1940 and that developed the fundamental viewpoints of my work, a bit crudely, perhaps, but unequivocally.[35] Three concrete studies applied these viewpoints to material. One, "On Popular Music," printed in the communications volume of the *Studies in Philosophy and Social Science*, was a kind of phenomenology of hit songs and presented the theory of standardization and pseudo-individualization and the resultant succinct distinction between light and serious music.[36] The category of pseudo-individualization was a preliminary form of the concept of personalization that later played a considerable role in *The Authoritarian Personality* and indeed gained a certain relevance for political sociology in general.[37] Then there was the study on the NBC "Music Appreciation Hour," the more voluminous American text of which unfortunately remained unpublished at the time.[38] What seemed to me essential I later inserted in German, with the kind permission of Lazarsfeld, in the chapter "Die gewürdigte Musik" of *Der getreue Korrepetitor*.[39] It was concerned with critical *content analysis**, strictly and simply with the demonstration that the popular and very esteemed—because a noncommercial contribution—"Damrosch Hour," which claimed to foster musical education, was propagating false information about music as well as a completely untrue image of it. The social reasons for such untruth were sought in the conformism of the views embraced by those responsible for that *Appreciation Hour**. Finally, the text "The Radio Symphony" was completed and printed in the volume *Radio Research 1941*.[40] Its thesis was that serious symphonic music, so far as it is broadcast on the radio, is not what it appears to be, and that therefore the claim of the radio industry to be bringing serious music to the people is dubious. This work immediately aroused indignation; thus the well-known music critic Haggin polemicized against it and termed it the kind of stuff that foundations fell for—a reproach that in my case was not at all accurate.[41] I incorporated the core of this work also in *Der getreue Korrepetitor*, in the last chapter, "Über die musikalische Verwendung des Radios."[42] Indeed one of the central ideas proved to be obsolete: my thesis that the radio symphony was not a symphony anymore, which I derived from the technological transformations of sound quality due to the recording tape still prevalent in radio at the time and which has since largely been overcome by the techniques of high fidelity and stereophonics. Yet I believe that this affects neither the theory of atomistic listening nor that of the particular "image character" of music on the radio, which should have survived the earlier distortion of sound.

Measured against what the music study was intended to accomplish, at least by design, these four studies were fragmentary or, as the Americans say, the result of a *salvaging action**. I did not succeed in presenting a systematically executed sociology and social psychology of music on the radio.[43] What resulted was more like models rather than a design for the whole I had felt obliged to produce. The reason for this shortcoming may well have been that I did not succeed in making the transition to listener research. That transition would be absolutely necessary, above all else in order to differentiate and correct the theorems.[44] It is an open question, which in fact can only be answered empirically, whether, to what extent, and in what dimensions the societal implications disclosed in musical *content analysis** are also understood by the listeners and how they react to them. It would be naive simply to presume an equivalence between the societal implications of the stimuli and the *"responses"**, though no less naive to regard the two as independent of each other in the absence of established research on the reactions. If in fact, as was explicated in the study "On Popular Music," the norms and rules of the hit music industry are sedimented results of audience preferences in a society not yet totally standardized and technologically organized, one can still suppose that the implications of the objective material do not completely diverge from the consciousness and unconscious of those to whom such material appeals—otherwise the popular would hardly be popular. There are established limits to manipulation. On the other hand, one must consider that the shallowness and superficiality of material that from the outset is calculated to be perceived in a condition of absentmindedness and entertainment permits the expectation of relatively shallow and superficial reactions. The ideology projected by the culture industry of music need not necessarily be the same as that of its listeners. To provide an analogy: the popular press in many countries, even in America and England, frequently propagates opinions of the extreme right, without this having any great consequences over the decades for the formation of the public will in those countries. My own position in the controversy between empirical and theoretical sociology—which is often, and especially here in Germany, thoroughly misrepresented—may be summarized roughly by saying that empirical investigations, even in the domain of cultural phenomena, are not only legitimate but essential. But they should not be hypostatized and treated as a universal key. Above all, they themselves must terminate in theoretical knowledge. Theory is not merely a vehicle that becomes superfluous as soon as the data are available.

It may be noted that the four musical studies from the Princeton project, together with the study in German on the fetish character of music, contained the core of the *Philosophy of New Music* that was completed only in 1948: the viewpoints under which I had treated questions of reproduction and consumption in the American texts on music were to be applied to the sphere of production itself. *Philosophy of New Music* then, completed in America, implicated everything I wrote about music later, including the *Introduction to the Sociology of Music*.[45]

The work of the music study was by no means entirely confined to what appeared under my name. There were two other investigations, one strictly empirical, that at least could be considered as stimulated by my work without my having had any authority over either of them—I was not a member of the editorial board of *Radio Research 1941*. Edward Suchman in "Invitation to Music" has made most likely the only attempt to date to confirm a thesis of the "Radio Symphony" with listener reactions.[46] He investigated the difference in the capacity for musical experience between those familiar with live serious music and those who were first initiated into it through the radio. The characterization of the problem was related to my own approach in that my work also treated the difference between live experience and the "reified" experience tinged with the mechanical means of reproduction and all that this implied. This thesis seems to have been confirmed by Suchman's investigation. The taste of those people who had listened to live serious music was superior to the taste of those who were familiar with serious music only through the New York radio station WQXR, which specialized in this music.[47] Yet it remains unclear whether that difference could in fact be attributed solely to the diverse modes of apprehending the music as explicated in my thesis and probably also in Suchman's reasoning, or whether, as I am prone to think now, a third factor plays a role: that those who generally go to concerts already belong to a tradition that makes them more familiar with serious music than the radio fans and that they moreover probably from the outset have a more specific interest in it than those who confine themselves to listening to the radio. Moreover, through this study, whose existence understandably pleased me, my misgivings about treating questions of the reification of consciousness with reified methods became quite concrete. According to the technique of the *Thurstone Scale**, which at that time was much more prevalent, a commission of experts were supposed to decide on the quality of the composers who were to be used for distinguishing between the standards of those people who had become initiated into music through live performance and through radio.[48] These experts were selected largely for their prominence and their authority in the public sphere of music. Here the question arose of whether such experts were not themselves imprinted with the same conventional attitudes attributable to that reified consciousness that actually constituted the object of the investigations. The high ranking accorded to Tchaikovsky in the scale seemed to me to justify such suspicions.

The study by Duncan MacDougald entitled "The Popular Music Industry" in *Radio Research 1941* served to concretize the thesis that musical taste was manipulated.[49] It was an initial contribution to the insight that what seemed immediate was in fact mediated, in that the study described in detail how hit songs were "made" at the time. With the methods of *high pressure** advertising, *"plugging"**, the most important channels for the popularity of hits, the bands, were worked on so that certain songs were played as often as possible, particularly on the radio, until in fact they had a chance of being accepted by the masses through the sheer power of incessant repetition.[50] Yet I felt some misgivings even about MacDougald's presentation. The facts he insisted on belong by their very structure to an earlier era than that of the centralized radio technology and the great monopolies in mass media. In his study the work of preposterously zealous agents, if not individual corruption, was still thought essential, whereas in truth the objective system and to some measure the technological conditions themselves had long since assumed this role. To this extent it would be necessary today to repeat the investigation and explore the objective mechanisms for popularizing the popular rather than the machinations and intrigues of those garrulous types whose *"sheet"** MacDougald so richly characterized.[51] In the face of the present social reality it easily looks old-fashioned and consequently rather conciliatory.[52]

In 1941 my activity at the Princeton Radio Research Project, from which the Bureau of Applied Social Research developed, came to an end, and my wife and I moved to California, where Horkheimer had already settled.

He and I spent the next years in Los Angeles almost exclusively working collaboratively on the *Dialectic of Enlightenment*; the book was completed in 1944, and the final supplements were written in 1945. Until the autumn of 1944 my contact with American science and research was interrupted and only then reestablished. Even during our time in New York, Horkheimer, in the face of the horrors happening in Europe, arranged for investigations into the problem of anti-Semitism. Together with other members of our institute we had developed and published the program for a research project to which we then often referred. It contained among other things a typology of anti-Semites, which then, substantially modified, recurred in later studies. Similar to the way the music study at the Princeton Radio Research Project was determined theoretically by the treatise "On the Fetish-Character in Music and the Regression of Listening," written in German, so it went this time. The chapter "Elements of Anti-Semitism" in the *Dialectic of Enlightenment*, which Horkheimer and I composed jointly in the strictest sense, namely by literally dictating it together, was determinative for my participation in the investigations carried out later with the Berkeley Public Opinion Study Group. They found their literary expression in *The Authoritarian Personality*.[53] The reference to the *Dialectic of Enlightenment*, which has not yet been translated into English,[54] does not seem superfluous to me because the book best obviates a misunderstanding *The Authoritarian Personality* was exposed to from the outset and for which it was perhaps not wholly unresponsible on account of its emphasis: namely the criticism that the authors had attempted to ground anti-Semitism, and beyond that fascism, merely subjectively, subscribing to the error that this political-economic phenomenon is primarily psychological. What I suggested about the conception of the music study of the Princeton project should suffice to show how little that was intended. The "Elements of Anti-Semitism" theoretically shifted racial prejudice into the context of an objectively oriented critical theory of society. To be sure, in contrast to a certain economic orthodoxy, we were not dismissive of psychology but acknowledged its proper place in our outline as an explanatory aspect. However, we never entertained doubts about the primacy of objective factors over psychological ones. We followed what I believe to be the plausible idea that in the present society the objective institutions and developmental tendencies have attained such an overwhelming power over individuals that people are becoming, and evidently in increasing measure, functionaries of the predominant tendencies operating over their heads. Less and less depends on their own particular conscious and unconscious being, their inner life. In the meantime the psychological, even the social-psychological explanation of social phenomena has become in many ways an ideological screen-image: the more dependent people are upon the total system and the less they can do something about it, the more they are intentionally and unintentionally led to believe that everything depends on them.[55] This does not render irrelevant the social-psychological questions that have been raised in connection with Freudian theory, especially those of depth psychology and characterology. Already in the long introduction to the volume of the Institute for Social Research, *Authority and Family* of 1935, Horkheimer had spoken of the "cement" that holds society together and had developed the thesis that, in the face of the divergence between what society promises its members and what it delivers to them, the system could hardly continue to function unless it had molded the people themselves down to their innermost being to conform to itself.[56] If at one time the bourgeois era, with the awakening need for independent wage earners, had produced people who corresponded to the requirements of the new means of production, then these people, generated as it were by the economic-societal system, were later the additional factor that contributed to the perpetuation of the conditions in whose image the subjects were created. We viewed social psychology as subjective mediation of the objective societal system, without whose mechanisms it would not have been possible to keep a hold on its subjects. To this extent our views approached subjectively oriented research methods as a corrective to a rigid thinking imposed from above, in which invoking the supremacy of the system becomes a substitute for insight into the concrete connection between the system and those who, after all, compose it. On the other hand, the subjectively oriented analyses have their valid place only within an objective theory. In *The Authoritarian Personality* this is emphasized repeatedly. The work's focus on the subjective moments was interpreted, along the lines of the predominant tendency of the times, as though social psychology was used as a philosopher's stone, whereas, in Freud's famous turn of phrase, it was simply trying to add something new to what was already known.

Horkheimer made contact with a group of researchers at the University of California at Berkeley composed principally of Nevitt Sanford, who has since passed away, Else Frenkel-Brunswick, and the then very young Daniel Levinson. I believe that the first point of contact was a study initiated by Sanford on the phenomenon of pessimism, which then recurred in a very modified form in the most important investigations in which the destructive drive was revealed to be one of the decisive dimensions of the authoritarian personality, though of course no longer in the sense of an "overt" pessimism but rather often precisely as the reactive suppression of it. In 1945 Horkheimer took over the direction of the

Research Division of the American Jewish Committee in New York and made it possible for the scientific resources of the Berkeley group and of our institute to be "pooled," so that over a period of years we were able to conduct extensive research related to our common theoretical reflections. He was responsible not only for the overall plan of the studies collected in the series "Studies in Prejudice" published by Harper's,[57] but *The Authoritarian Personality* in its specific content is also unthinkable without him, for Horkheimer's and my philosophical and sociological reflections had long since grown so integrated that neither of us could have said what came from one and what from the other. The Berkeley study was organized such that Sanford and I served as directors and Mrs. Brunswik and Daniel Levinson as principal colleagues. From the beginning, however, everything occurred in consummate *teamwork** without any hierarchical aspects. The title page of *The Authoritarian Personality* that gives equal *"credit"** to us all in fact completely expresses the actual situation. This kind of cooperation in a democratic spirit that does not get mired in formalities but rather extends into all the details of planning and execution, was for me probably the most fruitful thing I encountered in America, in contrast to the academic tradition in Europe. The present efforts toward an inner democratization of the German university are familiar to me from my American experience.[58] The cooperation in Berkeley knew no friction, no resistance, no scholarly rivalry. Dr. Sanford, for instance, sacrificed a great deal of his time in order to edit stylistically, in the kindest and most meticulous manner, all the chapters written by me. The reason for our *teamwork** was not only the American atmosphere but also scientific: our common orientation toward Freud. We four were agreed neither to tie ourselves fast to Freud nor, like the psychoanalytical revisionists, to dilute him. There was a certain measure of deviation from him in that we were pursuing a specifically sociological interest. The inclusion of objective elements, here especially of the "cultural climate," was incompatible with the Freudian view of sociology as merely applied psychology. Likewise the desiderata of quantification we submitted to differed somewhat from Freud, for whom the substance of research consists in qualitative investigations, *case studies**. Nevertheless we took the qualitative factor seriously throughout. The categories that underlay the quantitative investigations were in themselves of a qualitative character and derived from an analytical characterology. Moreover, already in the planning stage we were concerned to compensate for the danger of the mechanistic aspect of quantitative investigations with supplementary qualitative case studies. The aporia—that what was discovered purely by quantitative means seldom reaches the genetic deep mechanisms, while the qualitative discoveries can just as easily lose their generalizability and therefore also their objective sociological validity—we tried to overcome by applying a whole range of various techniques that were coordinated with each other only through the single underlying conception. Mrs. Brunswik undertook the remarkable attempt to quantify in turn the findings of the strictly qualitative, clinical analysis she obtained in her assigned sector, against which however I raised the objection that the complementary advantages of the qualitative analyses were once again lost through such quantification. Due to her early and tragic death we could not carry through this controversy between us. So far as I can tell, the issue still remains open.

The investigations on the authoritarian personality were pursued at various levels. While the center was in Berkeley, where I went once every fortnight, my friend Frederick Pollock also organized a study group in Los Angeles, where the social psychologist J. F. Brown, the psychologist Carol Creedon, and several other people actively participated. We came into contact already at that time with the psychoanalyst Dr. Frederick Hacker and his colleagues. Seminarlike discussions in the circle of all those interested often took place in Los Angeles. The idea of a large literary work that would integrate the individual investigations took shape only gradually and somewhat arbitrarily. The actual center of the common achievements was the F-scale that of all the parts of *The Authoritarian Personality* exercised the greatest influence—in any case it was applied and modified countless times and then later, after being adapted to the particular local conditions, formed the basis for the scale for measuring the authoritarian potential in Germany, about which the Institute for Social Research, newly founded in 1950 in Frankfurt, will soon release a large report.[59] Certain tests in American magazines, as well as unsystematic observations of several acquaintances, suggested to us the idea that without asking about anti-Semitic and other fascist opinions explicitly one could determine such tendencies indirectly, by determining the rigid views one can be fairly sure generally accompany those specific opinions and constitute with them a characterological unity. In Berkeley then we developed the F-scale in a free and relaxed environment deviating considerably from the conception of a pedantic science that must account for its every step. Probably the reason for this was what one liked to call the *"psychoanalytic background"** of us four directors of the study, particularly our familiarity with the method of free association. I emphasize this because a work like *The Authoritarian Personality*, which has been much faulted but whose familiarity with American material and American procedures has never been disputed, was produced in a manner that by no means coincides with the usual image of the positivism of the social sciences. *In praxi* such positivism

does not reign as unconditionally as the theoretical-methodological literature would have one believe. The conjecture is hardly too far-fetched
that whatever *The Authoritarian Personality* exhibits in originality,
unconventionality, imagination, and interest in important themes is due
precisely to that freedom. The element of playfulness that I would like to
think is essential to every intellectual productivity was in no way lacking
during the development of the F-scale. We spent hours thinking up
whole dimensions, *"variables"**, and syndromes as well as particular
questionnaire items, of which we were all the more proud the less apparent their relation to the main theme was, whereas theoretical reasons led
us to expect correlations with ethnocentrism, anti-Semitism, and reactionary political-economic views. Then we checked these *items** in established pretests and thereby achieved as well the technically requisite limitation of the questionnaire to a length that would still be reliable by
eliminating those *items** that proved not to be selective enough.

Of course, we had to water our wine somewhat in the process. For a
range of reasons, among which what was later called cultural susceptibil-
ity played no small role, we often had to give up precisely those items we
thought were the most profound and original, and give preference to
items that gained their greater selectivity by lying closer to the surface of
public opinions than those grounded in depth psychology. Thus, for
instance, we could not pursue further the dimension of revulsion felt by
authoritarian personalities to avant-garde art because this revulsion presupposed a cultural level—simply familiarity with such art—that had
been denied to the overwhelming majority of the people we interviewed.
While we believed that with the combination of quantitative and qualitative methods we were able to overcome the antagonism between what
can be generalized and what remains specifically relevant, that antagonism overtook us in the midst of our own endeavors. It seems to be the
affliction of every empirical sociology that it must choose between the
reliability and the profundity of its findings. Nonetheless, at that time we
could still work with the Likert form of operationally defined scales in a
way that simply allowed us to kill several birds with one stone, that is,
with one *item** to address at once several of the dimensions that according to our theoretical outline were indicative of the authoritarian personality, the *highs**, and its contrary, the *lows**. According to Guttman's criticism of the hitherto conventional procedure of *scaling**, the impartiality
of our F-scale could hardly still be entertained. It is difficult for me to
avoid the suspicion that the increasing exactness of methods in empirical
sociology, no matter how irrefutable their arguments may be, often
restrains scientific productivity.[60]

We had to bring the work to a close for publication relatively quickly.
It came out almost at the same time as I returned to Europe at the end of

1949. I did not directly observe its influence in the USA during the following years. The time pressure we experienced had a paradoxical result. There is a well-known British joke about the man who begins his letter by writing that he hasn't time to be brief; it was only because we could not return to the work yet again in order to condense the manuscript that the book became as ponderous and voluminous as it is now. But perhaps this shortcoming, of which we were all aware, is compensated for somewhat by the richness of the more or less independent methods and the materials they produced. What is perhaps lacking in the book by way of disciplined rigor and unity may partially be made good by the fact that so many concrete insights from the most diverse directions flow together and converge in the same main theses, until what remains unproven according to strict criteria nonetheless gains in plausibility. If *The Authoritarian Personality* made a contribution, then it is not to be found in the absolute conclusiveness of its positive insights, let alone in its measurements, but above all in the conception of the problem, which is marked by an essential interest in society and is related to a theory that had not previously been translated into quantitative investigations of this kind. In the meantime, surely not without the influence of *The Authoritarian Personality*, there have been several attempts to test psychoanalytical theorems with empirical methods. Our intention, similar to that of psychoanalysis, was to determine present opinions and dispositions. We were interested in the fascist *potential*. In order to be able to work against that potential, we also incorporated into the investigation, as far as was possible, the *genetic* dimension, that is, the emerging of the authoritarian personality. We all considered the work, despite its great size, a pilot study, more an exploration of possibilities than a collection of irrefutable results. Nevertheless our results were significant enough to justify our conclusions—as referring to tendencies and not as simple *statements of fact**. Else Frenkel-Brunswik paid particular attention to this point in her part of the work.

As in many investigations of this kind, there was a certain *handicap** in the sample, and we didn't gloss over it. Empirical sociological investigations at American universities, and not only there, chronically suffer from the fact that they must make do with students as subjects far more than could be justified by the principles of representative sampling of the entire population. Later in Frankfurt we tried to rectify this deficiency in similar investigations by organizing, through expressly designated contact persons, test groups arranged by quota from various segments of the population. All the same, it should be said that in Berkeley we were not actually striving for a representative sampling. We were far more interested in key groups: admittedly not as much as would perhaps have been good in the now often invoked *opinion leaders** as in the groups we presumed to be especially "susceptible," like prisoners in St. Quentin—who were in fact *"higher"* * than the average—or inmates of a psychiatric clinic, because we hoped from familiarity with pathological structures to gain information about "normal" structures.

Of greater importance is the objection concerning circularity raised by Jahoda and Christie: that the theory, which is presupposed by the research instruments, is validated by those same instruments.[61] This is not the place to go into this objection. Only this much may be said: we never considered the theory simply as a hypothesis but rather as in a certain sense something independent, and for that reason we also did not wish to prove or refute the theory through our results but to derive from the theory concrete research questions that then stand on their own and reveal certain general social-psychological structures. Of course, the criticism of the technical idea of the F-scale cannot be disputed: that to ascertain indirectly tendencies that cannot be broached for fear of the censoring mechanisms, which otherwise come into play, presupposes that one has already validated the tendencies via those direct opinions one assumes the test subjects hesitated to make known. To this extent the argument of circularity is justified. But here I would say that these requirements should not be pushed too far. Once a connection has been established between the overt and the latent in a limited number of pretests, one may pursue this connection in the main tests with entirely different people who will not be troubled by any overt questions. The only possibility would be that because in America people who were openly anti-Semitic and fascist in 1944 and 1945 hesitated to express their opinion, the original connection of the two types of questions could have led to excessively optimistic results, to an overvaluing of the potential of the *lows**. The criticism directed at us, however, went rather in the opposite direction: it faulted us for gearing our instruments all too much to the *highs**. These methodological problems, which are all structured on the model of presupposition—proof—conclusion, later helped occasion my philosophical critique of the conventional scientistic concept of the absolutely Primary, which I practiced in my books on epistemology.[62]

As in the case of the radio project, other investigations crystallized around *The Authoritarian Personality*, for example, the "Child Study," which Mrs. Brunswik and I initiated at the Child Welfare Institute at Berkeley and whose execution mainly fell to her; unfortunately the study remained incomplete. Only partial results of it have been published.[63] A certain mortality rate of individual studies is apparently unavoidable in large-scale research projects. Nowadays, since social science undergoes so much self-reflection, it would probably be well worthwhile to systematically inquire why so much that is started in it is not finished. The "Child Study" used the fundamental categories of *The Authoritarian Personality*. It gave rise to completely unexpected results. They refined the notion of the connection between conventionalism and the authoritarian attitude. Precisely the "good," that is, conventional children, were more free from aggression, one of the most essential aspects of the authoritarian personality, and vice versa. This can be explained plausibly in retrospect but not a priori. This aspect of the "Child Study" made me aware for the first time of something Robert Merton independently discerns as one of the most important justifications for empirical investigations: that more or less all findings, as soon as they are available, can be explained theoretically, but so also can their contrary.[64] Rarely have I so palpably experienced the legitimacy and necessity of empirical research that really answers theoretical questions. — Even before the collaboration with Berkeley began, I myself was writing a fairly large monograph on the social-psychological technique of Martin Luther Thomas, a fascist agitator who had recently been active on the American west coast. It was completed in 1943, a content analysis that treated the more or less standardized and by no means numerous stimuli used by fascist agitators. Here once again the conception that lay behind the music study of the Princeton Radio Research Project was of advantage: to treat types of reactions and objective effects in the same way. In connection with the "Studies in Prejudice" the two *"approaches"** were not accommodated to each other or integrated. Of course it remains to say that the articulated effects by agitators from the *"lunatic fringe"**[65] are by no means the only, presumably not even the essential objective elements promoting a fascistically inclined mentality in the population. The roots extend deep into the structure of society that generates the fascist mentality before demagogues willingly come to its aid. The views of demagogues are by no means limited to the *lunatic fringe**, as one might optimistically think. They can be found unmistakably, just not as compactly and aggressively formulated, in innumerable utterances of so-called respectable politicians. The analysis of Thomas suggested a great deal to me for *items**[66] that were useful in *The Authoritarian Personality*. The study must have been one of the first critical, qualitative content analyses to be carried out in the USA. It is still unpublished.[67]

In the late autumn of 1949 I returned to Germany and for years was completely taken up with the reconstruction of the Institute for Social Research, to which Horkheimer and I devoted all our time, and with my teaching activities at the University of Frankfurt. It was only in 1952, after a short visit in 1951, that I traveled back to Los Angeles for approx-

imately a year, as the scientific director of the Hacker Foundation in Beverly Hills.[68] It was established that I, although neither a psychiatrist nor
a therapist, would concentrate my work upon social psychology. On the
other hand, the colleagues at Dr. Hacker's clinic, to which the foundation
was attached, were fully occupied with practical duties, whether as psychoanalysts or *psychiatric social workers**. Whenever the cooperation
materialized, things went well. But the colleagues had far too little time
for research, and I for my part, as research director, did not have the
authority to tie down the clinicians with research projects. In this way
the possibilities of what could be done were necessarily more limited
than either Dr. Hacker or I had imagined. I saw myself forced into the situation that in America is called a *"one-man show"**: aside from the organization of lectures, I had to carry out the scientific studies of the foundation virtually alone. Thus I again found myself thrown back upon the
analysis of "stimuli." I wrapped up two content studies. One was on the
astrology column of the *Los Angeles Times,* and the English version
appeared in 1957 under the title "The Stars Down to Earth" in the *Jahrbuch für Amerikastudien* in Germany and later formed the basis for my
German treatment "Aberglaube aus zweiter Hand" in *Sociologica II.*[69]
My interest in this material dates back to the Berkeley study: above all to
the social-psychological interpretation of the destructive drive Freud had
discovered in *Civilization and Its Discontents* and which seems to me to
be the most dangerous subjective potential within the masses in the present political situation.[70] The method I followed was that of putting
myself in the position of the popular astrologer, who by what he writes
must immediately furnish his readers with a sort of gratification and who
constantly finds himself confronted with the difficulty of giving people,
about whom he knows nothing, seemingly specific advice suited to each
individual. The result was the reinforcing of conformist views through
the commercial and standardized astrology as well as the appearance in
the technique of the *column** writer, especially in the biphasic approach,
of certain contradictions in the consciousness of his audience, which in
turn hark back to societal contradictions.[71] I proceeded qualitatively,
although I did not fail to count at least in a very crude way the frequency
with which the basic tricks recurred in the material I had selected stretch-
ing over a period of two months. One of the justifications of quantitative
methods is that the very products of the culture industry are, as it were,
planned from a statistical viewpoint.[72] Quantitative analysis measures
them by their own standard. For instance, differences in the frequency
with which particular tricks recur derive in turn from a quasi-scientific
calculation of the effect on the part of the astrologer, who in many
respects resembles the demagogue and agitator, even though he avoids

openly political theses; incidentally, in *The Authoritarian Personality* we had already run into the tendency of the *"highs"**[73] to readily accept superstitious statements, above all those with a threatening and destructive content. The astrology study in this way is a continuation of the work I had pursued earlier in America.

This is also true for the study "How to Look at Television," published in the *Hollywood Quarterly of Film, Radio, and Television* in spring 1954, and likewise later utilized in the German study "Television as Ideology" in the volume *Interventions*.[74] It required all of Dr. Hacker's diplomacy to obtain for me a certain number of television scripts, which I analyzed with a view to their ideological implications, their various intentional levels. The industry does not in the least like to part with its scripts. Both studies belong to the realm of research on ideology.

In the fall of 1953 I returned to Europe. Since then I have not been back to America.

If I were to summarize what I hope I have learned in America, then I would first say it was something sociological and infinitely important for the sociologist: that over there, indeed beginning with my English stay, I was induced no longer to regard as natural the conditions that had developed historically, like those in Europe: *"not to take things for granted"**. My now departed friend Tillich once said that he was first deprovincialized in America; he surely meant something similar.[75] In America I was liberated from a naive belief in culture, acquired the ability to see culture from the outside. To make this clearer: in spite of all critique of society and all consciousness of the supremacy of the economy, the absolute importance of spirit was always natural and obvious to me. I was taught the lesson that this obviousness was not absolutely valid in America, where no reverential silence reigned before everything intellectual as it does in Central and Western Europe far beyond the so-called cultivated classes; the absence of this respect induces the spirit to critical self-reflection. This particularly affected the European presuppositions of musical culture in which I was immersed. Not that I denied these presuppositions, abandoned my ideas of such a culture, but it is a considerable difference whether one unreflectedly has these or becomes aware of them precisely in their discrepancy from the most technologically and industrially advanced country.[76] In saying this I do not ignore the displacement in the center of gravity of musical life effected in the meantime by the material resources of the USA. When I began to concern myself with the sociology of music in America thirty years ago, that was still unforeseeable.

More important and more gratifying was my experience of the substantiality of democratic forms: that in America they have seeped into life itself, whereas at least in Germany they were, and I fear still are, nothing more than formal rules of the game. Over there I became acquainted with a potential for real humanitarianism that is hardly to be found in old Europe. The political form of democracy is infinitely closer to the people. American everyday life, despite the oft lamented hustle and bustle, has an inherent element of peaceableness, good-naturedness, and generosity, in sharpest contrast to the pent-up malice and envy that exploded in Germany between 1933 and 1945. Surely America is no longer the land of unlimited possibilities,[77] but one still has the feeling that anything could be possible. If one encounters time and again in sociological studies in Germany the statement, "We are not yet mature enough for democracy," then such expressions of both the lust for power together with self-contempt are hardly conceivable in the allegedly much younger New World. I do not want to imply by this that America is somehow immune to the danger of veering toward totalitarian forms of domination. Such a danger lies in the tendency of modern society per se. But probably the power of resistance to fascist currents is stronger in America than in any European country, perhaps with the exception of England, which in more respects than we are accustomed to recognize, and not only through language, links America and continental Europe.

European intellectuals such as myself[78] are inclined to view the concept of *adjustment** [*Anpassung*] merely negatively, as the extinction of spontaneity and the autonomy of the individual person.[79] Yet it is an illusion sharply criticized by Goethe and Hegel that the process of humanization and cultivation necessarily and continually proceeds from the inside outward. It is accomplished also and precisely through "externalization," as Hegel called it. We become free human beings not by each of us realizing ourselves as individuals, according to the hideous phrase, but rather in that we go out of ourselves, enter into relation with others, and in a certain sense relinquish ourselves to them. Only through this process do we determine ourselves as individuals, not by watering ourselves like plants in order to become well-rounded cultivated personalities. A person who under extreme coercion or indeed through his egoistic interest is brought to behave in a friendly manner in the end attains a certain humanity in his relation to other people, more so than someone who, merely in order to be identical with himself—as though this identity was always desirable—makes a nasty, sour face and gives one to understand from the outset that one does not exist for him and has nothing to contribute to his inwardness, which often enough does not even exist. We in Germany should endeavor lest, in being indignant at American superficiality, we in turn do not become superficially and undialectically rigid ourselves.

To such general observations should be added something that concerns the specific situation of the sociologist or, less technically, of anyone who deems knowledge of society to be central for and inseparable from philosophy. Within the overall development of the bourgeois world the United States has unquestionably reached an extreme. The country displays capitalism, as it were, in its complete purity, without any precapitalist remnants. If one assumes, in contrast to a very widely and tenaciously held opinion, that the other noncommunist countries that do not belong to the Third World are also moving toward the same condition, then America offers the most advanced observation post for anyone who views neither America nor Europe with naiveté. In fact someone who returns to Europe can see many things approaching or already confirmed that he first encountered in America. Whatever objections a cultural criticism that takes seriously the concept of culture might have to raise when that concept is confronted with American conditions since Tocqueville and Kürnberger,[80] unless one withdraws behind a barricade of elitism one cannot avoid in America the question of whether the concept of culture in which one has grown up has not itself become obsolete; whether what today as a global tendency befalls culture is not what its very own failure brought upon it, the guilt it incurred by isolating itself as a special sphere of spirit without realizing itself in the organization of society. Certainly this has not happened even in America, but the horizon of such a realization is not as obstructed there as in Europe. In view of the quantitative thinking in America, with all its dangers of a loss of differentiation and an absolutizing of the average, the European must address the unsettling question to what extent qualitative differences are still significant at all in the contemporary social world. Already the airports everywhere in Europe, America, in the East, as well as in the states of the Third World, look interchangeably alike; already it is hardly a matter of days but of hours to travel from one country to the most remote parts of the globe. The differences not only in living standards but also in the specific qualities of peoples and their forms of existence assume an anachronistic aspect. Admittedly it is uncertain whether in fact the similarities are decisive and qualitative differences merely antiquated and, above all, whether in a rationally organized world what is qualitatively diverse and today only oppressed by the unity of technological reason would again come into its own. Reflections of this kind, however, would no longer be conceivable at all without the experience of America. It is hardly an exaggeration to claim that every consciousness today that has not appropriated the American experience, even if with resistance, has something reactionary to it.

In conclusion perhaps I should still add a word about the specific significance of the scientific experience in America for me personally and for my thinking. It strongly diverges from *common sense**. But Hegel, superior in this point to all later irrationalism and intuitionism, laid the greatest emphasis upon the idea that speculative thinking is not distinct from so-called healthy *common sense** [*gesunder Menschenverstand*] but rather essentially consists in its critical self-reflection and self-scrutiny. Even a consciousness that rejects the idealism of the total Hegelian conception should nonetheless not fall back behind this insight. Anybody who goes as far as I do in the critique of *common sense** must fulfill the simple requirement of having *common sense**. He should not claim to transcend something whose discipline he himself is unable to satisfy. It was only in America that I truly experienced for the first time the importance of what is called empiria, though from youth onward I was guided by the awareness that fruitful theoretical knowledge is impossible except in the closest contact with its materials. Conversely I had to recognize in the form empiricism took when translated into scientific praxis that the full unregulated scope of experience is more constricted by the empiricist ground rules than it is in the concept of experience itself. It would not be the most erroneous characterization to say that what I have in mind after all that is a kind a restitution of experience against its empiricist deformation. That was not the least important reason for returning to Germany, along with the possibility of pursuing my own interests in Europe without hindrance for the moment and of contributing something toward political enlightenment. But this did not in the least alter my gratitude, also my intellectual gratitude, nor do I believe that I ever will neglect as a scholar what I learned in and from America.

Dialectical Epilegomena

On Subject and Object

1

To lead in with reflections about subject and object raises the difficulty of stating what exactly the topic of discussion should be. The terms are patently equivocal. Thus "subject" can refer to the particular individual as well as to universal attributes of "consciousness in general," in the language of Kant's *Prolegomena*.[1] The equivocation cannot be removed simply through terminological clarification. For both meanings have reciprocal need of each other: one can hardly be comprehended without the other. No concept of the subject can have the element of individual humanity—what Schelling called "egoity"[2]—separated from it in thought; without any reference to it, subject would lose all significance. Conversely, the particular human individual, as soon as one reflects upon it under the guise of the universality of its concept, which does not signify merely some particular being *hic et nunc*, is already transformed into a universal, similar to what was expressed in the idealist concept of the subject; even the expression "particular person" requires the concept of species simply in order to be meaningful. The relation to that universal still inheres implicitly in proper names. They designate someone who has such and such a name and no other; and "someone" stands elliptically for "a person." On the other hand, if one wanted to escape complications of this kind by trying to define the two terms, then one would fall into an

aporia that attends the problematic of definition in modern philosophy
since Kant. The concepts of subject and object, or rather what they refer
to, have in a certain way priority over all definition. Defining means as
much as subjectively, by means of a rigidly applied concept, capturing
something objective, no matter what it may be in itself. Hence the resistance of subject and object to the act of defining. The determination of
their meanings requires reflection on the very thing the act of defining
truncates for the sake of conceptual manageability. Therefore it is advisable to start by taking up the words "subject" and "object" such as they
are handed down by the well-honed philosophical language, as a historical sediment; not, of course, sticking to such conventionalism but continuing further with a critical analysis. One could begin with the allegedly
naive, though already mediated, view that a knowing subject, whatever
kind it may be, stands confronting an object of knowledge, whatever kind
it may be. The reflection, which in philosophical terminology goes by the
name of *intentio obliqua*, is then a relating from that ambiguous concept
of object back to a no less ambiguous concept of subject. A second reflection reflects the first, more closely determining the vagueness for the
sake of the contents of the concepts of subject and object.

2

The separation of subject and object is both real and semblance. True,
because in the realm of cognition it lends expression to the real separation, the rivenness of the human condition, the result of a coercive historical process; untrue, because the historical separation must not be
hypostatized, not magically transformed into an invariant. This contradiction in the separation of subject and object is imparted to epistemology. Although as separated they cannot be thought away, the ψεῦδος of
the separation is manifested in their being mutually mediated, object by
subject, and even more and differently, subject by object. As soon as it is
fixed without mediation, the separation becomes ideology, its normal
form. Mind then arrogates to itself the status of being absolutely independent—which it is not: mind's claim to independence announces its
claim to domination. Once radically separated from the object, subject
reduces the object to itself; subject swallows object, forgetting how much
it is object itself. The image of a temporal or extratemporal original
state of blissful identity between subject and object is romantic, however:
at times a wishful projection, today just a lie. Before the subject constituted itself, undifferentiatedness was the terror of the blind nexus of
nature, was myth; it was in their protest against this myth that the great
religions had their truth content. After all, undifferentiatedness is not

unity, for the latter requires, even according to Platonic dialectic, diverse entities of which it is the unity. For those who experience it, the new horror of separation transfigures the old horror of chaos, and both are eternal sameness. The fear of gaping meaninglessness made one forget a fear that once was no less compelling: that of the vengeful gods Epicurean materialism and the Christian "fear not" wanted to spare mankind. This cannot be accomplished except through the subject. Were it liquidated instead of sublated into a higher form, the result would be not merely a regression of consciousness but a regression to real barbarism. Fate, the complicity of myth with nature, comes from the total political immaturity of society, from an age in which self-reflection had not yet opened its eyes, in which subject did not yet exist. Instead of conjuring the return of this age through collective praxis, the captivating spell of the old undifferentiatedness should be obliterated. Its prolongation is mind's identity-consciousness, which repressively makes its Other like itself. Were speculation concerning the state of reconciliation allowed, then it would be impossible to conceive that state as either the undifferentiated unity of subject and object or their hostile antithesis: rather it would be the communication of what is differentiated. Only then would the concept of communication, as an objective concept, come into its own. The present concept is so shameful because it betrays what is best—the potential for agreement between human beings and things—to the idea of imparting information between subjects according to the exigencies of subjective reason. In its proper place, even epistemologically, the relationship of subject and object would lie in a peace achieved between human beings as well as between them and their Other. Peace is the state of differentiation without domination, with the differentiated participating in each other.

3

In epistemology, 'subject' is usually understood to mean the transcendental subject. According to idealist doctrine, it either constructs the objective world out of an undifferentiated material as in Kant or, since Fichte, it engenders the world itself. The critique of idealism was not the first to discover that this transcendental subject, which constitutes all content of experience, is in turn abstracted from living individual human beings. It is evident that the abstract concept of the transcendental subject, that is, the forms of thought, their unity, and the originary productivity of consciousness, presupposes precisely what it promises to establish: actual, living individuals. The idealist philosophies were aware of this point. Indeed, Kant tried to develop a fundamental, constitutive, and hierarchic distinction between the transcendental and the empirical subject in his chapter on the psychological paralogisms.[3] His successors, however, particularly Fichte and Hegel, but also Schopenhauer, with subtle lines of argumentation endeavored to deal with the unavoidable problem of circularity. Frequently they returned to the Aristotelian motive that what comes first for consciousness—here, the empirical subject—is not the First in itself, and that it postulates the transcendental subject as its condition or origin. Even Husserl's polemic against psychologism, replete with the distinction between genesis and validity, continues this mode of argumentation.[4] It is apologetic. The conditioned is to be justified as unconditioned, the derivative as primary. Here a topos of the entire Western tradition is repeated, which holds that only the First or, as Nietzsche critically formulated it, only something that has not evolved, can be true.[5] The ideological function of the thesis cannot be overlooked. The more individuals are in effect degraded into functions within the societal totality as they are connected up to the system, the more the person pure and simple, as a principle, is consoled and exalted with the attributes of creative power, absolute rule, and spirit.

Nonetheless the question of the reality of the transcendental subject weighs heavier than it appears in its sublimation as pure spirit and, above all, in the critical revocation of idealism. In a certain sense, although idealism would be the last to admit it, the transcendental subject is more real, that is, it far more determines the real conduct of people and society than do those psychological individuals from whom the transcendental subject was abstracted and who have little to say in the world; for their part they have turned into appendages of the social machinery, ultimately into ideology. The living individual person, such as he is constrained to act and for which he was even internally molded, is as *homo oeconomicus* incarnate closer to the transcendental subject than the living individual he must immediately take himself to be. To this extent idealist theory was realistic and need not feel embarrassed when reproached for idealism by its opponents. The doctrine of the transcendental subject faithfully discloses the precedence of the abstract, rational relations that are abstracted from individuals and their conditions and for which exchange is the model. If the standard structure of society is the exchange form, its rationality constitutes people: what they are for themselves, what they think they are, is secondary. They are deformed at the outset by the mechanism that was then philosophically transfigured into the transcendental. What is supposedly most obvious, the empirical subject, would actually have to be considered as something not yet existing; from this aspect the transcendental subject is "constitutive." Allegedly the origin of all concrete objects, in its rigid timelessness it is concretely objectified, fully in keeping with the Kantian doctrine of the stable and immutable forms of transcendental consciousness. Its solidity and invariance, which according to transcendental philosophy engenders objects or at least prescribes their regularity, is the reflective form of the reification of human beings that has objectively occurred in the conditions of society. The fetish character, societally necessary semblance, historically has become the *prius* of what according to its concept would have to be the *posterius*. The philosophical problem of constitution has been inverted into its mirror image; yet in its inversion it expresses the truth about the historic stage that has been attained; a truth, to be sure, that a second Copernican turn might theoretically negate. It certainly also has its positive moment: that the antecedent society keeps itself and its members alive. The particular individual owes the possibility of his existence to the universal; proof of this is thought, which is itself a universal and to that extent a societal relation. Thought is given priority over the individual not only fetishistically. But idealism hypostatizes only one side, which is incomprehensible except in relation to the other. Yet the given, the *skandalon* of idealism it can, however, not remove, demonstrates again and again the failure of that hypostasis.

4

The insight into the primacy of the object does not restore the old *intentio recta*, the slavish confidence in the external world existing precisely as it appears this side of critique, an anthropological state devoid of the self-consciousness that first crystallizes in the context of the relationship leading from knowledge back to the knower. The crude confrontation of subject and object in naive realism is of course historically necessitated and cannot be dismissed by an act of will. But at the same time it is a product of false abstraction, already a piece of reification. Once this is seen through, then a consciousness objectified to itself, and precisely as such directed outward, virtually striking outward, could no longer be dragged along without self-reflection. The turn to the subject, though from the outset intent on its primacy, does not simply disappear with its revision; this revision occurs not least of all in the subjective interest in freedom. The primacy of the object means rather that subject for its part is object in a qualitatively different, more radical sense than object, because object cannot be known except through consciousness, hence is also subject. What is known through consciousness must be a something; mediation applies to something mediated. But subject, the epitome of mediation, is the 'How', and never, as contrasted to the object, the 'What' that is postulated by every conceivable idea for a concept of subject. Potentially, though not actually, objectivity can be conceived without a subject; but not likewise object without subjectivity. No matter how subject is defined, the existent being cannot be conjured away from it. If subject is not something, and "something" designates an irreducibly objective element, then it is nothing at all; even as *actus purus* it needs to refer to something that acts. The primacy of the object is the *intentio obliqua* of the *intentio obliqua*, not the warmed-over *intentio recta*; the corrective to the subjective reduction, not the denial of a subjective share. Object is also mediated; but, according to its own concept, it is not so thoroughly dependent upon subject as subject is dependent upon objectivity. Idealism ignored such a difference and thereby coarsened an intellectualization that functions as a disguise for abstraction. But this occasions a revision of the prevailing position toward the subject in traditional theory, which exalts the subject in ideology and defames it in epistemological praxis. If one wants to attain the object, however, then its subjective determinations or qualities are not to be eliminated: precisely that would be contrary to the primacy of the object. If subject has a core of object, then the subjective qualities in the object are all the more an objective moment. For object becomes something at all only through being determinate. In the determinations that seem merely to be affixed to it by the subject, the subject's own objectivity comes to the fore: they are all borrowed from the objectivity of the *intentio recta*. Even according to idealist doctrine the subjective determinations are not merely an afterthought; they are also always required by what is to be determined, and in this the primacy of the object asserts itself. Conversely, the supposedly pure object, free of any added thought or intuition, is the very reflection of abstract subjectivity: only it makes the Other like itself through abstraction. Unlike the indeterminate substrate of reductionism, the object of undiminished experience is more objective than that substrate. The qualities the traditional critique of epistemology eradicated from the object and credited to the subject are due in subjective experience to the primacy of the object; the reign of *intentio obliqua* deceived about this. Its legacy devolved upon a critique of experience that attained its own historical, and finally societal, conditionedness. For society is immanent to experience, not an ἄλλο γένος. Only the societal self-reflection of knowledge obtains that epistemological objectivity that escapes knowledge so long as it obeys the societal coercions at work in it and does not think through them. Critique of society is critique of knowledge, and vice versa.

5

The primacy of the object can be discussed legitimately only when that primacy—over the subject in the broadest sense of the term—is somehow determinable, that is, more than the Kantian thing-in-itself as the unknown cause of phenomenal appearance.[6] Despite Kant, to be sure, even the thing-in-itself bears a minimum of determinations simply by being distinguished from what is predicated by the categories; one such determination, of a negative kind, would be that of acausality. It is sufficient to establish an antithesis to the conventional view that agrees with subjectivism. The primacy of the object proves itself in that it qualitatively alters the opinions of reified consciousness that are smoothly consistent with subjectivism. Subjectivism does not affect naive realism at the level of content but rather simply attempts to provide formal criteria for its validity, as confirmed by the Kantian formula of empirical realism. One argument for the primacy of the object is indeed incompatible with Kant's doctrine of constitution: that in the modern natural sciences *ratio* peers over the wall it itself erects, that it snatches a snippet of what does not agree with its own ingrained categories. Such an expansion of *ratio* unsettles subjectivism. But what determines the antecedent object, as distinct from its being trussed up by the subject, can be grasped in what for its part determines the categorial apparatus by which the object is determined according to the subjectivist schema, namely in the conditionedness of what conditions the object. The categorial determinations, which according to Kant first bring about objectivity, are themselves something posited and thus, as it were, really are "merely subjective." The *reductio ad hominem* thus becomes the collapse of anthropocentrism. The fact that man as a *constituens* is in turn man-made disenchants the creationism of mind. But because the primacy of the object requires both reflection upon the subject and subjective reflection, subjectivity—differently than in the primitive materialism that actually does not permit dialectics—becomes a moment that is held fast.

6

Since the Copernican turn what goes by the name of phenomenalism—that nothing is known unless it goes through the knowing subject—has joined with the cult of the mind. Insight into the primacy of the object revolutionizes both of these views. What Hegel intended to maintain within subjective brackets has the critical consequence of shattering them. The general assurance that innervations, insights, cognitions are "only subjective" no longer helps as soon as subjectivity is seen through as a form of object. Semblance is the magical transformation of the subject into the ground of its own determination, its positing as true being. Subject itself must be brought to its objectivity, its stirrings must not be banished from cognition. But phenomenalism's semblance is a necessary one. It attests to the virtually irresistible nexus of deception that subject as false consciousness produces and likewise belongs to. The ideology of the subject is founded in such irresistibility. The consciousness of a defect—the awareness of the limits of cognition—becomes a merit, so as to make the defect more bearable. Collective narcissism was at work. But it could not have prevailed with such stringency, could not have brought forth the most powerful philosophies, if a truth, though distorted, did not underlie it. What transcendental philosophy praised in creative subjectivity is the subject's own self-concealed imprisonment within itself. The subject remains harnessed within everything objective it thinks, like an armored animal in its layers of carapace it vainly tries to shake loose; yet it never occurred to those animals to vaunt their captivity as freedom. It would be well to ask why human beings did so. Their mental captivity is exceedingly real. Their dependence as cognitive subjects upon space, time, and forms of thought marks their dependence on the species. The species finds its expression in these constituents, which are no less valid for that reason. The a priori and society interpenetrate. The universality and necessity of those forms, their Kantian fame, is none other than what unites human beings. They needed this unity for *survival**. Captivity was internalized: the individual is no less imprisoned within himself than he is within the universal, within society. Hence the interest in reinterpreting the captivity as freedom. The categorial captivity of individual consciousness repeats the real captivity of each individual. Even the view of consciousness that allows it to see through that captivity is determined by the forms it has implanted in the individual. Their individual self-captivity might make people cognizant of their societal captivity: the prevention of this was and remains a capital interest for the continuation of the status quo. For the sake of the status quo philosophy had to overstep its bounds, with hardly less necessity than that of the forms themselves. Idealism was this ideological even before it set about glorifying the world as absolute Idea. The original compensation already includes the presumption that reality, exalted into a product of the putatively free subject, in turn vindicates itself as free.

7

Identity thinking, screen-image of the dominant dichotomy, in the age of subjective impotence no longer poses as the absolutization of the subject. Instead what is taking shape is a type of seemingly anti-subjectivist, scientifically objective identity thinking, what is called reductionism; the early Russell was called a neorealist. It is the characteristic form of reified consciousness at present, false because of its latent and therefore all the more fatal subjectivism. The remainder is molded according to the standard of subjective reason's ordering principles and, being abstract itself, agrees with the abstractness of that reason. Reified consciousness, which mistakenly takes itself for nature, is naive: a historical formation and itself mediated through and through, it takes itself, to speak with Husserl, for an "ontological sphere of absolute origins" and takes the thing confronting it, which it itself has trussed up, for the coveted matter itself.[7] The ideal of depersonalizing knowledge for the sake of objectivity retains nothing but the *caput mortuum* of objectivity. If the dialectical primacy of the object is acknowledged, then the hypothesis of an unreflected practical science of the object as a residual determination after the subject has been subtracted away collapses. Subject is then no longer a subtractible addendum to objectivity. With the removal of one of its essential moments objectivity is falsified, not purified. The notion that guides the residual concept of objectivity has, then, its archetype in something posited and man-made: by no means in the idea of the in-itself, for which it substitutes the purified object. Rather it is the model of the profit that remains on the balance sheet after all production costs have been deducted. Profit, however, is subjective interest limited and reduced to the form of calculation. What counts for the sober matter-of-factness of profit thinking is anything but the matter:[8] it disappears into the return it yields. Cognition, however, must be guided by what exchange has not maimed or—since there is nothing left unmaimed anymore—by what is concealed within the exchange processes. Object is no more a subjectless residuum than it is posited by subject. The two conflicting determinations fit together: the residue, which science settles for as its truth, is a product of its manipulative procedures that are subjectively organized. To define what object is would in turn be itself part of that organization. Objectivity can be made out solely by reflecting, at every historical and cognitive stage, both upon what at that time is presented as subject and object as well as upon their mediations. To this extent object is in fact "infinitely given as a task," as neo-Kantianism taught.[9] At times subject, as unrestricted experience, will come closer to object than the residuum filtered and curtailed to suit the requirements of subjective reason. According to its present, and polemical, status in the philosophy of history, unreduced subjectivity is capable of functioning more objectively than objectivistic reductions. Not the least way all cognition is bewitched and spellbound is that the traditional epistemological theses have turned their subject matter upside down: *fair is foul, and foul is fair**. The objective contents of individual experience are produced not through the method of comparative generalization, but rather through the dissolution of what prevents that experience—as itself biased—from giving itself to the object without reservation, as Hegel said, with the freedom that would relax the cognitive subject until it truly fades into the object with which it is akin by virtue of its own objective being.[10] The key position of the subject in cognition is experience, not form; what for Kant is formation is essentially deformation. The exertion of cognition is predominantly the destruction of its usual exertion, of its using violence against the object. Knowledge of the object is brought closer by the act of the subject rending the veil it weaves about the object. It can do this only when, passive, without anxiety, it entrusts itself to its own experience. In the places where subjective reason senses subjective contingency, the primacy of the object shimmers through: that in the object which is not a subjective addition. Subject is the agent, not the constituent, of object; this has consequences for the relation between theory and practice as well.

8

Even after the second reflection of the Copernican turn, there still remains some truth to Kant's most contestable thesis: the distinction between the transcendental thing-in-itself and the constituted, concretely objective thing. For then object would finally be the nonidentical, liberated from the subjective spell and comprehensible through its own self-critique—if object is there at all and not rather what Kant outlined with the concept of idea.[11] Such nonidentity would quite closely approach the Kantian thing-in-itself, although he insisted on the vanishing point of its coincidence with subject. It would be no relic of a disenchanted *mundus intelligibilis*; rather it would be more real than the *mundus sensibilis* to the extent that Kant's Copernican turn abstracts from that nonidentity and therein finds its limit. Yet according to Kant, object is something "posited" by the subject, the weave of forms cast by the subject over the Something devoid of qualities,[12] finally the law that unites the appearances, which are disintegrated by their relation back to subject, into a concrete object. The attributes of necessity and universality Kant attaches to the emphatic concept of law possess thing-like solidity and are impenetrable just like the societal world the living collide with. That law, which according to Kant the subject prescribes to nature, the highest elevation of objectivity in his conception, is the perfect expression of subject as well as of its self-alienation: at the height of its formative pretension, the subject passes itself off as object. But nonetheless this again is paradoxically correct: in fact, subject is also object; it merely forgets, as it becomes autonomous form, how and by what it itself is constituted. Kant's Copernican turn precisely expresses the objectification of the subject, the reality of reification. Its truth content is by no means an ontological one but, on the contrary, the historically amassed block between subject and object. The subject erects that block when it claims supremacy over the object and thereby defrauds itself of it. As in truth nonidentical, the object distances itself farther from the subject the more the subject "constitutes" the object. The block against which the Kantian philosophy pounds its head is at the same time a product of that philosophy. Subject as pure spontaneity, originary apperception, apparently the absolutely dynamic principle is, however, by virtue of its chorismos from any material no less reified than the world of things constituted by the model of natural science. For through the chorismos the asserted absolute spontaneity is, in itself, though not for Kant, shut down; it is a form that is supposed to be the form of something, whereas by its own constitution it cannot enter into interaction with any Something. Its stark separation from the activity of individual subjects, where that activity must be devalued as being contingent and psychological, destroys the originary apperception, Kant's inmost principle. His apriorism deprives pure action of precisely the temporality without which absolutely nothing can be understood as "dynamic." Action recoils into a being of the second order; explicitly, as everyone knows, in the later Fichte's rejection of his own 1794 *Wissenschaftslehre*.[13] Kant codifies such objective ambiguity in the concept of object, and no theorem about the object should ignore this. Strictly speaking, primacy of the object would mean that there is no object understood as something abstractly opposed to the subject but that it necessarily appears as that; the necessity of this semblance should be removed.[14]

9

Just as little, to be sure, "is there" actually subject. Its hypostasis in idealism leads to absurdities. They may be summarized by saying that the definition of subject involves that against which it is posited; and by no means simply because as a *constituens* it presupposes the *constitutum*. Subject is itself object to the extent that the "there is," which the idealist doctrine of constitution implies—there has to be subject so that it can constitute something—in its turn was borrowed from the sphere of facticity. The concept of what there is means nothing other than the concept of what exists, and as existent subject falls at once under the heading of object. But as pure apperception subject should be the absolutely Other of all existents. Even here some truth appears in its negative guise: that the reification the sovereign subject has inflicted on everything, includ-

ing itself, is semblance. It transposes into the abyss of itself what would
be beyond reach of reification; with the absurd consequence, of course,
that it thereby licenses all other reification. Idealism takes the idea of the
correct life and wrongly projects it inward. The subject as productive
imagination, pure apperception, ultimately as free action,[15] enciphers
that activity in which the life of people actually reproduces itself, and
with good reason anticipates in it freedom. That is the reason why subject
will hardly simply vanish into object or into anything else allegedly
higher, into Being however it may be hypostatized.[16] Subject in its self-
positing is semblance and at the same time something historically
exceedingly real. It contains the potential for the sublation of its own
domination.

10

The difference between subject and object slices through subject as well
as through object. It can no more be absolutized than it can be removed
from thought. Actually everything that is in the subject can be attributed
to the object; whatever in it is not object semantically bursts open the
"is." The pure subjective form of traditional epistemology, according to
its own concept, is always only a form of something objective, never
without that objectivity, indeed not even thinkable without it. The solidity of the epistemological ego, the identity of self-consciousness, is obviously modeled after the unreflected experience of the enduring, identical
object; even Kant fundamentally relies on this. He could not have claimed
that the subjective forms are conditions of objectivity if he had not tacitly
granted them an objectivity borrowed from the one to which he contrasts
the subject. However, at the extreme where subjectivity contracts, from
the single point of its synthetic unity, what is taken together is always
only what in itself belongs together anyway. Otherwise synthesis would
be mere arbitrary classification. Of course, without the subjective act of
synthesis such a belonging together is just as inconceivable. Even the
subjective a priori can be claimed to have objective validity only in so far
as it has an objective side; without it the object constituted by the a priori
would be a pure tautology for subject. Finally, by virtue of its being indis-
soluble, given, and extraneous to the subject, its contents, what Kant calls
the matter of cognition, is likewise something objective in the subject.[17]
Accordingly, it is easy to think of the subject as nothing and of the object
as absolute, a tendency not far from Hegel's thoughts. But this is once
again transcendental illusion. Subject is reduced to nothing through its
hypostasis, making something out of no thing.[18] The hypostasis defaults
because it cannot satisfy the innermost, naive-realistic criterion of exis-

tence. The idealist construction of the subject founders on its falsely taking subject to be objective in the sense of something existing in-itself, precisely what it is not: measured against the standard of entities, the subject is condemned to nothingness. Subject is all the more the less it is, and all the less the more it believes itself to exist, to be for itself something objective. As an essential moment, however, it is ineradicable. Upon the elimination of the subjective moment the object would come apart diffusely like the fleeting stirrings and twinklings of subjective life.

11

Object, though attenuated, also is not without subject. If object itself lacked subject as a moment, then its objectivity would become nonsense. This is flagrantly obvious in the weakness of Hume's epistemology. It was subjectively oriented while still believing it could dispense with the subject.[19] Therefore it is necessary to judge the relationship between individual and transcendental subject. The individual subject, as has been stated since Kant in countless variations, is an integral component of the empirical world. Its function, however, its capacity for experience— which the transcendental subject lacks, for no purely logical entity could have any sort of experience—is in truth much more constitutive than the role idealism ascribed to the transcendental subject, which is itself a profoundly, precritically hypostatized abstraction of individual consciousness. Nevertheless the concept of the transcendental is a reminder that thinking, by virtue of its own immanent elements of universality, transcends its own inalienable individuation. The antithesis between universal and particular too is necessary as well as deceptive. Neither one can exist without the other, the particular only as determined and thus universal, the universal only as the determination of a particular and thus itself particular. Both of them are and are not. This is one of the strongest motives of a nonidealist dialectics.

12

The subject's reflection upon its own formalism is reflection upon society, with the paradox that, following the intention of the later Durkheim, on the one hand the formative constituents originate in society, while on the other hand, as current epistemology can boast, they are objectively valid; in Durkheim's arguments they are already presupposed in every proposition that demonstrates their conditionedness.[20] This paradox may well be one with the subject's objective captivity within itself. The cognitive function, without which there would be neither difference nor unity of the subject, for its part has arisen historically. It consists essentially in those formative constituents; to the extent that there is cognition, it must take place in accordance with them, even where it looks beyond them. They define the concept of cognition. Yet those formative constituents are not absolute but rather a historical development like the cognitive function itself. It is not beyond the pale of possibility that they could disappear. To predicate their absoluteness would posit the cognitive function, the subject, as absolute; to relativize them would dogmatically revoke the cognitive function. To counter this it is claimed that the argument involves a silly sociologism: that God created society and society created man and God in man's image. But the anteriority thesis is absurd only so long as the individual or its biological prototype is hypostatized. In view of evolutionary history it is more likely to assume the temporal *prius*, or at least the simultaneous copresence of the species. That "the" human being was there before the species is either a Biblical echo or sheer Platonism. Nature at its lower stages is full of nonindividuated organisms. If, as more recent biologists maintain, human beings in fact are born so much more ill-equipped than other creatures, then they probably could have survived only in association, through rudimentary social labor; the *principium individuationis* is secondary to that, hypothetically a kind of biological division of labor. It is improbable that some single human first emerged, archetypically. The belief in such an emergence mythically projects the *principium individuationis*, now historically fully developed, backward into the past or onto the celestial realm of eternal ideas. The species may have individuated itself through mutation, in order then, through individuation, to reproduce itself in individuals by relying on biological singularity. The human being is a result, not an εἶδος; the insights of Hegel and Marx penetrate all the way into the inmost aspects of the so-called questions of constitution. The ontology of "the" human being—the model for the construction of the transcendental subject—is centered on the developed individual, as is indicated linguistically by the ambiguity in the article "the," which names the species as well as the individual.[21] To this extent nominalism, much more than its opponent, ontology, includes the primacy of the species, of society. To be sure, ontology makes common cause with nominalism by at once denying the species, perhaps because it suggests animals: ontology, by exalting the individual into the form of unity and into a being-in-itself as opposed to the many; nominalism, by unreflectedly proclaiming the individual, on the model of the human individual, to be the true entity. It denies society in its concepts by degrading it into an abbreviation for the individual.

Marginalia to Theory and Praxis

For Ulrich Sonnemann

1

A simple consideration of history demonstrates just how much the question of theory and praxis depends upon the question of subject and object. At the same time as the Cartesian doctrine of two substances ratified the dichotomy of subject and object, literature for the first time portrayed praxis as a dubious undertaking on account of its tension with reflection. Despite all its eager realism, pure practical reason is devoid of object to the same degree that the world for manufacturing and industry becomes material devoid of quality and ready for processing, which in turn finds its legitimation nowhere else but in the marketplace. Whereas praxis promises to lead people out of their self-isolation, praxis itself has always been isolated; for this reason practical people are unresponsive and the relation of praxis to its object is a priori undermined. Indeed, one could ask whether in its indifference toward its object all nature-dominating praxis up to the present day is not in fact praxis in name only. Its illusory character is inherited by all the actions unreflectedly adopting the old violent gesture of praxis. Since its beginnings American pragmatism has been criticized—with good reason—for consecrating the existing conditions by making the practical applicability of knowledge its criterion for knowledge; supposedly nowhere else could the practical effectiveness of knowledge be tested. If in the end theory, which bears upon the totality if it does not want to be futile, is tied down to its effectiveness here and now, then the same thing befalls it despite its belief that it escapes the immanence of the system. Theory steals itself back from the system's immanence only where it shirks its pragmatic fetters, no matter how modified they may be. "All theory is gray," Goethe has Mephistopheles preach to the student he is leading around by the nose; the sentence was already ideology from the very beginning, fraud about the fact that the tree of life the practicians planted and the devil in the same breath compares to gold is hardly green at all;[1] the grayness of theory is for its part a function of the life that has been de-qualified.[2] Nothing should exist that cannot be fastened upon by both hands; not thought. The subject, thrown back upon itself, divided from its Other by an abyss, is supposedly incapable of action. *Hamlet* is as much the proto-history of the individual in its subjective reflection as it is the drama of the individual paralyzed into inaction by that reflection. In his process of self-externalization toward what differs from him, the individual senses this discrepancy and is inhibited from completing the process. Only a little later the novel describes how the individual reacts to this situation incorrectly termed 'alienation'—as though the age before individualism enjoyed an intimacy, which nonetheless can hardly be experienced other than by individuated beings: according to Borchardt animals are "lonely communities"—with pseudo-activity.[3] The follies of Don Quixote are the attempts at compensation for the lost Other, in the language of psychiatry, restitution phenomena.[4] What since then has been called the problem of praxis and today culminates in the question of the relation between theory and praxis coincides with the loss of experience caused by the rationality of the eternally same. Where experience is blocked or altogether absent, praxis is damaged and therefore longed for, distorted, and desperately overvalued. Thus what is called the problem of praxis is interwoven with the problem of knowledge. Abstract subjectivity, in which the process of rationalization terminates, strictly speaking can do just as little as the transcendental subject can conceivably have precisely what it is attested to have: spontaneity.[5] Ever since the Cartesian doctrine of the indubitable certainty of the subject—and the philosophy it described codified a historical culmination, a constellation of subject and object in which, following the ancient topos, only unlike can recognize unlike—praxis accrues a somewhat illusory character, as though it could not close the gap. Words like "industriousness" and "busyness" express the nuances quite succinctly.[6] The illusory realities of many mass movements of the twentieth century, which became the bloodiest reality and yet are overshadowed by something not completely real, delusional, were born in the moment when action was first called for. Whereas thinking restricts itself to subjective, practically applicable reason, the Other that escapes it is correlatively ascribed to an increasingly conceptless praxis that acknowledges no measure other than itself. As antinomian as the society undergirding it, the bourgeois spirit unifies autonomy and a pragmatistic hostility toward theory. The world, which subjective reason increasingly tends to reproduce only retrospectively, should continually be changed in keeping with its economically expansive tendencies and nonetheless should still remain what it is. Whatever disturbs this is cropped from thinking: especially theory that intends more than reproduction. A consciousness of theory and praxis must be produced that neither divides the two such that theory becomes powerless and praxis becomes arbitrary, nor refracts theory through the archbourgeois primacy of practical reason proclaimed by Kant and Fichte. Thinking is a doing, theory a form of praxis; already the ideology of the purity of thinking deceives about this. Thinking has a double character: it is immanently determined and rigorous, and yet an inalienably real mode of behavior in the midst of reality. To the extent that subject, the thinking substance of philosophers, is object, to the extent that it falls within object, subject is already also practical. The irrationality of praxis that continually resurfaces however—its aesthetic archetype are the sudden, random actions by which Hamlet carries out his plan and in carrying it out fails—unceasingly animates the illusion of the absolute division between subject and object. Where subject is inveigled into believing that object is something absolutely incommensurable, the communication between the two becomes the prey of blind fate.

2

It would be too coarse a generalization were one, for the sake of a historico-philosophical construction, to date the divergence between theory and praxis as late as the Renaissance. But the divergence was first reflected upon only after the collapse of that *ordo* that presumed to allocate the truth as well as good works their place in the hierarchy. The crisis of praxis was experienced as: not knowing what should be done. Together with the medieval hierarchy, which was connected to an elaborate casuistry, the practical guidelines disintegrated, which at that time, despite all their dubiousness, seemed at least to be suitable to the social structure. The much attacked formalism of Kantian ethical theory was the culmination of a movement that began irresistibly, and through legitimate critique, with the emancipation of autonomous reason. The inability to engage in praxis was first and foremost the consciousness of a lack of regulative principles, a weakness from the very beginning; from this weakness comes the hesitation, akin to reason in the guise of contemplation, and the inhibition of praxis. The formal character of pure practical reason constituted its failure before praxis; to be sure it also occasioned the self-reflection that leads beyond the culpable concept of praxis. If autarkic praxis has always manifested manic and compulsive traits, then self-reflection on the other hand signifies the interruption of action blindly directed outward; non-naiveté as the transition to the humane. Whoever does not want to romanticize the Middle Ages must trace the divergence between theory and praxis back to the oldest division between physical and intellectual labor, probably as far back as prehistoric obscurity. Praxis arose from labor. It attained its concept when labor no longer wanted to merely reproduce life directly but to produce its conditions: and this clashed with the already existing conditions. Its descent from labor is a heavy burden for all praxis. To this day it carries the baggage of an element of unfreedom: the fact that once it was necessary to struggle against the pleasure principle for the sake of one's own self-preservation, although labor that has been reduced to a minimum no longer needs to be tied to self-denial. Contemporary actionism also represses the fact that the longing for freedom is closely related to the aversion to praxis. Praxis was the reaction to deprivation; this still disfigures praxis even when it wants to do away with deprivation. To this extent art is the critique of praxis as unfreedom; this is where its truth begins. With a shock one can understand the abhorrence at the praxis so popular nowadays when one observes natural-historical phenomena such as beaver dams, the industriousness of ants and bees, or the grotesque struggles of the beetle as it carries a blade of grass. Modern and ancient intertwine in praxis; once again praxis becomes a sacred animal, just as in the time before recorded history it was thought a sacrilege not to devote oneself body and soul to the efforts of preserving the species. The physiognomy of praxis is brute earnestness. This earnestness dissolves where the genius of praxis emancipates itself: this is surely what Schiller meant with his theory of play.[7] The majority of actionists are humorless in a way that is no less alarming than are those who laugh along with everyone. The lack of self-reflection derives not only from their psychology. It is the mark of a praxis that, having become its own fetish, becomes a barricade to its own goal. The dialectic is hopeless: that through praxis alone is it possible to escape the captivating spell praxis imposes on people, but that meanwhile as praxis it compulsively contributes to reinforcing the spell, obtuse, narrow-minded, at the farthest remove from spirit. The recent hostility toward theory, which animates this process, makes a program out of it. But the practical goal, which includes the liberation from all narrow-mindedness, is not indifferent to the means intended to achieve it; otherwise this dialectic would degenerate into vulgar Jesuitism. The idiotic parliamentarian in Doré's caricature who boasts, "Gentlemen, I am above all practical," reveals himself as a scoundrel who cannot see beyond the immediate tasks and moreover is proud of it; his behavior denounces the very spirit of praxis as a demon.[8] Theory speaks for what is not narrow-minded. Despite all of its unfreedom, theory is the guarantor of freedom in the midst of unfreedom.

3

Today once again the antithesis between theory and praxis is being misused to denounce theory. When a student's room was smashed because he preferred to work rather than join in actions, on the wall was scrawled: "Whoever occupies himself with theory, without acting practically, is a traitor[a] to socialism." It is not only against him that praxis serves as an ideological pretext for exercising moral constraint. The thinking denigrated by actionists apparently demands of them too much undue effort: it requires too much work, is too practical. Whoever thinks, offers resistance; it is more comfortable to swim with the current, even when one declares oneself to be against the current. Moreover, by giving way to a regressive and distorted form of the pleasure principle, making things easier for oneself, letting oneself go, one can hope for a moral premium from those who are like-minded. In a crude reversal, the collective substitute superego demands what the old superego disapproved of: the very cession of oneself qualifies the willing adept as a better person. Even in Kant emphatic praxis was goodwill; but this signified as much as autonomous reason.[9] A concept of praxis that would not be narrow-minded can be applied only to politics, to the conditions of society that largely condemn the praxis of each individual to irrelevance. This is the locus of the difference between Kantian ethics and the views of Hegel who, as Kierkegaard also saw, no longer accepts the traditional under-

---

[a] The concept of the traitor comes from the eternal reserves of collective repression, whatever its coloration may be. The law of conspiratorial communities is irrevocability; for this reason conspirators enjoy warming up the mythical concept of the oath. Whoever thinks differently is not only excluded but exposed to the most severe moral sanctions. The concept of morality demands autonomy, which is, however, not tolerated by those who always have morality on the tip of their tongue. In truth it is the one who sins against his own autonomy who deserves to be called a traitor.

standing of ethics. Kant's writings on moral philosophy, in their conformity to the state of enlightenment in the eighteenth century and despite their anti-psychologism and all their endeavors to attain an absolutely conclusive and comprehensive validity, were individualistic to the extent that they addressed themselves to the individual as the substrate of correct—that is, for Kant, radically reasonable—action. All of Kant's examples come from the private and the business spheres; and this conditions the concept of an ethics based on dispositions, whose subject must be the individuated singular person. What comes to expression for the first time in Hegel is the experience that the behavior of the individual—even if he has a pure will—does not come near to a reality that prescribes and limits the conditions of any individual's action. Hegel in effect dissolves the concept of the moral by extending it into the political. Since then no unpolitical reflection upon praxis can be valid anymore. However, there should be just as little self-deception about the fact that the political extension of the concept of praxis introduces the repression of the particular by the universal. Humaneness, which does not exist without individuation, is being virtually recanted by the latter's snotty-nosed, casual dismissal. But once the action of the individual, and therefore of all individuals, is made contemptible, then collective action is likewise paralyzed. Spontaneity appears to be trivial at the outset in the face of the factual supremacy of the objective conditions. Kant's moral philosophy and Hegel's philosophy of right represent two dialectical stages of the bourgeois self-consciousness of praxis. Polarized according to the dichotomy of the particular and the universal that tears apart this consciousness, both philosophies are false. Each justifies itself against the other so long as a possible higher form of praxis does not reveal itself in reality; its revelation requires theoretical reflection. It is beyond doubt and controversy that a reasoned analysis of the situation is the precondition for political praxis at least: even in the military sphere, where the crude primacy of action holds sway, the procedure is the same. An analysis of the situation is not tantamount to conformity to that situation. In reflecting upon the situation, analysis emphasizes the aspects that might be able to lead beyond the given constraints of the situation. This is of incalculable relevance for the relationship of theory to praxis. Through its difference from immediate, situation-specific action, i.e., through its autonomization, theory becomes a transformative and practical productive force.[10] If thinking bears on anything of importance, then it initiates a practical impulse, no matter how hidden that impulse may remain to thinking. Those alone think who do not passively accept the already given: from the primitive who contemplates how he can protect his small fire from the rain or where he can find shelter from the storm to the Enlightenment philosopher who construes how humanity can move beyond its self-incurred tutelage by means of its interest in self-preservation.[11] Such motives continue to have an effect, and perhaps all the more so in cases where no practical grounds are immediately articulated. There is no thought, insofar as it is more than the organization of facts and a bit of technique, that does not have its practical telos. Every meditation upon freedom extends into the conception of its possible realization, so long as the meditation is not taken in hand by praxis and tailored to fit the results it enjoins. Just as the division of subject and object cannot be revoked immediately by a decree of thought, so too an immediate unity of theory and praxis is hardly possible: it would imitate the false identity of subject and object and would perpetuate the principle of domination that posits identity and that a true praxis must oppose. The truth content of the discourse about the unity of theory and praxis was bound to historical conditions. On the nodal points and fractures of this historical development reflection and action may ignite; but even then the two are not one.

4

The primacy of the object must be respected by praxis; this was first noted by the idealist Hegel's critique of Kant's ethics of conscience. To the extent that subject is for its part something mediated, praxis rightly understood is what the object wants: praxis follows the object's neediness. But not by the subject adapting itself, which would merely reinforce the heteronomous objectivity. The neediness of the object is mediated via the total societal system; for that reason it can be determined critically only by theory. Praxis without theory, lagging behind the most advanced state of cognition, cannot but fail, and praxis, in keeping with its own concept, would like to succeed. False praxis is no praxis. Desperation that, because it finds the exits blocked, blindly leaps into praxis, with the purest of intentions joins forces with catastrophe. The hostility to theory in the spirit of the times, the by no means coincidental withering away of theory, its banishment by an impatience that wants to change the world without having to interpret it while so far it has been chapter and verse that philosophers have *merely* interpreted—such hostility becomes praxis's weakness.[12] The requirement that theory should kowtow to praxis dissolves theory's truth content and condemns praxis to delusion; in practical terms, it is high time to voice this. A modicum of madness furnishes collective movements—apparently for the time being regardless of their contents—with their sinister power of attraction. Individuals

cope with their own disintegration, with their private paranoia, by integrating themselves into the collective delusion, the collective paranoia, as
Ernst Simmel realized.[13] At the moment it expresses itself first as the
incapacity to accept reflectively within consciousness objective contradictions the subject cannot resolve harmoniously; a unity that is convulsively defended against no aggressor is the screen-image of relentless
self-diremption. This sanctioned delusion exempts one from reality-testing, which necessarily generates unbearable antagonisms within the
weakened consciousness like that of subjective need and objective
refusal. A fawning and malicious servant of the pleasure principle, the
delusional element carries an infectious disease that mortally threatens
the ego by giving it the illusion that it is protected. Fear of this disease
would be the simplest—and therefore likewise repressed—means of self-
preservation: the unflinching refusal to cross the rapidly evaporating
Rubicon that separates reason and delusion. The transition to a praxis
without theory is motivated by the objective impotence of theory and
exponentially increases that impotence through the isolation and
fetishization of the subjective element of historical movement, spontaneity. The deformation of spontaneity should be seen as a reaction to the
administered world. But by frantically closing its eyes to the totality and
by behaving as though it stems immediately from people, spontaneity
falls into line with the objective tendency of progressive dehumanization: even in its practices. Spontaneity, which would be animated by the
neediness of the object, should attach itself to the vulnerable places of
rigidified reality, where the ruptures caused by the pressure of rigidifica-
tion appear externally; it should not thrash about indiscriminately,
abstractly, without any consideration of the contents of what is often
attacked merely for the sake of publicity.

5

If, to make an exception for once, one risks what is called a grand perspective, beyond the historical differences in which the concepts of theory
and praxis have their life, one discovers the infinitely progressive aspect
of the separation of theory and praxis, which was deplored by the
Romantics and denounced in their wake by the Socialists—except for the
mature Marx. Of course, the dispensation of spirit from material labor is
mere semblance since spirit presupposes material labor for its own existence. But that dispensation is not only semblance and serves not only
repression. The separation designates a stage in a process that leads out of
the blind predominance of material praxis, potentially onward to free-

dom. The fact that some live without material labor and, like Nietzsche's Zarathustra, take pleasure in their spirit—that unjust privilege—also indicates that this possibility exists for everyone;[14] all the more so when the technical forces of production are at a stage that makes it possible to foresee the global dispensation from material labor, its reduction to a limiting value. Revoking this separation by fiat is thought to be idealistic and is regressive. Spirit forcibly repatriated with praxis without surplus would be concretism. It would accord with the technocratic-positivistic tendency it believes to be opposing and with which it has more affinity—incidentally also in certain factions—than it dares imagine. Humaneness awakes with the separation of theory and praxis; it knows nothing of that indifferentiation that in truth bows before the primacy of praxis. Animals, similar to people with regressive brain injuries, are familiar only with objects directly related to action: perception, cunning, eating, all submit to the same constraint that weighs even heavier on the subjectless than on subjects. Cunning must have become autonomous in order for individual creatures to acquire that distance from eating whose telos would be the end of the domination in which natural history perpetuates itself. The palliative, benign, delicate, even the conciliatory element of praxis imitates spirit, a product of the separation whose revocation is pursued by an all too unreflected reflection. Desublimation, which in the present age hardly needs explicit recommendation, perpetuates the dark and backward conditions its advocates would like to clarify. The fact that Aristotle placed the dianoetic virtues highest certainly had its ideological side, the resignation of the Hellenistic private citizen, who out of fear must avoid influencing public issues and looks for ways to justify his withdrawal.[15] But his theory of virtue also opens up the horizon of a blissful contemplation; blissful because it would have escaped the exercising and suffering of violence. Aristotle's *Politics* is more humane than Plato's *Republic*, just as a quasi-bourgeois consciousness is more humane than a restaurative one that, in order to impose itself upon a world already enlightened, prototypically becomes totalitarian. The goal of real praxis would be its own abolition.

6

In his celebrated letter to Kugelmann, Marx warned of the threat of a relapse into barbarism, which already must have been foreseeable at that time.[16] Nothing could have better expressed the elective affinity between conservatism and revolution. Marx already saw this as the ultima ratio to deflect the collapse he had prognosticated. But the fear, which certainly was not the least thing motivating Marx, has been eclipsed. The relapse has already occurred. To still expect it in the future, even after Auschwitz and Hiroshima, is to take pitiable consolation in the thought that the worst is possibly yet to come. Humanity, which commits and endures wrong, in so doing already ratifies the worst: it is enough merely to listen to the nonsense being peddled about the dangers of détente. The sole adequate praxis would be to put all energies toward working our way out of barbarism. With the supersonic acceleration of history, barbarism has reached the point where it infects everything that conflicts with it. There are many who find the excuse plausible that only barbaric means are still effective against the barbaric totality. Yet in the meantime a threshold value of acceptance has been reached. What fifty years ago for a short period of time in the eyes of those who nourished the all too abstract and illusory hope for a total transformation might have appeared justified— that is, violence—after the experience of the National Socialist and Stalinist atrocities and in the face of the longevity of totalitarian repression is inextricably imbricated in what needs to be transformed. If society's nexus of complicity and with it the prospect for catastrophe has become truly total—and there is nothing that permits any doubt about this— then there is nothing to oppose it other than what denounces that nexus of blindness, rather than each in his own fashion participating in it. Either humanity renounces the eye for an eye of violence, or the allegedly radical political praxis renews the old terror. The petit bourgeois truism that fascism and communism are the same, or in its most recent version, that the ApO helps the NPD,[17] is shamefully confirmed: the bourgeois world has completely become what the bourgeoisie imagines it to be. Whoever does not make the transition to irrational and brutal violence sees himself forced into the vicinity of the reformism that for its part shares the guilt for perpetuating the deplorable totality. But no shortcut helps, and what does help is deeply obscured. Dialectic is perverted into sophistry as soon as it focuses pragmatically on the next step, beyond which the knowledge of the totality has long since moved.

7

The error of the primacy of praxis as it is exercised today appears clearly in the privilege accorded to tactics over everything else. The means have become autonomous to the extreme. Serving the ends without reflection, they have alienated themselves from them. Thus everywhere discussion is called for, certainly initially out of an anti-authoritarian impulse. But discussion, which by the way, like the public sphere, is an entirely bourgeois category, has been completely ruined by tactics.[18] What discussions could possibly produce, namely, decisions reached from a greater objectivity to the extent that intentions and arguments interpenetrate, does not interest those who automatically, and in completely inappropriate situations, call for discussions. Each of the hegemonic cliques has prepared in advance the results it desires. Discussion serves manipulation. Every argument, untroubled by the question of whether it is sound, is geared to a purpose. Whatever the opponent says is hardly perceived and then only so that formulaic clichés can be served up in retort. No one wants to learn, experience, insofar as experience is still possible at all. The opponent in a discussion becomes a functional component of the current plan: reified by the reified consciousness *malgré lui-même*. Either these cliques want to make him into something usable by means of engineered discussion and coerced solidarity, or to discredit him before their followers, or they simply speechify out the window for the sake of publicity, to which they are captive: pseudo-activity can stay alive only through incessant self-advertisement. If the opponent does not concede, then he will be disqualified and accused of lacking the qualities presupposed by the discussion. The concept of discussion is cleverly twisted so that the opponent is supposed to let himself be convinced; this degrades the discussion into farce. Behind this ploy lies an authoritarian principle: the dissenter must adopt the group's opinion. The unresponsive ones project their own unresponsiveness upon whomever will not let himself be terrorized. With all this, actionism acquiesces to the trend it intends or pretends to struggle against: the bourgeois instrumentalism that fetishizes means because its form of praxis cannot suffer reflection upon its ends.

8

Pseudo-activity, praxis that takes itself more seriously and insulates itself more diligently from theory and knowledge the more it loses contact with its object and a sense of proportion, is a product of objective societal conditions. It truly is conformist: to the situation of *huis clos*. The pseudo-revolutionary posture is complementary to that military-technical impossibility of spontaneous revolution Jürgen von Kempski identified years ago.[19] Barricades are ridiculous against those who administer the bomb; that is why the barricades are a game, and the lords of the manor let the gamesters go on playing for the time being. Things might be different with the guerrilla tactics of the Third World; nothing in the administered world functions wholly without disruption. This is why actionists in advanced industrial countries choose the underdeveloped ones for their models. But they are as impotent as the personality cult of leaders who are helplessly and shamefully murdered. Models that do not prove themselves even in the Bolivian bush cannot be exported.

Pseudo-activity is provoked and at the same time condemned to being illusory by the current state of the technical forces of production. Just as personalization offers false consolation for the fact that within the anonymous apparatus the individual does not count anymore, so pseudo-activity deceives about the debilitation of a praxis presupposing a free and autonomous agent that no longer exists. It is also relevant for political activity to know whether the circumnavigation of the moon had really required the astronauts at all, who not only had to subordinate themselves to their buttons and mechanisms but moreover received detailed orders from the control center on earth. The physiognomy and social character of a Columbus and a Borman are worlds apart. As a reflex reaction to the administered world pseudo-activity reproduces that world in itself. The prominent personalities of protest are virtuosos in rules of order and formal procedures. The sworn enemies of the institutions particularly like to demand the institutionalization of one thing or another, which usually are desires voiced by committees thrown together by happenstance; whatever is being discussed must at all costs be "binding." Subjectively, all this is promoted by the anthropological phenomenon of *gadgeteering**, the affective investment in technology that exceeds every form of reason and inhabits every facet of life. Ironically—civilization in its deepest degradation—McLuhan is right: *the medium is the message**. The substitution of means for ends replaces the qualities in people themselves. Interiorization would be the wrong word for it, because this mechanism does not even permit the constitution of a stable subjectivity: instrumentalization usurps its place. From pseudo-activity all the way to pseudo-revolution, the objective tendency of society coincides seamlessly with subjective regression. World history once again produces in parody the kind of people whom it in fact needs.

9

The objective theory of society, in as much as society is an autonomous totality confronting living individuals, has priority over psychology, which cannot address the decisive factors. Indeed, from this point of view, ever since Hegel resentment has often swung against the individual and his freedom, no matter how particularistic the latter may be, and especially against instinctual drives. This resentment accompanied bourgeois subjectivism like its shadow, and in the end was its bad conscience. Ascesis toward psychology, however, cannot be maintained even objectively.

Ever since the market economy was ruined and is now patched together from one provisional measure to the next, its laws alone no longer provide a sufficient explanation. Without psychology, in which the objective constraints are continually internalized anew, it would be impossible to understand how people passively accept a state of unchanging destructive irrationality and, moreover, how they integrate themselves into movements that stand in rather obvious contradiction to their own interests. The function of psychological determinants in the students is closely related to this situation. In relation to real power, which hardly feels a tickle, actionism is irrational. The more clever people realize the pointlessness of their activity, while others strenuously conceal it. Since the more important groups have hardly resolved themselves to martyrdom, psychological motivations must be taken into account; by the way, economic motivations are more directly in play than the blather about the affluent society would have us believe: there are still numerous students who eke out an existence on the threshold of starvation. Probably the construction of an illusory reality is ultimately necessitated by objective obstacles; it is mediated psychologically, the adjournment of thought is conditioned by the dynamic of the instinctual drives. In this a contradiction is flagrantly obvious. Whereas the actionists are exceedingly interested in themselves libidinally, in their spiritual needs, in the secondary pleasure gained through that concern with themselves, the subjective element—to the extent that it manifests itself in their opponents—arouses their spiteful fury. At once one recognizes here an extended application of Freud's thesis from *Group Psychology and the Analysis of the Ego*, that the imagines of authority have the subjective character of coldness, a lack of love and human relationships.[20] Just as those who are anti-authoritarian continue to embody authority, so they also rig out their negatively cathected imagines with the traditional leader qualities and grow uneasy as soon as authority figures are different, no longer correspond to what the anti-authoritarians nonetheless secretly desire from them. Those who protest most vehemently are similar to authoritarian personalities in their aversion to introspection; when they do consider themselves, it happens without criticism, and unreflectedly, aggressively is directed outward. They overestimate their own relevance narcissistically, without a sufficient sense of proportion. They impose their needs immediately, for instance, with the slogan of "learning processes," as the criterion of praxis; so far there has been little room left for the dialectical category of externalization. They reify their own psychology and expect reified consciousness from those who face them. Actually they taboo experience and become allergic as soon as anything refers to it. Experience for them comes down to what they call "privilege of information" without noticing that the concepts of information and communication they exploit are imported from the monopolistic culture industry and the science calibrated to it. Objectively they contribute to the regressive transformation of what still remains intact of the subject into contact points for *conditioned reflexes**.

10

The separation of theory and praxis in recent history and especially as it appears in sociology, which should have treated it thematically, finds its unreflected and most extreme scientific expression in Max Weber's theory of value neutrality. Almost seventy years old, this doctrine continues to be influential, even in the latest positivistic sociology.[21] Everything that has been brought forward against the theory has had little effect on established science. The more or less explicit, unmediated contrary position, that of a material ethic of values that would be immediately self-evident and would guide praxis, is discredited by its reactionary, arbitrary nature.[22] Weber's value neutrality was anchored to his notion of rationality. It remains an open question which of the two categories underpins the other in Weber's version. As is well known, rationality, the center of Weber's entire work, for him by and large means as much as instrumental reason. It is defined as a relation between appropriate means and ends. According to him, such ends are in principle external to rationality; they are left to a kind of decision whose dark implications, which Weber did not want, revealed themselves shortly after his death. Such an exemption of ends from *ratio*, which Weber in fact surrounded with qualifications and which yet unmistakably constituted the tenor of his theory of science and completely determined his scholarly strategy, is however no less arbitrary than the decree of values. Rationality cannot, any more than the subjective authority serving it, the ego, be simply split off from self-preservation; moreover, the anti-psychological but subject-oriented sociologist Weber did not try to do that. *Ratio* came into being in the first place as an instrument of self-preservation, that of reality-testing. Its universality, which suited Weber because it permitted him to delimit it from psychology, extended *ratio* beyond its immediate representative, the individual person. This emancipated *ratio*, probably for as long as it has existed, from the contingency of individually posed ends. In its immanent, intellectual universality, the subject of *ratio* pursuing its self-preservation is itself an actual universal, society—in its full logic, humanity. The preservation of humanity is inexorably inscribed within the meaning of rationality: it has its end in a reasonable organization of society, otherwise it would bring its own movement to an authoritarian standstill. Humanity is organized rationally solely to the extent that it

preserves its societalized subjects according to their unfettered potential-
ities. On the other hand, it would be delusional and irrational—and the
example is more than just an example—that the adequacy of the means
of destruction to the goal of destruction should be rational while, however, the ends of peace and the elimination of the antagonisms preventing it *ad kalendas Graecas* should be irrational. Weber, as loyal
spokesman of his class, inverted the relationship between rationality and
irrationality. Almost in vengeance and against his intentions, the ends-
means rationality undergoes dialectical reversal in his thought. The
development of bureaucracy, the purest form of rational domination,
into the society of the "iron cage" and which Weber prophesied with
obvious horror is irrational. Words such as "casing," "solidification,"
"autonomization of the apparatus," and their synonyms indicate that the
means so designated become ends in themselves instead of fulfilling their
ends-means rationality.[23] This is not a symptom of degeneration, however, as the bourgeoisie's self-image happily assumes. Weber recognized,
with an intensity of scrutiny matched only by his refusal to let it influence his conception, that the irrationality he both described and passed
over in silence follows from the determination of *ratio* as means, its
blindness to ends and to the critical consciousness of them. Weber's
resigned rationality becomes irrational precisely in that, as Weber postulated in angry identification with the aggressor, the ends remain irrational to rationality's ascesis. Without a hold on the determinateness of
its objects, *ratio* runs away from itself; its principle becomes one of bad
infinity. Weber's apparent de-ideologization of science was itself devised
as an ideology against Marxist analysis. But it unmasks itself, unsound
and self-contradictory, in its indifference toward the obvious madness.
Ratio should not be anything less than self-preservation, namely that of
the species, upon which the survival of each individual literally depends.
Through self-preservation the species indeed gains the potential for that
self-reflection that could finally transcend the self-preservation to which
it was reduced by being restricted simply to a means.

11

Actionism is regressive. Under the spell of the positivity that long ago
became part of the armature of ego-weakness, it refuses to reflect upon
its own impotence. Those who incessantly cry "too abstract!" strenuously cultivate concretism, an immediacy that is inferior to the available
theoretical means. The pseudo-praxis profits from this. Those who are
especially shrewd say—just as summarily as they judge art—that theory
is repressive; and which activity in the midst of the status quo is not so, in

its way? But immediate action, which always evokes taking a swing, is incomparably closer to oppression than the thought that catches its breath. The Archimedian point—how might a nonrepressive praxis be possible, how might one steer between the alternatives of spontaneity and organization—this point, if it exists at all, cannot be found other than through theory. If the concept is tossed aside, then traits, such as a unilateral solidarity degenerating into terror, will become manifest. What imposes itself straight away is the bourgeois supremacy of means over ends, that spirit actionists are, at least programmatically, opposed to. The university's technocratic reforms they, perhaps even bona fide, want to avert, are not even the retaliation to the protest. The protest promotes the reforms all on its own. Academic freedom is degraded into customer service and must submit to inspections.

12

Among the arguments available to actionism, there is one that indeed is quite removed from the political strategy it boasts of but that possesses a much greater suggestive power: it argues that one must opt for the protest movement precisely because one recognizes that it is objectively hopeless, following the model of Marx during the Paris Commune, or when the communist party stepped into the breach during the collapse of the anarcho-socialist councilor government in 1919 in Munich. Just as those responses had been triggered by desperation, so too those who despair of any possibility should support pointless action. The ineluctable defeat offers solidarity in the form of moral authority even to those who could have foreseen the catastrophe and would not have bowed before the dictate of a unilateral solidarity. But in truth the appeal to heroism prolongs that dictate; whoever has retained the sensibility for such types of appeal will not mistake its hollow tone. In the security of America an emigrant could endure the news of Auschwitz; it would be difficult to believe that Vietnam is robbing anyone of sleep, especially since every opponent of colonial wars must know that the Vietcong for their part use Chinese methods of torture. Whoever imagines that as a product of this society he is free of the bourgeois coldness harbors illusions about him-self as much as about the world; without such coldness one could not live. The ability of anyone, without exception, to identify with another's suf-fering is slight. The fact that one simply could not look on any longer, and that no one of goodwill should have to look on any longer, rationalizes the pang of conscience. The attitude at the edge of uttermost horror, such as was felt by the conspirators of 20 July who preferred to risk perishing under torture to doing nothing, was possible and admirable.[24] To claim from a distance that one feels the same as they do confuses the power of imagination with the violence of the immediate present. Pure self-protection prevents someone who was not there from imagining the worst, and even more, from taking actions that would expose him to the worst. Whoever is trying to understand the situation must acknowledge the objectively necessary limits to an identification that collides with his demand for self-preservation and happiness and should not behave as though he were already the type of person who perhaps can develop only in the condition of freedom, that is, without fear. One cannot be too afraid of the world, such as it is. If someone sacrifices not only his intellect but himself as well, then no one should prevent him, although objectively false martyrdom does exist. To make a commandment out of the sacrifice belongs to the fascist repertoire. Solidarity with a cause whose ineluctable failure is discernible may yield up some exquisite narcissistic gain; in itself the solidarity is as delusional as the praxis of which one comfortably awaits approbation, which most likely will be recanted in the next moment because no sacrifice of intellect is ever enough for the insatiable claims of inanity. Brecht, who as the situation at that time warranted was still involved with politics and not with its surrogate, once said, in effect, that when he was honest with himself he was *au fond* more interested in the theater than in changing the world.[b] Such a consciousness would be the best corrective for a theater that today confuses itself with reality, such as the *happenings** now and then staged by the actionists that muddle aesthetic semblance and reality. Whoever does not wish to fall short of Brecht's voluntary and audacious avowal will suspect most praxis today of lacking talent.

13

Contemporary practicality is based on an element that was baptized in the abominable language of sociology as the 'suspicion of ideology', as though the driving force in the critique of ideologies was not the experi-

---

[b] Cf. Walter Benjamin, *Versuche über Brecht* (Frankfurt: Suhrkamp, 1966), 118. [*Translator's note:* English: *Understanding Brecht*, trans. Anna Bostock (London: NLB, 1973). A reference to entry for 6 July in "Conversations with Brecht": "*6 July.* Brecht, in the course of yesterday's conversation: 'I often imagine being interrogated by a tribunal. "Now tell us, Mr Brecht, are you really in earnest?" I would have to admit that no, I'm not completely in earnest. I think too much about artistic problems, you know, about what is good for the theatre, to be completely in earnest. But having said "no" to that important question, I would add something still more important: namely, that my attitude is, *permissible*'" (106–107).]

ence of their untruth but rather the petit bourgeois disdain for all spirit because it is allegedly conditioned by interests, a view in fact motivated by an interest in skepticism and projected onto spirit. However, if praxis obscures its own present impossibility with the opiate of collectivity, it becomes in its turn ideology. There is a sure sign of this: the question "what is to be done?" as an automatic reflex to every critical thought before it is fully expressed, let alone comprehended. Nowhere is the obscurantism of the latest hostility to theory so flagrant. It recalls the gesture of someone demanding your papers. More implicit and therefore all the more powerful is the commandment: you must sign. The individual must cede himself to the collective; as recompense for his jumping into the *melting pot**, he is promised the grace of being chosen, of belonging. Weak and fearful people feel strong when they hold hands while running. This is the real turning point of dialectical reversal into irrationalism. Defended with a hundred sophisms, inculcated into adepts with a hundred techniques for exerting moral pressure, is the idea that by abandoning one's own reason and judgment one is blessed with a higher, that is, collective reason; whereas in order to know the truth one needs that irreducibly individual reason that, it is nowadays incessantly belabored, is supposedly obsolete and whose message has long since been refuted and laid to rest by the comrades' superior wisdom. One falls back upon that disciplinarian attitude the communists once practiced. What once was deadly serious and bore terrible consequences when the situation still seemed undecided is now repeated as comedy in the pseudo-revolutions, according to a maxim of Marx.[25] Instead of arguments one meets standardized slogans, which apparently are distributed by leaders and their acolytes.

14

If theory and praxis are neither immediately one nor absolutely different, then their relation is one of discontinuity. No continuous path leads from praxis to theory—what has to be added is what is called the spontaneous moment. But theory is part of the nexus of society and at the same time is autonomous. Nevertheless praxis does not proceed independently of theory, nor theory independently of praxis. Were praxis the criterion of theory, then for the sake of the *thema probandum* it would become the swindle denounced by Marx and therefore would not be able to attain what it wants; were praxis simply to follow the instructions of theory, then it would become rigidly doctrinaire and furthermore would falsify theory. What Robespierre and St. Just did with the Rousseauist *volonté* *générale*, which certainly did not lack a repressive streak itself, is the most famous but by no means the only example. The dogma of the unity of theory and praxis, contrary to the doctrine on which it is based, is undialectical: it underhandedly appropriates simple identity where contradiction alone has the chance of becoming productive. Whereas theory cannot be extracted from the entire societal process, it also maintains an independence within this process; it is not only a means of the totality but also a moment of it; otherwise it could not resist to any degree the captivating spell of that totality. The relationship between theory and practice, after both have once distanced themselves from each other, is that of qualitative reversal, not transition, and surely not subordination. They stand in a polar relationship. The theory that is not conceived as an instruction for its realization should have the most hope for realization, analogous to what occurred in the natural sciences between atomic theory and nuclear fission; what they had in common, the backtracking to a possible praxis, lay in the technologically oriented reason in-itself, not in any thoughts about application. The Marxist doctrine of the unity of theory and praxis was no doubt credible because of the presentiment that it could be too late, that it was now or never. To that extent it was certainly practical, but the theory as it is actually explicated, the *Critique of Political Economy*, lacks all concrete transitions to that praxis that, according to the eleventh thesis on Feuerbach, should constitute its raison d'être.[26] Marx's reticence concerning theoretical recipes for praxis was hardly less than that concerning a positive description of a classless society. *Capital* contains numerous invectives, most often against economists and philosophers, but no program for action; every speaker of the ApO who has learned his vocabulary would have to chide that book for being abstract. The theory of surplus value does not tell how one should start a revolution. In regard to praxis generally—not in specific political questions—the anti-philosophical Marx hardly moves beyond the philosopheme that only the proletariat itself can be the cause of its emancipation; and at that time the proletariat was still visible. In recent decades the *Studies on Authority and Family*, the *Authoritarian Personality*, even the *Dialectic of Enlightenment* with its in many respects heterodox theory of domination were written without practical intentions and nonetheless exercised some practical influence. That influence came from the fact that in a world where even thoughts have become commodities and provoke *sales resistance** no one could suppose when reading these volumes that he was being sold or talked into something. Wherever I have directly intervened in a narrow sense and with a visible practical influence, it happened only through theory: in the polemic against the musical Youth Movement and its followers, in the critique of the newfangled German jargon of authenticity, a critique that spoiled the pleasure of a very virulent ideology by charting its derivation and restoring it to its proper concept. If these ideologies are in fact false consciousness, then their dissolution, which diffuses widely in the medium of thought, inaugurates a certain movement toward political maturity, and that, in any case, is practical. The stale Marxist pun about "critical critique," the witlessly pleonastic, hackneyed witticism that believes theory is annihilated because it is theory, merely conceals the insecurity involved in the direct translation of theory into praxis.[27] And even later, despite the Internationale, with whom he had a falling-out, Marx by no means surrendered himself to praxis. Praxis is a source of power for theory but cannot be prescribed by it. It appears in theory merely, and indeed necessarily, as a blind spot, as an obsession with what is being criticized; no critical theory can be practiced in particular detail without overestimating the particular, but without the particularity it would be nothing. This admixture of delusion, however, warns of the excesses in which it incessantly grows.

Critical Models 3

Critique

Something should be said about critique in its connection with politics. Since, however, politics is not a self-enclosed, isolated sphere, as it manifests itself for instance in political institutions, processes, and procedural rules, but rather can be conceived only in its relationship to the societal play of forces making up the substance of everything political and veiled by political surface phenomena, so too the concept of critique cannot be restricted to a narrow political field.

Critique is essential to all democracy. Not only does democracy require the freedom to criticize and need critical impulses. Democracy is nothing less than defined by critique. This can be recalled simply in the historical fact that the conception of the separation of powers, upon which every democracy is based, from Locke and Montesquieu and the American constitution up to today, has its lifeblood in critique. The *system of checks and balances**, the reciprocal overview of the executive, the legislative, and the judiciary, means as much as that each of these powers subjects the others to critique and thereby reduces the despotism that each power, without this critical element, gravitates to. Critique and the prerequisite of democracy, political maturity, belong together. Politically mature is the person who speaks for himself, because he has thought for himself and is not merely repeating someone else; he stands free of any guardian.[1] This is demonstrated in the power to resist established opinions and, one and the same, also to resist existing institutions, to resist everything that is merely posited, that justifies itself with its existence. Such resistance, as the ability to distinguish between what is known and what is accepted merely by convention or under the constraint of authority, is one with critique, whose concept indeed comes from the Greek *krino*, "to decide." He who equates the modern concept of reason with critique is scarcely exaggerating. The Enlightenment thinker Kant, who wanted to see society emancipated from its self-incurred immaturity and who taught autonomy,[2] that is, judgment according to one's own insight in contrast to heteronomy, obedience to what is urged by others, named his three major works critiques. This was true not only for the intellectual capacities, whose limits he intended to measure off and whose procedures to construe. The power of Kant, as for instance Kleist vividly sensed, was that of critique in a very concrete sense.[3] He criticized the dogmatism of the rationalistic systems that were accepted prior to him: the *Critique of Pure Reason* was more than anything else a blistering critique of Leibniz and Wolf. The influence of Kant's main work was due to its negative results, and one of its most important parts, which dealt with pure thought's transgressions of its own limits, was thoroughly negative.

But critique, cornerstone of reason and bourgeois thinking *tout court*, by no means dominated spirit as much as one would assume from that spirit's self-image. Even the all-destroyer, as Kant was called two hundred years ago, often showed the gestures of one who blamed critique for being improper. His vocabulary shows this in malicious expressions like "subtle reasoning" [*Vernünfteln*], which not only punish reason's exceeding its bounds but also want to bridle its use that, in Kant's own understanding, irresistibly surges past its own limits. Finally Hegel, in whom the movement commencing with Kant culminates, and who in many passages equates thinking altogether with negativity and hence with critique, likewise has the opposite tendency: to bring critique to a halt. Whoever relies on the limited activity of one's own understanding Hegel calls, using a political epithet, *Raisonneur* [carper, argufier] and accuses of vanity because he does not reflect on his own finitude, is incapable of subordinating himself to something higher, the totality.[4] However, for Hegel this higher thing is the present conditions. Hegel's aversion to critique goes together with his thesis that the real is rational.[5] According to Hegel's authoritarian directive, that person is truly in control of his reason who does not insist on reason's antithesis to what presently exists, but rather within given reality recognizes his own reason. The individual citizen is supposed to capitulate before reality. The renunciation of critique is twisted into a higher wisdom; the young Marx's phrase about the ruthless critique of everything existing was the simple reply to this, and even the mature Marx subtitled his main work a "critique."[6]

The substantive import of those passages in Hegel, especially in the book that concentrates his anti-critical tendency, the *Philosophy of Right*, is societal.[7] One need not be a sociologist to hear in his ridicule of the *Raisonneur* and the starry-eyed reformer the unctuous sermon admonishing the underling to keep still, who out of stupidity—the modification of which obviously does not concern his guardian—objects to the decrees descending upon him from the authorities on high, because said underling is incapable of recognizing that ultimately everything is and happens for the best and that those who are above his station in life also should be his intellectual superiors. Something of the contradiction between the modern emancipation of critical spirit and its simultaneous dampening is characteristic of the entire bourgeois period: from an early period onward the bourgeoisie must have feared that the logic of its own principles could lead beyond its own sphere of interests. Habermas has demonstrated contradictions of this sort in the notion of the public sphere—the most important medium of all politically effective criticism—that on the one hand should concentrate the critical political maturity of society's subjects and, on the other, has become a commodity and works against the critical principle in order to better market itself.[8]

It is easily forgotten in Germany that critique, as a central motif of spirit, is not very popular anywhere in the world. But there is reason to reflect on a specifically German phenomenon in the hostility to critique especially in the political arena. Full-fledged bourgeois emancipation was not successful in Germany, or only in a historical period in which its prerequisite, the liberalism of diffused free enterprise, was already undermined. Likewise the unification into a nation-state—which in many other countries was attained parallel to the strengthening of the bourgeoisie—limped behind history and became a short intermezzo. This may have caused the German trauma of unity and unanimity that scents weakness in that multiplicity whose resultant outcome is democratic will formation. Whoever criticizes violates the taboo of unity, which tends toward totalitarian organization. The critic becomes a divisive influence and, with a totalitarian phrase, a subversive. The denunciation of alleged quarrels in the party was an indispensable propaganda tool for the National Socialists. The unity-trauma has survived Hitler and has possibly even been intensified by the division of Germany following the war Hitler unleashed. It is a banality that democracy was a belated arrival in Germany. There is probably less general awareness, however, that the consequences of this belatedness extended even into the ramifications of mind. Besides the economic and straightforward societal problems democracy in Germany confronts in order to permeate the sovereign people [Volk], not inconsiderable is the additional difficulty that predemocratic and undemocratic forms of consciousness—in particular those that stem from statism and a thinking that conforms to authority—survive in the midst of a suddenly implanted democracy and prevent people from making it their own. One such vestigial pattern of behavior is the mistrust of critique and the inclination to throttle it under some pretense or other. The fact that Goebbels could degrade the concept of critic into that of criticaster, could maliciously associate it with the concept of the grumbler, and wanted to prohibit the criticism of all art was not only meant to take independent intellectual impulses in hand. The propagandist was calculating in terms of social psychology. He could tap into the general German prejudice against critique that dates back to absolutism. He was expressing the heartfelt convictions of those already being led by the hand.

If one wanted to sketch an anatomy of the German hostility to critique, one would find it unquestionably bound up with the rancor against the intellectual. In public or, in Franz Böhm's expression, non-public opinion, the suspect intellectual is probably equated with the person who criticizes.[9] It seems plausible that anti-intellectualism derives originally from a submissiveness to officialdom. Again and again the injunction is intoned that critique must be responsible. But that always amounts to meaning that only those are actually justified to criticize who happen to be in a responsible position, just as even anti-intellectualism until quite recently didn't extend to state-employed intellectuals like professors.[10] According to the subject matter of their work, professors would have to be counted among the intellectuals. However, in general, because of their prestige as government officials, they were highly respected in established public opinion as long as conflicts with students didn't convince them of their actual powerlessness. Critique is being departmentalized, as it were. It is being transformed from the human right and human duty of every citizen into a privilege of those who are qualified by virtue of the recognized and protected positions they occupy. Whoever practices critique without having the power to carry through his opinion, and without integrating himself into the official hierarchy, should keep silent—that is the form in which the variation of the cliché about servants' limited powers of understanding returns in the Germany that formally has equal rights. Obviously, people who are institutionally intertwined with present conditions will in general hesitate to criticize them. Even more than administrative-legal conflicts they fear conflicts with the opinions of their own group. By means of the division between responsible critique, namely, that practiced by those who bear public responsibility, and irresponsible critique, namely, that practiced by those who cannot be held accountable for the consequences, critique is already neutralized. The unspoken abrogation of the right to critique for those who have no position makes the privilege of education, especially the career insulated by official examinations, into the authority defining who may criticize, whereas the truth content of critique alone should be that authority. All this is unspoken and not institutionally anchored but so deeply present in the preconscious of innumerable people that it exercises a kind of social control. In recent years there has been no lack of cases where people outside of the hierarchy—which, incidentally, in the age of celebrities is certainly not limited to officials—practiced critique, for instance, criticizing the juridical practices in a certain city. They were immediately rebuffed as grumblers. It is not enough to answer this by indicating the mechanisms that in Germany create the suspicion that the independent individualist or dissenting person is a fool. The state of affairs is much more grave: through the anti-critical structure of public opinion the dissenter as a type is *really* brought into the situation of the grumbler and takes on the characteristics of a malcontent, to the extent that those characteristics have not already driven him to stubborn critique. Unwavering critical freedom easily slides by its own dynamic into the attitude of Michael Kohlhaas, who not coincidentally was a German.[11] One of the most important conditions for changing the structure of public opinion in Germany would be if the facts I've indicated here became generally conscious, for instance, were treated in civics education, and thereby would lose some of their disastrously blind power. Occasionally the relationship of German public opinion to critique virtually seems to be stood on its head. The right to free critique is unilaterally invoked for the good of those who oppose the critical spirit of a democratic society. However, the vigilance that rebels against such misuse requires the strength of public opinion that is still lacking in Germany and that can hardly be produced by mere appeal.

Indicative of the concealed relationship of public opinion to critique is the attitude of its organs that actually lay claim to a tradition of freedom. Many newspapers that by no means wish to be thought reactionary assiduously cultivate a tone that in America, where analogies are not lacking, one calls *pontifical**. They speak as though they stood above the controversies, assume a posture of sage experience that would befit the epithet "old-maidish." Their supercilious remove usually only benefits the defense of the official state of affairs. At most the powers are solemnly encouraged not to let themselves be swayed from their good intentions. The language of such newspapers sounds like that of governmental announcements, even where nothing is being announced about any government. Behind the pontifical posture stands the authoritarian one: both in those who assume it and in the consumers who are being cleverly targeted. Identification with power prevails in Germany now just as it did before; in this lurks the dangerous potential of identifying oneself with power politics inwardly and outwardly. The caution exercised in reforming institutions, where the reform is demanded by critical consciousness and to a considerable degree is acknowledged by the executive powers, is based on the fear of the voting masses; this fear easily renders critique without consequence. It also indicates how widespread the anti-critical spirit is in those whose interest should lie in critique.

Critique's lack of consequence in Germany has a specific model, presumably of military origin: the tendency to protect at any cost subordinates who are charged with misbehavior or offense. In military hierarchies the oppressive element of such an esprit de corps may be found everywhere; however, if I am not mistaken, then it is specifically German that this military behavior pattern also thoroughly dominates the civil, especially the specifically political spheres. One cannot shake the feeling that in answer to every public critique the higher authorities, who stand above the person being criticized and who ultimately bear the responsibility, first and foremost, irrespective of the facts of the case, defend the criticized person and strike outward. This mechanism, which sociology really should study thoroughly, is so ingrained that it automatically threatens political criticism with a fate similar to that granted the soldier who dared to complain about his superior during the Wilhelminian era. The rancor toward the institution of defense commissioner is symbolic for this entire sphere.

Perhaps the damaged German relationship to critique is most comprehensible in its lack of consequence. If Germany deserves the title "land of unlimited presumabilities" that Ulrich Sonnemann formulated, then this too is related.[12] It may be simply a phrase that someone has been swept away by the pressure of public opinion; however, worse than the phrase is when no public opinion forms to exert that kind of pressure, or, when no consequences are drawn if it does happen. A topic for political science would be research studies comparing the consequences of public opinion, unofficial critique in the old democracies of England, France, America with the consequences in Germany. I do not dare to anticipate the result of such a study, but I can imagine it. If the *Spiegel* affair is held out as the one exception, then it should be kept in mind that in that case the protesting newspapers, bearers of public opinion, showed their rare verve not out of any solidarity with the freedom to criticize and its prerequisite, unimpeded information, but rather because they saw themselves

threatened in their own concrete interests, *news value**, the market value
of information.[13] I am not underestimating attempts at effective public
critique in Germany. They include the fall of a radical right-wing minister of culture in one federal state. However, since that solidarity between
students and professors does not exist anywhere now the way it did then
in Göttingen, it is doubtful whether something similar could happen
again today.[14] It looks to me as though the spirit of public critique, after it
was monopolized by political groups and thereby became publicly compromised, has suffered severe setbacks; I hope I am mistaken.

Essentially German, although once again not so completely as one
who has not had the opportunity to observe similar phenomena in other
countries might easily suppose, is an anti-critical schema from philosophy—precisely the philosophy that besmirched the *Raisonneur*—that
has sunk into blather: the appeal to the positive. One continually finds
the word *critique*, if it is tolerated at all, accompanied by the word *con-
structive*. The insinuation is that only someone can practice critique who
can propose something better than what is being criticized; Lessing
derided this two hundred years ago in aesthetics.[15] By making the positive a condition for it, critique is tamed from the very beginning and loses
its vehemence. In Gottfried Keller there is a passage where he calls the
demand for something edifying a "gingerbread word." He roughly
argues that much would already be gained if the mustiness were cleared
away where something that has gone bad blocks the light and fresh air.[16]
In fact, it is by no means always possible to add to critique the immediate
practical recommendation of something better, although in many cases
critique can proceed by way of confronting realities with the norms to
which those realities appeal: following the norms would already be better. The word *positive*, which not only Karl Kraus decades ago but also a
hardly radical writer like Erich Kästner polemicized against, has in the
meantime in Germany been made into a magic charm.[17] It automatically
snaps into place. Its dubiousness can be seen in the fact that in the present
situation the higher form, toward which society should move according
to progressive thought, can no longer be read out of reality as a concrete
tendency. If one wanted for that reason to renounce the critique of society, then one would only reinforce society in precisely the dubiousness
that obstructs its transition to a higher form. The objective obstruction of
what is better does not abstractly affect the larger whole. In every individual phenomenon one criticizes, one swiftly runs up against that limitation. Again and again the demand for positive proposals proves unful-
fillable, and for that reason critique is all the more comfortably defamed.
Perhaps the observation suffices here that from a social-psychological
perspective the craving for the positive is a screen-image of the destruc-

tive instinct working under a thin veil.[18] Those talking most about the positive are in agreement with destructive power. The collective compulsion for a positivity that allows its immediate translation into practice has in the meantime gripped precisely those people who believe they stand in the starkest opposition to society. This is not the least way in which their actionism fits so smoothly into society's prevailing trend. This should be opposed by the idea, in a variation of a famous proposition of Spinoza, that the false, once determinately known and precisely expressed, is already an index of what is right and better.[19]

Resignation

We older representatives of what the name
"Frankfurt School" has come to designate have recently and eagerly been
accused of resignation. We had indeed developed elements of a critical
theory of society, the accusation runs, but we were not ready to draw the
practical consequences from it. And so, we neither provided actionist programs nor did we even support actions by those who felt inspired by critical theory. I will not address the question of whether that can be
demanded from theoretical thinkers, who are relatively sensitive and by
no means shockproof instruments. The purpose that has fallen to them in
a society based on the division of labor may be questionable; they themselves may be deformed by it. But they are also formed by it; of course,
they could not by sheer will abolish what they have become. I do not
want to deny the element of subjective weakness that clings to the nar-
rowed focus on theory. I think the objective side is more important. The
objection, effortlessly rattled off, runs along these lines: the person who
at this hour doubts the possibility of radical change in society and who
therefore neither participates in spectacular, violent actions nor recom-
mends them has resigned. What he has in mind he thinks cannot be realized; actually he doesn't even want to realize it. By leaving the conditions
untouched, he condones them without admitting it.

Distance from praxis is disreputable to everyone. Whoever doesn't
want to really knuckle down and get his hands dirty, is suspect, as though

the aversion were not legitimate and only distorted by privilege. The distrust of whoever distrusts praxis extends from those on the opposite side who repeat the old slogan "enough talking already" all the way to the objective spirit of advertising that propagates the image—they call it a "guiding image"—of the active, practical person, be he an industrial leader or an athlete. One should join in. Whoever only thinks, removes himself, is considered weak, cowardly, virtually a traitor. The hostile cliché of the intellectual works its way deeply into that oppositional group, without them having noticed it, and who in turn are slandered as "intellectuals."

Thinking actionists answer: among the things to be changed include precisely the present conditions of the separation of theory and praxis. Praxis is needed, they say, precisely in order to do away with the domination by practical people and the practical ideal. But then this is quickly transformed into a prohibition on thinking. A minimum is sufficient to turn the resistance to repression repressively against those who, as little as they wish to glorify their individual being, nonetheless do not renounce what they have become. The much invoked unity of theory and praxis has the tendency of slipping into the predominance of praxis. Many movements defame theory itself as a form of oppression, as though praxis were not much more directly related to oppression. In Marx the doctrine of this unity was inspired by the real possibility of action, which even at that time was not actualized.[1] Today what is emerging is more the direct contrary. One clings to action for the sake of the impossibility of action. Admittedly, already in Marx there lies concealed a wound. He may have presented the eleventh thesis on Feuerbach so authoritatively because he knew he wasn't entirely sure about it. In his youth he had demanded the "ruthless criticism of everything existing."[2] Now he was mocking criticism. But his famous witticism against the young Hegelians, the phrase "critical critique," was a dud, went up in smoke as nothing but a tautology.[3] The forced primacy of praxis irrationally stopped the critique that Marx himself practiced. In Russia and in the orthodoxy of other countries the malicious derision of critical critique became an instrument so that the existing conditions could establish themselves so terrifyingly. The only thing praxis still meant was: increased production of the means of production; critique was not tolerated anymore except for the criticism that people were not yet working hard enough. So easily does the subordination of theory to praxis invert into service rendered to renewed oppression.

The repressive intolerance to the thought that is not immediately accompanied by instructions for action is founded on anxiety. Untrammeled thought and the posture that will not let it be bargained away must be feared because of what one deeply knows but cannot openly admit: that the thought is right. An age-old bourgeois mechanism with which the eighteenth century enlightenment thinkers were quite familiar operates once again, but unchanged: the suffering caused by a negative situation—this time by obstructed reality—becomes rage leveled at the person who expresses it. Thought, enlightenment conscious of itself, threatens to disenchant the pseudo-reality within which actionism moves, in the words of Habermas.[4] The actionism is tolerated only because it is considered pseudo-reality. Pseudo-reality is conjoined with, as its subjective attitude, pseudo-activity: action that overdoes and aggravates itself for the sake of its own *publicity**, without admitting to itself to what extent it serves as a substitute satisfaction, elevating itself into an end in itself. People locked in desperately want to get out. In such situations one doesn't think anymore, or does so only under fictive premises. Within absolutized praxis only reaction is possible and therefore false. Only thinking could find an exit, and moreover a thinking whose results are not stipulated, as is so often the case in discussions in which it is already settled who should be right, discussions that therefore do not advance the cause but rather inevitably degenerate into tactics. If the doors are barricaded, then thought more than ever should not stop short. It should analyze the reasons and subsequently draw the conclusions. It is up to thought not to accept the situation as final. The situation can be changed, if at all, by undiminished insight. The leap into praxis does not cure thought of resignation as long as it is paid for with the secret knowledge that that really isn't the right way to go.

Pseudo-activity is generally the attempt to rescue enclaves of immediacy in the midst of a thoroughly mediated and rigidified society. Such attempts are rationalized by saying that the small change is one step in the long path toward the transformation of the whole. The disastrous model of pseudo-activity is the *"do-it-yourself"** [*Mach es selber*]: activities that do what has long been done better by the means of industrial production only in order to inspire in the unfree individuals, paralyzed in their spontaneity, the assurance that everything depends on them. The nonsense of do-it-yourself in the production of material goods, even in the carrying out of many repairs, is patently obvious. Admittedly the nonsense is not total. With the reduction of so-called *services** [*Dienstleistungen*], sometimes measures carried out by the private person that are superfluous considering the available technology nonetheless fulfill a quasi-rational purpose. The do-it-yourself approach in politics is not completely of the same caliber. The society that impenetrably confronts people is nonetheless these very people. The trust in the limited action of small groups recalls the spontaneity that withers beneath the encrusted totality and without which this totality cannot become something differ-ent. The administered world has the tendency to strangle all spontaneity, or at least to channel it into pseudo-activities. At least this does not func-tion as smoothly as the agents of the administered world would hope. However, spontaneity should not be absolutized, just as little as it should be split off from the objective situation or idolized the way the adminis-tered world itself is. Otherwise the axe in the house that never saves the carpenter will smash in the nearest door, and the riot squad will be at the ready.[5] Even political undertakings can sink into pseudo-activities, into theater. It is no coincidence that the ideals of immediate action, even the propaganda of the act, have been resurrected after the willing integration of formerly progressive organizations that now in all countries of the earth are developing the characteristic traits of what they once opposed. Yet this does not invalidate the critique of anarchism. Its return is that of a ghost. The impatience with theory that manifests itself in its return does not advance thought beyond itself. By forgetting thought, the impa-tience falls back below it.

This is made easier for the individual by his capitulation to the collec-tive with which he identifies himself. He is spared from recognizing his powerlessness; the few become the many in their own eyes. This act, not unwavering thought, is resignative. No transparent relationship obtains between the interests of the ego and the collective it surrenders itself to. The ego must abolish itself so that it may be blessed with the grace of being chosen by the collective. Tacitly a hardly Kantian categorical imperative has erected itself: you must sign. The sense of a new security is purchased with the sacrifice of autonomous thinking. The consolation that thinking improves in the context of collective action is deceptive: thinking, as a mere instrument of activist actions, atrophies like all instrumental reason. At this time no higher form of society is concretely visible: for that reason whatever acts as though it were in easy reach has something regressive about it. But according to Freud, whoever regresses has not reached his instinctual aim. Objectively regression is renuncia-tion, even when it thinks itself the opposite and innocently propagates the pleasure principle.[6]

By contrast the uncompromisingly critical thinker, who neither signs over his consciousness nor lets himself be terrorized into action, is in truth the one who does not give in. Thinking is not the intellectual repro-duction of what already exists anyway. As long as it doesn't break off, thinking has a secure hold on possibility. Its insatiable aspect, its aversion to being quickly and easily satisfied, refuses the foolish wisdom of resig-nation. The utopian moment in thinking is stronger the less it—this too a form of relapse—objectifies itself into a utopia and hence sabotages its realization. Open thinking points beyond itself. For its part a comportment, a form of praxis, it is more akin to transformative praxis than a comportment that is compliant for the sake of praxis. Prior to all particular content, thinking is actually the force of resistance, from which it has been alienated only with great effort. Such an emphatic concept of thinking admittedly is not secured, not by the existing conditions, nor by ends yet to be achieved, nor by any kind of battalions. Whatever has once been thought can be suppressed, forgotten, can vanish. But it cannot be denied that something of it survives. For thinking has the element of the universal. What once was thought cogently must be thought elsewhere, by others: this confidence accompanies even the most solitary and powerless thought. Whoever thinks is not enraged in all his critique: thinking has sublimated the rage. Because the thinking person does not need to inflict rage upon himself, he does not wish to inflict it on others. The happiness that dawns in the eye of the thinking person is the happiness of humanity. The universal tendency of oppression is opposed to thought as such. Thought is happiness, even where it defines unhappiness: by enunciating it. By this alone happiness reaches into the universal unhappiness. Whoever does not let it atrophy has not resigned.

Appendix 1   *Discussion of Professor Adorno's Lecture "The Meaning of Working Through the Past"*

TRANSLATOR'S NOTE: The first published version of "The Meaning of Working Through the Past" includes the following transcription of the discussion that followed the lecture.

Professor Adorno's lecture was first discussed in four study groups. Each of these groups prepared several questions, which were then presented to the lecturer in the plenary meeting.

FIRST QUESTION: Would the question of coming to terms with the German past arise if there had not been a National Socialist period?

PROF. ADORNO: I can only respond to that by saying that Hegel handled this problem with the concept of "abstract possibility."[1] I mean, I simply cannot answer this question. If world history had not been shattered into pieces, then the problem of collective amnesia probably would not have arisen, but in the end it is no coincidence that everything happened the way it did. I would like to propose that we set this question aside, because I think answering it will not help us much.

SECOND QUESTION: The focus of our discussion was on the concept you called the "self-alienation of society." Could you please explain this in a bit more detail?

PROF. ADORNO: I spoke of the self-alienation of society here in connection
with the problem of democracy, and I meant that because of
the preponderance of innumerable societal processes over the
particular individuals, people in their societal role are not
identical with what they are as immediate, living people.
Democracy, according to its very idea, promises people that
they themselves would make decisions about their world. But
democracy actually prevents them from this "deciding for
oneself about the world." In other words, with the concept of
self-alienation—and perhaps I should not have done so—I
was really referring to a very fundamental philosophical state
of affairs, in terms of social philosophy, that perhaps we
should not go into here, because I don't think that here,
where we are of course concerned ultimately with deriving
applications, that within such a group we have the possibility
of coming to grips with this phenomenon of self-alienation in
the real world. However, I don't want to evade your question.
I think that this question can be changed into something far
more empirical, which to be sure is only indirectly related to
this highly theoretical concept of self-alienation I allowed
myself to use in a sentence just that once. It is in fact a peda-
gogical-psychological question I have in mind here. You
must excuse me, if I churn butter out of the Milky Way and
now speak directly *terre à terre*. It seems to me to be the case
that in the development of children, their first experience of
alienation generally is when they enter school. For the first
time the child is torn away from the protection of the family,
from the extended womb, so to say, and comes to feel the
coldness of a world with which he or she is not identical. And
it seems to me to be the case that genetically the first expressions of anti-Semitism or of racial hatred at all, as for
instance the persecution of black children or red-haired children or whatever it may be, takes place precisely at this stage.
Now in part this has the quite solid reason that in school, for
one reason or another, there is always a child who has
already picked that up from home—this prejudice—and who
then spreads it further. But I think that generally a factor
comes in here, that people have the tendency to pass onto
others whatever has happened to them, to do once more to
others what was done to them. Thus, the child who in school
experiences coldness, anxiety, the pressure of the collective,
psychologically saves himself by displacing it onto others,
and groups form in order, as it were, to pass this burden of
alienation onto others. I would at least construe as a problem—God knows I would not presume to solve it, but I would
like to mention it for the educators among you—whether, if
possible, precisely in the first years of school forms might not

be developed that would prevent this oppression of the individual, and moreover of every individual, by the collective. Perhaps thereby at a very crucial place genetically in the development of the child one could counteract the emergence of racial prejudices. Here I would like just to toss these thoughts into the debate, so to speak, as a first practical application of the problem of alienation, for indeed here one could really, as it were, get at the alienation. I mean here, that is, here one could really come to grips with it in manageably small groups, whereas of course the socially dictated alienation within society at large, in which we live, cannot be overcome through any kind of educational work.

THIRD QUESTION: Within the system underlying your observations, where is there room for individual responsibility? To what extent are the societal processes and conditions so overwhelming that for the individual there remains no possibility whatsoever to make one's own decisions and to act with personal responsibility?

PROF. ADORNO: I think this question in fact repeats the question I raised myself. It would be extremely irresponsible and careless of me to say to you: yes, but the individual's responsibility is something inalienable, but it really is curtailed precisely under the preponderance of this process, and when I told you that the reflections I've shared with you are not of an edifying nature, but rather very earnest, then I was referring exactly to this. Nonetheless I think that if people finally are able really to see through their entanglement in the objective conditions I tried, however sketchily, to explain to you, that the consciousness that raises itself above this compulsion by seeing through it at the same time also produces the potential that can be used to resist it. I would say, and I also tried to suggest this in the last sentence of my lecture, that what you have termed autonomy and self-responsibility today essentially consists altogether in the resistance of people, in that they try to see through these mechanisms and that they themselves yet somehow rebel against these mechanisms. Morality has transformed itself nowadays into the resistance against this blind force, against this predominance of the merely existent, under which in fact we all must suffer today. This is of course very abstract and unsatisfying, and is no fanfare at all, for how far this resistance goes, that's another story. But I would still like to say, if one once at some point or other—and I return to what I said about the paranoia being infectious—pursues something specific with a little bit of craziness, if you will allow me, without letting oneself get all confused, then strangely enough one comes further than in fact would be expected if one reflected about these things objectively. I could give you quite curious evidence of this from my own experience, I don't want to do that, lest it divert us from our subject. I really believe that when one has this power of consciousness on his side, that is, when one really has the better insight on his side and when one today is committed—a word I do not like at all—that the scope of such a commitment is larger than the mere analysis of objectivity would lead one to suppose. We are not only spectators looking upon this predominance of the institutional and the objective that confronts us; rather it is after all constituted out of us, this societal objectivity is made up of us ourselves. In this doubledness, that we are subject and object of this society, surely lies precisely also the possibility of perhaps changing it.

ADDITIONAL QUESTION: If the conditions of society remain unchanged, then the latent danger of a resurgence still exists. Does this danger also exist in other countries with similar societal conditions?

PROF. ADORNO: I would answer with an emphatic yes: that the danger also exists in other countries, and it is even probably important for the practical work in Germany that the issue is not a purely German phenomenon and that it is not a matter of some particular characteristics of the German national character, but that this threat lies precisely in a society where simply the immense concentration of economical and administrative power leaves the individual no more room to maneuver, that the structure of such a society also tends toward totalitarian forms of domination. But it is better to indicate this danger and become conscious of it than to act naively and innocently as though the danger did not exist.

FOURTH QUESTION: What possibility do you see of lessening the universal anxiety? Someone in our group said that rational means don't work against feelings and that distinctions must be made between older and younger people, since the latter surely have less anxiety.

PROF. ADORNO: I think that any irrationality that is recommended for rational reasons, that is, because people cannot be changed by rational means, is always something very dubious. Irrationality that, as it were, is rationally prescribed—that is exactly what I described in my short characterization of propaganda—introduces into the work, which is so vitally important for us, an element of dishonesty and ambiguity that would give me serious pause. Well, I would say, and I agree completely with you, one cannot simply overcome very strong irrational forces by rational means. I said this over and over again in my lecture as well. So, psychologically speaking, in terms of the economy of drives there exist needs for things like racial prejudices that are simply far too powerful for one to be able deal with them by making clear to people that Rothschild did not start the battle of Waterloo and that *The Protocols of Zion* are counterfeit. By the way, the fact that the general refutation of the *Protocols* did not alter in the least their effectiveness is in itself a very interesting thing. But that does not condemn us to irrationality; instead the consequence to be drawn would really be what I tried to characterize as the turn to the subject, that is, the crucial thing is to be rational, not in the superficial sense, as when people who believe untrue things for irrational reasons are then confronted with the truth, but instead that people be brought to the point in themselves, through self-reflection, of gaining insight into what they can do in this respect. And this seems to me certainly to be the most important task for education that would begin relatively early in childhood, that is, rationality not in the sense of a rationalistic insistence on facts, but rationality in the sense of people being led to self-reflection and thereby being prevented from becoming blind victims of this instinctual impulse. By the way, I of course do not want to speak in favor of a crude and philistine rational-ism, rather I mean only that the irrationality, which I con-sider a very serious danger, of course does not lie in the fact that people have instincts and passions and whatever else, but rather that the irrationality—and perhaps I have not stressed this enough, in the emphatic sense, in which I meant it as something negative—this irrationality is the instinctual impulses and the affects that are repressed—I simply must speak Freudian here—and that teem about in the darkness and emerge again in distorted, twisted, altered form as aggression, as projection, as displacement, all those things we are so familiar with, and wreak havoc. And so when I spoke of the need to resist irrationality, I meant irrationality in this repressed, this twisted sense that was first wonderfully described by Nietzsche and then thoroughly analyzed by Freud. I therefore do not mean that people should become merely cold rationalists and shouldn't have affects and pas-sions any more. On the contrary, if they have more affects and more passions, they will have less prejudices. I would like to say, if they allow themselves more of their affects and pas-sions, if they do not once again repeat in themselves the pres-sure that society exerts upon them, then they will be far less

evil, far less sadistic, and far less malicious than they sometimes are today.

ADDITIONAL   Would you please briefly address the question of whether
QUESTION: young people suffer less from universal anxiety than the
                older generation?

PROF. ADORNO: One can answer such questions only with reservations if one
                really does not want to speak irresponsibly. I would say that
                nonetheless the young people have also received a great deal
                of this anxiety. The anxiety itself—I tried to explain this—
                has its basis in reality. The anxiety today is not at all neurotic
                anymore. The anxiety that people have, that they will be
                killed by atomic bombs—for that I don't need any existen-
                tialist philosophy that issues mysterious statements about
                the essence of anxiety. This anxiety is in itself quite reason-
                able. The excessive need for security, for safety, that can be
                seen in many people, that they always want to be holding
                something solid in their hands, that they are anxious about
                getting involved in anything they cannot get an overall view
                of beforehand, the tendency to marry as soon as possible,
                before one is mature enough—I could provide countless
                other, and above all intellectual moments—all this seems to
                me to indicate a repressed anxiety, and this repressed anxiety
                certainly is closely connected to this potential for disaster. I
                don't believe that here a great distinction can seriously be
                made between the forty-year-olds and the twenty-year-olds
                today.

FIFTH QUESTION: How can the working-through succeed if self-examination
                already assumes abilities the majority of people doesn't
                have?

PROF. ADORNO: This is of course correct. And here you precisely define the
                problem, that is, it would be wholly wrong if we were to
                preach self-examination and then expect that because of this
                sermon people will examine themselves. That is illusory.
                What we can do is give people contents, give them categories,
                give them forms of consciousness, by means of which they
                can approach self-reflection. The question you pose seems to
                me in turn to be extraordinarily grave because we know from
                psychology that something like analysis and also self-analy-
                sis faces extraordinarily great difficulties for reasons I do not
                want to go into here. I know the forces that repress the
                unconscious are the same forces that then prevent us from
                becoming conscious of these things, and to be sure when we
                talk here we cannot forget what we have learned from psy-

chology. In our work we must not, so to say, be more naive
than the most advanced psychology. But I think, we should
be a little more liberal on this point. For example, as I could
observe in America, if something has once been established
in public opinion, for instance, that anti-Semitism is bad, that
anti-Semitism is a symptom indicating that something is
wrong with the person himself, then certainly these potentials will not be cured at the level of depth psychology, but,
and I intentionally am expressing myself a bit casually here,
people won't dare to do it anymore. And I think, in a sphere
where murder occurs, it is nevertheless pretty good if people
won't dare to do it anymore.

SIXTH QUESTION: In our group there were questions about standards of value.
How far do you believe the ethical values of Christianity can
be brought to bear in the intellectual exchange with anti-
Semites? If in your opinion the preconditions for fascist
thinking are still present today, don't we need to ground our
behavior more deeply in terms of ethics?

PROF. ADORNO: Well, you are putting me in a difficult position as a professor
of philosophy. Ex officio, so to speak, I would be obliged to
speak for such an ethics. However, I am terribly sorry, I cannot do it. First, because I believe the problem of a correct life
cannot be expressed in a doctrine of value. I certainly think
that Christianity, simply because it is a power in the tradition
and also in its contemporary organizational form, is also a
part of those forces that check anti-Semitism, although I am
honest enough to tell you that I think Christianity has fed a
whole series of motives into anti-Semitism. But I do not
think one gets very far with anti-Semites by appealing to
Christianity, because they in fact confirm a condition, they
bring to a culmination a condition in which the binding force
of all these things no longer exists. If one reads the book by
Kogon on the SS state,[2] stories play a great role in it, stories
like: there's smoke coming out of the crematorium again,
probably it's some serious Biblical scholar winding his way
up to the heavens. It's in all the Nazi atrocities, for instance,
also in that they hauled off eighty- and ninety-year-olds into
the camps and killed them, even this is part of it, as it were to
challenge the Christian or Jewish God: come on, show us
what You can do. And if He allows it and there's no bolt of
lightning, then it is a sort of triumph. I mean by this that the
people who do it, that is, the actually dangerous types, are
from the very beginning those who have already extirpated
in themselves precisely the element of truth that is present in
the great religions, they have already annulled beforehand

the motive of pity, the motive of reconciliation. And I'd have to wholly ignore this syndrome were I to presume that these people are responsive to this approach. They would be responsive only if they could be brought somewhat to self-reflection, and they are responsive to the demonstration that their entire practical reason they apply ultimately brings disaster upon them as well. By appealing to a religious tradition they in fact already have rejected and against which they already react with a kind of spite, I don't think one will get to them. I don't want to deny that in particular cases it can be otherwise. There are of course many people, for instance, those of conservative intellectual temperament, who stand in the Christian tradition and on the other hand precisely in connection with their conservatism indulge in a certain social anti-Semitism. Such people can of course be made aware of this contradiction and probably can also be motivated to change. In general I do not think this will do it, but rather that the consciousness of anti-Semites really is precisely the regression into a crude rationalism. And I think it can only be fought on its own ground, that one applies the standard of *ratio* that at bottom is the only standard anti-Semitism acknowledges.

ADDITIONAL
QUESTION:

One probably cannot convince incorrigible anti-Semites with a Christian or another religious ethos. They will also hardly react to utilitarian arguments of advantage, for they received enough advantage during the years of Hitlerism. Perhaps the problem should be put this way: do you believe that the youth can be convinced by a religious ethos rather than by utilitarian arguments?

PROF. ADORNO:

You see, we're getting at a very difficult matter indeed. One cannot pronounce something like a religious ideal for the sake of the effect it has. There is only one legitimation for pronouncing an ideal, and that is its own truth. I would say that the collective role Christianity plays today in a large measure is that people seek and accept it because they believe they find a bond in it. But not at all for the sake of its own truth, and I think that in this tendency there is something that is extraordinarily dangerous for these very religions. And I think, the theologians would grant me this most heartily, that enlisting so to speak religious motives in order to confirm something else, as long as these religious motives are not entirely transparent and as long as they are not based on the truth, that this is a very double-edged matter. But here we are at an extremely difficult juncture, and I know far too well that many among you, and precisely among the most impassioned, do this out of specifically Christian impulses, and so I do not dare draw from that fact general conclusions, which would be completely illegitimate. You asked me, and I, who am not involved in such a bond, cannot answer otherwise. But to be sure religion should not be used in any sense as a means to an end, neither on account of the religion nor on account of the cause for which it is used.

SEVENTH QUESTION: Doesn't the claim that the appeal to purely blatant interests can contribute more to the overcoming of fascism than the appeal to ideals contradict our conception of education?

PROF. ADORNO: Yes, I'd like to say something here generally about the question of education. Of course, our education contains something that could be called ideals, although in general I prefer to avoid using this word. We educate people toward the possibility of something better, instead of having them swear an oath to what exists. But I also really did not speak of our fundamental idea of education. I agree with you wholeheartedly, we must educate people toward the idea that they are more than what simply exists. Otherwise education is altogether complete nonsense. Rather I really spoke from familiarity with the specifically susceptible character type, and I certainly would say that this type is characterized by the fact that he is constantly talking about ideals, and the really archetypical anti-Semite, if he were here among us, would say that we lack ideals. At the same time he would also be the person who in an emergency would have not the least respect for anything that turns out not to belong to the sphere of power, reality, and realism. And since here it comes down to dealing with this potential, I would say—the subjective aspect, of reaching people, is indeed only a small part of the whole problem—but as soon as it's about that, one must in God's name tell people that this pitiful reason, which racial prejudice, which fascism and everything connected with it obeys, precisely is so particular and narrow that it is also at the same time unreason and that it turns against the people who proclaim it; and by making this narrow reason transparent as such and by juxtaposing to it, first of all according to its own standard, a higher reason, through this probably one would really achieve in education what is meant by the concept of ideal.

ADDITIONAL
QUESTION: Instead of speaking in general of ideals, could we take one concretely, namely the ideal of justice? Do you see a possibility of building up reserves against totalitarian thinking by drawing on legal thought and people's sense of justice?

PROF. ADORNO: Here I would say, I indeed think that the concept of justice occupies such a privileged position among the ideals because the concept of justice always also includes one's own interest, that is, because when they are referred to the concept "justice" people see that their own interests are sublated into the general interest. That is probably why the concept of justice should really be invoked. But at this point I would like to say something that will perhaps surprise you, after I've spoken so much about enlightenment. For I don't know whether one doesn't end up in a hopeless position when one goes into these things in the discussion, for instance, to say that certainly it really is an absolute norm that no one should be killed, but in war people are killed, and there do exist exceptional situations—which norm, which ethical law contains the ultimate justification for them? I think, when one gets involved in, I would like to say, adolescent discussions, in such infantile discussions, where the most drastic things are at issue, when one right away asks about the stars and the absolutely ultimate values, then one is already in the devil's kitchen, and I think that in answer to this a certain minimum amount of enlightenment suffices, namely, when one simply says, listen, whether one should murder people or not murder people, that's something I won't discuss, that is a vulgarity I cannot abide—that this is basically also philosophically the higher standpoint, rather than if one were to derive from a system of ethics, first, second, and third volume, that is, general, specific, and very specific parts, that one should not murder the Jews. I mean, to get involved in theoretical discussions about whether people should be tortured or not, let's rather stop that. I think that then certainly in a higher sense breaking off rationality at such places better serves reason than a kind of pseudo-rationality that erects systems where it is first and foremost a question of immediate reaction.

EIGHTH QUESTION: You said that conditions of our society have changed only superficially. But haven't these changes also had more profound effects?

        You said that objective societal preconditions are a necessary but not sufficient cause for National Socialism. This leads to the question of what should be seen as the final cause for the emergence of National Socialism and whether it is possible to overcome National Socialism when the objective societal preconditions have remained unchanged.

PROF. ADORNO: I cannot recall that I said the necessary but not sufficient precondition. You are probably thinking of my having said that I do not consider National Socialism to be a specifically German phenomenon. I would respond to this by saying that here probably the sufficient explanation was the worsening of the political-economic situation in Germany and also certain theological traditions. I also actually feel that in relation to the militant nationalism that was found everywhere in the Germany of the Weimar Republic people have now somehow become gentler. Above all, certain traditions of a certain militant nationalism have grown weaker. This is probably connected with the fact that Imperial Germany plays only a very slight role in collective memory and also with the objective situation that people no longer seriously think that we will defeat France and that people can no longer imagine that Germany can conquer the world, simply because of the whole reality. To that extent I think that something certainly has changed, and moreover in the sense that we are genuinely becoming more similar to America, which I by no means put down to the so-called American influence, but rather to the fact that in countless aspects the structure of German society is approaching that of American society. On the other hand, I would say that in comparison with the Germany of 1933 the decisive cause of fascism, namely the concentration of economic and administrative power on the one side and complete impotence on the other side, has progressed. But I would still think that this altered subjective potential nonetheless can have as much force as it does in America. After all, for the last fifty or sixty years America has been the country of trusts and trust-legislation, of this immense concentration of economic power, and nevertheless the democratic rules have functioned so well up to now that the danger of fascism in America is, at the moment in any case, very slight. I don't see why at least such a chance shouldn't exist for us, where indeed there live so many "burnt children" in the fullest sense of the phrase.[3] Excuse me, the answer came out a bit complicated and complex, but the world simply is that complex, and it is not always possible to reduce these things to a simple and easy formula.

NINTH QUESTION: It was said that even exaggeration is a means for teaching and education. Could you explain this a bit more?

PROF. ADORNO: I would like to try to forestall a misunderstanding. I would not be able to accept the responsibility for recommending exaggeration in education. On the contrary, where consciousness is so sensitive, as in these places, if someone says, say, that six million Jews were killed and not five million, then the five million wouldn't be believed either. With this I only wanted to say, in consideration of the by no means opti-

mistic overall picture that I gave, that I perhaps exaggerated
and this exaggeration seems to me to be a necessary medium
for social-theoretical and philosophical presentation, because
the moderate, normal surface existence in general conceals
such potentials and because in the face of neutral, average
everydayness to indicate the threat lying below it at first
blush always has the character of exaggeration. I would
urgently warn against exaggeration in pedagogical work, for
instance. On the contrary, I would say the less the idea of
propaganda here even arises, the more stringently one holds
to the facts—which God knows speak for themselves, or
against themselves—the better. If you will recall from the
war, which I of course did not experience in Germany, the
authority the BBC, the English radio, enjoyed precisely
because it did not make propaganda but because one knew
that it was telling the truth, then I think this expressed something very central to our problem.

Appendix 2
Introduction to the Lecture "The Meaning of Working Through the Past"

TRANSLATOR'S NOTE: The following remarks were added by Adorno as an introduction when he repeated the lecture "The Meaning of Working Through the Past" on 24 May 1962, in Berlin at the invitation of the Socialist German Student Association [Sozialistischer Deutscher Studentenbund] (SDS).

The lecture you are about to hear was given on 6 November 1959, that is, before the filthy wave of anti-Semitism lent it a sad topicality. Permit me to indicate at the beginning that I made the attempt to derive the phenomena, which have unsettled us during recent months, from objective social and social-psychological conditions. So in this case sociological theory to a certain extent has preceded empirical reality and been confirmed by it. To be sure, studies such as the one undertaken in the *Group Experiment* by the Institute for Social Research, but also the surveys by several public opinion research institutes, have long since accumulated enough material to justify fears of this sort.[1] The theoretical anticipation is perhaps not irrelevant for the controversy about the nature and significance of recent events because they were inferred from structural elements that explain more deeply and more seriously than theses that join the symptoms of the day. In particular the ever recurring question of whether what is at issue is a planned and directed undertaking—or just pranks by those whose very characterization as "rowdy kids" in fact already characterizes the actions they then perform—hardly does justice to the events. If indeed, as I will lay out for you, objective conditions and tendencies produce the relapse into catastrophe, then such alternatives surely lose their meaning. On the one hand, there undoubtedly exist groups who identify themselves with these tendencies, who support them and who further them in the service of their own political will to power. In the well-known German love of organizations one can surely assume, without falling into persecution fantasies, that such groups are far more organized than they appear; that they are so difficult to apprehend is probably due to careful organization on their part. On the other hand, the social-psychological elements that in turn follow from the objective societal situation, and about which I will say a few things, create a reservoir of people who can be recruited for the aims of such organizers. There prevails a kind of preestablished harmony between this reservoir and those who exploit it. The two interact such that it is difficult to assign responsibility to one side or the other. Just as even the National Socialist conspirators were not essentially different from the people who flocked to them, rather they simply had the ill-fated gift of being able to find the brazen slogan for what was already lying ready, silently and insidiously, in others. One takes the twelve years of terror all too lightly if all the blame is laid at the feet of Hitler and his paladins and if one overlooks the fact that in their clique something coalesced that reached far beyond their private wills and their special interests. Conversely, that wide reservoir alone never would have gained such destructive power if it had not been channeled and constantly pushed beyond its immediate contents at the time.

So please understand my reflections as a contribution to the attempt to deal with the threat not through fruitless indignation and cosmetic measures, but rather by comprehending it in its deeper dimensions. Some suggestions for praxis nonetheless may follow, even if one does not imagine the path from insight to action to be as short as so many well-meaning people today seem to believe it to be.

Publication Information

Interventions

Why Still Philosophy

Radio lecture: (shortened version) "Wozu Philosophie heute?" Hessischer Rundfunk, 2 January 1962.
First published version: "Wozu noch Philosophie?" *Merkur* 16 (1962): 1001–1011.
Earlier translation: "Why Philosophy?" trans. Margaret D. Senft-Howie, in *German Opinion on Problems of Today*, ed. Walter Leifer, vol. 4, *Man and Philosophy* (Munich: Hueber, 1964), 11–24; reprinted in *Critical Theory: The Essential Readings*, ed. David Ingram and Julia Simon-Ingram (New York: Paragon House, 1991), 20–30.

Philosophy and Teachers

Radio lecture: "Lehrer und Philosophie: Ansprache an Studenten," originally a lecture in the Studentenhaus, Frankfurt; broadcast by Hessischer Rundfunk on 7 December 1961.
First published version: "Lehrer und Philosophie," *Neue Sammlung* 2 (1962): 101–114.

Note on Human Science and Culture

First published version: "Notiz über Geisteswissenschaft und Bildung," in *4 Daten: Standorte—Konsequenzen* (Hamburg: Internationaler Studenten-Arbeitskreis, 1962).

Those Twenties

First published version: "Jene zwanziger Jahre," Merkur 16 (1962): 46–51.
Earlier English translation (shortened version) appeared in The Times Literary Supplement, Friday, 13 October 1961, pp. 716–717. No translator named.

Prologue to Television

First published version: "Prolog zum Fernsehen," Rundfunk und Fernsehen 2 (1953): 1–8.

Television as Ideology

First published version: "Fernsehen als Ideologie" Rundfunk und Fernsehen 4 (1953): 1–11. The German essay developed out of an American work by Adorno: "How to Look at Television," The Quarterly of Film, Radio, and Television 8 (Spring 1940): 214–235.

Sexual Taboos and Law Today

First published version: (shorter version) "Sexualtabus und Recht heute," in Sexualität und Verbrechen: Beiträge zur Strafrechtsreform, ed. Fritz Bauer, Hans Bürger-Prinz, Hans Giese, and Herbert Jäger (Frankfurt: Fischer Bücherei, 1963), 299–317.

The Meaning of Working Through the Past

First published version: "Was bedeutet: Aufarbeitung der Vergangenheit?" Bericht über die Erzieherkonferenz am 6. und 7. November 1959 in Wiesbaden veranstaltet vom Deutschen Koordinierungsrat, herausgegeben vom Deutschen Koordinierungsrat der Gesellschaften für Christlich-Jüdische Zusammenarbeit (Frankfurt: Verlag Moritz Diesterweg, 1959).
Radio lecture: "Was bedeutet: 'Aufarbeitung der Vergangenheit'?" Hessischer Rundfunk, 7 February 1960.
Earlier translation: "What Does Coming to Terms with the Past Mean?" trans. Timothy Bahti and Geoffrey Hartman, in Bitburg in Moral and Political Perspective, ed. Geoffrey Hartman (Bloomington: Indiana University Press, 1986).

Opinion Delusion Society

Lecture held in Bad Wildungen during the "University-Weeks for Continuing Education in Political Science," conference sponsored by the Hessen State government, October 1960.
First published version: "Meinung Wahn Gesellschaft," Der Monat 14 (December 1961): 17–26.

Catchwords

Notes to Philosophical Thinking

Radio lecture: (shortened version), "Meditationen über das Denken," Deutschland-funk, 9 October 1964.
First published version: "Anmerkungen zum philosophischen Denken," *Neue deutsche Hefte* 107 (1965): 5–14.

Reason and Revelation:

Theses for a discussion with Eugen Kogon in Münster, which was broadcast by West-deutscher Rundfunk on 20 November 1957.
First published version: Theodor W. Adorno and Eugen Kogon, "Offenbarung oder autonome Vernunft," *Frankfurter Hefte* 13 (1958): 392–402 [position papers by both speakers] and 484–498 [discussion].

Progress

Lecture at the Münster Philosophers' Congress, 22 October 1962.
First published version: "Fortschritt," in *Argumentationen: Festschrift für Josef König*, ed. Harald Delius and Günther Patzig (Göttingen: Vandenhoeck & Ruprecht, 1964), 1–19.
Earlier translation: "Progress," trans. Eric Krakauer, *The Philosophical Forum* 15 (Fall/Winter 1983–84): 55–70; reprinted in *Benjamin: Philosophy, History, Aesthetics*, ed. Gary Smith (Chicago: University of Chicago Press, 1989), 84–101.

Gloss on Personality

Radio lecture: "Persönlichkeit: Höchstes Glück der Erdenkinder?" Westdeutscher Rundfunk, 2 January 1966.
First published version: "Glosse über Persönlichkeit," *Neue deutsche Hefte* 109 (1966): 47–53.

Free Time

Radio lecture: "Freizeit: Zeit der Freiheit? Leben als Konterbande," Deutschland-funk, 25 May 1969.
Earlier translation: "Free Time," trans. Gordon Finlayson, in *The Culture Industry: Selected Essays on Mass Culture*, ed. J. M. Bernstein (London: Routledge, 1991), 162–170.

Taboos on the Teaching Vocation

Radio lecture: "Der Lehrerberuf und seine Tabus," Hessischer Rundfunk, 9 September 1965.
First published version: "Tabus über dem Lehrberuf," *Neue Sammlung* 5 (1965): 486–498. With the following preface by Adorno: "The lecture here printed was

completely freely improvised on 21 May 1965, in the Institute for Pedagogical Research [Institut für Bildungsforschung] in Berlin. The author, who strictly distinguishes between the written and the spoken word, abstained from any attempt to give the lecture retrospectively the consistent and integral character he necessarily demands of a text and restricted himself to absolutely minimal corrections. Even the loose, associative transitions, which may be permitted in extemporaneous speech only, have been kept here. The author is all too aware of the resultant deficiencies. Yet perhaps precisely these deficiencies may benefit its practical effects."

Education After Auschwitz

Radio lecture: (shortened version) "Pädagogik nach Auschwitz," Hessischer Rundfunk, 18 April 1966.
First published version: "Erziehung nach Auschwitz," in *Zum Bildungsbegriff der Gegenwart*, ed. Heinz-Joachim Heydorn, Berthold Simonsohn, Friedrich Hahn, and Anselmus Hertz (Frankfurt: Verlag Moritz Diesterweg, 1967), 111–123.

On the Question: "What is German?"

Radio lecture: "Was ist Deutsch? Versuch einer Definition." A contribution to the series of the same title. Deutschlandfunk, broadcast on 9 May 1965.
First published version: "Was ist deutsch?" *Liberal* 7 (1965): 470–479.
Earlier Translation: "On the Question: 'What is German?'" trans. Thomas Y. Levin, *New German Critique* 36 (Fall 1985): 111–131.

Scientific Experiences of a European Scholar in America

Radio lecture: (shortened) "Wissenschaftliche Erfahrungen in den USA," Hessischer Rundfunk, broadcast on 31 January 1968.
First published version: "Wissenschaftliche Erfahrungen in Amerika," *Neue deutsche Hefte* 122 (1969): 3–42.
Earlier translation: "Scientific Experiences of a European Scholar in America," trans. Donald Fleming, *Perspectives in American History* 2 (1968): 338–70; reprinted in *The Intellectual Migration: Europe and America, 1930–1960*, ed. Donald Fleming and Bernard Bailyn (Cambridge, Mass.: Belknap Press and Harvard University Press, 1969), 338–370. This is a very reliable translation of the radio version of the article.

On Subject and Object

Unpublished.
Earlier translation: "Subject and Object," in *The Essential Frankfurt School Reader*, ed. Andrew Arato and Eike Gebhardt (New York: Urizen Books, 1978), 497–511.

Marginalia to Theory and Praxis

Unpublished.

Eingriffe and *Stichworte* have appeared in French translation in a single volume: *Modèles Critiques*, trans. Marc Jimenez and Eliane Kaufholz (Paris: Payot, 1984).

Critical Models 3

Critique

Radio lecture: "Kritik," broadcast in the series *Politik für Nichtpolitiker* by Süddeutscher Rundfunk, 26 May 1969.
First published version: "Kritik," *Die Zeit*, 27 June 1969: 22–23; reprinted in *Politik für Nichtpolitiker: Ein ABC zur aktuellen Diskussion*, ed. Hans Jürgen Schultz (Stuttgart/Berlin: Kreuz Verlag, 1969), 1:261–267.

Resignation

Radio lecture: "Aus gegebenem Anlaß," broadcast by Sender Freies Berlin, 9 February 1969.
First published version: "Resignation," in *Politik, Wissenschaft, Erziehung: Festschrift für Ernst Schütte* (Frankfurt: Verlag Moritz Diesterweg, 1969), 62–65.
Earlier translation: "Resignation," trans. Wes Blomster, *Telos* 35 (1978): 165–8; reprinted in *The Culture Industry: Selected Essays on Mass Culture*, ed. J. M. Bernstein (London: Routledge, 1991), 171–175.

Appendixes

Appendix 1

From the first published version of the essay, "What Does Coming to Terms with the Past Mean?" *Was bedeutet: Aufarbeitung der Vergangenheit? Bericht über die Erzieherkonferenz am 6. und 7. November 1959 in Wiesbaden*, veranstaltet vom Deutschen Koordinierungsrat, herausgegeben vom Deutschen Koordinierungsrat der Gesellschaften für Christlich-Jüdische Zusammenarbeit (Frankfurt: Verlag Moritz Diesterweg, 1959), here pp. 24–33.

Appendix 2

Reprinted in *GS* 10.2:816–817.

Translator's Notes

Preface

1. Letter of Adorno to Kracauer, 19 July 1951, from the Adorno-Kracauer correspondence located in the Deutsches Literaturarchiv, Marbach am Neckar (hereafter abbreviated DLA).

2. Letter of Adorno to Kracauer, 14 November 1963 (DLA). Suhrkamp Verlag cannot confirm these figures because of incomplete records.

3. For instance, between 1928–1932 Adorno published in and edited the musical journal *Anbruch* while in Vienna. The dates and Adorno's exact duties are somewhat controversial: cf. Heinz Steinert, *Adorno in Wien: Über die (Un-)Möglichkeit von Kunst, Kultur, und Befreiung* (Frankfurt: Fischer, 1993), 152–176. During the early thirties Adorno gave several radio talks and regularly published under Siegfried Kracauer's editorship in the *Frankfurter Zeitung*, and as his correspondence records, he entertained the idea of becoming a journalist like Kracauer and Georg Simmel rather than an academic.

4. Gerd Kadelbach, "Persönliche Begegnungen mit Theodor W. Adorno im Frankfurter Funkhaus," in , *Politische Pädagogik: Beiträge zur Humanisierung der Gesellschaft*, ed. Friedhelm Zubke (Frankfurt: Deutscher Studien Verlag, 1990), 51–52.

5. Letter of Adorno to Kracauer, 17 December 1963 (DLA). Adorno's modus operandi since the late thirties was to collect copious notes, then dictate, and repeatedly edit the typescripts. For most of the essays in the present volume there are between three and seven extant typescript versions.

6. Adorno most clearly describes his practical engagement in the mass media for the purpose of what he calls "debarbarization" in texts collected in Adorno, *Erzieh-*

ung zur Mündigkeit: Vorträge und Gespräche mit Hellmut Becker, 1959–1969 (Frankfurt: Suhrkamp, 1970), in which the radio lecture versions of several essays from the present volume are reprinted.

7. Adorno in his response also appends the paragraph from "Sexual Taboos and Law Today" dealing with the law on homosexuality; *Weder Krankheit noch Verbrechen: Plädoyer für eine Minderheit*, ed. Rolf Italiaander (Hamburg: Gala Verlag, 1969), 227–228.

8. "The demand for binding cogency without system is the demand for thought models [*Denkmodelle*]. These are not merely monadological in kind. The model concerns the specific and more than the specific, without evaporating into its more universal generic concept. Philosophical thinking means as much as thinking in models, and negative dialectics an ensemble of model analyses [*Modellanalysen*]" (T. W. Adorno, *Negative Dialectics*, trans. E. B. Ashton [New York: Seabury Press, 1973], 29; translation modified). On the double gesture of critique see p. 154: "The ideas live in the cavities between what things claim to be and what they are."

9. *Negative Dialectics*, 29 (trans. modified). Kracauer too recognized the affinity and praised the author of *Jargon of Authenticity* for being a genuine "*moraliste*." Kracauer to Adorno, 22 November 1963, in DLA.

10. As Adorno himself wrote: "No improvement is too small or trivial to be worthwhile. Of a hundred alterations each may seem trifling or pedantic by itself; together they can raise the text to a new level" (Adorno, *Minima Moralia*, trans. E. F. N. Jephcott [London: NLB, 1974], 85).

11. "The Essay as Form," in Adorno, *Notes to Literature*, trans. Shierry Weber Nicholsen (New York: Columbia University Press, 1991), 1:13. Cf. a similar formulation in *Negative Dialectics*, 45.

12. "Punctuation Marks," in *Notes to Literature*, 1:91–97. All citations in this paragraph are from that essay.

13. For a useful introduction to this vocabulary see Raymond Williams, *Keywords: A Vocabulary of Culture and Society*, rev. ed. (Oxford: Oxford University Press, 1985); Howard Caygill, *A Kant Dictionary* (Oxford: Blackwell, 1995); and Michael Inwood, *A Hegel Dictionary* (Oxford: Blackwell, 1992).

14. Cf. "Words from Abroad," in *Notes to Literature*, 1:185–199; "On the Use of Foreign Words," in *Notes to Literature*, 2:286–291, and his apothegm "German words of foreign derivation are the Jews of language" in *Minima Moralia*, 110.

Interventions

Introduction

1. "*Ausgebaut und vertieft*" (literally "built up and deepened"): hackneyed *contradictio in conjunctio* used incessantly by diplomats and journalists to refer to the German-Austrian alliance in 1918 and savagely dissected by Karl Kraus in "Ausgebaut und Vertieft," *Die Fackel* (September 1918), reprinted in Kraus, *Weltgericht: Polemische Aufsätze und Satiren aus den Jahren 1914–1919 gegen den Krieg*, ed. Heinrich Fischer (Munich/Vienna: Langen-Müller, 1965), 237–246. The phrase also suffers dramatic "tender persecution" in act 5, scene 9 of Kraus's *Die Letzten Tage*

der Menschheit (1926). Cf. also Adorno, *Minima Moralia*, trans. E. F. N. Jephcott (London: NLB, 1974), 85, where he discusses the same phrase.

2. The "clump" results from the density of the German semantics: *Eingriff*, literally "intervention," also can mean "abortion," as in the expression *verbotener Eingriff*, literally "prohibited intervention" yet actually meaning "illegal abortion"; *Verhältnis* in the plural means "relations, conditions" (e.g., of society in Marxist philosophy); in the singular (as here in the original) it can mean "relationship," "liaison" in the sexual sense. English "relations" conveys only some of this ambiguity.

3. Adorno is here playing on the dialectical relationship between essence (*Wesen*) and appearance (*Erscheinung*), as for instance in Hegel's *Science of Logic*, with, however, the further qualification that the essence is a "malfeasance" (*Unwesen*).

Why Still Philosophy

1. Radio version has "intellectual Vatican City" instead of "enclave."

2. Allusion to Heidegger's neologisms and his etymological argumentation in his later interpretations of pre-Socratic philosophy. Adorno's "resolute beings" [*Entschlossene*] puns on Heidegger's decisionistic "resoluteness" [*Entschlossenheit*] as in sections 60 and 62 of his *Sein und Zeit* (1926); English: *Being and Time*, trans. John Macquarrie and Edward Robinson (New York: Harper & Row, 1962).

3. Allusion to Hegel's famous dictum,

Was vernünftig ist, das ist wirklich;
und was wirklich ist, das ist vernünftig.
[What is rational is actual;
and what is actual is rational.]

It appears in the preface to the *Grundlinien der Philosophie des Rechts* (G. W. F. Hegel, *Werke* [Frankfurt: Suhrkamp, 1970], 7:24) and is returned to in the introduction (§6) of the *Enzyklopädie der philosophischen Wissenschaften* (*Werke*, 8:47ff.). English: G. W. F. Hegel, *Elements of the Philosophy of Right*, ed. Allen W. Wood, trans. H. B. Nisbet (Cambridge: Cambridge University Press, 1991), 20.

4. Radio lecture and first published version are more to the point here: "In the face of the unspeakable that occurred and can happen again just as easily . . . ."

5. Cf. Martin Heidegger, "Die Kehre," in *Die Technik und die Kehre* (Pfullingen: Verlag Günther Neske, 1962). Heidegger's 'turn' is generally taken to be from human existence (*Dasein*) to Being (*Sein*) itself. English: "The Turning," in Martin Heidegger, *The Question Concerning Technology and Other Essays*, ed. and trans. W. Lovitt (New York: Harper & Row, 1977), 36–49.

6. Rudolf Carnap, "Überwindung der Metaphysik durch logische Analyse der Sprache," *Erkenntnis* 2 (1931): 219–241. English translation in *Heidegger and Modern Philosophy*, ed. Michael Murray (New Haven: Yale University Press, 1978), 23–34.

7. Adorno several times obliquely cites the first proposition of Wittgenstein's *Tractatus logico-philosophicus* (trans. D. F. Pears and B. F. McGuiness [London: Routledge & Kegan Paul, 1969], 6–7): "Die Welt ist alles, was der Fall ist" ("The world is everything that is the case").

8. Cf. preface in the *Phänomenologie des Geistes*, G. W. F. Hegel, *Werke*, (Frankfurt: Suhrkamp, 1970), 3:56. English: "What, therefore, is important in the *study* of *science*, is that one should take on oneself the strenuous effort of the concept" (G. W. F. Hegel, *The Phenomenology of Spirit*, trans. A. V. Miller [Oxford: Oxford University Press, 1977], 35; translation modified).

9. Walter Bröcker, *Dialektik—Positivismus—Mythologie* (Frankfurt: Vittorio Klostermann, 1958).

10. Adorno is parodically referring to Heidegger's "hut" in the Black Forest, using the medieval term *"Gehäus"* as in Dürer's 1514 etching of St. Jerome, *Hieronymus im Gehäus*, as well as to the *"stahlhartes Gehäuse"* ("iron cage" [*sic*]) of modernity in the conclusion of Max Weber's *Die protestantische Ethik und der "Geist" des Kapitalismus*. English: *The Protestant Ethic and the Spirit of Capitalism*, trans. Talcott Parsons (New York: Routledge Chapman & Hall, 1993).

11. A Kantian term, *das Mannigfaltige* is sometimes rendered in English as "the [sensible] manifold."

12. The "something" (*"Etwas"*) is a topos in Kantian epistemology resulting from the division between the intelligible world of objects in themselves (*noumena*) and the sensible world of appearances (*phenomena*). "And we indeed, rightly considering objects of sense as mere appearances, confess thereby that they are based on a thing in itself, though we know not this thing as it is in itself but only know its appearances, viz., the way in which our senses are affected by this unknown something" (Immanuel Kant, *Prolegomena to Any Future Metaphysics*, trans. Paul Carus [Indianapolis: Hackett, 1977], 57). The original is in *Prolegomena zu einer jeden künftigen Metaphysik, die als Wissenschaft wird auftreten können* (1783), §32 (A. A. 4:314f.). For the same topos in Kant's moral theory, cf. the *Grundlegung zur Metaphysik der Sitten* (A. A. 8:461f.); English: *Grounding for the Metaphysics of Morals*, trans. James W. Ellington (Indianapolis: Hackett, 1993), 60.

13. Günther Anders, "On the Pseudo-Concreteness of Heidegger's Philosophy," in *Philosophy and Phenomenological Research*, vol. 8 (1947/48). Cf. also Günther Anders, *Die Antiquiertheit des Menschen*, vol. 1, *Über die Seele im Zeitalter der zweiten industriellen Revolution*, 5th (expanded) ed. (Munich: Beck, 1980), 21–96; and vol. 2, *Über die Zerstörung des Lebens im Zeitalter der dritten industriellen Revolution* (Munich: Beck, 1981), 335–354.

14. Cf. Immanuel Kant, *Critique of Practical Reason*, trans. Lewis White Beck, 3d ed. (New York: Macmillan, 1993), 53 (A. A. 5:51).

15. Adorno's citation of *"Dabeisein"* alludes to a passage from Hegel: "The principle of *experience* contains the infinitely important determination that, for a content to be accepted and held to be true, man must himself *be* actively involved *with it* [*dabei sein*], more precisely, that he must find any such content to be at one and in unity with *the certainty of his own self*. He must himself be involved with it, whether only with his external senses, or with his deeper spirit, with his essential consciousness of self as well" (G.W.F. Hegel, *The Encyclopedia Logic: Part I the Encyclopedia of Philosophical Sciences, with the Zusätze*, trans. T.F. Geraets, W.A. Suchting, and H.S. Harris [Indianapolis: Hackett, 1991], §7, p. 31). German: Hegel, *Enzyklopädie der philosophischen Wissenschaften I, Werke* (Frankfurt: Suhrkamp, 1970), 8:49–50.

16. Radio and first published versions continue here: "Students experience this for themselves when they come to the university with the unconscious hope that

their eyes will be opened, and instead they are put off with methodologies that ignore their actual concerns and consign them to the contingency of reviled aperçus and in fact isolate the students' original inquisitiveness and degrade it into prattle about worldviews."

17. Husserl's famous injunction underlying his phenomenological method.

18. "This is an expression of the impracticality of idealistic construction as soon as it reached complete consistency. What is not proper to the subject appears phantasmagorically as reflection in transcendental phenomenology, though it fancies itself breaking directly out of the phantasmagoria in the mirroring of 'what gives itself as such.'

This is true to Benjamin's definition of *Jugendstil* as the dream in which the dreamer dreams that he has awakened" (T. W. Adorno, *Against Epistemology* [Cambridge, Mass.: MIT Press, 1982], 138). Adorno here footnotes Benjamin, "Paris, die Hauptstadt des XIX. Jahrhunderts," Konvolut K, B1.2 (now: Benjamin, *Gesammelte Schriften*, vol. V/1 [Frankfurt: Suhrkamp, 1982], 496).

19. '*Wesenschau*' is variously translated as 'essential insight', 'intuition of essences', and 'eidetic intuition' and refers to Husserl's phenomenological reduction as the method to intuit the forms of consciousness underlying perceptual cognition.

20. Radio and first published version of this sentence: "Marx's thesis against Feuerbach, that philosophers have merely interpreted the world in various ways while it is a question of changing the world, already foresees the end of philosophy."

21. *Diamat* is the abbreviation of "*dialektischer Materialismus*" (dialectical materialism) common in the Socialist countries.

22. With "consciousness of needs" ("*Bewußtsein von Nöten*") Adorno quotes a nonexistent Hegel passage several times at strategic junctures in his argumentation for the role of modern art (e.g., *Philosophie der neuen Musik*, GS 12:22 [where Adorno provides the reference to Hegel's *Ästhetik*] and *Ästhetische Theorie*, GS 7:35, 309) because the edition of Hegel's *Ästhetik* he used (ed. Hoth, 2d ed. [Berlin, 1842]) misinterprets Hegel's text: Hegel speaks of "*Bewußtseyn von Nöthen*," an older orthography conforming to the modern phrase "*etwas vonnöten haben*" ("something is needed, required") and not, as Hoth (and hence Adorno and his readers) take it, meaning "Bewußtsein von Nöten," "consciousness of needs." Hegel is speaking of the fact that consciousness is necessary (more in the learning of the art of poetry than in the art of music) while Adorno takes him to be saying that art in general exists as long as it is accompanied by the "consciousness of needs." Cf. Jürgen Trabant, " 'Bewußtseyn von Nöthen,'" *Theodor W. Adorno*, ed. Heinz Ludwig Arnold, Sonderband aus der Reihe text + kritik (Munich: text + kritik, 1977), 130–135.

23. Radio version interjects: "spirit, the consciousness of people about themselves. . . ."

24. Radio version is slightly different: "Only thinking that does not forsake the impulse toward the unconditioned without, however, elevating itself as unconditioned is able to call the universally conditioned by its own name. It is as irreconcilable with reified consciousness as Platonic enthusiasm once was. But what exists would have as its purpose to exist for its own sake."

25. Adorno is here drawing on the entire semantic field of German "*Schuld*": "wrong," "guilt," "sin," and "debt."

26. G. W. F. Hegel, *Grundlinien der Philosophie des Rechts oder Naturrecht und Staatswissenschaft im Grundrisse, Werke*, vol. 7 (Frankfurt: Suhrkamp, 1970). Here from the "Preface" (*Vorrede*), p. 26. English: "To comprehend *what is* is the task of philosophy, for *what is* is reason. As far as the individual is concerned, each individual is in any case a *child of his time*; thus philosophy, too, is *its own time comprehended in thoughts*" (G. W. F. Hegel, *Elements of the Philosophy of Right*, 21).

27. Allusion to Heidegger's text, in explanation of his turning down the second offer of a philosophy chair in Berlin, "Schöpferische Landschaft: Warum Bleiben wir in der Provinz?" (1933) originally in *Der Alemanne: Kampfblatt der Nationalsozialisten Oberbadens*, 67a, "Zu neuen Ufern: Die wöchentlich erscheinende Kulturbeilage der Alemannen," 9 (Freiburg, 1934; reprinted in *Nachlese zu Heidegger*, ed. Guido Schneeberger [Bern, 1962], 216–218; and in Martin Heidegger, *Aus der Erfahrung des Denkens, Gesamtausgabe* [Frankfurt: Vittorio Klostermann, 1983], 13:9–13). English: "Why Do I Stay in the Provinces? (1934)," trans. Thomas J. Sheehan *Listening: Journal of Religion and Culture* (River Forest), 112 (3) (1977): 122–125. In an introductory lecture course in philosophy Adorno used this text to excoriate Heidegger's latent fascism: in the work "you can see how the supposedly pure ontological in the texts of Heidegger himself moves into a laudatio of the simple peasant life, that is, into a kind of blood-and-soil ideology" (*Philosophische Terminologie* [Frankfurt: Suhrkamp, 1973], 1:152).

28. Cf. Friedrich Nietzsche, "Von den Hinterweltern," *Also Sprach Zarathustra*, vol. 4 of *Sämtliche Werke: Kritische Studienausgabe*, ed. Giorgio Colli and Mazzino Montinari (Berlin/New York: de Gruyter, 1967–1977), 35–38. English: "On the Afterworldly," in *Thus Spake Zarathustra*, trans. Walter Kaufmann (New York: Viking Press, 1966), 30–33.

29. Adorno plays on the resonance between *das Heile*, "the safe and sound," and *das Unheil*, "the calamity."

30. Presumably an allusion to the conservative Springer Verlag.

31. Robert Drill, *Aus der Philosophen-Ecke: Kritische Glossen zu den geistigen Strömungen unserer Zeit* (Frankfurt: Frankfurter Societäts-Verlag, 1923). Drill was a national economist who turned to neo-Kantianism (in the person of Ernst Marcus) in search of a secure "standpoint." The book is a loose collection of digressive occasional pieces, reviews, critical comments on anthroposophy, expressionism, Spengler, the "woman question," etc., as well as expository appreciations of philosophers and social theorists of the German idealist tradition. Kantian "criticism" and psychoanalysis (topics that may have drawn Adorno's attention to the book initially) serve more as invocations to "healthy common sense" than as argumentative means.

32. Adorno plays here on the resonance between *Weisheit*, "wisdom," and *Wohlweisheit*, his neologistic substantivization of the adverb *wohlweislich*, meaning "prudently" and implying cautious conservatism.

33. *Der Blaue Engel* (*The Blue Angel*), Joseph von Sternberg's 1930 film version of Heinrich Mann's novella *Professor Unrat oder das Ende eines Tyrannen* (1905). Cf. Adorno's polemic against the reissuing of the novel with the title altered to *Der Blaue Engel* in "Ein Titel," and "Unrat und Engel," in *Noten zur Literatur*, GS 11:654–660. English: "A Title," and "Unrat and Angel," in *Notes to Literature*, trans. Shierry Weber Nicholsen (New York: Columbia University Press, 1992), 2:299–304.

Philosophy and Teachers

1. Secondary school (in its three varieties: *humanistisches Gymnasium, das Realgymnasium, die Oberrealschule*) in Germany extends to the pupil's eighteenth year of age. Students who successfully complete the school receive the *Abitur*, roughly equivalent to British A-levels or the first two years of undergraduate study in the United States.

2. Cf. Friedrich Nietzsche, "Von der Nächstenliebe," in *Also Sprach Zarathustra*, vol. 4 of *Sämtliche Werke: Kritische Studienausgabe*, ed. Giorgio Colli and Mazzino Montinari (Berlin/New York: de Gruyter, 1967–1977), 76–79. English: "Do I recommend love of the neighbor to you? Sooner I should even recommend flight from the neighbor and love of the farthest. Higher than love of the neighbor is love of the farthest and the future: higher yet than the love of human beings I esteem the love of things and ghosts" ("On Love of the Neighbor," in *Thus Spake Zarathustra*, trans. Walter Kaufmann [New York: Viking Press, 1966], 61).

3. Presumably an allusion to the character of Tesman in Ibsen's play *Hedda Gabler*. In act 2 Hedda says of her husband, the scholar, "Tesman is a specialist . . . and specialists are not at all amusing to travel with. Not in the long run, at any rate." Quoted from vol. 10 of the William Archer edition of *The Works of Henrik Ibsen* (New York: Viking, 1911–12), 92f. Adorno is also probably referring to the section "Acclimatization and Specialization" in Löwenthal's study of Ibsen; cf. Leo Löwenthal, *Literature and the Image of Man: Communication in Society* (New Brunswick, N. J.: Transaction Books, 1986), 2:163ff. An earlier version was published in the Institute journal: Leo Löwenthal, "Das Individuum in der individualistischen Gesellschaft: Bemerkungen über Ibsen," *Zeitschrift für Sozialforschung* 5 (1936): 321–363.

4. A posthumous tract: *Deducirter Plan einer zu Berlin zu errichtenden höheren Lehranstalt: Geschrieben im Jahre 1807 von Johann Gottlieb Fichte* (Stuttgart: Cotta, 1817). The text was reprinted in a modern collection on "the idea of the German university," a topic under extreme scrutiny at the time Adorno was writing the present essay. Cf. *Die Idee der deutschen Universität: Die fünf Grundschriften aus der Zeit ihrer Neubegründung durch klassischen Idealismus und romantischen Realismus*, ed. Ernst Anrich (Darmstadt: Wissenschaftliche Buchgesellschaft, 1956).

5. In the twenty-fifth "adventure" of the *Nibelungenlied* Hagen, the vassal of King Gunther, leads the royal retinue to visit the king's sister Kriemhild, who, following the murder of her husband Siegfried by Hagen, has married the Hun Etzel and, notwithstanding twelve years of marriage, still plans to avenge Siegfried's murder. While searching for a ford or ferry across the swollen Danube, Hagen meets two water nymphs who warn him that all the company will be killed by the Huns with the sole exception of the king's chaplain. To test the prophecy Hagen hurls the chaplain into the raging waters of the Danube as they cross by ferry, and the chaplain, who cannot swim, remarkably survives and remains on the near side of the river. Thus Hagen knows that the entire retinue is fated to perish and vows to fight to the bitter end.

6. Hugo von Hofmannsthal, *"Elektra": Tragödie in einem Aufzug frei nach Sophokles*, orig. 1904, in *Gesammelte Werke in Einzelausgaben*, ed. Herbert Steiner,

vol. 3 of *Dramen* (Frankfurt: Fischer, 1959), 29–30. The reference is to Clytemnestra's words in her response to Electra's intimation that a sacrifice must be made to appease the situation, meaning the murder of her mother:

CLYTEMNESTRA: We need only make subservient to us
the powers that are scattered somewhere. There are
rites. There must be proper rites for everything.
(Electra: A Tragedy in One Act, trans. Alfred Schwarz, in Hugo von Hofmannsthal, Selected Plays and Libretti, ed. Michael Hamburger [New York: Pantheon Books, 1963], 27–28)

7. Adorno's citation: "*Ich will ja gar kein Mensch sein*"; the full citation is "*Oh, Jungens, ich will doch gar kein Mensch sein*" and is spoken by Paul in scene 8 of *Aufstieg und Fall der Stadt Mahagonny*, originally in *Versuche*, Heft 2 (Berlin: Kiepenheuer Verlag, 1930); now in Bertolt Brecht, *Werke: Stücke 2* (Berlin, Weimar, Frankfurt: Aufbau-Verlag, Suhrkamp, 1988), 351.

8. Adorno's *Fachmenschentum* (specialized personnel) alludes to Max Weber's coinage in the opening pages of his introduction to the *Gesammelte Aufsätze zur Religionssoziologie* (Tübingen: Mohr, 1920–21); English: introduction to *The Protestant Ethic and the Spirit of Capitalism*, trans. Talcott Parsons (New York: Scribner's, 1958), where he very ambivalently evaluates the unique conjunction of specialization and thoroughgoing administrative organization in Western rationality. Adorno's pun rests on the idiomatic phrase "*seine Orgien feiern*" (celebrate one's orgies, go wild): in this case, "orally."

9. Hans Cornelius (1863–1947), professor of philosophy at the University of Frankfurt, under whom Horkheimer and Adorno wrote their dissertations.

10. Cf. Adorno, *Jargon der Eigentlichkeit: Zur deutschen Ideologie*, in *GS* 6:413–526. English: *The Jargon of Authenticity*, trans. Knut Tarnowski and Frederic Will (London: Routledge & Kegan Paul, 1973).

11. Adorno here contrasts the Hegelian notion of externalization (*Entäußerung*), in which a person develops through a dialectic of self-abandonment to an external subject and self-transformation, with merely indifferent rote learning of independent information. For the latter activity Adorno uses the cliché "*sich mit etwas auseinandersetzen*," "to confront, come to terms with something," but literally "to set oneself apart from something," precisely the opposite of "externalization."

12. University degree required for the teaching profession.

13. Adorno here echoes Hegel's Hellenophilic stylistics: the German *Paränese* (*Paränesen* here, in plural) has an equally abstruse English equivalent: paraenesis: exhortation, advice, counsel, a hortatory composition, from the Greek παραίνεσις (advice, counsel).

14. The German originals are: "*in etwa*," "*echtes Anliegen*," and "*Begegnung*." The latter two carry existentialist overtones.

15. *Ebbes* in the dialect of Hessen is equivalent to the standard High German *etwas*, "something."

16. The German idiom is "*wie einem der Schnabel gewachsen ist*," literally, "just as the beak has grown on one," which does not have the connotation of spontaneity that the English idiom does.

17. First published version directly cites the neo-Marxist phrase "sedimented cultural goods of the privileged class."

18. Radio and first published version has "are not natural [*naturhaft*]" instead of "are not invariants."

19. Plato: *daimon* in *Apology* 31d as Socrates' inner voice, divine advisor, in *Symposium* 202e *eros* is called a *daimon* (mediator between mortals and immortals) that impels the lover of wisdom to attain cognition of the good and the beautiful. Cf. also *mania* in *Ion* 533dff. and *Phaedrus* 244ff.

20. *Vorlesungen über die Methode des akademischen Studiums*, in *Schellings Werke*, ed. Manfred Schröter, vol. 3, *Schriften zur Identitätsphilosophie, 1801–1806* (Munich: Beck and Oldenbourg, 1927), 229–374. English: F. W. J. Schelling, *On University Studies*, trans. E. S. Morgan, ed. Norbert Gutermann (Athens, Ohio: Ohio University Press, 1966).

Note on Human Science and Culture

1. This essay especially relies on the fabric of the German language and the German intellectual tradition. *Geist* is "spirit," "mind," or "intellect" as opposed to matter or nature; *geistige Gebilde* are the fabrications, works, creations that are infused, shaped by spirit. *Wissenschaft* means both "science" and "scholarship." Though Wilhelm Dilthey did not invent the term, in 1883 he secured the meaning of *Geisteswissenschaften* as the "sciences of the spirit" (including the humanities, history, the arts, etc., and here rendered "human sciences") as opposed to sciences of nature in his *Introduction to the Human Sciences: An Attempt to Lay the Foundation for the Study of Society and History* (ed. and trans. Ramon J. Betanzos [Detroit, Mich.: Wayne State University Press, 1988]). In later development the term came to designate all hermeneutical inquiries into human society and cultural production as opposed to analytical and positivistic methodologies, a distinction Adorno elaborated in his contribution to the "positivism controversy" in German sociology. Adorno adds a further twist by using the word in its uncustomary singular in the title and at strategic junctures in the essay, in analogy to "natural science" (*Naturwissenschaft*): a linguistic performance of the essay's argument that the consolidation of a false model of scientific method homogenizes and reifies the diverse and irreducibly dialectical human sciences. Adorno coins the verb *entgeisten* and the substantive *Entgeistung*, "dispirit," "deprivation of spirit," as the ultimate step in a worldview characterized by the human self-image as "the ghost in the machine." The semantics of *Bildung*, "formation," "development," "culture," "self-cultivation," "education" and its related verb *bilden*, is also specific to the German intellectual tradition and is differentiated from education in the sense of practical training (*Ausbildung*) and specialized training (*Fachbildung*). The distinction is paralleled by that of autonomy and heteronomy. The theory of *Bildung* as the development of a learned and cultivated personality through *Wissenschaft* was characteristic of German Idealism and Humboldt's university reforms.

2. On the network of meanings to the term *Entäußerung* see Georg Lukács, *The Young Hegel: Studies in the Relations between Dialectics and Economics*, trans. Rodney Livingstone (London: Merlin Press, 1975), 537–568. Lukács draws the parallels between Goethe and Hegel in his *Goethe and his Age*, trans. Robert Anchor (London: Merlin Press, 1979), 157–255.

3. Adorno's neologisms *entgeisten, Entgeistung* (rendered "dispirit," "dispiriting") here echo Nietzsche's lament of the "despiritualization" [*Entgeistigung,* also a neologism] of German education; cf. section 3 of "Was den Deutschen abgeht" in *Götzen-Dämmerung* in Nietzsche, *Sämtliche Werke: Kritische Studienausgabe,* ed. Giorgio Colli and Mazzino Montinari (Berlin/New York: de Gruyter: 1967–1977), 6:105. English: "For seventeen years I have not tired of shedding light on the *despiritualizing* influence of our contemporary science business. The burdensome serfdom to which the immense range of the sciences condemns every individual today is the main reason why natures with fuller, richer, *deeper* constitutions can no longer find any suitable education *or educators.* Nothing makes our culture suffer *more* than the oversupply of arrogant loafers and fragments of humanity; our universities, *despite* themselves, are really the greenhouses for this sort of stunting of spiritual instincts" (Friedrich Nietzsche, *Twilight of the Idols, or How to Philosophize with the Hammer,* trans. Richard Polt [Indianapolis: Hackett, 1997], 45).

4. Adorno's verb here, *gleichschalten,* belonged to the Nazi vocabulary and meant forcing institutions to toe the party line after 1933.

5. First published version of this article has instead of "the same" (*das Gleiche*), "Being" (*das Sein*).

Those Twenties

1. Adolf Frisé (born 1910), German writer, editor of Robert Musil's *Collected Works,* and director of the cultural program of the regional radio studio Hessischer Rundfunk 1956–1975. Lotte Lenya (1898–1981), Austrian actress and singer, wife of Kurt Weill, famous as interpreter of the Brecht/Weill plays (*Mahagonny, Threepenny Opera, Seven Deadly Sins,* etc.), emigrated in 1933 and came to the USA in 1935.

The radio discussion was between Frisé, Lenya, and Adorno, part of the "evening studio" program of Hessischer Rundfunk, and was broadcast on July 26, 1960. The Hessischer Rundfunk's catalog gives the following summary of the dialogue: "An attempt to illuminate anew the reality of the twenties against the background of the experiences of a contemporary witness. To start off the discussion Adorno formulates the idea of imagelessness, the lack of traditional 'imagines' in America, from which result worlds of synthetic images, for instance, that of the wild West and the image of the 'golden twenties.' Addressing the question of the fascination of the twenties, the attempt is made to separate the real characteristics of this period from the aspects of a synthetically produced imagistic world of the 'golden twenties.' Arguing for a relativistic interpretation, Adorno speaks of aesthetic and thematic 'archetypes,' which were laid out in the twenties and only today are becoming productive for art. As an example he notes Stockhausen's collective compositional technique as a continuation of Brecht's collective work."

2. IGNM = Internationale Gesellschaft für neue Musik (International Society of New Music). *In nuce* Adorno's argument in his article is that the new music, for all its apparently radical innovations, occurs within the established order of society: "The music has *stabilized,* and has submitted to the requirements of the likewise freshly stabilized society; to be sure, the music has caught up to the development of society and has liberated itself from the petit bourgeois privacy of the nineteenth century as

well as from the undynamic rigidity of its musical system; the stabilized music of today relates to the stable music of the nineteenth century no differently than the most progressive theory of marginal utility relates to classical economic theory. However, within the frame of such change everything has remained as it was" (Adorno, "Die stabilisierte Musik," in GS 18, Musikalische Schriften 5:721–728, here p. 725). According to the editorial afterword, this article was written in 1928 but never published. Cf. also "Das Altern der neuen Musik" in Dissonanzen, in GS 14:143–168; English: "The Aging of the New Music," Telos 28 (Summer 1976): 113–124.

3. Allusion to Adorno's essay "Zeitlose Mode: Zum Jazz" in GS 10.1:123–137. English: "Perennial Fashion: Jazz," in Prisms, trans. Samuel and Shierry Weber (Cambridge, Mass.: MIT Press, 1981), 119–132.

4. Allan Bott, Our Fathers (1870–1900): Manners and Customs of the Ancient Victorians: A Survey in Pictures and Text of their History, Morals, Wars, Sports, Inventions, and Politics (London: Heinemann, 1931; reprint, New York: Blom, 1972).

5. "Alienation" [Verfremdung] in the sense of Brecht's alienation effect: a familiar object, practice, etc. is "defamiliarized" by detaching it from its everyday context or by breaking the conventions through which it is unrefractedly experienced.

6. Die Dreigroschenoper (1928) by Bertolt Brecht, music by Kurt Weill; Aufstieg und Fall der Stadt Mahagonny (1929) by Brecht and Weill; Ernst Krenek, Jonny spielt auf (1926), opus 45, piano and vocal score. English: Johnny Strikes up the Band: An Opera in Two Parts, book and music by Ernst Krenek, English version by Frederick H. Martens (New York: Bullman, 1928).

7. Cf. the refrain "alles dürfen darf" from the men's chorus in act 2, scene 13 of the opera Aufstieg und Fall der Stadt Mahagonny in Bertolt Brecht, Werke, ed. Werner Hecht, Jan Kopf, Werner Mittenzwei, Klaus-Detlef Müller, vol. 2, Stücke 2 (Berlin/Weimar: Aufbau Verlag, and Frankfurt: Suhrkamp, 1988), 362; English: Bertolt Brecht, The Rise and Fall of the City of Mahagonny, trans. W. H. Auden and Chester Kallman (Boston: Godine, 1976), 68:

One means to eat all you are able;
Two, to change your loves about;
Three means the ring and gaming table;
Four, to drink until you pass out.
Moreover, better get it clear
That Don'ts are not permitted here.
Moreover, better get it clear
That Don'ts are not permitted here!

8. Wunschbild, "ideal-image," "image of desire," a terminus technicus in Freud denoting the ideal image of a love-object as constructed by the libido. Cf. Die Traumdeutung (1900); English: The Interpretations of Dreams, vols. 4 and 5 of The Standard Edition of the Complete Psychological Works of Sigmund Freud, trans. James Strachey (London: Hogarth Press, 1975).

9. According to Brecht, his early drama Baal (1918) was an "antithesis" or "materialistic" "counter-design" to the drama Der Einsame: Ein Menschenuntergang (1917) by Johst, an idealistic expressionist dramatization of the life of the poet

Hans Christian Grabbe (1801–1836). Brecht said he wanted to "undermine the weak successful drama [. . .] with a ridiculous treatment of genius and the amoral," *Schriften zum Theater* 15 (Frankfurt: Suhrkamp 1963), 69.

After being attacked by Nazi ideologues for his early expressionist plays, Hanns Johst (1890–1978) began writing in praise of Hitler and the National Socialist cause. His play *Schlageter* (1933), glorifying the early Nazi martyr, was performed regularly in the theaters of the Third Reich. In 1933 Johst was named producer of the Prussian State Theater and made president of the Academy of German Literature; in 1934 he was appointed to the Prussian State Council, and in 1935 he became president of the Reich Theater Chamber. He called for a "reawakening of confidence" as the condition for a new *völkisch* theater under National Socialism and is said to have boasted that whenever someone mentioned the word *culture* to him, he was inclined to reach for his revolver.

10. The German *Umbruch* means literally the breaking up, plowing up of soil for aeration and replanting and figuratively a radical change or shake-up.

11. Adorno articulates his abhorrence at the idea of a "guiding image" (*Leitbild*) in the text that opens his essay collection *Ohne Leitbild* (1967, 1968), now in *GS* 10.1.

Prologue to Television

1. Johann Wolfgang von Goethe, *Maximen und Reflexionen*, 902, vol. 12 of *Goethe's Werke*, ed. Erich Trunz (Munich: Beck, 1973), 497.

2. First published version: "The more seamless the imagistic world, the more fragile it becomes at the same time."

3. First published version interjects here: "one hit song was called '*Especially For You*'* . . . ."

4. First published version is slightly different: "The reading of a number of admittedly better than average television drama scripts . . . ."

5. Georg Legman, *Love and Death: A Study in Censorship* (New York: Hacker Art Books, 1963). An extremely witty study of the negation of sex and the institutionalization of violence in American life, as reflected in murder mysteries, comic books, films, etc., and the patent absurdity of censoring sex while promoting violence. He also offers trenchant social-psychological interpretations of the figure of the "bitch-heroine" and innumerable high (Hemingway) and low (*Gone with the Wind*) manifestations of misogyny and gynophobia. "My dear fellow, it is not easy to take the adolescent's mind off sex. It takes death, death, death, and more death. For adults, more still" (93). "Violence and death have saved us from sex" (94).

6. First published version is more Freudian here: "which condition the instinctual impulses of the public according to the requirements . . . ."

7. An ironic allusion to Zarathustra's self-injunction "Werde, der du bist!" in his address to the "human sea" in *Also Sprach Zarathustra* (in Nietzsche, *Sämtliche Werke: Kritische Studienausgabe*, ed. Giorgio Colli and Mazzino Montinari [Berlin/New York: de Gruyter: 1967–1977], 4:297). "Open up and cast up to me your fish and glittering crabs! With my best bait I shall today bait the queerest human fish. My happiness itself I cast out far and wide, between sunrise, noon, and sunset, to see if many human fish might not learn to wriggle and wiggle from my happiness until, biting at my sharp hidden hooks, they must come up to *my* height—the most color-

ful abysmal groundlings, to the most sarcastic of all who fish for men. For that is what I am through and through: reeling, reeling in, raising up, raising, a raiser, culti-vator, and disciplinarian, who once counseled himself, not for nothing: Become who you are!" (*Thus Spake Zarathustra*, trans. Walter Kaufmann [New York: Viking Press, 1966], 239).

8. First published version is slightly different: "and changing its destructive force for the good, . . ."

9. First published version interjects the following sentence: "In the words of Leo Löwenthal, psychoanalysis in reverse is carried out."

10. First published version interjects a further "maxim": "that fathers are wax in the hands of their cruelly enchanting daughters . . . ."

11. One of the maxims "From Makarie's Archive" [*Aus Makariens Archiv*] in book 3 of *Wilhelm Meisters Wanderjahre*, no. 172, p. 485 of vol. 8 of *Goethe's Werke*. The maxim is reprinted as no. 137 in *Maximen und Reflexionen*, vol. 12 of *Goethe's Werke*. English: J. W. von Goethe, *Conversations of German Refugees: Wilhelm Meister's Journeyman Years, or The Renunciants*, trans. Krishna Winston, ed. Jane K. Brown (New York: Suhrkamp, 1989), 435.

12. Like English, the German "to watch television" [*fernsehen*] means literally to "see far, into the distance."

Television as Ideology

1. First published version begins with the following two sentences: " 'Prologue to Television' theoretically developed some things the new medium inflicts upon the consciousness of those exposed to it. Concrete proof of these implications must be added to those theses."

2. First published version has "barbaric" instead of "philistine."

3. First published version has the following: "They were carried out in a pilot study at the Hacker Foundation in Beverly Hills during the time from November 1952 to August 1953. The author must thank Bernice T. Eiduson, George Gerbner, Merril B. Friend, and Liesel Seham for their assistance."

4. Dallas W. Smythe and Angus Campbell, *Los Angeles Television* (Ann Arbor: Edwards Brothers, 1951). Other research studies include: *New York Television, January 4–10, 1951–52* (Urbana, Ill.: National Association of Educational Broadcasters, 1952); *New Haven Television, May 15–21, 1952* (Urbana, Ill.: National Association of Educational Broadcasters, 1952); *Three Years of New York Television, 1951–53* (Urbana, Ill.: National Association of Educational Broadcasters, 1953). Interpretive studies by Smythe include: "Television in Relation to Other Media and Recreation in American Life," *Hollywood Quarterly* 4 (Spring 1950): 256–261; "An Analysis of Television Programs," *Scientific American* 1951 (June): 15–17; "The Consumer's Stake in Radio and Television," *Quarterly Review of Film, Radio, and Television* 6 (Winter 1951): 109–128; "What TV Programming is Like," *Quarterly Review of Film, Radio, and Television* 3 (Summer 1952): 25–31; "The Content and Effects of Broadcasting," *Mass Media and Education*, National Security for the Study of Education, 53d Yearbook (1954): 192–217; "Reality as Presented by TV," *Public Opinion Quarterly* 18, no. 2 (Summer 1954): 143–156.

5. First published version has "older films" instead of "films."

6. The footnote in the original manuscript report presented to the Hacker Foundation on April 13, 1953, and now located in the Adorno Archive in Frankfurt, runs as follows:

According to the December 1951 issue of *Los Angeles Television* by Dallas W. Smythe and Angus Campbell and published by the National Association of Educational Broadcasters, "drama programs took the largest piece of available television time. Approximately one fourth (26%) of the total television program time during the test week was devoted to general adult drama programs." "During the evening hours this percentage increased to 34.5% of programming with an additional 1.7% in children's drama." "Within the broad class of drama, the Western drama led all subclasses of programs. . . . Together with crime drama, these two forms of drama contribute 1/5 of all television programming." "In addition, drama took over one half of the children-hours programming." "If the television user tuned in at random between 7:00 and 11:00 P.M. any day of the week, the probability would be one out of three that he would encounter drama."

7. Hans Weigel (1908–1991), novelist, dramatic critic, satirist, and playwright, who lived in Vienna except for the period between 1938 and 1945 when he was in political exile in Switzerland. Adorno is presumably alluding to a scathing review of the film version of J. S. Bach's *St. Matthew's Passion* by Ernst Marischka ("Für und wider Marischkas *Matthäus-Passion*") originally in *Welt am Montag*, (Dec. 7 and 14, 1949), reprinted in Hans Weigel, *1000 Premieren: Hymnen und Verrisse* (Graz: Styria, 1983), 2:393–397. Weigel argues principally against the practice of making a "film version" of classical musical works and in particular here that the excellent musical and choral production (Herbert Karajan directing) is mutilated by the commercial need to tell and show a "story."

8. "Refunction" [*umfunktionieren*] in Brecht refers to the practice of alienating a term, situation, etc. from its habitual context and redeploying it in a critical fashion; "Brecht has coined the phrase 'functional transformation' [*Umfunktionierung*] to describe the transformation of forms and instruments of production by a progressive intelligentsia—an intelligentsia interested in liberating the means of production and hence active in the class struggle" (Walter Benjamin, "The Author as Producer," *Understanding Brecht*, trans. Anna Bostock [London: NLB, 1973], 93).

9. The earlier English study, on which this essay is based, offers a useful comparative exposition of the interrelationship Adorno sees between aesthetic complexity (or "multilayered structure") and the multilayered personality:

When we speak of the multilayered structure of television shows, we are thinking of various superimposed layers of different degrees of manifestness or hiddenness that are utilized by mass culture as a technological means of "handling" the audience. This was expressed felicitously by Leo Löwenthal when he coined the term "psychoanalysis in reverse." The implication is that somehow the psychoanalytic concept of a multilayered personality has been taken up by cultural industry [*sic*], but that the concept is used in order to ensnare the consumer as completely as possible and in order to engage him psychodynamically in the service of premeditated effects. A clear-cut division into allowed gratifications, forbidden gratifications, and recurrence of the forbidden gratification in a somewhat modified and deflected form is carried through.

("How to Look at Television," The Quarterly of Film, Radio, and Television 8 [Spring 1954]: 213–235, here p. 223)

10. Georg Legman, *Love and Death: A Study in Censorship* (New York: Hacker Art Books, 1963). In particular the chapter "Avatars of the Bitch":

The "spirited" heroine—let us be frank, the *bitch-heroine*—appearing on the champ de Mars some twelve years ago, has carried popular literature before her; outselling, outswearing, and outswinging all competition. But she has not yet removed her mask. After a dozen years of spying out the land she still pretends to be merely a historical hussy, merely an exceptional vixen; or, if her methods are too bloodthirsty for the mild disguise of historical or individual peculiarity, she presents herself as a poor, helpless, pathological case. Let us not be fooled. She is no accident, neither of history, nor personality, nor pathology. She is a wishful dream—Venus Dominatrix—cunningly contrived out of the substance of women's longings. She is presented to the "emancipated" but still enslaved wives-mothers-and-mistresses as a fantasy escape from their servitude to men, to fashion, traditional morality, and the paralyzing uselessness of being nothing but the show-horses of their owners' success.   *(58)*

Avatars include: Scarlett O'Hara in *Gone with the Wind, Dutchess Hotspur,* diverse *femmes fatales* in Dashiell Hammett, etc.

11. Theodor Fontane, *Frau Jenny Treibel* (1893), in vol. 7 of *Sämtliche Werke* (Munich: Nymphenburger Verlagshandlung, 1959). English: Theodor Fontane, *Short Novels and Other Writings,* ed. P. Demetz (New York: Continuum, 1982).

The eponymous protagonist of Fontane's novel is a society woman who constantly upholds literature and sentiment while unhesitatingly seeking material advantage. Fontane ironically portrays her attempts to undermine her son's betrothal to the richly cultured and intelligent daughter of a teacher, alas of modest means.

12. Johann Andreas Eisenbart (1661–1727) was an itinerant practitioner of the curative arts, oculist, and gem cutter, a "country doctor from Great Britain and Hannöverian-Münden" as his gravestone attests. An important surgeon in his time, he is now remembered as a type of medical charlatan, above all because of a song about him that first appeared in a fraternity songbook in 1818, the first quatrain of which is as follows:

Ich bin der Doktor Eisenbart,
Kurier' die Leut' nach meiner Art,
Kann machen, daß die Blinden gehn,
Und daß die Lahmen wieder sehn.

[I am the Doctor Eisenbart,
heal the folks by my own art,

Make it so the dumb can walk,
And make it so the lame can talk.]

13. First published version explicitly cites the (unlocated) neo-Marxist passage.

14. Cf. Søren Kierkegaard, "A Crisis in the Life of an Actress," in Kierkegaard, *Crisis in the Life of an Actress and Other Essays on Drama*, trans. Stephen Crites (London: Collins, 1967), 67–91.

15. First published version: "Precisely in Germany, where television is not yet institutionalized, where the procedure has not yet become established, and where economic interests do not directly control the programming, ..."

16. First published version specifies: "Instead of tracking down vulgar words and indecency like the Johnson Code, the 'self-censor' of the producers should be vigilant. . . ."

17. Reference to Paul Lazarsfeld's project of wedding "administrative research" to critical theory. Cf. Paul F. Lazarsfeld, "Remarks on Administrative and Critical Communications Research," *Studies in Philosophy and Social Science* 9 (1941): 2–16; and Adorno's account of the divorce in "Scientific Experiences of a European Scholar in America," below. For a historical treatment of the failed marriage, cf. David E. Morrison, "Kultur and Culture: The Case of Theodor W. Adorno and Paul F. Lazarsfeld," *Social Research* 45 (1978): 330–355.

Sexual Taboos and Law Today

1. *Denker in dürftiger Zeit*, itself an allusion to Hölderlin's "what use are poets in indigent times?" [*"wozu Dichter in dürftiger Zeit?"*] from his poem "Bread and Wine" [*"Brot und Wein"*], here alludes to Karl Löwith's critical assessment *Heidegger: Denker in dürftiger Zeit* (1935; 2d. ed. 1960), in *Sämtliche Schriften* (Stuttgart: Metzlersche Verlagsbuchhandlung, 1984), 8:124–234.

2. *Partialtrieb*, "component or partial instinct," a *terminus technicus* introduced by Freud in the first edition of *Drei Abhandlungen zur Sexualtheorie* (1905); English: *Three Essays on the Theory of Sexuality*, vol. 7 of *The Standard Edition of the Complete Psychological Works of Sigmund Freud*, trans. James Strachey (London: Hogarth Press, 1975). The sexual drive is there analyzed into component or partial instincts, each with its own source (e.g., oral, anal, etc.) and goal (e.g., *Bemächtigungstrieb*, the instinct to master). The free interplay of the partial instincts explains the "polymorphous perversion" of childhood sexuality as well as the adult phenomena of fore-pleasure [*Vorlust*] and various perversions.

3. Karl Kraus, *Sittlichkeit und Kriminalität*, *Werke*, vol. 11 (Munich/Vienna: Langen-Müller, 1963). Cf. Adorno's review of this volume: "Sittlichkeit und Kriminalität: Zum elften Band der Werke von Karl Kraus," in *Noten zur Literatur*, GS 11:367–387; in English: "Morals and Criminality: On the Eleventh Volume of the Works of Karl Kraus," in *Notes to Literature*, trans. Shierry Weber Nicholsen (New York: Columbia University Press, 1992), 2:40–57.

4. Cf. Hans Magnus Enzensberger, "Bildung als Konsumgut: Analyse der Taschenbuch-Produktion," in Enzensberger, *Einzelheiten* (Frankfurt: Suhrkamp, 1962), 110–136. As part of his critique of the commodification of consciousness, Enzensberger takes to task Ernesto Grassi, the editor of the recently published

Rowohlts deutsche Enzyklopädie. Grassi's explanatory justification of the modern encyclopedia, *Die zweite Aufklärung: Enzyklopädie heute* [The Second Enlightenment: the Encyclopedia Today] defends the new encyclopedia's (in Enzensberger's words "haphazard") concatenation of articles as being a "meaningful construct," the only mode of presentation equal to modernity's rapid production of knowledge, to which Enzensberger responds: "That he would like to be allowed to stipulate what an encyclopedia should be is of course understandable. We however would rather stay with Diderot and d'Alembert, even though these authors don't get much attention from Grassi, just as we prefer the first Enlightenment to the second, which he threatens to continue to produce and which comes down to nothing more than reversing the idea and intention of its illustrious predecessor" (127). Later (pp. 129–130) in the article he faults another encyclopedia for leaving "the inner law of the mass media" unexplained and refers approvingly to the work of Anders and Adorno.

5. Martha Wolfenstein and Nathan Leites, *Movies: A Psychological Study* (Glencoe, Ill.: Free Press, 1950; reprint, New York: Hafner, 1971):

> The solution of love problems tends to be phrased mainly in terms of female types and functions. Thus two current love requirements, which in part conflict with one another, find satisfaction in various film heroines. There is on the one hand the impact of what we call goodness morality, which leads to high estimation of the charms of wickedness as well as to guilt about pursuing them. The good-bad girl represents a solution to the problem which goodness morality poses to the man. On the other hand, expressing a more recent trend, there are the demands of what we call fun morality: you've got to have fun (whether you like it or not). If you are not having fun, you must ask yourself what is wrong with you. The strength of impulse, which seemed so assured when faced with the barriers of goodness morality, often dwindles before the imperative of fun morality. A relatively new type of heroine has appeared to help the man over this difficulty. She boldly takes the initiative in love relations and assures the man of her confidence in his masculinity even when he is not proving it. She estimates appraisingly the quantity of pleasure produced by a kiss, but does not seem to demand any all-out letting go of emotion, which might be difficult to achieve. Thus she approaches sex with a man's point of view, helps the man who is inhibited when confronted by an excess of femininity, and makes the requisite achievement of fun seem not too much of a strain.   *(21–22)*

> The good-bad girl and the girl with the masculine approach, while they are frequently combined in a single prize package, satisfy to some extent different needs. The good-bad girl fulfills the wish of enjoying what is forbidden and at the same time meeting the demands of what we may call (with some apparent redundancy) goodness morality. The good-bad girl is what the man thinks he wants when he is told by society and conscience that he must be good. The girl with the masculine approach satisfies a different need. She is related to what we may call (with some apparent contradiction) fun morality. You ought to have fun. If you are not having fun, something is the matter with you. Fun morality, widely current in America today, makes one feel guilty for not having fun.   *(82)*

6. Fore-pleasure (*Vorlust*), a term introduced by Freud to designate an increment of pleasure accompanying increasing tension, particularly during sexual stimulation, prior to the "end pleasure" connected with the release of the tension. Freud interpreted this "incentive bonus" as the result of the interplay of the partial instincts after they have been integrated into genital sexuality and suspected that it "corresponds with an arrangement that holds good in many widely separated departments of mental life." He saw "the fore-pleasure principle" operative in the way tendentious jokes use humor to suggestively evoke suppressed or repressed instinctual urges and in the way the writer's reworked daydreams provide aesthetic pleasure that seduces the reader into a release of additional instinctual energy. Freud, *Three Essays on the Theory of Sexuality* (1905), *Standard Edition* 7:149–156, 210–234; *The Joke and its Relationship to the Unconscious* (1905), *Standard Edition* 8:167–169; "Creative Writers and Daydreaming" (1908), *Standard Edition* 9:153.

7. August Aichhorn (1878–1949), Viennese educational and social worker, became the director of an institution for children showing a tendency to become delinquent. He came to see how psychoanalysis offered insight into juvenile delinquency, and based on his experiences at the school he wrote *Wayward Youth*, in which he advocated psychoanalytic treatment instead of punishment in cases of juvenile delinquency.

In *Wayward Youth* (foreword by Freud, trans. and ed. E. Bryant, J. Deming, M. O. Hawkins, G. J. Mohr, E. J. Mohr, H. Ross, and H. Thun [New York: Viking Press, 1935]; from the original German: *Verwahrloste Jugend* [Vienna: Internationaler Psychoanalytischer Verlag, 1925]) Aichhorn offers psychoanalytically derived etiologies of juvenile delinquents in his care and described the means by which his school sought to modify character and behavior among its pupils through work-oriented therapy and positive transference. Cf. also Aichhorn, "Über die Erziehung in Besserungsanstalten," *Imago* 9 (11) (1923): 189–221.

8. Freud, *Massenpsychologie und Ich-Analyse* (1921); English: *Group Psychology and the Analysis of the Ego*, vol. 18 of the *Standard Edition*.

9. The association *Lebensborn e.V.* was founded in 1935 by Heinrich Himmler with the chief goals of furthering the "nordic" race, strengthening the campaign against abortion, and creating the next generation of German military forces, and it was the first step in the National-Socialist politics of "planned reproduction" ["*gelenkte Fortpflanzung*"]. The association was subordinated to the Central Office of Race and Settlement [*Rasse- und Siedlungs-Hauptamt*] and after 1938 was administratively answerable to the Central Office for Economics and Administration [*Wirtschafts- und Verwaltungs-Hauptamt*], both of the SS. The association actively promoted large families (at least four children) among SS officers and police, the support of unmarried mothers, and quite openly propagated the procreation of children out of wedlock. All full-time SS officers were obligated to join, and dues were inversely scaled to the given officer's number of children.

The *Lebensborn e.V.* maintained its own maternity homes (in 1943 nine in the "greater German empire" and four in occupied territories), which took in, following a blood test administered by SS doctors, not only all wives and fiancées of SS and police members but also other women who fulfilled selection requirements and needed to keep their pregnancy a secret. In total about 8,000 children (60% of whom were born out of wedlock) were born in the maternity homes. Illegitimate children were either raised in SS children's homes or placed with SS families. In addition, beginning in 1941, several hundred "racially valuable" children from populations in the occupied territories were taken into *Lebensborn e.V.* homes for compulsory "Germanization" ["*Eindeutschung*"]: for this several leading functionaries of the program were charged with kidnapping at the Nuremburg trials.

10. In a footnote in the first published version Adorno refers here to the first published version of "Working Through the Past."

11. "Moral Rearmament" (MRA), also known as "Buchmanism" and the "Oxford Group," was a vigorous modern revivalistic movement founded by the Lutheran evangelist Frank N. D. Buchman (1878–1961). The movement strove to bring about a moral transformation of society via a return to the Christian fundamental principles (the four "absoluta") of honesty, sexual purity, selflessness, and neighborly love. The movement's practice of public speaking and group confessing influenced the founding of Alcoholics Anonymous.

12. First published version has "the old wound" instead of "the old ache."

13. The behavioristic "sociology of knowledge" movement (influenced by Talcott Parsons) proclaimed the victory of the empirical scientific method and the "end of ideology." Opponents, including members of the postwar Frankfurt School, attacked the position for a "positivistically truncated rationalism" (Habermas) stripped of enlightenment critique and itself ideological and apologetic, since unacknowledged social prejudices inform the theory, which then seeks and implacably finds their empirical confirmation in the society that generated them. On the political level, the "end of ideology" thesis claimed that the monolithic ideologies were bankrupt (Marxism because of the Moscow show trials, liberal mercantilism because of the growing role played by state planning in western democracies) and advocated in their stead pragmatic flexibility. Cf. C. I. Waxman, ed., *The End of Ideology Debate* (New York: Funk & Wagnalls, 1968).

14. First published version is more specific here: "People delight in the *Threepenny Opera*, the records of Brecht and Weill songs, as though they were the mementos of a golden erotic age: at the same time prostitution, which was more or less left in peace in the era when sexual repression was allegedly harsher, is being persecuted everywhere."

15. First published version has "pregenital sexuality" instead of "sexuality alienated from its proper purpose" [*zweckentfremdet*].

16. 'Anaclisis' [*Anlehnung*], a *terminus technicus* to indicate how the sexual drives "lean on" the subject's vital functions of self-preservation, through which the sexual drives receive an organic source, an orientation, and even the choice of love-object. Cf. S. Freud, *Drei Abhandlungen zur Sexualtheorie* (1905); English: *Three Essays on the Theory of Sexuality*, vol. 7 of the *Standard Edition*.

17. *Triebregung*, a *terminus technicus* by which Freud refers to the dynamic aspect of instincts [*Triebe*] to the extent that an instinct is actualized and specified within a determinate inner excitation [*Reiz*]. Cf. Freud, "Triebe und Triebschicksale" (1915); English: "Instincts and their Vicissitudes," in vol. 14 of the *Standard Edition*.

18. *Wunschbild*, "ideal-image," "image of desire," a *terminus technicus* in Freud denoting the ideal image of a love-object as constructed by the libido. Cf. *Die Traumdeutung* (1900); English: *The Interpretations of Dreams*, vols. 4 and 5 of the *Standard Edition*.

19. *Lolita* by Vladimir Nabokov (1955). Tatjana is presumably a reference to the female figure in Tchaikovsky's opera *Evgenij Onegin*, based on Aleksandr Pushkin's

"novel in verse" of the same name. *Baby Doll* is a screenplay by Tennessee Williams about the awakening of a Mississippi woman to her sexuality. Although the film was banned in 1956 by the Catholic church, the screenplay was nominated for an Academy Award. Cf. Tennessee Williams, *Baby Doll* (New York: New Directions 1956); *Baby Doll and Tiger Tail: A Screenplay and Play* (New York: New Directions, 1991).

20. Adorno alludes to a ballad by Theodor Fontane that was familiar to German children; "Herr von Ribbeck auf Ribbeck im Havelland," in Theodor Fontane, *Sämtliche Werke*, vol. 20, *Balladen und Gedichte*, ed. Edgar Groß und Kurt Schreinert (Munich: Nymphenburger Verlagshandlung, 1962), 249–250. My English, which cannot capture the dialect adequately:

HERR VON RIBBECK OF RIBBECK IN HAVELLAND

Herr von Ribbeck of Ribbeck in Havelland,
A pear tree in his garden did stand,
And when the golden autumn arrived,
and the pears shone far and wide,
Then, noonday chiming from the tower bell
Von Ribbeck stuffed both his pockets full,
And if a boy came along with clogs o'foot,
Then he called, "Lad, d'ya wan' so' fruit?"
And come a girl, then he called: "Com' ov'r here,
Little lass, come, I git a pear."

And so it went for many a year, 'till honest
old von Ribbeck of Ribbeck came to rest.
He sensed his end. Autumn had arrived,
again the pears were laughing far and wide,
von Ribbeck said: "It's time for me to leave.
Lay a pear in my grave beside me."
And they carried von Ribbeck out, three days after,
From his house with the doubled rafters.
Peasants and townsfolk of solemn face
sang: "Jesus, in thee lieth my faith."
And the children cried, hearts heavy to bear:
"An' now he's dead. Who's gonna giv's a pear?"

Thus the children cried. That wasn't rightly,
Ach, they knew old Ribbeck too slightly.
The *new* one, a scrooge, stingy and tight,
guards park and pear-tree day and night.
But the *old* one, with a sense of omen,
and full of mistrust for his very own son,
he knew exactly what he was doing there
when he asked that his grave get a pear,
and in the third year, from that peaceful abode
a little pear-tree sprig did sprightly unfold.

And the years, each comes and each goes,
Over the grave a pear tree grows,
and in the autumn's golden light
it shines again far and wide.
And if in the churchyard a boy sets foot,
the tree whispers: " d'ya wan' so' fruit?"
and comes a girl, then: "Com' ov'r her',
Li'l lass, com' an' I'll giv' ya a pear."

Thus blessings still flow from the hand
of von Ribbeck of Ribbeck in Havelland.

21. "Conversion" [*Konversion*], a *terminus technicus* to explain (according to Freud's economical model) the "leap from the psychical to the somatic innervation," that is, the libido is separated from its idea or presentation [*Vorstellung*] during the process of repression, and the resultant liberated libidinal energy is "converted" into somatic innervations, physical symptoms of psychical disfigurement. "Conversion hysteria" [*Konversionshysterie*] is a form of hysteria characterized by conversion symptoms. On conversion cf. Freud, *Die Abwehr-Neuropsychosen* (1894) and "Bruchstück einer Hysterie-Analyse" (1905); English: "Fragment of an Analysis of a Case of Hysteria," in vol. 7 of *The Standard Edition*. On conversion hysteria cf. Freud, "Analyse der Phobie eines fünfjährigen Knaben" (1909); English: "Analysis of a Phobia in a Five-Year-Old Boy," in vol. 10 of *The Standard Edition*.

22. Dante, *Inferno*, canto 5.

23. Paragraph 174 of the Criminal Code, entitled "illicit sexual relations with dependents" [*Unzucht mit Abhängigen*], defines dependent as someone entrusted to another through education, training, charge, or care, or dependent on another through official or institutional position, and includes seven pages of commentary on the law's application. Cf. *Strafgesetzbuch*, vol. 10 of *Beck'sche Kurzkommentare* (Munich/Berlin: Beck'sche Verlagsbuchhandlung, 1963), 511–517.

24. Cf. Karl Kraus, "Kinderfreude," in *Sittlichkeit und Kriminalität, Werke*, vol. 11 (Munich/Vienna: Langen-Müller, 1963).

25. Cf.: "But it must be remembered that it is the usual practice of the fascist to dress his most antidemocratic actions in a legalistic cloak." (Adorno et al., *The Authoritarian Personality* [New York: Harper & Brothers, 1950], 974). See further the work on prejudice by the social psychologist Gordon W. Allport, *The Nature of Prejudice* (Boston: Addison-Wesley Publishing, 1954), e.g., in the chapter entitled "The Prejudiced Personality":

The Nazis were noted for their emphasis upon conventional virtues. Hitler preached and in many respects practiced asceticism. Overt sex perversion was violently condemned, sometimes punished with death. A rigid protocol dominated every phase of military and social life. The Jews were constantly accused of violating conventional codes—with their dirtiness, miserliness, dishonesty, immorality. But while pretentious moralism ran high, there seemed to be little integration with private conduct. It was sham propriety, illustrated by the urge to make all expropriation and torture of the Jews appear "legal." *(399)*

See also p. 235; the chapter affirmatively summarizes *The Authoritarian Personality*. Adorno is certainly drawing on the work of two emigré legal scholars who were his colleagues at the Institute for Social Research in New York City. Franz Neumann's comprehensive study *Behemoth: The Structure and Practice of National Socialism, 1933–1944*, 2d rev. ed. (New York: Oxford University Press, 1944) undertook a sociological interpretation of "the political pattern of National Socialism." Otto Kirchheimer wrote several analyses, including "The Legal Order of National Socialism," held as a public lecture at Columbia University in December 1941 and published in the Institute's *Studies in Philosophy and Social Science* (9 [1941]: 456–75). These early essays are collected with biographical and bibliographical material in *Politics, Law, and Social Change: Selected Essays of Otto Kirchheimer*, ed. F. Burin and Kurt Shell (New York/London: Columbia University Press, 1969). In the 1955 *Festschrift* to Horkheimer, Kirchheimer published an article to which Adorno may be alluding, "Politische Justiz" (in *Sociologica: Aufsätze, Max Horkheimer zum 60. Geburtstag gewidmet*, vol. 1 of *Frankfurter Beiträge zur Soziologie* [Frankfurt: Suhrkamp, 1955], 171–99; English version, "Politics and Justice," *Social Research* 22 [1955]: 377–98 and reprinted in *Politics, Law, and Social Change*, 408–27). The argument was expanded in Kirchheimer's best known work, *Political Justice: The Use of Legal Procedure for Political Ends* (Princeton: Princeton University Press, 1961). For a historical and theoretical treatment, see William E. Scheuermann, *Between the Norm and the Exception: The Frankfurt School and the Rule of Law* (Cambridge, Mass.: MIT Press, 1994).

26. On folkways, note the seminal study by William Graham Sumner, *Folkways: A Study of the Sociological Importance of Usages, Manners, Customs, Mores, and Morals* (Boston: Ginn, 1906), one of a group of American works of sociology the restored Frankfurt Institute planned to translate into German during the 1950s. The project never materialized, and these books remain unavailable in German.

On Durkheim's concept of *fait sociaux* cf. the first chapter of Emile Durkheim, *The Rules of Sociological Method*, ed. Steven Lukes, trans. W. D. Halls (New York: Free Press, 1982). Cf. also Adorno's introduction to Emile Durkheim, *Soziologie und Philosophie* (Frankfurt: Suhrkamp, 1967); reprinted in *GS* 8:245–279.

27. See for example section 4 of the second essay in Friedrich Nietzsche, *On the Genealogy of Morals*, trans. Walter Kaufmann (New York: Vintage, 1967).

28. Cf. the "Dialectic of Pure Practical Reason" in Immanuel Kant, *Critique of Practical Reason*, trans. Lewis White Beck, 3d ed. (New York: Macmillan, 1993).

29. A snub at Max Scheler's "material theory of value ethics": *Der Formalismus in der Ethik und die materiale Wertethik: Neuer Versuch der Grundlegung eines ethischen Personalismus* (1916), reprinted in *Gesammelte Schriften*, vol. 2 (Bern/Munich: Francke Verlag, 1966). English: *Formalism in Ethics and Non-Formal Ethics of Values: A New Attempt Toward the Foundation of an Ethical Personalism*, trans. Manfred S. Frings and Roger L. Funk (Evanston, Ill.: Northwestern University Press, 1973).

30. In his voluntaristic radicalization of Kant's principle of the moral law, Johann Gottlieb Fichte claimed that since deontological morality is based solely on reason, it is unconditioned, self-evident, and self-affirming. Cf. in particular J. G. Fichte, *System der Sittenlehre: Über den Grund unseres Glaubens an eine göttliche Weltregierung* (1798).

31. The F-scale (F for fascism) was developed in the Berkeley Study Group to detect through content analysis, opinion polls, and interviews latent (fascist) authoritarian impulses in the American population.

32. The "Case of Vera Brühne" or the "Brühne Affair" was the media sensation of the summer of 1962, though she was only the secondary defendant in a five-week-long Munich murder trial covered extensively by the German press. Her friend, Hans Ferbach, was accused of murdering the Munich doctor Otto Praun and his companion Elfriede Kloo. Ferbach was allegedly acting on behalf of Brühne, who was Praun's mistress and had been promised the inheritance of a property in Spain by him, only to learn that he wanted to sell the real estate. Praun and Kloo were found dead on Maundy Thursday 1960, and the case was first deemed by local police a homicide and suicide by Praun. Two years later rumors and accusations led the police to reopen the case and prosecute, when neither Ferbach nor Brühne could at that time provide a reliable alibi for the night of the killings. There was no evidence linking Ferbach, let alone Brühne, to the deaths aside from Brühne's putative motive. The prosecution paraded several "girlfriends" of Brühne who dilated at length upon the dissolute character of the codefendant. The defense responded by introducing a secondary line of slanderers who suitably besmirched the characters of the initial witnesses. Other highlights of the trial included Vera Brühne's daughter, Sylvia Cosiolkofsky, who had first told police investigators that her mother had confessed the murders to her but then rescinded her statement when put on the stand. Between the contradictory statements there was enough time for the daughter to fatally run down a pensioner in her mother's automobile while intoxicated. The prosecution's star witness, Siegfried Schramm, testified that Ferbach confessed the crime to him when both were being held in custody while awaiting trial. However, Schramm's testimony too was liable to skepticism since he was an acknowledged police informant and professional con man with four convictions for fraud, who five days after testifying was again convicted of fraud and forgery.

Vera Brühne became a celebrity, and newspapers and magazines of the stature of *Die Zeit* and *Der Spiegel* joined the tabloids in reporting regularly on her alleged "unbourgeois" lifestyle. On June 8, 1962, Ludwig Ferbach and Vera Brühne were found guilty and sentenced to life imprisonment.

On the juridical dubiousness of the verdict cf. Frank Arnau, *Der Fall Brühne-Ferbach: Autopsie eines Urteils* (Munich: Verlag "gestern und heute," Kurt Hirsch, 1965). Adorno also refers to the case of Vera Brühne at the conclusion of his review of Karl Kraus's *Sittlichkeit und Kriminalität* (*Morals and Criminality*) in *Noten zur Literatur*. Cf. *Notes to Literature*, trans. by Shierry Weber Nicholsen (New York: Columbia University Press, 1992), 2:56–57.

The Meaning of Working Through the Past

1. "*Aufarbeitung*" is here translated as "working through" and requires clarification since it does not wholly coincide with the psychoanalytical term "working through" (*Durcharbeitung*), though it is related. Its common meaning is that of working through in the sense of dispatching tasks that have built up and demand attention, catching up on accumulated paperwork, etc. It thus conveys the sense of getting through an unpleasant obligation, clearing one's desk, etc., and some politi-

cians and historians with less sensitivity to language than Adorno began using the term in reference to the need to reappraise, or "master" the past (the German for the latter being *Vergangenheitsbewältigung*, which connotes both confrontation and overcoming). At the outset of the essay Adorno contrasts "working through" (*aufarbeiten*) with a serious "working upon" (*verarbeiten*) of the past in the sense of assimilating, coming to terms with it.

2. Adorno's reply to the highly critical appraisal of the postwar Frankfurt Institute's *Gruppenexperiment* by the respected, conservative psychologist Peter R. Hofstätter, who defended what Adorno had disparagingly called the "positivist-atomistic" method of orthodox opinion survey (which defines public opinion as the sum of individual opinions). Hofstätter reinterpreted the material to indicate that by the study's own standards only 15% of the participants could legitimately be considered authoritarian or undemocratic, a percentage fully comparable to that in any other Western country: there was no "legacy of fascist ideology" in Germany, no danger from the right. Furthermore, Hofstätter attacked the study's authors as totalitarian moralists and idealists themselves. He described the qualitative analysis (Adorno's contribution to the study) as "nothing but an accusation, or a demand for genuine mental remorse" and countered that "there is simply no individual feeling that could satisfactorily correspond to constantly looking at the annihilation of a million people"; therefore "the indignation of the sociological analyst" seemed "misplaced or pointless," because according to Hofstätter, moral reflection on personal guilt was a private affair. Peter R. Hofstätter, "Zum 'Gruppenexperiment' von Friedrich Pollock: Eine kritische Würdigung," *Kölner Zeitschrift für Soziologie und Sozialpsychologie* 9 (1957): 97–104.

Adorno's reply is no less polemical: "The method is declared to be useless so that the existence of the phenomenon that emerges can be denied." According to him, Hofstätter's criticism indicates the appeal to collective narcissism: "Hofstätter considers 'it is hardly possible that a single individual could take upon himself the horror of Auschwitz.' It is the victims of Auschwitz who had to take its horror upon themselves, not those who, to their own disgrace and that of their nation, prefer not to admit it. The 'question of guilt' was 'laden with despair' for the victims, not for the survivors, and it takes some doing to have blurred this distinction with the existential category of despair, which is not without reason a popular one. But in the house of the hangman one should not mention the noose; one might be suspected of harboring resentment" (Adorno, "Replik zu Peter R. Hofstätters Kritik des Gruppenexperiments," *Kölner Zeitschrift für Soziologie und Sozialpsychologie* 9 [1957]: 105–117; reprinted in *GS* 9.2:378–394, here 392–393).

3. Radio version: "I do not do wish to go into the question of neo-Nazi organizations. From the communication by Harry Pross you've learned more, and more starkly, about it than presumably most of us knew. Those of us who have gathered here see very little of what we want not to happen again—the fact that we do not want it already separates us from the others. But I consider . . . ."

4. Radio and first published versions continue: "Compared with this, the continued existence of radical-right groups, which by the way during the last weeks suffered a severe rebuff from the voters of Bremen and Schleswig-Holstein, seems to me to be only a surface phenomenon."

5. Cf. *Gruppenexperiment: Ein Studienbericht*, bearbeitet von Friedrich Pollock, vol. 2 of *Frankfurter Beiträge zur Soziologie*, im Auftrag des Instituts für Sozial-

forschung herausgegeben von Theodor W. Adorno und Walter Dirks (Frankfurt: Europäische Verlagsanstalt, 1955).

6. Radio version: "You all, ladies and gentlemen, are familiar with . . . ."

7. Radio version adds: "or at least it is hardly reflected upon."

8. Radio and first published versions have "naive" instead of "lax."

9. Reference to Mephistopheles's reaction to Faust's death in part 2, after the latter finally says "Abide, you are so fair!" ["*Verweile doch, du bist so schön!*"] when contemplating his intentions for bettering the lot of humanity:

> MEPH.:   Now it is over. What meaning can you see?
> It is as if it had not come to be,
> And yet it circulates as if it were.
> I should prefer—Eternal Emptiness.
>
> (Goethe's Faust, *trans. Walter Kaufmann [New York: Doubleday, 1961],*
> *468–471, ll. 11595–11603)*

10. Cf. several essays included in the following collections: Hermann Heimpel, *Der Mensch in seiner Gegenwart: Acht historische Essais* (Göttingen: Vandenhoeck & Ruprecht, 1954, 1957); *Kapitulation vor der Geschichte? Gedanken zur Zeit* (Göttingen: Vandenhoeck & Ruprecht, 1956, 1957, 1960).

11. Radio and first published versions interject the following paragraph:

This German development, flagrant after the Second World War, coincides with the lack of historical awareness [*Geschichtsfremdheit*] in the American consciousness, well known since Henry Ford's "*History is bunk*,*" the nightmare of a humanity without memory. It is no mere phenomenon of decline, not a reaction of a humanity that, as one says, is flooded with stimuli and cannot cope with them. Rather it is necessarily connected to the advancement of the bourgeois principle. Bourgeois society is universally situated under the law of exchange, of the like-for-like of accounts that match and that leave no remainder. In its very essence exchange is something timeless; like ratio itself, like the operations of mathematics according to their pure form, they remove the aspect of time. Similarly, concrete time vanishes from industrial production. It transpires more and more in identical and spasmodic, potentially simultaneous cycles and hardly requires accumulated experience any more. Economists and sociologists, such as Werner Sombart and Max Weber, have ascribed the principle of traditionalism to feudal forms and the principle of rationality to bourgeois forms of society. But this means nothing less than that recollection, time, memory is being liquidated by advancing bourgeois society itself, as a kind of irrational residue, similar to the way advancing rationalization of the industrial means of production reduces along with the remains of the artisanal also categories like apprenticeship [the radio version interjects: "that is, the gaining of experience"]. If humanity divests itself of memory and breathlessly exhausts itself in continually conforming to what is immediately present, then in doing so it reflects an objective developmental law.

12. For instance: "Here came to consciousness and received its plain expression, what *German* is: to wit, the thing one does for its own sake, for the very joy of doing

it; whereas Utilitarianism, namely the principle whereby a thing is done for the sake of some personal end, ulterior to the thing itself, was shewn to be un-German." Wagner goes on, first, to identify this "German virtue" with the highest principle of Kantian aesthetics, the autonomy of art, and, second, to advocate this principle as a national policy "which assuredly presupposes a solid ordering of every nearer, every relation that serves life's necessary ends" ("German Art and German Policy" in *Richard Wagner's Prose Works*, trans. William Ashton Ellis, vol. 4, *Art and Politics* [New York: Broude Brothers, 1966; reprint of 1895 London edition by Routledge & Kegan Paul], 35–148, here pp. 107–108). Cf. also Adorno's "What is German?" in *Catchwords* (this volume).

13. Cf. Franz Böhm in his preface to *Gruppenexperiment*, the published results of a study undertaken by the Institute for Social Research exploring ideologies of various population groups in postwar Germany:

> What is it then that produces the shock when reading the present investigation? I would like to think that it is a double aspect.
>
> First of all the overly clear perception that alongside the so-called public opinion, which expresses itself in elections, referenda, public speeches, newspaper articles, radio broadcasts, the platforms of political parties and groups, parliamentary discussions, political meetings, there is also a *non-public opinion*, whose contents can diverge very considerably from the contents of the actual public opinion, whose statements however circulate alongside the statements of the public opinion like the monetary units of a *second currency*—indeed they have perhaps a more fixed and stable rate than the values of actual public opinion, which we flaunt according to propriety in public, especially for the audience abroad, and of which we imagine they represent our own and only currency, as though they expressed what we really mean to say, although, after all, they are only formal expressions we use when we are wearing our Sunday clothes. Yes, it almost appears as though what circulates about us as public opinion represents the sum of those (mutually contradictory) opinions we wish people would believe are our true opinions, whereas non-public opinion is about the sum of those (likewise mutually contradictory) opinions that we actually have.
>
> Second, the likewise overly clear perception of what the non-public opinion actually looks like. So that is what many of us actually think!
>
> In other words: the one shock results from the perception that we have *two currencies of opinion*, each encompassing a whole bundle of diverse opinions. And the other shock overcomes us when we look at the values comprising the unofficial opinion.
>
> *(Franz Böhm, "Geleitwort," in* Gruppenexperiment: Ein Studienbericht, *bearbeitet von Friedrich Pollock, vol. 2 of* Frankfurter Beiträge zur Soziologie *[Frankfurt: Europäische Verlagsanstalt, 1955], here excerpted from pp. xi–xii)*

Cf. also Franz Böhm, "Das Vorurteil als Element totaler Herrschaft," in vol. 17 of *Vorträge gehalten anläßlich der Hessischen Hochschulwochen für staatswissenschaftliche Fortbildung* (Bad Homburg vor der Höhe: Verlag Dr. Max Gehlen, 1957), 149–167.

14. First published version is more cautious: "Certainly one may hope that democracy is more deeply rooted . . . ."

15. Radio and first published version: "with Western democracy" instead of "with the West."

16. Radio and first published version: "deadly serious" instead of "obvious."

17. *Wir Wunderkinder*: a film satire of the so-called economic miracle in West Germany, it depicts the unprincipled career of a small-town operator during four decades of German history: first a dashing Nazi leader, then a successful financier in postwar West Germany, his unswerving self-interest and opportunism insure his success. Directed by Kurt Hoffmann; 1958 Filmaufbau.

18. *KdF = "Kraft durch Freude"* ["Strength through Joy"], National Socialist recreational organization (whose name supposedly was invented by Hitler himself) set up in imitation of a similar Italian organization *"Dopolavoro"* founded by Mussolini with the purpose of stimulating workers' morale. A new form of industrial relations and mass tourism, the KdF program encompassed package holiday tours on its own ocean liners and via the state railway system as well as subsidized theater and concert performances, exhibitions, sports, hiking, folk dancing, and adult education courses. The organization, part of the German Labor Front (*Deutsche Arbeitsfront*), received massive state subsidies for the purpose of demonstrating the enlightened labor policies of the National Socialists in eliminating classes within the Third Reich.

The KdF was comprised of the following offices: (1) the "After Work" department organized theater performances, concerts, etc. as well as political education courses for ca. 38 million people (1933–1938); the "Sport" department organized factory sports for "military training" and "racial perfection"; the "Beauty of Labor" department sought to improve working conditions and the aesthetic contours of the workplace; the "Military Homes" department promoted contacts to the armed forces and the State Labor Service; the department "Tour, Travel, Vacation" until 1938 organized vacation trips for ca. 10 million people. As the German Labor Front put it in 1940, "We did not send our workers off on vacation on our own ships or build them massive sea resorts just for the fun of it. . . . We did it only in order for them to return to their workplaces invigorated and with a new orientation."

19. *Massenpsychologie und Ich-Analyse* (1921); English in vol. 18 of *The Standard Edition of the Complete Psychological Works of Sigmund Freud*, trans. James Strachey (London: Hogarth Press, 1975).

20. Radio and first published version: "automatically" instead of "pharisaically."

21. Radio and first published version: "features of horror" instead of "grotesque features."

22. Radio and first published version: "Just as the witch trials took place not during the high point of Scholasticism but during the Counter-Reformation, that is when what they wanted to reinforce was already undermined, so too has nationalism first become completely sadistic and destructive in an age in which it was already toppling."

23. In his article, "Anti-Semitism and Mass Psychopathology" in *Anti-Semitism: A Social Disease*, ed. Ernst Simmel (New York: International Universities Press, 1946), Simmel draws on Le Bon and Freud to arrive at the following interpretation:

By identifying himself with the mass, the individual in his retreat from reality employs the same escape mechanism as the psychotic, i.e., regression to that infantile level of ego development when the superego was still represented by external parental power.

However, through this temporary regression he gains one advantage the individual psychotic does not have. The submergence of his ego into the group enables him to overcome his actual infantile impotence toward reality; he attains instinct freedom with the power of an adult. *This circumstance allows him, by way of a mass psychosis, to return to reality, from which the individual psychotic must flee.*   *(47)*

Summarizing the parallelisms between a collective psychosis and an individual psychosis, we can say: The mass and the psychotic think and act irrationally because of regressively disintegrated ego systems. In the individual psychotic mind the process of regression is of a primary nature and is constant. In the collective psychotic mind regression is secondary and occurs only temporarily. The reason for this is that in the individual psychotic, the ego breaks with reality because of its pathological weakness, whereas *in the mass member, reality breaks first with the ego.* This ego, by submerging itself into a pathological mass, saves itself from individual regression by regressing collectively. *Flight into mass psychosis is therefore an escape not only from reality, but also from individual insanity.*

This insight gives us our answer to the enigmatic question why apparently normal individuals can react like psychotics under the spell of mass formation. *Their ego is immature* as a result of superego weakness. The immature individual who, under the stress of environmental circumstances, is on the verge of losing contact with reality, can find his way back to it when his ego, carried by the spirit of the group, finds opportunity for the discharge of pent-up aggressive instinct energies into the object world.   *(49–50)*

24. Radio and first published version: "the self-reflection" instead of "the autonomy."

25. Radio version adds: "They experience their own autonomy in a certain sense as a burden."

26. Radio version interjects: "if it hasn't always been so."

27. Radio and first published version: "objects" instead of "subjects."

28. Radio version interjects: "to use an example Franz Böhm likes to adduce . . . ."

29. First published version has "anti-Semitism" instead of "fascism," and the radio version continues here: "In our work this is that danger for which in America they use the saying '*preaching to the saved*,*' [*also, denen predigen, die ohnehin bereits gerettet sind*]."

30. Snub at Heideggerian existentialism.

31. Radio version interjects: "subjectively, that is, the appeal to individuals . . . ."

32. Radio version interjects: "individuation, that is, that it concerns this specific girl and not everyone."

33. Cf. #233 of La Rochefoucauld's *Maximes* (1678):

Afflictions give rise to various kinds of hypocrisy: in one, pretending to weep over the loss of someone dear to us we really weep for ourselves, since we miss that person's good opinion of us or deplore some curtailment of our wealth, pleasure, or position. The dead, therefore, are honoured by tears shed for the living alone. I call this a kind of hypocrisy because in afflictions of this sort we deceive ourselves. There is another hypocrisy, less innocent because aimed at the world at large: the affliction of certain persons who aspire to the glory of a beautiful, immortal sorrow. Time, the universal destroyer, has taken away the grief they really felt, but still they obstinately go on weeping, wailing, and sighing; they are acting a mournful part and striving to make all their actions prove that their distress will only end with their lives. This miserable and tiresome vanity is usually found in ambitious women, for as their sex precludes them from all roads to glory they seek celebrity by a display of inconsolable affliction. There is yet another kind of tears that rise from shallow springs and flow or dry up at will: people shed them so as to have a reputation for being tender-hearted, so as to be pitied or wept over, or, finally, to avoid the disgrace of not weeping.

(La Rochefoucauld, Maxims, *trans. Leonard Tancock [London: Penguin, 1959], 67–68)*

34. Radio version and first published version have the following addition to the conclusion: "Whatever aims at the more humanly decent organization of the whole, be it theoretically or practical-politically, is at once also resistance against the relapse."

Opinion Delusion Society

1. The liberal *Berliner Tageblatt und Handelszeitung* ran from 1872 to 1939. In 1933 its owners were bought out, and it was "brought into line" by the Nazi regime.
2. Presumably Adorno is referring to Sartre's anecdote of his friend's cousin Jules in Jean-Paul Sartre, *Réflexions sur la question juive* (Paris: Éditions Gallimard, 1954), 60ff. English: *Anti-Semite and Jew,* trans. George Becker (New York: Schocken, 1948). The translated excerpt with which Adorno was acquainted (it is also cited in *The Authoritarian Personality*) after portraying the anti-Semite per se turns to "secondhand antisemites" who "are no one; and since in spite of everything, one must appear to be something, they murmur, without thinking of evil, without thinking at all, they go about repeating some formulas they have learned and that give them the right to enter certain drawing rooms," and recounts the anecdote as follows:

These secondhand antisemites take on, without much cost to themselves, an aggressive personality. One of my friends often cites the example of an old cousin who came to dine with his family and about whom they said with a certain air: "Jules cannot abide the English." My friend cannot remember ever hearing anything else about Cousin Jules. But that was enough: there was a tacit agreement between Jules and his family. They ostensibly avoided talking about the English in front of him, and this precaution gave him a semblance of existence in the eyes of his relatives and at the same time gave them an agreeable feeling of taking part in a sacred ceremony. And if someone, under certain specific circumstances, after careful deliberation and as it were inadvertently, made an allusion to Great Britain or its Dominions, Uncle Jules pretended to go into a fury and felt himself come to life for a moment. Everyone was happy. Many people are antisemites in the same way as Uncle Jules was an Anglophobe, and of course they have not the faintest idea what their attitude really implies. Simple reflections, reeds bent in the wind, they would certainly never have invented antisemitism if conscious antisemitism had not already existed. But they are the ones who, in all indifference, insure the survival of anti-semitism and carry it forward through the generations.

(Jean-Paul Sartre, "Portrait of the Antisemite," trans. Mary Guggenheim
Partisan Review 13 [1946]: 163–178, here 176–177)

3. "Rationalization" [Rationalisierung]: process through which the subject attempts to provide a logically coherent or morally acceptable explanation for behavior, actions, thoughts, feelings, etc., whose real motives are unknown. Freud particularly speaks of the rationalization of a symptom, a defense mechanism, a reaction-formation. Delusion also can be rationalized in that it creates for itself a more or less extensive systemic structure of explanation. Cf. especially Freud, "Psychoanalytische Bemerkungen über einen autobiographisch beschriebenen Fall von Paranoia (Dementia paranoides)" (1911); English: "Psycho-Analytic Notes on an Autobiographical Account of a Case of Paranoia (Dementia Paranoides)," in vol. 12 of The Standard Edition of the Complete Psychological Works of Sigmund Freud, trans. James Strachey (London: Hogarth Press, 1975). The term was popularized by Ernest Jones in his Rationalization in Everyday Life (1908).

4. German traffic signals include a cautionary yellow light after the red and before the green.

5. Presumably alluding to the following passage from the "Preface" to the Phänomenologie des Geistes (1807) (Werke [Frankfurt: Suhrkamp, 1970], 3:56):

That habit should be called material thinking, a contingent consciousness that is absorbed only in material stuff, and therefore finds it hard work to lift the self clear of such matter, and to be with itself alone. At the opposite extreme, argumentation [Räsonieren] is freedom from all content [of thought], and a sense of vanity toward it. From it is demanded [by Hegel's method] the effort to relinquish this freedom and, instead of being the arbitrarily moving principle of the content, to sink this freedom in the content and let it move by its own nature, that is, by the self as its own, and to observe this movement. This refusal to intrude into the immanent rhythm of the concept, either arbitrarily or with wisdom obtained from elsewhere, constitutes a restraint that is itself an essential moment of the concept.

(G. W. F. Hegel, The Phenomenology of Spirit, trans. A. V. Miller [Oxford:
Oxford University Press, 1977], 35–36; translation modified)

6. Cf. Bertolt Brecht's two "teaching-plays" entitled Der Jasager and Der Nein-sager (1929–1930); English: He Who Says Yes and He Who Says No, trans. Wolfgang Sauerlander, in The Measures Taken and other Lehrstücke (London: Eyre Methuen, 1977), 61–79.

7. First published version interjects a sentence at this point: "In the persistent irrationality of society that is rational merely in its means, not in its ends, especially opaque is the societal fate of the individual; he remains a fate as in the myths from time immemorial."

8. According to Mannheim, the majority is treated as a privileged group in order to counteract feelings of atomization and personal insecurity as part of the techniques of modern mass manipulation. Cf. Karl Mannheim, *Mensch und Gesellschaft im Zeitalter des Umbaus* (Leiden, 1935); English: *Man and Society*, trans. Edward Shils (London: Routledge & Kegan Paul, 1940). Adorno criticizes Mannheim extensively in "Sociology of Knowledge and its Consciousness," *Prisms*, trans. Samuel and Shierry Weber (Cambridge, Mass.: MIT Press, 1981).

9. Cf. "Apology for Raymond Sebond" in *The Complete Essays of Montaigne*, trans. Donald M. Frame (Stanford, Ca.: Stanford University Press, 1957), 318–457. Cf. Max Horkheimer, "Montaigne and the Function of Skepticism," in Horkheimer, *Between Philosophy and the Social Sciences: Selected Early Writings*, trans. G. Frederick Hunter, Matthew S. Kramer, and John Torpey (Cambridge, Mass.: MIT Press, 1993).

10. Adorno is alluding obliquely to Hegel's notion of "determinate negation" [*bestimmte Negation*]. Consciousness applies its own standard of truth to itself and discovers itself to be one-sided and incomplete such that when "the result is conceived as it is in truth, namely, as a *determinate* negation, a new form [of consciousness] has thereby immediately arisen, and in the negation the transition is made through which the progress through the complete series of forms comes about of itself" (G. W. F. Hegel, "Introduction," *The Phenomenology of Spirit*, 50–51; German: *Phänomenologie des Geistes*, 3:74).

11. The preceding paragraph did not appear in the first published version.

12. First published version ends this sentence slightly differently after the comma: "whose substantiality has dissolved into the movement of spirit."

13. Adorno's (mis-)citation of "*was wird schon sein*" presumably refers to the above passage, which in a very similar context he correctly cites and interprets along similar lines in "Trying to Understand *Endgame*," in *Notes to Literature*, trans. Shierry Weber Nicholsen (New York: Columbia University Press, 1991), 1:262, referring to *Endspiel*, trans. Elmar Tophoven (Frankfurt: Suhrkamp, 1957).

14. Vilfredo Pareto (1848–1923), sociologist and theoretician of science, advocated the mathematical and econometrical analysis of society, based on the tenet that economic relations are paradigmatic of all social relations. Karl Mannheim (1893–1947), founder of the sociology of knowledge. Mannheim believed that only the free-floating intelligentsia was capable of transforming the conflict of societal interests into a conflict of ideas because it was classless and free of self-interest, and therefore could gain insight into the total ideology of society at any given time.

15. Immanuel Kant, *Träume eines Geistersehers, erläutert durch Träume der Metaphysik* (1766); English: *Dreams of a Spirit-Seer*, trans. E. F. Goerwitz (London: Swan Sonnenschein, 1900).

16. Erich Jaensch (1893–1940), phenomenologist and psychologist who gained prominence in Nazi Germany with his book *Der Gegentypus* (Leipzig: Barth, 1938), which evaluated character typologies based on successful personality "integration," with German nationalist and peasant types topping the list. The "anti-type," which Jaensch explicitly associated with Jews and foreigners, was characterized by synesthetic perception, capacity for ambiguity, "lability," and individuality. Adorno may be alluding to the sustained comparison drawn by one of his colleagues from the *Authoritarian Personality* project: "Jaensch concentrates on a very articulate

description of the most desirable type from the standpoint of Nazi ideology and this type shows marked similarities to our description of the authoritarian personality. The fact that Jaensch glorifies this pattern while our attitude is one of reserve, or criticism, add to the interest of the parallelism. The parallel delineation lends confidence to our interpretation of our results, since they are concurred in by psychologists glorifying the authoritarian personality" (E. Frenkel-Brunswick, "Further Explorations by a Contributor to 'The Authoritarian Personality'" in *Studies in the Scope and Method of "The Authoritarian Personality,"* ed. Richard Christie and Marie Jahoda [Glencoe, Ill.: Free Press, 1954; reprint, Westport, Conn.: Greenwood Press, 1981], 225–275, here p. 252).

17. First published version: "perduring" instead of "tenacious."

18. Franz Leonard Schlüter was named by the regional coalition government to the post of minister of culture in Lower Saxony in May 1955. Schlüter, a frustrated patriot (judged by the Nazis unfit for military service because of his Jewish mother) who had failed his doctoral exams and been under investigation for improper conduct as head of the criminal police in Göttingen after the war, had been a vociferous member of the nationalist "German Party of the Right" (Deutsche Rechtspartei) before joining the right wing of the liberal Free Democrat Party (FDP) in 1951. At that time he also founded a Göttingen publishing house that printed several works by former Nazi ideologues and functionaries as well as by professors who were forbidden to lecture by denazification strictures. In protest to Schlüter's appointment, the rector of Göttingen university, Prof. Dr. Emil Woermann, and the entire university senate resigned. The Göttingen Student Union, broadly supported by the professors, initiated large-scale student strikes and demonstrations. On 9 June 1955, fifteen days after assuming the post of minister of culture, Schlüter submitted his resignation and a month later resigned also from the FDP leadership. On the third anniversary of his "fall," Schlüter's publishing house brought out under an anonymous author a three-hundred page book (*Die große Hetze: Der niedersächsische Ministersturz, Ein Tatsachenbericht zum Fall Schlüter* [Göttingen: Göttinger Verlagsanstalt, 1958]) recounting in detail the compromised writings published during the Nazi regime by Woermann and other prominent Göttingen professors.

19. First published version does not have this paragraph.

20. The German proverb is *"Gemeinnutz vor Eigennutz."*

21. Anatole France, *L' île des pingouins* (Paris: Calmann-Lévy, 1908); English: *Penguin Island,* trans. A. W. Evans (New York: Dodd Mead, 1925).

22. First published version continues here with the following sentence, "If this is correct, then it is based on a situation that can hardly be changed by mere consciousness alone," and the text continues with the sentence "The reification of consciousness that deserts and defects . . . ." The final published version adds new material between the first sentence of the paragraph and this latter sentence.

23. Cf. Adorno's aphorism in *Minima Moralia,* trans. E. F. N. Jephcott (London: NLB, 1974), 39: "Wrong life cannot be lived rightly" (original in *GS* 4:43). The saying gained a certain notoriety, as Adorno commented at the beginning of a lecture course on ethics in 1963: *Probleme der Moralphilosophie,* ed. Thomas Schröder (Frankfurt: Suhrkamp, 1996), 9.

24. First published version interjects: "similar to the way existential philosophy and logical positivism come together in several philosophies . . . ."

25. First published version ends here.

Catchwords

Introduction

1. "Content of thought" cannot convey the density of Adorno's expression *das Gedachte*, which is the substantivized past participle of the verb "to think" (*denken*) but also of the verb "to remember, be mindful of" (*gedenken*); the interrelationship between these two actions is central to the argument of *Dialectic of Enlightenment* and Adorno's philosophy of nature.

2. *Negative Dialektik*, in *GS* 6; English: T. W. Adorno, *Negative Dialectics*, trans. E. B. Ashton (New York: Seabury Press, 1973).

3. Cf. "Résumé über Kulturindustrie," in *Ohne Leitbild: Parva Aesthetica*, in *GS* 10.1:337–345. English: "Culture Industry Reconsidered," trans. Anson Rabinbach, *New German Critique* 6 (Fall 1975): 12–19, reprinted in *Critical Theory and Society: A Reader*, ed. Stephen Eric Bronner and Douglas MacKay Kellner (New York: Routledge, 1989), 128–135; and in *The Culture Industry: Selected Essays on Mass Culture*, ed. J.M. Bernstein (London: Routledge, 1991), 85–92.

4. "Refunction" (*umfunktionieren*) in Brecht refers to the practice of alienating a term, situation, etc. from its habitual context and redeploying it in a critical fashion; "Brecht has coined the phrase 'functional transformation' (*Umfunktionierung*) to describe the transformation of forms and instruments of production by a progressive intelligentsia—an intelligentsia interested in liberating the means of production and hence active in the class struggle" (Walter Benjamin, "The Author as Producer," *Understanding Brecht*, trans. Anna Bostock [London: NLB, 1973], 93).

5. Adorno's philosophy lecture course "Introduction to Dialectics" was disrupted in April 1969 by members of the Women's Council of the SDS (Sozialistischer Deutscher Studentenbund, the Socialist German Student Association), following months of tension between student protesters and members of the Institute for Social Research, including the student occupation of the sociology department's building, confrontations with Habermas and Adorno, etc. See Rolf Wiggershaus, *The Frankfurt School: Its History, Theories, and Political Significance*, trans. Michael Robertson (Cambridge, Mass.: MIT Press, 1994), 609–635. For Adorno's reaction, see in particular his interview "Keine Angst vor dem Elfenbeinturm," *Der Spiegel*, no. 19 (1969): 204–209 (reprinted in *GS* 20.1:402–409). English: "Of Barricades and Ivory Towers: An Interview with T. W. Adorno." *Encounter* 33 (September 1969): 63–69.

Notes on Philosophical Thinking

1. First published version has a different "dedication": "Rejected by the editors of the Festschrift for Herbert Marcuse; all the more warmly dedicated to him."

2. Radio version: "The division between that about which and that which is thought."

3. Radio version and first published version: "demythologization" instead of "enlightenment."

4. Radio version abbreviates, goes to "Philosophical thinking begins . . . ."

5. In *The Critique of Pure Reason* (trans. Norman Kemp Smith [New York: St. Martin's, 1965], 92–3, 153) Kant defines the "spontaneity of the concepts" (as

opposed to the 'receptivity'—the capacity of receiving sensible impressions) as the faculty of knowing an object by producing concepts that organize those sensible impressions:

> If the *receptivity* of our mind, its power of receiving representations in so far as it is in any wise affected, is to be entitled sensibility, then the mind's power of producing representations from itself, the *spontaneity* of knowledge, should be called the understanding. Our nature is so constituted that our *intuition* can never be other than sensible; that is, it contains only the mode in which we are affected by objects. The faculty, on the other hand, which enables us to *think* the object of sensible intuition is the understanding. To neither of these powers may a preference be given over the other. Without sensibility no object would be thought. Thoughts without content are empty, intuitions without concepts are blind.   *(A 50–1, B 74–5)*

Spontaneity can be either *empirical* (containing sensations, i.e. requiring the physical presence of the intuited object) or *pure* (relations of concepts without appeal to sensible intuition). In the second edition Kant specifies the relationship between pure spontaneity and self-consciousness:

> That representation which can be given prior to all thought is entitled intuition. All the manifold of intuition has, therefore, a necessary relation to the "I think" in the same subject in which this manifold is found. But this representation is an act of *spontaneity*, that is, it cannot be regarded as belonging to sensibility. I call it *pure apperception*, to distinguish it from empirical apperception, or, again, *original apperception*, because it is that self-consciousness which, while generating the representation *"I think"* (a representation which must be capable of accompanying all other representations, and which in all consciousness is one and the same), cannot itself be accompanied by any further representation. The unity of this apperception I likewise entitle the *transcendental* unity of self-consciousness, in order to indicate the possibility of *a priori* knowledge arising from it.   *(B 132)*

6. Kant (*Critique of Pure Reason*, 182–183) speaks of the "depth" of human understanding in the context of his discussion of the schemata of the understanding, the means by which empirical objects have categories of the understanding applied to them and thus become conceptually recognizable:

> These conditions of sensibility constitute the universal condition under which alone the category can be applied to any object. This formal and pure condition of sensibility to which the employment of the concept of understanding is restricted, we shall entitle the *schema* of the concept. The procedure of understanding in these *schemata* we shall entitle the schematism of pure understanding. . . .
> The concept "dog" signifies a rule according to which my imagination can delineate the figure of a four-footed animal in a general manner, without limitation to any single determinate figure such as experience, or any possible image that I can represent *in concreto*, actually presents. This schematism of

our understanding, in its application to appearances and their mere form, is an art concealed in the depths of the human soul, whose real modes of activity nature is hardly likely ever to allow us to discover, and to have open to our gaze.   *(A 140, B 179ff.)*

7. The transcendental apperception (see note 5 above) represents the formal, necessary synthesizing unity of a consciousness such that it can organize and recognize its intuitions and representations as belonging to it: "For the manifold representations, which are given in an intuition, would not be one and all *my* representations, if they did not all belong to one self-consciousness . . . only in so far as I can grasp the manifold of the representations in one consciousness, do I call them one and all *mine*" (B 132, 134). However, the unity is a functional one only, an "I think" that necessary accompanies my representations, but no substantive intuition of an "I." This entails the impossibility of the subject of awareness (i.e., the private world) connecting with the objective (common) world in a representational-mimetic fashion. Whoever seeks introspective self-knowledge expects to find a subject of awareness, an ego, but only finds more and more objects and never any subject. Hume established this point (*Treatise of Human Nature*, I.iv), and Kant accepted it and explained why the transcendental subject can never be an object. Cf. the "Transcendental Dialectic," book 2, chapter 1 in the *Critique of Pure Reason*.

8. First published version: "therein presumably lies the mystery [*Geheimnis*] of thinking," a formulation that perhaps drew too close to Heidegger's exegesis in *Kant und das Problem der Metaphysik* (1929); English: *Kant and the Problem of Metaphysics*, trans. J. S. Churchill (Bloomington, Ind.: Indiana University Press, 1962). The radio version does not include this paragraph.

9. Object-relationship (*Objektbeziehung*) in psychoanalysis refers to the type of relationship between a subject and its environment, whereby the relationship represents a complex result of a certain organization of personality, a more or less fantasized apprehension of objects (object-choice and object-love) and certain privileged forms of psychic defense. The relationship is wholly reciprocal: not merely how a subject comes to choose or construct its objects, but also how the objects inform the psychic activities of the subject. In Melanie Klein this thought is expressed much more strongly: objects that are "projected" or "introjected" literally exert an influence (e.g., persecutory, compensatory, calming, etc.) on the subject.
Mentioned by Freud, e.g., in "Trauer und Melancholie" (1917); English: "Mourning and Melancholia," in vol. 14 of *The Standard Edition of the Complete Psychological Works of Sigmund Freud*, trans. James Strachey (London: Hogarth Press, 1975), but not really a fully developed part of his conceptual apparatus.

10. Radio version and first published version: "determine" instead of "establish."

11. In the radio version the paragraph ends here.

12. Cf. Kant's preface to the second edition of the *Critique of Pure Reason* (B xvi–B xxiv) and in particular the following footnote:

Similarly, the fundamental laws of the motions of the heavenly bodies gave established certainty to what Copernicus had at first assumed only as an hypothesis, and at the same time yielded proof of the invisible force (the Newtonian attraction) which holds the universe together. The latter would have remained for ever undiscovered if Copernicus had not dared, in a manner contradictory of the senses, but yet true, to seek the observed movements, not in the heavenly bodies, but in the spectator. The change in point of view, analogous to this hypothesis, which is expounded in the *Critique*, I put forward in this preface as an hypothesis only, in order to draw attention to the character of these first attempts at such a change, which are always hypothetical. But in the *Critique* itself it will be proved, apodeictically not hypothetically, from the nature of our representations of space and time and from the elementary concepts of the understanding.   *(Immanuel Kant,* Critique of Pure Reason, *25)*

13. The German is *"Genie ist Fleiß."*
14. Radio and first published version: "primitive" instead of "naively imputed."
15. In the radio version the paragraph ends here.
16. Cf. Hegel's "Preface" to the *Phänomenologie des Geistes (Werke* [Frankfurt: Suhrkamp, 1970], 3:17–18):

> Still less must this complacency which abjures science claim that rapturous haziness is superior to science. This prophetic talk supposes that it is staying right in the center and in the depths, looks disdainfully at determinateness (*Horos*), and deliberately holds aloof from concept and necessity as from reflection, which is at home only in finitude. But just as there is an empty breadth, so too is there an empty depth; and just as there is an extension of substance that pours forth as a finite diversity without the force to hold the diversity together, so there is an intensity without content, one that holds itself in as a sheer force without spreading out, and this is in no way distinguishable from superficiality. The power of spirit is only as great as its expression, its depth only as deep as it dares to spread out and lose itself in its exposition [*Auslegung*].
>
> *(G. W. F. Hegel,* Phenomenology of Spirit, *trans. A. V. Miller [Oxford: Oxford University Press, 1977], 6; translation modified)*

Commentators note that Hegel's critique is directed against J. Görres and C. A. Eschenmayer, who turned the Kantian negative knowledge (that we cannot know things in themselves, but only as they appear to us) into a positive claim for the power of enthusiasm and prayer as the closest we are able come in knowing divinity and things as they really are. The Greek ὅρος is apparently introduced by Hegel here in the sense of 'conceptual definition'; further connotations include "goal," "end," "purpose," as well as "border," "measure."
In the radio version this paragraph ends here.
17. A thinly veiled allusion to the "originary" phenomenology of Martin Heidegger.
18. Antonio Canova (1757–1833) and Bertel Thorwaldsen (1768–1844): leading neoclassicist sculptors of their age.
19. Cf. the final sections of Hegel's *Phenomenology of Spirit,* trans. A. V. Miller (Oxford: Oxford University Press, 1977) and *Science of Logic,* trans. A. V. Miller (New York: Humanities Press, 1969).
20. Radio version excises next two sentences, goes to "Where the philosophical thought . . . ."
21. In the radio version the paragraph ends here.

22. Cf. Aphorism 283 in the fourth book of *Die Fröhliche Wissenschaft* (1882); Friedrich Nietzsche, *The Gay Science: With a Prelude in Rhymes and an Appendix of Songs*, trans. Walter Kaufmann (New York: Random House: 1974), 228–229.

23. Radio and first published version: "with every necessary reservation" instead of "with every expectation of cheap ridicule."

24. Adorno plays on the ambiguity of the preposition and verbal prefix *nach*, which can mean (among much else) "after" in the temporal and spatial senses. So *denken* "to think" but *nachdenken* "to reflect deeply upon"; *Vollzug* "action, performance" is the nominalization of the verb *vollziehen*, "to perform, carry out"; *nachvollziehen*, "to comprehend, understand something that has occurred as though one had done it oneself," from which Adorno coins the analogous noun *Nachvollzug*, here translated as "reconstruction."

25. Radio version of this sentence: "Nonetheless to him who observes it in itself, to the extent that he really knows [*weiß*] what he wants to come to know [*erkennen*], philosophical thinking seems also to be able to come to know it."

First published version of this sentence: "Nonetheless to him who observes it in itself, philosophical thinking seems to be able to come to know [*erkennen*] what he wants to come to know, to the extent that he really knows [*weiß*] what he wants to come to know."

26. *Darstellung* is rendered "exhibition" in Kant, and elsewhere "presentation," at times "representation." Both Benjamin and Adorno devoted significant texts to the question of the adequate philosophical presentation of a given problem. Walter Benjamin, "Epistemo-Critical Prologue," in *The Origin of German Tragic Drama*, trans. John Osborne (London/New York: NLB, 1977; Verso, 1985). T. W. Adorno, "The Essay as Form," in *Notes to Literature*, vol. 1, trans. Shierry Weber Nicholsen (New York: Columbia University Press, 1991).

27. Radio and first published version: "if not indeed" instead of "possibly."

28. Radio version excises the following and goes to "Benjamin once alluded . . . ."

29. Cf. Adorno: "The greater demands Benjamin makes of the speculative concept, the more unreservedly, one might almost say blindly, does this thought succumb to its material. He once said, not out of coquettishness but with absolute seriousness, that he needed a proper dose of stupidity to be able to think a decent thought" ("Introduction to Benjamin's *Schriften*," *Notes to Literature*, trans. Shierry Weber Nicholsen [New York: Columbia University Press, 1992], 2:225).

30. Adorno plays on *Gegenstand*, "concrete object," and *Vergegenständlichung*, "concretion, concretization." The mentioning of *Ursprünglichkeit*, "primordiality," confirms that Adorno is taking yet another swipe at Heidegger's ontology.

31. Cf. Immanuel Kant, *The Critique of Pure Reason*:

Hitherto the concept of philosophy has been a merely scholastic concept [*Schulbegriff*]—a concept of a system of knowledge which is sought solely in its character as a science, and which has therefore in view only the systematic unity appropriate to science, and consequently no more than the *logical* perfection of knowledge. But there is likewise another concept of philosophy, a cosmical concept [*Weltbegriff*] (*conceptus cosmicus*), which has always formed the real basis of the term "philosophy," especially when it has been as it were personified and its archetype represented in the ideal *philosopher*. On this view, philosophy is the science of the relation of all knowledge to the essential ends of human reason (*teleologia rationis humanae*), and the philosopher is not an artificer in the field of reason, but himself the lawgiver of human reason. In this sense of the term it would be very vainglorious to entitle oneself a philosopher, and to pretend to have equalled the pattern which exists in the idea alone.   (Critique of Pure Reason, *657–658 [A 839/B 867]*)

Cf. also Kant, *Logik*, A 23–24 for a similar presentation of the opposition. In "What is Enlightenment" (1784) he uses similar language to define the "public use" of learned reason.

Reason and Revelation

1. G. W. F. Hegel, "Revealed Religion," in *Phenomenology of Spirit*, trans. A. V. Miller (Oxford: Oxford University Press, 1977), 453–478.

2. Cf. the chapter "Die absolute Freiheit und der Schrecken" in G. W. F. Hegel, *Phänomenologie des Geistes, Werke* (Frankfurt: Suhrkamp, 1970), 3:435–6. "Kein positives Werk noch Tat kann also die allgemeine Freiheit hervorbringen; es bleibt ihr nur das *negative Tun*; sie ist nur die *Furie* des Verschwindens." English: "Universal freedom, therefore, can produce neither a positive work nor a deed; there is left for it only *negative* action; it is merely the *fury* of destruction" (G. W. F. Hegel, *Phenomenology of Spirit*, 359).

3. Radio and first published version: "far more pitiless and evil" instead of "far more vicious."

4. Radio and first published version: "suppress with violence" instead of "suppress through intimidation."

5. Radio and first published version: "an essential element" instead of "some."

6. Radio and first published version: "this moment only seemingly [*nur scheinhaft*] has become independent in relation to the totality" instead of "admittedly even this moment has become independent in relation to the totality."

7. "Transcendental homelessness," a concept made famous by Georg Lukács in his *Theorie des Romans* (1920). English: Georg Lukács, *The Theory of the Novel: A Historico-philosophical Essay on the Forms of Great Epic Literature*, trans. Anna Bostock (Cambridge, Mass.: MIT Press, 1971).

8. "Über die Lehre Spenglers" (1924), reprinted in Thomas Mann, *Gesammelte Werke* (Frankfurt: Fischer, 1960), 10:172–179. English: "On the Theory of Spengler," in Thomas Mann, *Past Masters and Other Papers*, trans. H. T. Lowe-Porter (New York: Knopf, 1933), 217–230.

9. Radio and first published version: "monstrous" instead of "colossal."

10. Cf. Immanuel Kant, *Grounding for the Metaphysics of Morals* (1785), trans. James W. Ellington (Indianapolis: Hackett, 1993), 23–24 [*Grundlegung zur Metaphysik der Sitten*, A. A. 8:412f.]. There Kant defines the will as the capacity to choose what reason alone, independent of subjective desires, recognizes as practically necessary or "good." Because human beings are not completely rational creatures, constraint plays a role: "if the will does not of itself completely accord with reason (as is actually the case with men), then actions which are recognized as objectively necessary are subjectively contingent, and the determination of such a will according to objective laws is necessitation [*Nötigung*]. That is to say that the relation of objective laws to a will not thoroughly good is represented as the determination of the will of a

rational being by principles of reason which the will does not necessarily follow because of its nature."

11. For Hegel, "ethical substance" [*Sittlichkeit*] is "substantial" [*substantiell*] if its rules, or virtues, are embedded in the community as such, without the need for anything like a (Kantian) transcendental derivation of "the moral law."

12. Radio and first published version: "as for instance in the American magazine *Time*."

13. Radio and first published version: "its pragmatic elements" instead of "its factual content."

14. Radio and first published version: "the transparently agrarian relations" instead of "the transparent relations of the '*primary community**.'"

15. Cf. "Franz Kafka," in Walter Benjamin, *Gesammelte Schriften*, ed. Rolf Tiedemann and Hermann Schweppenhäuser (Frankfurt: Suhrkamp, 1977), II/2:423. English: " 'In Kafka,' said Soma Morgenstern, 'there is the air of a village, as with all great founders of religions"' ("Franz Kafka: On the Tenth Anniversary of his Death," in *Illuminations: Essays and Reflections*, trans. Harry Zohn, ed. Hannah Arendt [New York: Schocken, 1968], 125–26).

Cf. also Benjamin *Gesammelte Schriften*, II/3:1231f.; and Adorno/Benjamin, *Briefwechsel, 1928–1940* (Frankfurt: Suhrkamp, 1994), 94.

Soma Morgenstern (1890–1976), Jewish lawyer turned writer, whom Adorno met in 1925 during his stay in Vienna; Morgenstern later worked as the Viennese correspondent for the *Frankfurter Zeitung*; in 1938 he emigrated to Paris, where he met Benjamin, and in 1941 to New York.

16. Cf. T. W. Adorno, *Kierkegaard: Konstruktion des Ästhetischen* (1962), GS 2:166. English: Adorno, *Kierkegaard: Construction of the Aesthetic*, trans. Robert Hullot-Kentor (Minneapolis: University of Minnesota Press, 1989), 117.

Progress

1. Throughout this essay Adorno plays on the double meaning of *Menschheit*, which like its usual translation, "humanity," can signify an abstract principle as well as the sum of existing human beings (that is, "humanness" on the one hand, "humankind" on the other). In the first "model" of *Negative Dialectics*, in a section entitled "Ontical and Ideal Moments," Adorno explores this ambiguity of *Menschheit* in Kant's moral theory, concluding "Kant must have noticed the double meaning of the word 'humanity,' as the idea of being human and as the totality of all men; he introduced it into theory in a manner that was dialectically profound, even though playful. His subsequent usage vacillates between ontical manners of speech and others that refer to the idea. . . . He wants neither to cede the idea of humanity to the existing society nor to vaporize it into a phantasm" (*Negative Dialectics*, trans. E. B. Ashton [New York: Seabury Press, 1973], 258). In this essay *Menschheit* is consistently translated as "humanity" to preserve the doubleness. By contrast German *Humanität*, which also occurs in the essay, derives from the Latin *humanitas*, and signifies not the ontic human species but rather the ideal of humane refinement as a mark of civilization; it is translated as "humanitarianism."

2. Here, as in his essay on Kafka in *Prisms* (and GS 8:229), Adorno's partial quotation neglects Kafka's emphasis on the mutual implication of progress and belief.

Kafka's aphorism is quoted in its entirety by Benjamin in "Franz Kafka: On the Tenth Anniversary of his Death": " 'To believe in progress is not to believe that progress has already taken place. That would be no belief.' Kafka did not consider the age in which he lived as an advance over the beginnings of time. His novels are set in a swamp world. In his works, created things appear at the stage Bachofen has termed the hetaeric stage. The fact that it is now forgotten does not mean that it does not extend into the present. On the contrary: it is actual by virtue of this very oblivion" (*Illuminations*, 130).

    3. "Und wer's nie gekonnt, der stehle weinend sich aus diesem Bund" from Friedrich Schiller's ode "An die Freude" (1786).

    4. First published version has: "For the element of enlightenment within it, that of demythologization, which terminates . . . . "

    5. "Und alles Drängen, alles Ringen / Ist ewige Ruh in Gott dem Herrn" from "Zahme Xenien VI," translated in *Goethe: Selected Verse*, ed. David Luke (New York: Penguin, 1981), 280.

    6. "The fact that the subjective purpose, as the power over these processes (in which the *objective* gets used up through mutual friction and sublates itself), keeps itself *outside of them* and *preserves itself* in them is the *cunning* of reason.

"In this sense we can say that, with regard to the world and its process, divine Providence behaves with absolute cunning. God lets men, who have their particular passions and interests, do as they please, and what results is the accomplishment of *his* intentions, which are something other than those whom he employs were directly concerned about" (G. W. F. Hegel, *The Encyclopedia Logic: Part I of the Encyclopedia of Philosophical Sciences, with the Zusätze*, trans. T. F. Geraets, W. A. Suchting, and H. S. Harris [Indianapolis: Hackett, 1991], here p. 284). German: G. W. F. Hegel, *Enzyklopädie der philosophischen Wissenschaften I, Werke* (Frankfurt: Suhrkamp, 1970), 8:365 (§209 and Zusatz). Cf. also *Wissenschaft der Logik II, Werke* 6:452 ("C. Der ausgeführte Zweck") and *Philosophie der Geschichte, Werke* 12:49 and 119.

    7. I.e., the fifth and sixth theses.

    8. Cf. the fifth proposition of Kant's "Idea for a Universal History":

The greatest problem for the human species, the solution of which nature compels him to seek, is that of attaining a civil society which can administer justice universally.

    The highest purpose of nature—i.e. the development of all natural capacities—can be fulfilled for mankind only in society, and nature intends that man should accomplish this, and indeed all his appointed ends, by his own efforts. This purpose can be fulfilled only in a society which has not only the greatest freedom, and therefore a continual antagonism among its members, but also the most precise specification and preservation of the limits of this freedom in order that it can co-exist with the freedom of others. The highest task which nature has set for mankind must therefore be that of establishing a society in which *freedom under external laws* would be combined to the greatest possible extent with irresistible force, in other words of establishing a perfectly *just civil constitution*. For only through the solution and fulfillment of this task can nature accomplish its other intentions with our species. Man, who is otherwise so enamoured with unrestrained freedom, is forced to enter this state of restriction by sheer necessity. And this is indeed the most stringent of all forms of necessity, for it is imposed by men upon themselves, in that their inclinations make it impossible for them to exist side by side for long in a state of wild freedom. But once enclosed within a precinct like that of civil union, the same inclinations have the most beneficial effect. In the same way, trees in a forest, by seeking to deprive each other of air and sunlight, compel each other to find these by upward growth, so that they grow beautiful and straight— whereas those which put out branches at will, in freedom and in isolation from others, grow stunted, bent and twisted. All the culture and art which adorn mankind and the finest social order man creates are fruits of his unsociability. For it is compelled by its own nature to discipline itself, and thus, by enforced art, to develop completely the germs which nature implanted.

(From "Idea for a Universal History with a Cosmopolitan Purpose," trans. H. B. Nisbet, in Kant, Political Writings, ed. Hans Reiss, 2d ed. [Cambridge: Cambridge University Press, 1991], 45–46)

9. Adorno alludes to Heidegger's *Kant und das Problem der Metaphysik* (1929); English: *Kant and the Problem of Metaphysics*, trans. J. S. Churchill (Bloomington, Ind.: Indiana University Press, 1962).

10. Cf. Walter Benjamin, "Theological-political Fragment" in *Reflections: Essays, Aphorisms, Autobiographical Writings*, trans. E. Jephcott, ed. Peter Demetz (New York: Schocken, 1978), 312–313.

11. Adorno here alludes to a seminar presentation made by one of his students, Karl Heinz Haag, that has been preserved in the Adorno Archive in Frankfurt. Haag later briefly touches on some aspects of this paper in his *Der Fortschritt in der Philosophie* (Frankfurt: Suhrkamp, 1983), esp. 37–39.

12. Cf. Schopenhauer in *The World as Will and Representation* (trans. E. F. J. Payne [New York: Dover, 1969]), 1:185 (§36, on art):

Whilst science, following the restless and unstable stream of the fourfold forms of reasons or grounds and consequents, is with every end it attains again and again directed farther, and can never find an ultimate goal or complete satisfaction, any more than by running we can reach the point where the clouds touch the horizon; art, on the contrary, is everywhere at its goal. For it plucks the object of its contemplation from the stream of the world's course, and holds it isolated before it. This particular thing, which in that stream was an infinitesimal part, becomes for art a representative of the whole, an equivalent of the infinitely many in space and time. It therefore pauses at this particular thing; it stops the wheel of time; for it the relations vanish; its object is only the essential, the Idea. We can therefore define it accurately as *the way of considering things independently of the principle of sufficient reason*, in contrast to the way of considering them which proceeds in exact accordance with this principle, and is the way of science and experience.

And in chapter 41, "On Death and Its Relation to the Indestructibility of Our Inner Nature," "There is no greater contrast than that between the ceaseless, irresistible flight of time carrying its whole content away with it and the rigid immobility of what is actually existing, which is at all times one and the same; and if, from this point of view, we fix our really objective glance on the immediate events of life, the *Nunc stans* becomes clear and visible to us in the center of the wheel of time" (ibid., 2:481).

13. Adorno surely relies here on the severely abbreviated version of the essay "Die Rückschritte der Poesie" ["The Regression of Poetry"] by Carl Gustav Jochmann (1789–1830), which Walter Benjamin published with an introduction in the *Zeitschrift für Sozialforschung* 8 (1939/40): 92—114. Benjamin presented what originally appeared as the fourth of five sections comprising Jochmann's anonymous book *Über die Sprache* (Heidelberg: C. F. Winter, 1828). Jochmann makes the distinction between material progress in the natural sciences and the lack of progress in the "spiritual domain": whereas the natural sciences progress in terms of technical ability, knowledge, and the domination of nature, the intellectual "internal development" operates in the opposite direction, as the destruction of reigning prejudices, as the reinvestment of the world with imagination. The investment through fantasy was the chief characteristic of lyric poetry, and Benjamin's excision of this section of Jochmann's text misled Adorno to think that Jochmann had prophesied the end of art (cf. Benjamin, *Gesammelte Schriften* II/3:1393; and Adorno, *Ästhetische Theorie*, GS 7:501).

14. First published version has slightly different sentence: "it is the Hegelian 'Furie des Verschwindens,' which plunges one concept after another into the Orcus of the mythical."

15. Cf. "On the Tarantulas" and "On Redemption" in Friedrich Nietzsche, *Thus Spake Zarathustra*, trans. Walter Kaufmann (New York: Viking Press, 1966), 99–102, 137–142.

16. First published version: "behavior" instead of "attitude."

17. Adorno here both invokes and corrects Walter Benjamin's theory of the "dialectical image," the cognitive armature of the studies composing his unfinished *Arcades Project* [*Passagenarbeit*]. Benjamin, who Adorno felt was too much under the sway of the surrealists, had suggested that juxtapositions of historical material in "constellations" would release the archaic dream and wish images lodged in the collective unconscious at the threshold to modernity. In a now renowned exchange of letters, Adorno rejected the theory's implied idealism: "If you transpose the dialectical image into consciousness as a 'dream,' then not only has the concept been disenchanted and made more tractable, it has also thereby forfeited precisely the objective interpretive power which could legitimate it in materialistic terms. The fetish character of the commodity is not a fact of consciousness but rather dialectical, in the eminent sense that it produces consciousness" (*Aesthetics and Politics: Debates between Bloch, Lukács, Brecht, Benjamin, Adorno*, ed. Ronald Taylor [London: NLB, 1977; Verso, 1980], 140–41). Indeed the present essay can be considered a practical exposition of Adorno's viewpoint.

18. Karl Marx, *Critique of the Gotha Programme: With Appendixes by Marx, Engels, and Lenin* (New York: International Publishers, 1970).

19. First published version: "is one with" instead of "reinforces."

Gloss on Personality

1. Cf. Karl Kraus, "Niemand geringerer als" in *Die Fackel* 20, no. 474–483 (23 May 1918): 23–25.

2. In the first published version, Adorno provides the source in a footnote: Kant, *Kritik der praktischen Vernunft*, ed. Karl Vorländer (Hamburg: Meiner, 1952), 101

[A. A.: V, 87]. English: Immanuel Kant, *Critique of Practical Reason*, trans. Lewis White Beck, 3d. ed. (New York: Macmillan, 1993), 90; translation modified.

3. German *Person, persönlich, Persönlichkeit*: "person," "personal," "personality."

4. Cf. Immanuel Kant, *Grounding for the Metaphysics of Morals*, trans. James W. Ellington (Indianapolis: Hackett, 1993), 40–41; German: *Grundlegung der Metaphysik der Sitten*, BA 78 [A. A. IV: 434–435]:

> In the kingdom of ends everything has either a price or a dignity. Whatever has a price can be replaced by something else as its equivalent; on the other hand, whatever is above all price, and therefore admits of no equivalent, has a dignity.
>
> Whatever has reference to general human inclinations and needs has a market price. Whatever, without presupposing any need, accords with a certain taste, i.e., a delight in the mere unpurposive play of our powers, has an affective price; but that which constitutes the condition under which alone something can be an end in itself has not merely a relative worth, i.e., a price, but has an intrinsic worth, i.e., dignity.
>
> Now morality is the condition under which alone a rational being can be an end in himself, for only thereby can he be a legislating member in the kingdom of ends. Hence morality and humanity, insofar as it is capable of morality, alone have dignity.

5. Cf. Johann Wolfgang von Goethe, *West-Eastern Divan/West-östlicher Divan*, rendered into English by J. Whaley (London: Oswald Wolff, 1974), 130–133. The relevant passage:

> SULEIKA: Volk und Knecht und Überwinder,
> Sie gestehn zu jeder Zeit:
> Höchstes Glück der Erdenkinder
> Sei nur die Persönlichkeit.
>
> Jedes Leben sei zu führen,
> Wenn man sich nicht selbst vermißt:
> Alles könne man verlieren,
> Wenn man bliebe, was man ist.

Translation:

> Nations, ruler, slave subjected,
> All on this one point agree:
> Joy of earthlings is perfected
> In the personality.
>
> Every life is worth the choosing
> If oneself one does not miss;
> Everything is worth the losing
> To continue as one is.

6. First published version has footnote: Wilhelm von Humboldt, *Werke I* (Darmstadt, 1960), 235.

7. "Theorie der Bildung des Menschen," in *Wilhelm von Humboldts Gesammelte Schriften*, ed. Königlich Preussische Akademie der Wissenschaften, part 1: *Wilhelm von Humboldts Werke*, ed. Albert Leitzmann, vol. 1, 1785–1795 (Berlin: Behr's Verlag, 1903), 282–287 [citation from p. 283]. First published version gives footnote: ibid. [*Werke* 1 (Darmstadt 1960)], 235.

8. Cf. Friedrich Nietzsche, "On Old and New Tablets," no. 20, in *Thus Spake Zarathustra*, trans. Walter Kaufmann (New York: Viking Press, 1966), 209.

9. Adorno's term "specialized personnel" [*Fachmenschentum*] alludes to Max Weber's coinage in the opening pages of his introduction to the *Gesammelte Aufsätze zur Religionssoziologie* (Tübingen: Mohr, 1920–21); English: introduction to *The Protestant Ethic and the Spirit of Capitalism*, trans. Talcott Parsons (New York: Scribner's, 1958), where he very ambivalently evaluates the unique conjunction of specialization and thoroughgoing administrative organization in Western rationality.

10. Adorno is here alluding to the policy aim of a "fully formed society" (*formierte Gesellschaft*) ironically since he replaces the conclusive past participle with the open-ended present participle. The concept of *formierte Gesellschaft* was introduced in 1965 by Chancellor Ludwig Erhard under the influence of the economist Götz Briefs and the philosopher Eric Voegelin (whose diagnoses suggest the influence of Carl Schmitt). It held that following the eclipse of the estates in early modernity and the class system in postwar German society, organized special interest groups, industrial cartels, unions, etc., all seeking power and benefits from the welfare state, represented an increasing potential for dissent and threatened economic and social order and even parliamentary rule. Before Erhard could bring concrete proposals to the Bundestag for reinforcing social and economic stability, his policy statement was attacked by the Left as undemocratic and his political position weakened drastically.

11. First published version differs slightly: "nor would he fortify himself in his pure selfhood, his being so and not differently."

12. "Drum, so wandle nur wehrlos / Fort durchs Leben, und fürchte nichts!" from Hölderlin's poem "Dichtermuth." First published version has footnote: Hölderlin, *Sämtliche Werke*, vol. 2, Kleine Stuttgarter Ausgabe (Stuttgart, 1955), 68. English: Friedrich Hölderlin, *Poems and Fragments*, trans. Michael Hamburger (London: Routledge & Kegan Paul, 1966), 200–203.

Free Time

1. Radio version has "conformist sociologies" instead of "conciliatory sociologies," presumably an allusion to Erving Goffman's theory of 'social roles'; cf. his *The Presentation of Self in Everyday Life* (Garden City: Anchor Books, 1959).

2. Radio version: "the difference between work and free time has been branded, become a taboo" instead of "branded as a norm."

3. Radio version: "Organized free time is branded with compulsion" instead of "organized free time is compulsory."

4. The Youth Movement [*Jugendbewegung*] was a protest movement around the turn of the century, influenced by the cultural pessimism of Nietzsche and progressive-alternative educational theories, largely undertaken by middle-class urban adolescents who rejected the industrial, Wilhelminian bourgeois lifestyle in favor of a romantic "return" to nature, simplicity, sincerity, and self-reliance. By 1914 the movement had over 25,000 members and after the war split along confessional (Protestant and Catholic) and political (socialist, communist, conservative) lines. Certain *völkisch* aspects of the conservative wing of the movement fed easily into the National Socialist ideology, and in 1933 all those groups that had not incorporated themselves into the Hitler Youth [*Hitler Jugend*] were disbanded.

5. Radio version: "more important than the situations, which . . . ." instead of "than the flirtation."

6. Cf. for instance Baudelaire's poem "Le Voyage," in *Les Fleurs du Mal* (1861).

7. Schopenhauer on boredom: §57 of *The World as Will and Representation* (trans. E. F. J. Payne [New York: Dover, 1969]) in general is a discussion of desire and pain (want, need) and boredom as the fundamental constitutive qualities of human existence. Cf. also Horkheimer: "Perhaps Helvétius was not wrong when he connected boredom, which Schopenhauer sees only as evil and at most responsible for superstitions, as a reason for imagination, to real culture. The division between leisure [*Muße*] and boredom [*Langeweile*] is not distinct; people don't attain either of them. In technical civilization they are so fundamentally 'cured' of their heaviness, that they forget how to resist. But resistance is the soul of Schopenhauer's philosophy" (Horkheimer, "Schopenhauer und die Gesellschaft," in Horkheimer and Adorno, *Sociologica II: Reden und Vorträge* [Frankfurt: Europäische Verlagsanstalt, 1962], here p. 122).

8. Cf. Schopenhauer: "As we have said, the common, ordinary man, that manufactured article of nature which she daily produces in the thousands, is not capable, at any rate continuously, of a consideration of things wholly disinterested in every sense, such as is contemplation proper. He can direct his attention to things only in so far as they have some relation to his will, although that relation may be only very indirect" (Schopenhauer, *The World as Will and Representation*, 1:187 [§36]). Cf. also 2:426.

9. Radio version: "to the objective eternal sameness" instead of "to objective dullness."

10. Cf. act 3, scene 1 of Schiller's *Wilhelm Tell* (1804):

A man with eyesight clear and sense alert,
Who trusts in God and his own supple strength,
Will find some way to slip the noose of danger.
Mountain-born was never scared of mountains.
(*Having finished his work he puts the tools away.*)
There now! That gate should serve another twelvemonth.
An axe in the house will save a joiner's labor.
(*Reaches for his hat.*)
(*Johann Christoph Friedrich von Schiller*, Wilhelm Tell, *trans. and ed.*
William F. Mainland [Chicago: University of Chicago Press, 1972], 64–65 [ll.
1508–1513])

11. Perhaps Adorno's clearest explanation of pseudo-activity can be found in prose piece #91, "Vandals," in *Minima Moralia* (composed during his American emigration, published in 1951):

Doing things and going places is an attempt by the sensorium to set up a kind of counter-irritant against a threatening collectivization, to get in training for it by using the hours apparently left to freedom to coach oneself as a member of the mass. The technique is to try to outdo the danger. One lives in a sense even worse, that is, with even less self, than one expects to have to live. At the same time one learns through this playful excess of self-loss that to live in earnest without a self could be easier, not more difficult. All this is done in great haste, for no warning bells will announce the earthquake. If one does not take part, and that means, if one does not swim bodily in the human stream, one fears, as when delaying too long to join a totalitarian party, missing the bus and bringing on oneself the vengeance of the collective. Pseudo-activity is an insurance, the expression of a readiness for self-surrender, in which one senses the only guarantee of self-preservation. Security is glimpsed in adaptation to the utmost insecurity.

(Minima Moralia, *trans. E. F. N. Jephcott [London: NLB, 1974], 139 [GS 4:155–156])*

Cf. also pp. 130–1 (*GS* 4:145) and Adorno, *The Stars Down to Earth and other Essays on the Irrational in Culture,* ed. Stephen Crook (London/New York: Routledge, 1994), 63. The concept is clearly related to Adorno's analysis of the "manipulative type" in Adorno et al., *The Authoritarian Personality* (New York: Harper & Brothers, 1950), 767. The concept in fact was first defined by Erich Fromm in his analysis of *Scheinaktivität* in "Zum Gefühl der Ohnmacht," *Zeitschrift für Sozialforschung* 6 (1937): 95–118.

Adorno returns to the concept in his diagnosis of student actionism in the essays "Marginalia to Theory and Praxis" and "Resignation," this volume.

12. The study in March 1966 was never evaluated and published, though its data were incorporated, together with several other Institute studies using the new A-Scale (studies of Germans' reactions to the Eichmann trial, political tendencies among German youth, pupils' reactions to civic education in select *Gymnasien*, German prejudices toward *Gastarbeiter*, and stereotypes of Chinese), in the appendixes to Michaela von Freyhold, *Autoritarismus und politische Apathie: Analyse einer Skala zur Ermittlung autoritätsgebundener Verhaltensweisen,* vol. 22 of *Frankfurter Beiträge zur Soziologie* (Frankfurt: Europäische Verlagsanstalt, 1971), esp. 273, 300, 303, 307, 317.

Taboos on the Teaching Vocation

1. German *Lehrer* refers exclusively to primary and secondary education. *Professoren* (professors) have "teaching duties" [*Lehrtätigkeiten*], but these generally stand below research in terms of importance.

2. University degree required for the teaching profession.

3. Radio version: "reasons" instead of "motives."

4. Hellmut Becker (1913–1993), lawyer, who defended among others Foreign Service Secretary of State Freiherr von Weizsäcker in the Nuremburg trials, then went on to pursue legal and cultural-political aspects of education and education reform. He was a close associate of Adorno's, and the two often debated issues of educational reform, the societal role of education, etc. in lectures and radio programs. Cf. Adorno, *Erziehung zur Mündigkeit: Vorträge und Gespräche mit Hellmut Becker, 1959–1969*, ed. Gerd Kadelbach (Frankfurt: Suhrkamp, 1970).

Explicit allusions to the "administered school" can be found in his *Probleme einer Schulreform* (Stuttgart: Alfred Kröner Verlag, 1959), 105–118. Cf. also "Die verwaltete Schule," in Hellmut Becker, *Kulturpolitik und Schule: Probleme der verwalteten Welt*, Serie Fragen an die Zeit, ed. Theodor Eschenburg (Stuttgart: Deutsche Verlagsanstalt, 1956).

5. German *Korps* and *Korporationen* were originally dueling societies, and though today they are roughly equivalent to fraternities or student social clubs at the university, many maintain an aristocratic-militaristic ethos.

6. *Gymnasium*: German secondary school with emphasis on classical humanist education. Its contrastive counterpart is the *Realschule*, with emphasis on mathematics and natural sciences.

7. Radio and first published versions: "one would need to investigate it empirically; I doubt it."

8. Cf. the preface to the second edition of *The World as Will and Representation*, trans. E. F. J. Payne (New York: Dover, 1969), 1:xixf.

9. The anecdote, which Adorno relates in the untranslatable dialect of his native Hessen, refers to the following chapter in the poet's biography. In 1796 Hölderlin received a position as private tutor for the patrician Gontard family in Frankfurt. He fell in love with his pupil's mother, Susette Gontard, whom he glorified in his lyrics as "Diotima." The husband Jakob Gontard apparently confronted Hölderlin about the liaison, and he was forced to leave his position in 1798. Hölderlin maintained clandestine contact with Susette Gontard until her death in 1802, which it is believed contributed to his final mental collapse.

10. Radio and first published version: "In the sense of this image world [*Bilderwelt*], this *imagerie*, the teacher . . . ."

11. In the twenty-fifth "adventure" of the *Nibelungenlied* Hagen, the vassal of King Gunther, leads the royal retinue to visit the king's sister Kriemhild, who, following the murder of her husband Siegfried by Hagen, has married the Hun Etzel and, notwithstanding twelve years of marriage, still plans to avenge Siegfried's death. While searching for a ford or ferry across the swollen Danube, Hagen meets two water nymphs who warn him that all the company will be killed by the Huns with the sole exception of the king's chaplain. To test the prophecy Hagen hurls the chaplain into the raging waters of the Danube as they cross by ferry, and the chaplain, who cannot swim, remarkably survives and remains on the near side of the river. Thus Hagen knows that the entire retinue is fated to perish and vows to fight to the bitter end.

12. On Hartmann von der Aue (late 12th c. Swabian Minnesänger) and literacy, cf. the opening of his *Der arme Heinrich*, here in prose translation:

"There was once a knight so well-educated that he could read whatever he found in the way of books. His name was Hartmann, and he was a vassal at Aue. He would

frequently consult books of various kinds in which he hoped to find anything calculated to promote the glory of God and at the same time enhance his own standing in
the eyes of his fellowmen. Now he is prepared to recount for you something he found
in a text. He has named himself in order that the effort he has put into it may not go
unrewarded, so that anyone hearing or reading it after his death may pray to God for
his soul's salvation. They say that he who prays on behalf of another is at the same
time acting as his own advocate and redeeming himself thereby as well" (*The Narra-
tive Works of Hartmann von Aue*, trans. R. W. Fisher [Göppingen: Kümmerle Verlag, 1983], 158).

13. First published version includes the following footnote by Adorno, which was
removed from subsequent editions: "My thanks to Jacob Taubes for this reference."

14. "Limit situation" [*Grenzsituation*], a term of art from existential phenomenology, introduced by Karl Jaspers (in his *Psychologie der Weltanschauungen* of
1919 and *Philosophie* of 1932) and adopted by Max Scheler and Martin Heidegger,
indicating those situations where one's existence (*Dasein*) becomes "transparent" to
its own historicity and contingency: e.g., battle, suffering, dread, etc.

15. "Ein Landarzt," in Franz Kafka, *Gesammelte Schriften*, edited by Max Brod
together with Heinz Politzer (Berlin: Schocken, 1935), vol. 1. English translations
generally have the title "A Country Doctor."

16. Thomas Mann, *Buddenbrooks: The Decline of a Family*, trans. John E. Woods
(New York: Knopf, 1993). Originally published in 1899.

17. Cf. chapter 5 of *The Trial* (ca. 1914) in Franz Kafka, *The Trial*, trans. Douglas
Scott and Chris Waller (London: Picador, 1977).

18. In the radio version Adorno interjects—"'a gentleman is never intentionally
rude*,' is an English saying—. . . ."

19. In the radio version Adorno uses the colloquial and gender specific *Backfisch*
(half-grown, teenage girl) instead of the foreign "teenager."

20. Heinrich Mann, *Professor Unrat oder das Ende eines Tyrannen* (1905). In
1947 the book was reissued under the title of its film version *Der blaue Engel* (1930,
directed by Josef von Sternberg), in which Marlene Dietrich played the chanteuse
Rosa Fröhlich. English: *The Blue Angel: The novel by Heinrich Mann; The film by
Josef von Sternberg* (New York: Ungar, 1979). Cf. Adorno's polemic against the reissuing of the novel with the title altered to *Der Blaue Engel* in "Ein Titel," and "Unrat
und Engel," in *Noten zur Literatur*, GS 11:654–660; English: "A Title," and "Unrat
and Angel," in *Notes to Literature*, trans. Shierry Weber Nicholsen (New York:
Columbia University Press, 1992), 2:299–304.

21. Radio version begins the next paragraph as follows: "This partiality, however,
is detested most of all in the person with a claim to intellectual authority. He is seen
in general to be someone who lives in an unreal world, like the unlucky hero . . . ."

22. *Traumulus* (1924), a tragic comedy written by Arno Holz and Oskar Jerschke.
A sexual indiscretion by a schoolboy and the subsequent small-town gossip about
him lead inevitably to his suicide.

23. Karl Kraus, *Sittlichkeit und Kriminalität*, *Werke*, vol. 11 (Munich/Vienna:
Langen-Müller, 1963). Cf. Adorno's review of this volume: "Sittlichkeit und Kriminalität: Zum elften Band der Werke von Karl Kraus," in *Noten zur Literatur*, GS
11:367–387; in English: "Morals and Criminality: On the Eleventh Volume of the
Works of Karl Kraus," in *Notes to Literature*, 2:40–57.

24. Adorno's *Fachmensch* (specialized person) alludes to Max Weber's coinage "*Fachmenschentum*" ("specialized personnel") in the opening pages of his introduction to the *Gesammelte Aufsätze zur Religionssoziologie* (Tübingen: Mohr, 1920–21); English: introduction to *The Protestant Ethic and the Spirit of Capitalism*, trans. Talcott Parsons (New York: Scribner's, 1958), where he very ambivalently evaluates the unique conjunction of specialization and thoroughgoing administrative organization in Western rationality.

25. Radio version interjects: "—I mean the idiosyncratic sensibility of the children."

26. Radio version: "The school has an immanent tendency to close itself off with an astounding violence"; first published version: "The school has an immanent tendency to seal itself off."

27. Tucholsky and a female acquaintance meet a child who has run away from the children's home. The director of the home, Frau Adriani, demands the child's return, and Tucholsky records their conversation when he brings the child back:

"So the child fled to you! That's just great! It's lucky for you that you brought her back on my instructions right away! She won't run away any more—that I can promise you. What a creature! Well you just wait . . ."—"But the child must have had a reason to run away!" I said. "No, she had none whatsoever. She didn't have any reason." "Hm. And what will you do with her?"—"I will punish her," said Frau Adriani, at once both satiated and hungry. She stretched in her chair. "Please permit me a question: how will you punish her?" "I don't need to answer that question—I don't have to. But I will tell you, for it is in accordance with Frau Collin's wishes that the child be dealt with strictly. So she will be confined to her room [*Zimmerarrest*, a military term], and will receive the small penalties, work, she cannot go outside with the others—that's how it's done here."—"And if we asked you to waive the punishment . . . would you do that?—"No. I could not decide to do that. You can ask all you want . . . Is that what you came to ask me?" she added with a sneer.

(Kurt Tucholsky, Gesammelte Werke in 10 Bänden, *ed. Mary Gerold-Tucholsky and Fritz J. Raddatz [1931] [Hamburg: Rowohlt, 1960], 9:87)*

28. Gustav Wyneken (1875–1964), educator, in 1906 founded and oversaw the progressive "Free School Community Wikkersdorf." In his book about the school, *Der Gedankenkreis der Freien Schulgemeinde* (1914), he presented his theory of the independent "culture of youth," which had a wide influence on the Youth Movement.

29. Richard Matthias Müller, *Über Deutschland: 103 Dialoge* (Olten and Freiburg i. Br.: Walter, 1965), 2d ed. (Frankfurt: Fischer, 1966). Short, sardonic dialogues between a Catholic father and his son that expose the hypocrisy of the Federal Republic's contemporary political palaver regarding the recent past, relations with the German Democratic Republic, the Allied powers, etc.

30. Radio and first published versions: "This is implied by an experience that no one can evade. We all have experienced the relapse of humanity into barbarism, in the literal, indescribable, and true sense. Nothing can be added to the word 'Auschwitz.' But barbarism is a condition . . . ."

31. *Entbarbarisieren*, Adorno's neologism, modeled on and likely a corrective deepening of "denazification" [*entnazifizieren*]. The radio version is more direct: "thus, that something like Auschwitz does not happen again in the world, essentially depends on individuals becoming debarbarized."

32. Radio and first published versions have the following sentence next: "Boger's ideology was that of pedagogical corporal punishment; even at his trial he was clamoring about the youth's lack of discipline."

Education After Auschwitz

1. Sigmund Freud, *Massenpsychologie und Ich-Analyse* (1921) and *Das Unbehagen in der Kultur* (1930); English: vols. 18 and 21, respectively, of *The Standard Edition of the Complete Psychological Works of Sigmund Freud*, trans. James Strachey (London: Hogarth Press, 1975).

2. First published version: "helpless" and "helplessness" instead of "desperate" and "desperation."

3. *Die Vierzig Tage des Musa Dagh* (1933) by Franz Werfel. Set in Syria in 1915, the novel recounts the resistance offered by the Armenians against more numerous and better equipped Young Turk forces. The Armenian forces entrench themselves on the mountain Musa Dagh for forty days and, on the verge of being overwhelmed, are rescued by an Anglo-French naval squadron. English: *The Forty Days of Musa Dagh*, trans. Geoffrey Dunlop (New York: Viking, 1934).

4. See the essay, "The Meaning of Working Through the Past," this volume.

5. First published version: "resistance, rebellion" instead of "spiteful resentment."

6. German translation *Tote ohne Begräbnis* of Jean Paul Sartre, *Morts sans sépulchre* in *Théatre*, vol. 1 (Paris: Gallimard, 1946). English: *The Victors*, in *Three Plays*, trans. Lionel Abel (New York: Knopf, 1949).

7. Eugen Kogon, *Der SS-Staat: Das System der deutschen Konzentrationslager* (Frankfurt: Europäische Verlagsanstalt, 1946); numerous reprints. English: Eugen Kogon, *The Theory and Practice of Hell: The German Concentration Camps and the System Behind them*, trans. Heinz Norden (New York: Berkley, 1950).

8. First published version: simply "has not yet succeeded" without the comparative.

9. Cf. Max Horkheimer and Theodor W. Adorno, *Dialectic of Enlightenment*, trans. John Cumming (New York: Seabury Press, 1972; reprint, New York: Continuum, 1989), esp. 231–236.

10. Cf. William Graham Sumner, *Folkways: A Study of the Sociological Importance of Usages, Manners, Customs, Mores, and Morals* (Boston: Ginn, 1906). Cf. also *Soziologische Exkurse: Nach Vorträgen und Diskussionen*, vol. 4 of *Frankfurter Beiträge zur Soziologie* (Frankfurt: Europäische Verlagsanstalt, 1956), 157; and T. W. Adorno, *Einführung in die Soziologie* (Frankfurt: Suhrkamp, 1993), 77. Adorno planned to have Sumner's book translated into German when he returned to Frankfurt after the war.

11. *Rauhnächte*: hazing ritual during the nights of Christmastide; *Haberfeldtreiben*: old Bavarian custom of censuring those perceived by the community as (often moral or sexual) reprobates who have been overlooked by the law. Cf. T. W.

Adorno, *Einführung in die Soziologie*, 65, where Adorno speaks of "Oberbayerische Haberfeldtreiben" in the context of the conceptual opacity of Durkheim's *faits sociaux*.

12. Cf. Friedrich Nietzsche, *Beyond Good and Evil*, trans. Walter Kaufmann (New York: Vintage, 1966), numbers 82, 210, 260, 269; *The Gay Science*, trans. Walter Kaufmann (New York: Random House, 1974), number 26; "On the Old and New Tablets," no. 29, in *Thus Spake Zarathustra*, trans. Walter Kaufmann (New York: Viking, 1966), 214.

13. Wilhelm Boger was in charge of the "escape department" at Auschwitz and took pride in the fact that it had the fewest escapes of any concentration camp. As one of the twenty-one former SS men brought before the "Frankfurt" or "Auschwitz" trials (1963–1965), Boger was accused of having taken part in numerous selections and executions at Auschwitz as well as having mistreated prisoners so severely on the "Boger swing" (a torture device he invented) during interrogation that they subsequently died. The court found him guilty of murder on at least 144 separate occasions, of complicity in the murder of at least 1,000 prisoners, and of complicity in the joint murder of at least 10 persons. Boger was sentenced to life imprisonment and an additional five years of hard labor.

14. First published version: "objects" instead of "material."

15. See Adorno's interpretation of "The 'Manipulative' Type" in *The Authoritarian Personality*, by T. W. Adorno, Else Frenkel-Brunswik, Daniel J. Levinson, and R. Nevitt Sanford, in collaboration with Betty Aron, Maria Hertz Levinson, and William Morrow, *Studies in Prejudice*, ed. Max Horkheimer and Samuel H. Flowerman (New York: Harper & Brothers, 1950), 767–771.

16. See part 3 of "Egoism and the Freedom Movement: On the Anthropology of the Bourgeois Era," (1936) in Max Horkheimer, *Between Philosophy and Social Science: Selected Early Writings*, trans. G. Frederick Hunter, Matthew S. Kramer, and John Torpey (Cambridge, Mass.: MIT Press, 1993).

17. Original reflections on "L'inhumaine" in Paul Valéry, "Rhumbs" in *Œuvres II*, ed. Jean Hytier (Paris: Gallimard 1960), 620–621.

Cf. Adorno's review of recent German translations of Valéry, "Valéry's Abweichungen" in *Noten zur Literatur*, GS 11:158–202, esp. 177–178, where he cites the passage as translated by Bernhard Böschenstein (*Windstriche* [Frankfurt: Insel Verlag, 1959]; reprinted in Paul Valéry, *Werke*, vol. 5, *Zur Theorie der Dichtkunst und vermischte Gedanken*, ed. Jürgen Schmidt-Radefeldt [Frankfurt: Insel Verlag 1991]). The English version of Adorno's essay ("Valéry's Deviations," in *Notes to Literature*, trans. Shierry Weber Nicholsen [New York: Columbia University Press, 1991] 1:137–173, here p. 153) quotes Valéry from the *Collected Works of Paul Valéry*, ed. Jackson Matthews, Bollingen Series 45, here vol. 14, *Analects*, trans. Stuart Gilbert ([Princeton, N.J.: Princeton University Press, 1970], 190): "The revolt of common sense is the instinctive recoil of man confronted by the inhuman; for common sense takes stock only of the human, of man's ancestors and yardsticks; of man's powers and interrelations. But research and the very powers that he possesses lead away from the human. Humanity will survive as best it can—perhaps there's a fine future in store for inhumanity" [translation corrected].

18. The "technological veil," as Adorno and Horkheimer first conceived it, is the "excess power which technology as a whole, along with the capital that stands behind

it, exercises over every individual thing" so that the world of the commodity, manufactured by mass production and manipulated by mass advertising, comes to be equated with reality per se: "Reality becomes its own ideology through the spell cast by its faithful duplication. This is how the technological veil and the myth of the positive is woven. If the real becomes an image insofar as in its particularity it becomes as equivalent to the whole as one Ford car to all the others of the same range, then the image on the other hand turns into immediate reality" ("The Schema of Mass Culture" (1942), trans. Nicholas Walker, now in Adorno, *The Culture Industry: Selected Essays on Mass Culture*, ed. J. M. Bernstein [London: Routledge, 1991], here p. 55). Original in *GS* 3:301. Adorno used the concept throughout his works, e.g., the 1942 text "Reflexionen zur Klassentheorie," *GS* 8:390, and the 1968 text "Spätkapitalismus oder Industriegesellschaft," where he defines it as follows: "The false identity between the organization of the world and its inhabitants caused by the total expansion of technology amounts to upholding the relations of production, whose beneficiaries in the meantime one searches for almost as much in vain as the proletariat has become invisible" (*GS* 8:369).

19. Radio version is stronger here: "If I may voice a suspicion here, concerning how this fetishization of technology comes about, then I would like to say that people who cannot love, that is those who constitutively, essentially, are cold, must themselves negate even the possibility of love, that is, withdraw their love of other people from the very outset, because they cannot love them at all, and at the same time apply to means whatever has managed to survive of their ability to love."

20. Cf. Adorno's qualitative evaluation of the clinical interview with "Mack," the exemplary subject prone to fascism as presented in *Authoritarian Personality*, 789; cf. also pp. 55, 802.

21. According to Aristotle, "man is by nature a political animal. And therefore men, even when they do not require one another's help, desire to live together," where "common advantage" and "friendship as political justice" hold states together. Cf. *Politics*, 1278b16–25 and *Nicomachean Ethics*, 1155a21–28 and 1160a9–14.

22. David Riesman, *The Lonely Crowd: A Study of the Changing American Character* (New Haven: Yale University Press, 1950).

23. Radio version and first published version continue as follows: "Similar behavior can be observed in innumerable automobile drivers, who are ready to run someone over if they have the green light on their side."

24. Charles Fourier, *Le nouveau monde industriel et sociétaire; ou, Invention du procédé d'industrie attrayante et naturelle distribuée en séries passionnées* (1829). English: Charles Fourier, *The Passions of the Human Soul, and their Influence on Society and Civilization*, trans. Hugh Doherty (London: Hippolythe Baillière, 1855).

25. Radio version: "First of all, it is necessary to learn about the objective and subjective mechanisms that led to this, as well as to learn about the stereotypical defense mechanisms that prevent working against such consciousness."

26. First published version: "then people perhaps will not give vent to these traits so unrestrainedly." Radio version: "When one no longer has the feeling that countless people are all similarly waiting for outrages to be committed, rather when one knows that they are deformations and the entire cultural consciousness is permeated with the intimation of the pathogenic character of these traits, then people will perhaps not give vent to it so unrestrainedly."

On the Question: "What is German?"

1. The proverb is even more ill-fated in German, literally: "No crow pecks out the eye of another."

2. Radio and first published version: "rage" instead of "indignation."

3. A loose quotation of Wagner, which in its entirety reads: "What German is: to wit, the thing one does for its own sake and for the very joy of doing it" (Richard Wagner, "Deutsche Kunst und Deutsche Politik," translated by William Ashton Ellis as "German Art and German Policy," in volume 4 [*Art and Politics*] of *Richard Wagner's Prose Works* [New York: Broude Brothers, 1966; reprint of 1895 ed. by Routledge & Kegan Paul], 4:107). Related observations can also be found in Wagner's essay "Was ist Deutsch?" (1865/78) translated as "What is German?" ibid., 149–169.

4. Adorno here nominalizes Hegel's terms for the relationship between consciousness and knowledge: *an sich* ("in-itself"), *für anderes* ("for-something-else") with the modification *für andere* ("for-others").

5. Radio and first published version: "realizations" instead of "manifestations."

6. Allusion to Hölderlin's "An die Deutschen." English: "To the Germans," in Friedrich Hölderlin, *Poems and Fragments*, trans. Michael Hamburger (Cambridge: Cambridge University Press, 1980), 59 and 123.

7. Radio and first published version: "the radical seriousness of spirit" instead of "the unwavering radicalism of spirit."

8. In the radio version Adorno pronounces this explicitly as a foreign word.

9. In the first published and radio broadcast versions of this article the paragraph continues as follows: "Years ago Max Frisch had already sharply criticized the kind of culture of the spirit that itself becomes a value and a substitute satisfaction, by pointing out that several of those responsible for the Nazi atrocities were excellent pianists or were connoisseurs who listened to records of Beethoven or Bruckner symphonies in their headquarters."

10. Reprinted in *GS* 8:20–41. The original lecture appeared in *Psyche* 6 (April 1946).

11. Radio version does not have this paragraph.

12. A graphic illustration of Adorno's point: Hegel's work has been translated into English under the two titles, *Phenomenology of Mind* and *Phenomenology of Spirit*.

13. Ulrich Sonnemann, "Zum 60. Geburtstag von Theodor Wiesengrund Adorno," reprinted in Sonnemann, *Müllberge des Vergessens: Elf Einsprüche* (Stuttgart: Metzler, 1995), 41–47.

14. *Jargon der Eigentlichkeit: Zur deutschen Ideologie* (1964), *GS* 6:413–526. English: *Jargon of Authenticity*, trans. Knut Tarnowski and Frederic Will (London: Routledge & Kegan Paul, 1973).

15. Reference to Hans Pfitzner's *Von deutscher Seele* (1921), a "romantic cantata" based on motifs from the poet J. von Eichendorff for four solo voices, mixed chorus, orchestra, and organ. Adorno may be responding to Thomas Mann, who championed Pfitzner in the essays "Von der Tugend" and "Ästhetizistische Politik," in his *Betrachtungen eines Unpolitischen* (1918–1920), reprinted in *Gesammelte Werke* (Frankfurt: Fischer, 1960), 12:375–427, 537–567; English: "On Virtue" and "The Politics of Estheticism," in Thomas Mann, *Reflections of a Nonpolitical Man*, trans. Walter D. Morris (New York: Frederick Unger, 1983), 273–314, 396–418.

16. Cf. for example, "What the Germans are Missing," in Friedrich Nietzsche, *Twilight of the Idols, or How to Philosophize with the Hammer*, trans. Richard Polt (Indianapolis: Hackett, 1997), 43–49. Also on the sphere of profundity [*Tiefe, Tiefsinn*] cf. section 15 of the first volume and aphorism 289 of the second volume in Nietzsche, *Human, All Too Human: A Book for Free Spirits*, trans. R. J. Hollingdale (Cambridge: Cambridge University Press, 1986), 19, 280.

Scientific Experiences of a European Scholar in America

1. Radio version and first published version: "I never denied it, and would not have been able to either."
2. Radio version: "to hold onto my own existence" instead of "intellectual continuity."
3. Radio and first published version has extra sentence: "Even if I had wanted to, I would hardly have been able to."
4. "Adjustment" is Adorno's own translation for the German *Anpassung*, which carries stronger tones, such as "conformity," "adaptation."
5. "Zur gesellschaftlichen Lage der Musik," *Zeitschrift für Sozialforschung* 1 (1932): 104–124, 356–78, now in *GS* 18:729–777. English: "On the Social Situation of Music," trans. Wes Blomster *Telos*, no. 35 (1975): 128–64.
6. With the verb *erscheinen*, "to appear," Adorno plays on the distinction between phenomenal appearance (*Erscheinung*) and (often aesthetic) illusion or semblance (*Schein*).
7. Radio and first published version: "alien" instead of "contrary."
8. Radio and first published version: "necessarily had attracted me" instead of "necessarily had affected me."
9. Literally "research project" or "research undertaking."
10. On this point see Adorno's review of Sargeant's book *Jazz Hot and Hybrid* in *Zeitschrift für Sozialforschung* 9 (1941): 167–178.
11. "Über Jazz" published under the pseudonym Hektor Rottweiler in *Zeitschrift für Sozialforschung* 5 (1936): 235–259, now in *GS* 17, *Musikalische Schriften* 4:74–108. English: "On Jazz," trans. Jamie Owen Daniel, *Discourse* 12, no. 1 (1989–90): 45–69.
12. Allusion to Brecht's alienation effect [*Verfremdungseffekt*]: a familiar object, practice, etc. is "defamiliarized" by detaching it from its everyday context, or by breaking the conventions through which it is unrefractedly experienced.
13. Radio version: "Hadley Cantril of Princeton University."
14. Radio version: "whose president he is today."
15. Radio version continues here: "It hardly requires many words to say that what is called culture industry, consciousness industry, manipulated mass culture, can be studied nowhere better than in America, where this form of directed culture of the mass media already at that time was by far the most advanced."
16. "Über den Fetischcharakter in der Musik und die Regression des Hörens," in *Zeitschrift für Sozialforschung* 7 (1938): 321–356. Reprinted in *Dissonanzen: Musik in der verwalteten Welt*, *GS* 14 (1973): 7–167. English: "On the Fetish-Character in Music and the Regression of Listening," in *The Essential Frankfurt School Reader*, ed. Andrew Arato and Eike Gerhardt (New York: Urizen Books, 1978), 270–299.

Reprinted in Adorno, *The Culture Industry*, ed. J. M. Bernstein (London: Routledge, 1991), 26–52.

17. *Versuch über Wagner* (1952), reprinted in *GS* 13 (1971): 7–148. English: *In Search of Wagner*, trans. Rodney Livingstone (London: NLB, 1981).

18. Walter Benjamin, "L'œuvre d'art à l'époque de sa reproduction mécanisée" in *Zeitschrift für Sozialforschung* 5 (1936): 40–68; English translation of a later, reworked version of the essay: "The Work of Art in the Age of Mechanical Reproduction," in *Illuminations*, ed. Hannah Arendt, trans. Harry Zohn (New York: Schocken Books, 1969), 217–252.

19. Cf. the exchange of letters between Adorno and Benjamin presented in *Aesthetics and Politics: Debates between Bloch, Lukács, Brecht, Benjamin, Adorno*, ed. Ronald Taylor (London: NLB, 1977; Verso, 1980).

20. Cf. the conclusion of Franz Kafka's unfinished novel *Der Verschollene* (written 1912–1914, first chapter published separately as "Der Heizer" in 1913), which Max Brod published in 1927 under the title *Amerika*. English: *America*, trans. E. Muir (New York: New Directions, 1962).

21. Paul Felix Lazarsfeld, "Remarks on Administrative and Critical Communications Research," in *Studies in Philosophy and Social Science* 9 (1941): 2–16.

22. The original is *"Musikerlebnis,"* one of the concepts Adorno attacked in his polemic against the Musical Youth Movement.

23. In the radio version Adorno translates: "die Programmanalysiermaschine."

24. Radio version interjects: "As an aside, if one could assume that test subjects in music-sociological studies could read the music, and then simply mark the passages that they like or dislike, then such a machine would be superfluous. But over there I had to quickly realize—which is probably the same for us too—that the number of those who can read music at all in comparison with the entire population really is hardly significant."

25. In the radio version Adorno translates: "Inhaltsanalyse."

26. Franz Neumann, *Behemoth: The Structure and Practice of National Socialism, 1933–1944*, 2d rev. ed. (New York: Oxford University Press, 1944). The book was reviewed in *Zeitschrift für Sozialforschung* 9 (1941): 526–7.

27. First published version: "resistance" instead of "unwillingness."

28. Radio version continues: "and which I would never have been able to give account of if I had not been in America."

29. In the first version of this article Adorno here quotes the following passage from Durkheim: "Moreover, there is another reason for not confusing the objective response and the average response: it is that the reactions of the average individual remain individual reactions. . . . There is no essential difference between the two propositions 'I like this' and 'a certain number of us like this'" (Emile Durkheim, *Sociologie et philosophie* [Paris, 1963], 121–122).

30. Radio version interjects: "such as indeed predominates in America . . . ."

31. All quotations in English in the original.

32. Radio version continues: "Much later, back in Germany, I dealt with this inhomogeneity, as opposed for instance to the views of Talcott Parsons, in methodological articles."

The first English translation interjects the following: "Much later, back in Germany, I dealt with this discontinuity, opposing the views of Talcott Parsons in methodological articles of which I may mention 'Soziologie und empirische Forschung.' It is now in *Sociologica II* by Horkheimer and myself, in the series *Frankfurter Beiträge zur Soziologie* edited by the Institut für Sozialforschung."

33. For other perspectives on Adorno's difficulties, cf. David E. Morrison, "Kultur und Culture: The Case of Theodor W. Adorno and Paul F. Lazarsfeld," *Social Research* 45 (1978): 331–355.

34. Emile Durkheim, *The Division of Labor in Society*, trans. George Simpson (Glencoe, Ill.: Free Press, 1933).

35. "A Social Critique of Radio Music," *Kenyon Review* 7 (1945): 208–217; reprinted in *Reader in Public Opinion and Communication*, eds. Bernard Berelson and Morris Janowitz (Glencoe, Ill.: Free Press, 1950), 309–316. Written in 1938–1941 with the assistance of George Simpson, this essay belongs to the corpus of texts from the Princeton Radio Research Project that will eventually be published as *Current of Music: Elements of a Radio Theory* as volume 3 of Adorno's *Nachlaß*.

36. "On Popular Music," with the assistance of George Simpson, *Studies in Philosophy and Social Science* 9 (1941): 17–48. Not reprinted in *GS*. In the article Adorno actually provides two types of "pseudo-individualization," both correlates of standardization in the culture industry:

(1) standardization of a product and even of its possible superficial varieties that gives the semblance of individualization where there is none: "Thus, standardization of the norm enhances in a purely technical way standardization of its own deviation—pseudo-individualization." (25)

(2) labelling technique of styles and name-brands of products that in fact differ only negligibly provides the illusion of consumer choice: "It provides trade-marks of identification for differentiating between the actually undifferentiated. . . . Popular music becomes a multiple choice questionnaire." (26)

37. *The Authoritarian Personality* by T. W. Adorno, Else Frenkel-Brunswik, Daniel J. Levinson, and R. Nevitt Sanford, in collaboration with Betty Aron, Maria Hertz Levinson, and William Morrow, *Studies in Prejudice*, ed. Max Horkheimer and Samuel H. Flowerman, vol. 1 (New York: Harper & Brothers, 1950). Chapters 1, 7, 16, 17, 18, and 19 appear in *GS* 9.1 (1975): 143–509 under the title *Studies in the Authoritarian Personality*.

38. Earlier English translation adds: "and certainly today would be too outdated in many respects to have any effect in America."

39. In *GS* 15:163–187. The original English manuscript of the study has been published and introduced by Thomas Y. Levin and Michael von der Linn as Theodor W. Adorno, "Analytical Study of the NBC *Music Appreciation Hour*," *The Musical Quarterly* 78 (Summer 1994): 316–377.

40. "The Radio Symphony: An Experiment in Theory," in *Radio Research 1941*, ed. Paul. F. Lazarsfeld and Frank N. Stanton (New York: Duell, Sloan, and Pearce, 1941), 110–139.

41. The exact quote is:

Adorno's tripe is the sort of thing that social science research institutes, foundations, and journals go for. He is, we are told, "associated with the Institute for Social Research at Columbia University" and "has been in charge of the music research at the Office of Radio Research"; his influence in this research,

his status and power are attested by the other writers' genuflections to his suggestions, ideas, and writings: even MacDougald cannot mention the song publisher's dictation to the song writer without a "Cf. T. W. Adorno, 'The Fetish
Character of Music and the Retrogression [sic] of Listening,' [in] Zeitschrift
für Sozialforschung, 7 (1938): 336."[Second emendation in original.]
    And the matter goes further than Adorno. But that will have to wait.
    (B. H. Haggin, Music in the Nation [New York: William Sloan, 1949], 94–95)

The full scope of Haggin's diatribe becomes clear in his vitriolic reviews on 25 July
and 10 October 1942 (published in Music in the Nation), of Dr. Herbert Graf's book
The Opera and its Future in America, wherein the author is taken to task for "a German inclination to operate with concepts and systems" (104) such that "whatever
facts Dr. Graf deals with often acquire false meaning in the process of being incorporated in the conceptual systematizations that are developed without regard for their
lack of relation to fact" (105); and Haggin then launches into his true polemic: "Dr.
Graf's performance is typical of German writing. As a stage director he is cloudy
where the Professor Doktor is heavily pedantic; but the striking thing about German
writing is the combination of its pedantic fact-grubbing with a concept-spinning so
freed from connection with fact, sometimes, as to become utterly fantastic, and
indeed often manipulating facts, and misrepresenting them, for its purposes. An
extreme example of this writing was Adorno's discussion of the effect of radio on the
symphony" (107). And, concluding the column: "This preoccupation with what is
remote from the realities of an art that interest and affect us, this scorn for these realities is typical of the musicological writing that I have been planning to discuss. Any
day now" (108).
    42. In GS 15:369–401.
    43. Radio version and earlier English version: "To what extent the later book
Introduction to the Sociology of Music meets such a need is not for me to judge."
    44. Radio version: "and I am delighted that moves in this direction are now dis-
cernible in Marburg. First of all it would be important to differentiate and correct the
theorems I developed."
    45. Philosophie der neuen Musik (1949), now GS 12; Philosophy of Modern
Music, trans. Anne G. Mitchell and Wesley V. Blomster (New York: Seabury Press,
1973). Einleitung in die Musiksoziologie: Zwölf theoretische Vorlesungen (1962),
now in GS 14 (1973): 169–433. Introduction to the Sociology of Music, trans. E. B.
Ashton (New York: Seabury Press, 1976).
    46. Edward A. Suchman, "Invitation to Music: A Study of the Creation of New
Music Listeners by the Radio," in Radio Research 1941, ed. Paul F. Lazarsfeld and
Frank N. Stanton (New York: Duell, Sloan, and Pearce, 1941), 140–188.
    47. Radio version continues: "This result was obtained, although here research
methods were used that in turn arose precisely from that model of reified consciousness it was our task to investigate."
    48. Thurstone devised a method for measuring the attitude of a group toward a
specific issue by charting the frequency distribution along a linear continuum, a limitation entailing that only those aspects of attitude can be measured for which one
can compare individuals by "the 'more and less' type of judgment." Subjects were
presented with statements of opinion they could either endorse or reject. Their col-

lected responses were then plotted against other subjects' responses, allowing relative measures only (i.e., person x is "more religious" than person y).

L. L. Thurstone and E. J. Chave, *The Measurement of Attitude: A Psychophysical Method and Some Experiments with a Scale for Measuring Attitude toward the Church* (Chicago: University of Chicago Press, 1929). See also note 60 below.

49. Duncan MacDougald, Jr., "The Popular Music Industry," in *Radio Research 1941*, 65–109.

50. Earlier English version inserts following sentence: "Thus MacDougald had the merit of giving the first circumstantial demonstration of such mechanisms in the musical world."

51. "The sheet is a list of the currently popular songs with the number of radio performances (10 or more) received by each one over the three major networks . . . from 5:00 P.M. to 1:00 A.M. 'Making the sheet' each week is the principal goal in life of every song plugger, and his success is judged by his ability to get songs on the sheet and keep them in high positions in this tabulation of plugs" (Duncan MacDougald, Jr., "The Popular Music Industry," *Radio Research 1941*, 99).

Radio version has "spiel" instead of "sheet," and the earlier English translation follows this.

52. Radio version: "Therefore this study, which has to do with old-fashioned, reporter-like types—or perhaps not reporter-like, but rather advertising agent-like types—looks easily old-fashioned and, I'd almost like to say, conciliatory."

53. In the radio version Adorno translates the title as *Die autoritätsgebundene Persönlichkeit*.

54. Max Horkheimer and Theodor W. Adorno, *Dialectic of Enlightenment*, trans. John Cumming (New York: Seabury Press, 1972; reprint, New York: Continuum, 1989). A new translation is under way, a chapter of which has been published. Cf. "Odysseus or Myth and Enlightenment," trans. Robert Hullot-Kentor, *New German Critique* 56 (Spring-Summer 1992): 109–142, and his introduction, 101–108.

55. Radio version: "I once put it very pointedly: 'Man is the ideology of dehumanization.'" Cf. *Jargon der Eigentlichkeit*, GS 6:452; English: *The Jargon of Authenticity*, trans. Knut Tarnowski and Frederic Will (London: Routledge & Kegan Paul, 1973), 59.

56. *Studien über Authorität und Familie*, ed. Max Horkheimer (Paris: Alcan, 1936). The "Allgemeiner Teil" was later retitled "Autorität und Familie" and anthologized. English: "Authority and the Family," in *Critical Theory: Selected Essays*, trans. Matthew J. O'Connell and others (New York: Seabury Press, 1972).

57. The series *Studies in Prejudice*, edited by Max Horkheimer and Samuel H. Flowerman, and published by Harper's (New York) was sponsored by the American Jewish Committee and presented the results of research into prejudice and social discrimination, particularly anti-Semitism. The volumes eventually published included: *The Authoritarian Personality* by T. W. Adorno, Else Frenkel-Brunswik, Daniel J. Levinson, and R. Nevitt Sanford; *Dynamics of Prejudice: A Psychological and Sociological Study of Veterans* by Bruno Bettelheim and Morris Janowitz; *Anti-Semitism and Emotional Disorder: A Psychoanalytic Interpretation* by Nathan W. Ackerman and Marie Jahoda; *Prophets of Deceit: A Study of the Techniques of the American Agitator* by Leo Löwenthal and Norbert Gutermann; and *Rehearsal for Destruction: A Study of Political Anti-Semitism in Imperial Germany* by Paul W. Massing.

58. Radio and earlier English translation: "and although twenty years have gone by, I truly feel it to be a continuation of a tradition to which I belonged in America to work as hard as I can for a similar democratization in Germany."

59. On the enormous influence of *The Authoritarian Personality*, see: Richard Christie and Peggy Cook, "A Guide to Published Literature Relating to the Authoritarian Personality Through 1956," in *The Journal of Psychology* 45 (1958): 171–199.
The study Adorno alludes to is: Michaela von Freyhold, *Autoritarismus und politische Apathie: Analyse einer Skala zur Ermittlung autoritätsgebundener Verhaltensweisen*, vol. 22 of *Frankfurter Beiträge zur Soziologie* (Frankfurt: Europäische Verlagsanstalt, 1971).

60. The Thurstone (cf. note 48 above), Likert, and Guttman scales were scaling techniques developed and refined in order to guarantee unequivocal results from empirical opinion surveys. For the details of these techniques, see e.g. chapter 12, "Placing Individuals on Scales," in Claire Sellitz, Lawrence S. Wrightman, and Stuart W. Cook, *Research Methods in Social Relations*, 1–3d ed. (New York: Holt, Rinehart and Winston, 1951, 1959, 1976). Compare Adorno's own résumé of the different attitude scales in part 8 ("Construction of Scales") in his article "Empirische Sozialforschung," written with J. Décamps, L. Herberger, et al. for the *Handwörterbuch der Sozialwissenschaften* (1954) and reprinted in *GS* 9.2:

a. With the *Thurstone scale (method of equal appearing intervals*)* the scalar values of the *"items,"** the individual questions or statements, are determined by the central value of the judgments of a relatively large jury of experts, and the values are distributed in approximately equal intervals across the entire scale. The positions of the questioned individuals or groups on the scale derive from the agreement or rejection of the *"items,"** which are fixed in a particular sequence.

b. In the *Likert scale (method of summated ratings*)* those *"items"** are selected that best correlate with the overall values (they are usually located at the end-points of the Thurstone scale) and that show the greatest selectivity. The subjects are asked to respond to each of the *"items"** by selecting a response that is qualified usually into five degrees. The weighted individual results are summed up along the lines of point values in sports, the position of the individual or group on the scale is then determined by the magnitude of the point score.

c. With the *Guttman scale (scalogram analysis*)* the *"items"** must be one-dimensional, that is, the agreement with a specific *"item"** must include the agreement with all the other less extreme *"items"** and match the rejection of all more extreme *"items."** A greater methodical rigor is gained at the price of breadth of the content.   *(GS 9.2:348)*

61. Richard Christie and Marie Jahoda, eds., *Studies in the Scope and Method of "The Authoritarian Personality"* (Glencoe, Ill.: Free Press, 1954; reprint, Westport, Conn.: Greenwood Press, 1981).

62. Cf. for example, *Zur Metakritik der Erkenntnistheorie: Studien über Husserl und die phänomenologischen Antinomien* (1956), GS 5 (1970): 7–245. *Against Epistemology: A Metacritique; Studies in Husserl and the Phenomenological Antino-*

mies, trans. Willis Domingo (Oxford: Blackwell, 1982; Cambridge, Mass.: MIT Press, 1983).

63. The child studies published by Else Frenkel-Brunswik (1908–1958) comprise the following: "A Study of Prejudice in Children," *Human Relations* 1 (1948): 295–306; "Patterns of Social and Cognitive Outlooks in Children," *American Journal of Orthopsychiatry* 21 (1951): 543–548; and together with J. Havel, "Authoritarianism in the Interviews of Children: 1. Attitudes toward Minority Groups," *Journal of General Psychology* 82 (1953): 91–136; "Further Explorations by a Contributor to 'The Authoritarian Personality,'" in *Studies in the Scope and Method of "The Authoritarian Personality,"* ed. Richard Christie and Marie Jahoda, 226–275.

64. Cf. the chapters "The Bearing of Sociological Theory on Empirical Research" and "The Bearing of Empirical Research on Sociological Theory" in Robert K. Merton, *Social Theory and Social Structure* (New York: Free Press, 1949, 1957, 1968).

65. In the radio version Adorno translates this as *"Rand der Verrückten,"* later as *"Rand der Wahnsinnigen."*

66. In the radio version Adorno translates *"Testsätze."*

67. "The Psychological Technique of Martin Luther Thomas' Radio Addresses" (1943), in *GS* 9.1 (1975): 7–141.

68. Radio version and earlier English translation: "The situation I faced there was entirely different from that of the Princeton project or *The Authoritarian Personality.*"

69. "The Stars Down to Earth," *Jahrbuch für Amerikastudien* (Heidelberg: Carl Winter, 1957), 2:19–88. Reprinted in *GS* 9.2:7–120. An abbreviated German version was published in 1962 as "Aberglaube aus zweiter Hand" in Max Horkheimer and Theodor W. Adorno, *Sociologica II: Reden und Vorträge* (Frankfurt: Europäische Verlagsanstalt, 1962). It is reprinted in *GS* 8:147–76. See also "The Stars Down to Earth: The *Los Angeles Times* Astrology Column," *Telos,* 19 (Spring 1974): 13–90; reprinted in T. W. Adorno, *The Stars Down to Earth and Other Essays on the Irrational in Culture,* ed. Stephen Crook (London/New York: Routledge, 1994), 34–127.

70. Cf. Freud's theory of the "death drive" [*Todestrieb*] in *Das Unbehagen in der Kultur* (1930); English: vol. 21 of *The Standard Edition of the Complete Psychological Works of Sigmund Freud.*

71. Adorno applies the "biphasic" behavior the depth psychologist Otto Fenichel (*Psychoanalytic Theory of Neuroses* [New York: Norton, 1945]) notes in compulsive neurotics ("The patient behaves alternately as though he were a naughty child and a strict punitive disciplinarian" [ibid., 291]) to the rationalized time schedule of modern bourgeois life, which establishes antinomies of work and pleasure. Astrology columnists offer a solution by emphasizing ego ideal responsibilities for the morning, and the pleasure principle for the evening. Adorno: "*The problem of how to dispense with contradictory requirements of life is solved by the simple device of distributing these requirements over different periods mostly of the same day.*" [Adorno's emphasis] *GS* 9.2:56; Crook, ibid., 67.

72. Radio version interjects: "that the products of the culture industry, of the secondhand *'popular culture'*,* . . . . "

73. In the radio version Adorno translates *"vorurteilsvollen."*

74. "How to Look at Television," *Quarterly of Film, Radio, and Television* 8 (Spring 1954): 213–235. Reprinted as "Television and the Patterns of Mass Culture"

in *Mass Culture: The Popular Arts in America,* ed. Bernard Rosenberg and David Manning White (Glencoe, Ill.: Free Press, 1957), 474–487.
"Fernsehen als Ideologie": "Television as Ideology" in this volume.

75. Paul Tillich (1886–1965), German Protestant theologian and philosopher, leader of the "League of Religious Socialists" [Bund religiöser Sozialisten] in Berlin. In 1929 he was named professor of religious studies and social philosophy at the University of Frankfurt. In 1933 he was suspended by the National Socialists and emigrated to the United States, becoming a US citizen in 1940. From 1937 to 1955 he was professor for philosophical theology at the Union Theological Seminary (New York), from 1955 to 1962 at Harvard University, and from 1962 until his death at the University of Chicago. In 1931 Adorno wrote his *Habilitation* under Tillich, which appeared in book form in 1933: *Kierkegaard: Construction of the Aesthetic,* trans. Robert Hullot-Kentor (Minneapolis: University of Minnesota Press, 1989); the original is *GS* 2.

76. Radio version interjects: "and thereby learns for the first time how to put the specifically cultural into conceptual terms."

77. Radio version interjects: "and there too nothing is for free, rather the commodities are exchanged equivalently."

78. Radio version: "We Europeans."

79. Radio version continues: "indeed as an expression of mechanization."

80. Charles Alexis Henri Clével de Tocqueville (1805–1859), French writer and politician. After his visit to America in 1831–1832, he wrote his famous *On Democracy in America* (1835–1840), in which he described American society as the model of an inevitably expansive democracy, and surmised an inevitable loss of individualism.

Ferdinand Kürnberger (1821–1879), Austrian liberal-minded author of novels, plays, and satirical feuilletons, who achieved fame for his *roman à clef* about Nicolaus Lenau's travels to the United States entitled *Der Amerika-Müde* (1855). Whereas the popular literature about America at the time juxtaposed a free and democratic society and natural wholesomeness to a repressive civilization of restoration Europe, Kürnberger's novel portrays America as a land without culture where egoism and materialism prevail.

On Subject and Object

1. "Consciousness in general" is Kant's designation for the universal validity of "judgments of experience" as opposed to the subjective validity of individual, psychological "judgments of perception" (as in Locke's 'ideas' and Hume's 'perceptions'). Judgments of perception refer directly to sensible intuitions and are made according to the individual's "association of ideas," whereas judgments of experience are made by the faculty of understanding, which subsumes intuitions under universal concepts of the understanding, such as causality. Such concepts are logical universals and therefore transcend individual, subjective experience and consciousness, belonging rather to "experience in general" and "consciousness in general":

The sum of the matter is this: the business of the senses is to intuit, that of the understanding is to think. But thinking is uniting representations in a consciousness. This unification originates either merely relative to the subject and is contingent and subjective, or it happens absolutely and is necessary or objective. The uniting of representations in a consciousness is judgment. Thinking therefore is the same as judging, or referring representations to judgments in general. Hence judgments are either merely subjective when representations are referred to a consciousness in one subject only and united in it, or they are objective when they are united in a consciousness in general, that is, necessarily. The logical moments of all judgments are so many possible ways of uniting representations in consciousness.

(Immanuel Kant, Prolegomena zu einer jeden künftigen Metaphysik, die als Wissenschaft wird auftreten können [1783], §22 [A 88; A. A. 4:304–5]; English: Prolegomena to Any Future Metaphysics, Carus translation revised by James W. Ellington [Indianapolis: Hackett, 1977], 48)

2. Cf. Schelling's 1810 *Stuttgarter Privatvorlesungen* in *Schellings Werke*, ed. Manfred Schröter, vol. 4, *Schriften zur Philosophie der Freiheit, 1804–1815* (Munich: Beck'sche Verlagsbuchhandlung, 1929; reprint, 1978), 309–376, esp. 330ff.: "On this view then, there are two principles in God. The first principle or the first primordial force is that through which He exists as a particular, single, individual being. We can call this force the Selfhood, the Egoism in God," (330) and it has the form of "Egoity" *[Egoität]* (332) under which the being or essence *[Wesen]* of God is posited. The second and opposed principle is that of love, and Schelling assures the reader that egoism and love are the "human expressions" for the real and the ideal, respectively, in God.

3. "The Paralogisms of Pure Reason," *Critique of Pure Reason*, trans. Norman Kemp Smith (New York: St. Martin's, 1965), 328–383.

4. On Husserl's attack on psychologism and his distinction between genesis and validity *[Genesis/Geltung]* cf. Adorno, *Zur Metakritik der Erkenntnistheorie, GS* 5:7–245, esp. 81–95. English: *Against Epistemology: A Metacritique; Studies in Husserl and the Phenomenological Antinomies*, trans. Willis Domingo (Oxford: Basil Blackwell, 1982; Cambridge, Mass: MIT Press, 1983), esp. 74–78.

5. Cf. sections 2 and 16 of the first part of Friedrich Nietzsche, *Human, All Too Human: A Book for Free Spirits*, trans. R. J. Hollingdale (Cambridge: Cambridge University Press, 1986).

6. Cf. Kant, *Critique of Pure Reason*, A 20: "The effect of an object upon the faculty of representation, so far as we are affected by it, is *sensation [Empfindung]*. That intuition which is in relation to the object through sensation, is entitled *empirical*. The undetermined object of an empirical intuition is entitled *appearance [Erscheinung]*" (*Critique of Reason*, 65).

7. "*Seinssphäre absoluter Ursprünge*," Husserl's term for consciousness understood as an absolute first cause. Cf. Edmund Husserl, *Ideen zur einer reinen Phänomenologie und phänomenologischen Philosophie, Husserliana*, vol. 3/1, ed. Karl Schuhmann (The Hague: Martinus Nijhoff, 1976), 107 (in the original pagination of the 1922 Halle edition). English: *Ideas: General Introduction to Pure Phenomenology*, trans. W. R. Boyce Gibson (New York: Collier, 1962). Adorno quotes this phrase on the first page of his Husserl critique: *Zur Metakritik der Erkenntnistheorie: Studien über Husserl und die phänomenologischen Antinomien* (1956), *GS* 5 (1970): 7–245. English: *Against Epistemology: A Metacritique*.

8. Adorno plays on the resonance between *Sachlichkeit*, which means an objective, unemotional attitude (as in the *Neue Sachlichkeit* movement, sometimes translated as "The New Functionalism") and *Sache*, "subject matter, matter-at-hand."

9. Allusion to the Marburg School (H. Cohen, R. Natorp, E. Cassirer, K. Vorländer) who mobilized Kant's transcendental epistemology against materialist theories and in favor of a strict, value-free, verifiable empiricism. "Infinitely given as a task" [*unendlich aufgegeben*] echoes Kant's claim that transcendental ideas of reason operate "regulatively" rather than "constitutively": they are not given [*gegeben*] in experience but given as a task [*aufgegeben*] to thought by which mind can think beyond what it receives in phenomenal experience.

10. Presumably alluding to the following passage from the "Preface" to the *Phänomenologie des Geistes* (1807) (*Werke* [Frankfurt: Suhrkamp, 1970], 3:56):

> That habit should be called material thinking, a contingent consciousness that is absorbed only in material stuff, and therefore finds it hard work to lift the self clear of such matter, and to be with itself alone. At the opposite extreme, argumentation [*Räsonieren*] is freedom from all content [of thought], and a sense of vanity toward it. From it is demanded [by Hegel's method] the effort to relinquish this freedom and, instead of being the arbitrarily moving principle of the content, to sink this freedom in the content and let it move by its own nature, that is, by the self as its own, and to observe this movement. This refusal to intrude into the immanent rhythm of the concept, either arbitrarily or with wisdom obtained from elsewhere, constitutes a restraint that is itself an essential moment of the concept.
>
> (G. W. F. Hegel, Phenomenology of Spirit, *trans. A. V. Miller [Oxford: Oxford University Press, 1977], 35–36; translation modified*)

11. Cf. the first book of "The Transcendental Dialectic" in the *Critique of Pure Reason*.

12. Drawing on the distinction between sensible appearance (*phenomenon*) and intelligible essence (*noumenon*), Kant maintains "we indeed, rightly considering objects of sense as mere appearances, confess thereby that they are based upon a thing in itself, though we know not this thing as it is in itself but only its appearances, viz., the way in which our senses are affected by this unknown something" (*Prolegomena to Any Future Metaphysics*, 57 [§32, A. A. 4:314f.]). For the same structure of intelligible/sensible in terms of the moral law see Immanuel Kant, *Grounding for the Metaphysics of Morals*, trans. James W. Ellington, 3d. ed. (Indianapolis: Hackett, 1993), 61 (A. A. 4:462).

13. In his later versions of the *Wissenschaftslehre* (especially that of 1810) Johann Gottlieb Fichte's idealism becomes more extreme and finally, religious. In his *Die Anweisung zum seligen Leben* (1806) Fichte's original principle of the intellectual and moral self-positing of the Ego (subjective idealism) is shown to rely on what is absolute, unconditioned, and can only be affirmed in thought—what Fichte now calls God.

14. Adorno plays here on the resonance between the verb *erscheinen*, "to appear phenomenally" (hence in Kant "phenomenon"—"appearance" as opposed to "noumenon," "essence"—is called *Erscheinung*), and *Schein* (and the related verb *scheinen*, "to seem") "semblance," "illusion" (here "seeming appearance" as opposed to "being").

15. "Free action" [*freie Tathandlung*], a phrase from Fichte's metaphysical theory as presented in his *Wissenschaftslehre* (1794), which holds that the fundamental principle underlying all reality derives from the self-positing and self-affirming of the Ego, i.e., subjective idealism. Such positing precedes and itself conditions the resultant dualism between Ego (subject) and non-Ego (object); since the positing itself is unconditioned, Fichte calls it a "free action."

16. Thinly veiled allusion to Heidegger.

17. Cf. Kant, *Critique of Pure Reason*, A20–21.

18. Adorno's pun: "*die Verdinglichung des Undinglichen*," literally, "the reification of what is not thingly," but also playing on the colloquial *Unding*, "absurdity."

19. According to David Hume (1711–1776), the mind's primary data is comprised solely of sensory impressions, feelings, or ideas, the latter being nothing but memories of previous impressions. Therefore Hume concluded that the mind is nothing other than a bundle of subjective perceptions related through resemblance, succession, and causation and lacks any substantive identity of the self (what Kant inherited as the problem of the unity of consciousness). Cf. David Hume, *A Treatise of Human Nature* (1739), bk. 1, pt. 4; Hume, *Enquiry Concerning Human Understanding* (1748), section 12.

20. Adorno here echoes one of his critiques of Durkheim's concept of *faits sociaux* as expounded in his *Les règles de la méthode sociologique* (1901) and *Sociologie et philosophie* (1924). For Adorno's appraisal of Durkheim's sociology, cf. his "Einleitung zu Emile Durkheim, 'Soziologie und Philosophie,'" *GS* 8:245–279 and "Zum gegenwärtigen Stand der deutschen Soziologie" in *GS* 8:500–531, esp. 503.

21. In German, like French, the article is used to indicate species as well as individual, thus, *der Mensch* [or *l'homme*] means both "man" as well as "mankind."

Marginalia to Theory and Praxis

1. "Grau, teurer Freund, ist alle Theorie / Und grün des Lebens goldner Baum." *Faust, Erster Teil*, ll. 2038–2039. In Walter Kaufman's translation: "Gray, my dear friend, is every theory, / And green alone life's golden tree," in *Goethe's Faust*, trans. Walter Kaufmann (New York: Doubleday, 1961), 206.

2. Adorno's neologistic *entqualifizieren* suggests not only the English "disqualify" but here primarily "removing the qualities, distinctions from," "de-differentiating."

3. Alluding to line 16 of Rudolf Borchardt's poem "Auf eine angeschossene Schwalbe, die der Dichter fand," here given in a literal translation:

TO A SWALLOW SHOT AND WOUNDED, FOUND BY THE POET

Now there you lie, a small broken arrow;
Your tendon cut clean through
And no more wing is healthy
For one alone cannot carry you.

You meet my monstrous closeness
With a mien of deathly fear

My hesitation to you means claw and tooth
My leaning forward hunger for you,

And no more flight; for you are not swift;
You and your nest-mate
Could win life only
By outstripping, by escaping:

With enmity through the desert of your world
Shooting, always before the enemy,
In the shrill, shrill cry alone
You stay together, lonely community!

How, in my hand, which renders warmth,
The life-black eye is surprised!
I am not god, who disowns you,
Like hundreds upon hundreds every day,—

You had flight, and what can sustain you,
From him, the serene sustainer of your foe,
Past the spot, where your impotence lay,
went your god, flew your sibling,

And those you never honored with your thievery,
When you rounded the curve in the blueness,
Already a birth of dust crept upon you,
To it you are carrion, soon as it sees you wounded!—

Tiny tongue, that boldly feasts upon my finger
You are full of tidings without speaking;
So that you once trust stronger ones,
Must god break the ring of his own providence,—

To rectify, where even he pities
The mockery and wrong of his own work,
he has need of his great son,
whom the common kingdom does not completely compass.

Here he thanks me, what he gave me:
That he granted me his soul,
Drew taught the bridge between you and him,
The bridge he himself could not build.

He who sets each body before death
Does not let his own be gambled away:
He, who banished his creature, created
Also the creature, to save the banished.

Rudolf Borchardt, *Ausgewählte Gedichte*, selected and introduced by Theodor W. Adorno (Frankfurt: Suhrkamp, 1968), 76–77. Adorno's introduction to his selection of Borchardt's poems is reprinted in *Noten zur Literatur*, now *GS* 11:536–555. English: "Charmed Language: On the Poetry of Rudolf Borchardt," in Adorno, *Notes to Literature*, trans. Shierry Weber Nicholsen (New York: Columbia University Press, 1992), 2:193–210.

4. "Restitution phenomena" in psychology originally referred to the (partial) recovery of cognitive function after traumatic brain injury and was metaphorically adopted to indicate analogous psychiatric processes, for instance, a schizophrenic's (partial) regaining of a sense of reality.

5. Cf. Kant, *Critique of Pure Reason*, 92 (A51/B75).

6. Adorno plays on the commercial undertones of the terms: *Betriebsamkeit*, "bustle, industriousness," from *Betrieb* meaning both "enterprise, business" and "hustle, bustle"; *Geschäftigkeit*, "busyness, zealousness," from *Geschäft* meaning "business, undertaking" and "business, shop, office."

7. Cf. Schiller's concept of the "play-drive" [*Spieltrieb*] in his *Briefe über die ästhetische Erziehung des Menschen* (1794/95). English: Friedrich Schiller, *On the Aesthetic Education of Man: In a Series of Letters*, ed. and trans. Elizabeth M. Wilkinson and L. A. Willoughby (Oxford: Clarendon, 1967).

8. "*Messieurs, avant tout je suis practique*"; from *Versailles et Paris en 1871: D'après les dessins originaux de Gustave Doré* (Paris: Libraire Plon, Plon-Nourrit, 1907); reprinted in Gustave Doré, *Das graphische Werk* (Munich: Rogner & Bernhard, 1975), 2:1377. In his condemnation, Adorno deploys one of his favorite puns, that of *Geist* (spirit) and *Ungeist* (boor, demon).

9. Cf. the opening of Kant's *Grundlegung zur Metaphysik der Sitten* (1785): "There is no possibility of thinking of anything at all in the world, or even out of it, which can be regarded as good without qualification, except a *good will*." Immanuel Kant, *Grounding for the Metaphysics of Morals*, 7 [A. A. 4:393]).

10. *Produktivkraft*, "productive force, productive power" (and the plural, usually rendered "forces of production" in contrast to "modes of production") is a technical term in Marx, referring to the result of practical human energy, specifically in labor. To the extent that productive power is appropriated in the form of objectified labor by capital as surplus value, it constitutes the productive force of capital (surplus value creating wealth); to the extent that it is not so appropriated, it represents a potential point of conflict with existing modes of production.

11. "*Enlightenment is man's emergence from his self-incurred immaturity. Immaturity* is the inability to use one's own understanding without the guidance of another. This immaturity is *self-incurred* if its cause is not lack of understanding, but lack of resolution and courage to use it without the guidance of another. The motto of enlightenment is therefore: *Sapere aude!* Have courage to use your *own* understanding!" (Immanuel Kant, "An Answer to the Question: 'What is Enlightenment?'" trans. H. B. Nisbet in Kant, *Political Writings*, ed. Hans Reiss, 2d ed. [Cambridge: Cambridge University Press, 1991], 54 [A.A. 8:35]).

12. Allusion to Marx's eleventh thesis on Feuerbach: "The philosophers have merely *interpreted* the world, in various ways; the point, however, is to *change* it."

13. Cf. Ernst Simmel, "Anti-Semitism and Mass Psychopathology," in *Anti-*

Semitism: A Social Disease, ed. Ernst Simmel (New York: International Universities Press, 1946):

> Summarizing the parallelisms between a collective psychosis and an individual psychosis, we can say: The mass and the psychotic think and act irrationally, because of regressively disintegrated ego systems. In the individual psychotic mind, the process of regression is of a primary nature and is constant. In the collective psychotic mind regression is secondary and occurs only temporarily. The reason for this is that in the individual psychotic, the ego breaks with reality because of its pathological weakness, whereas *in the mass member, reality breaks first with the ego.* This ego, by submerging itself into a pathological mass, saves itself from individual regression by regressing collectively. *Flight into mass psychosis is therefore an escape not only from reality, but also from individual insanity.*
>
> This insight gives us our answer to the enigmatic question why apparently normal individuals can react like psychotics under the spell of mass formation. *Their ego is immature* as a result of superego weakness. The immature individual who, under the stress of environmental circumstances, is on the verge of losing contact with reality, can find his way back to it when his ego, carried by the spirit of the group, finds opportunity for the discharge of pent-up aggressive instinct energies into the object world.   *(49–50)*

14. Cf. for example, the first words of "Zarathustra's Preface": "When Zarathustra was thirty years old he left his home and the lake of his home and went into the mountains. Here he enjoyed his spirit and his solitude, and for ten years did not tire of it" (Friedrich Nietzsche, *Thus Spake Zarathustra*, trans. Walter Kaufmann [New York: Viking Press, 1966], 9).

15. Aristotle divides the 'virtues', or 'excellences' (ἀρεταί) into dianoetic, or those of intellect (διανοητική) and moral, or those of character (ἠθική). The intellectual excellences involve reason and belong to the rational part of the soul, the moral excellences involve inclinations and habit, belong to the irrational part of the soul, and are obedient to reason, which is considered the divine part of man. Cf. *Nicomachean Ethics*, 1103a3ff.; *Eudemian Ethics*, 1120b5ff.; *Politics*, 1333a16ff.

16. The reference has not been found. Perhaps Adorno is referring to comments by Rosa Luxemburg in her so-called Junius pamphlet entitled "The Crisis of Social Democracy" (1916) where she writes: "Friedrich Engels once said, bourgeois society confronts a dilemma: either the transition to socialism or relapse into barbarism. What does a 'relapse into barbarism' mean at our height of European civilization? . . . This world war—this is a relapse into barbarism" (*Politische Schriften*, vol. 2, ed. Ossip Flechtheim [Frankfurt: Europäische Verlagsanstalt, 1966], 31). However, the Engels source has not been found.

17. ApO = *Außerparlamentarische Opposition* (Extra-parliamentary Opposition), a loosely organized activist movement that formed in reaction to the lack of effective parliamentary opposition as a consequence of the grand coalition of the SPD and CDU/CSU parties in 1966 and constituted an important part of the German New Left in 1968. It reached its culmination in the protest actions following the murder of

Rudi Dutschke and against the conservative publishing conglomerate Springer Verlag in 1968.

NPD = *Nationaldemokratische Partei Deutschlands* (National Democratic Party of Germany), the collective party of the extreme right, including ex-Nazi and neofascist groups. It developed a strong following, gaining representation in seven *Länder* of the Federal Republic from 1966 to 1968.

18. Allusion to the recent publication by his colleague at the Institute for Social Research; Jürgen Habermas, *Strukturwandel der Öffentlichkeit: Untersuchungen zur einer Kategorie der bürgerlichen Gesellschaft* (Frankfurt: Suhrkamp, 1962). English: *The Structural Transformation of the Public Sphere*, trans. T. Burger (Cambridge, Mass.: MIT Press, 1988).

19. Cf. "Betrachtungen zum 20. Juli," in Jürgen von Kempski, *Recht und Politik: Studien zur Einheit der Sozialwissenschaft, Schriften 2*, ed. Achim Eschbach (Frankfurt: Suhrkamp, 1992), 321–333. Originally published in *Merkur* (1949). Von Kempski argues that the attempted coup d'état of 20 July 1944 by Wehrmacht officers was foiled because Hitler had created diverse command structures, i.e., a bureaucracy. The final section of the article speculates about possible lessons for democratic states:

> It is worth considering whether splitting up the command structures as a technique for safeguarding a totalitarian regime from coups d'état can also mutatis mutandis be translated onto democracies. As far as the safeguarding of a democratic state from overthrow is concerned, the constitutional thinkers still operate under the idea that the threat of overthrow comes from below, from the "masses." However, under modern technological conditions, "revolutions" can scarcely still be carried out successfully; the superiority of the state in weapons technology is too great. Moreover, for the industrial states the classical age of the revolutionary situation is long past. What threatens is the transition to totalitarian forms of government by completely or half 'legal' paths, the cold revolution from above. This threat demands different means than those used against revolutions from below.   *(332)*

20. Freud, *Massenpsychologie und Ich-Analyse* (1921); English: *Group Psychology and the Analysis of the Ego*, vol. 18 of *The Standard Edition of the Complete Psychological Works of Sigmund Freud*, trans. James Strachey (London: Hogarth Press, 1975).

21. Max Weber advocated "value-free" judgments in sociology on the model of scientific objectivity, polemicizing, on the one hand, against utilitarians who identified value with use and, on the other hand, against the unscientific particularism of the older generation of sociologists belonging to the so-called "Historical School" (e.g., Gustav Schmoller, Adolph Wagner, Georg Friedrich Knapp). Weber presents his arguments in two articles: "Die 'Objektivität' sozialwissenschaftlicher and sozialpolitischer Erkenntnis," in *Archiv für Sozialwissenschaft und Sozialpolitik* 19 (1904): 22–87; "Der Sinn der 'Wertfreiheit' der soziologischen und ökonomischen Wissenschaften," in *Logos* 7 (1917–18): 40–88 (both reprinted in *Gesammelte Aufsätze zur Wissenschaftslehre* [Tübingen: 1968], 146–214 and 489–590). In English cf. Max Weber, *The Methodology of the Social Sciences*, trans. and ed. Edward Shils and H. A. Finch (Glencoe, Ill.: Free Press, 1949). Adorno's comments here echo his argu-

ments in the dispute concerning positivism in sociology. Cf. Theodor W. Adorno et al., *Der Positivismusstreit in der deutschen Soziologie* (Neuwied, Berlin: Luchterhand, 1969). Adorno's contributions are reprinted in *GS* 8; English: Theodor W. Adorno et al., *The Positivist Dispute in German Sociology*, trans. Glyn Adey and David Frisby (London: Heinemann, 1976).

22. A salvo in Adorno's ongoing critique of Max Scheler's *Der Formalismus in der Ethik und die materiale Wertethik: Neuer Versuch der Grundlegung eines ethischen Personalismus* (1916), reprinted in *Gesammelte Schriften*, vol. 2 (Bern/Munich: Francke Verlag, 1966). English: *Formalism in Ethics and Non-Formal Ethics of Value: A New Attempt Toward the Foundation of an Ethical Personalism*, trans. Manfred S. Frings and Roger L. Funk (Evanston, Ill.: Northwestern University Press, 1973).

23. The terms "casing" [*Gehäuse*], "solidification, hardening" [*Verfestigung*] and "autonomization of the apparatus" [*Verselbständigung der Apparatur*] derive from Weber-inspired sociological theory of bureaucratization. "*Stahlhartes Gehäuse*," an expression made famous by Weber in *The Protestant Ethic and the Spirit of Capitalism*, is translated in English as the "iron cage"[*sic*] of modernity.

24. Reference to the attempted coup d'état of 20 July 1944 by Wehrmacht officers, most notably Claus Schenk Graf von Stauffenberg. The attempt on Hitler's life failed, and the conspirators were executed.

25. Allusion to the famous opening of Marx's *The Eighteenth Brumaire of Louis Bonaparte* (1852): "Hegel remarks somewhere that all great, world-historical facts and personages occur, as it were, twice. He has forgotten to add: the first time as tragedy, the second as farce."

26. See note 12 above.

27. Cf. the first joint publication by Marx and Engels, a satirical polemic against Bruno Bauer and the Young Hegelians: *Die Heilige Familie; oder, Kritik der kritischen Kritik* (1845). English: *The Holy Family: A Critique of Critical Criticism*, in *The Collected Works of Karl Marx and Friedrich Engels*, ed. Y. Dakhina and T. Chikileva, vol. 4 (New York: International Publishers, 1975).

Critique

1. Adorno here draws on the definition of "political maturity" [*Mündigkeit*] from Kant's essay "What is Enlightenment?" (1784) and draws implications from the formulation itself: *mündig*, literally "come of age" means no longer requiring a guardian [*Vormund*], who makes one's decisions for one [*bevormunden*]. All these expressions in turn stem from mouth [*Mund*]; hence political maturity also means speaking for oneself, not parroting another.

2. "*Enlightenment is man's emergence from his self-incurred immaturity. Immaturity* is the inability to use one's own understanding without the guidance of another. This immaturity is *self-incurred* if its cause is not lack of understanding, but lack of resolution and courage to use it without the guidance of another. The motto of enlightenment is therefore: *Sapere aude!* Have courage to use your *own* understanding!" (Immanuel Kant, "An Answer to the Question: 'What is Enlightenment?'" trans. H. B. Nisbet in Kant, *Political Writings*, ed. Hans Reiss, 2d ed. [Cambridge: Cambridge University Press, 1991], 54 [A.A. 8:35]).

3. Allusion to Heinrich von Kleist's (idiosyncratic) reading of Kant in March 1801, the solipsistic and relativistic consequences of which "so profoundly, so painfully shocked" him, as he reported in a letter to Wilhelmine von Zenge (22 March 1801). Friedrich Nietzsche quotes the letter as evidence of the power philosophy can have in "Schopenhauer as Educator," in Friedrich Nietzsche, *Untimely Meditations*, trans. R. J. Hollingdale (Cambridge: Cambridge University Press, 1983), 140–141.

4. Compare Hegel's definition of "argufying" [*Räsonieren*] as "freedom from all content [of thought], and a sense of vanity toward it. From it is demanded [by Hegel's method] the effort to relinquish this freedom and, instead of being the arbitrarily moving principle of the content, to sink this freedom in the content and let it move by its own nature, that is, by the self as its own, and to observe this movement" (G. W. F. Hegel, "Preface," *Phenomenology of Spirit*, trans. A. V. Miller [Oxford: Oxford University Press, 1977], 35–36; translation modified). Original: Hegel, *Phänomenologie des Geistes, Werke* (Frankfurt: Suhrkamp, 1970), 3:56.

5. Allusion to Hegel's famous dictum,

Was vernünftig ist, das ist wirklich;
und was wirklich ist, das ist vernünftig.
[What is rational is actual;
and what is actual is rational.]

It appears in the preface to the *Grundlinien der Philosophie des Rechts* (Hegel, *Werke*, 7:24) and is returned to in the introduction (§6) of the *Enzyklopädie der philosophischen Wissenschaften* (*Werke*, 8:47ff.). English: G. W. F. Hegel, *Elements of the Philosophy of Right*, ed. Allen W. Wood, trans. H. B. Nisbet (Cambridge: Cambridge University Press, 1991), 20.

6. Allusion to Marx's letter to Arnold Ruge, part of public correspondence between them and Bakunin and Feuerbach, published in the *Deutsch-Französische Jahrbücher* (1844): "If we have no business with the construction of the future or with organizing it for all time there can still be no doubt about the task confronting us at present: I mean the *ruthless critique of everything existing*, ruthless in that it will shrink neither from its own discoveries nor from conflict with the powers that be" (Marx, *Early Writings*, trans. R. Livingstone and G. Benton [London: Penguin Books, 1992], 207). Marx's late work *Capital* bears the subtitle "Critique of Political Economy."

7. *Grundlinien der Philosophie des Rechts* (1821); English: G. W. F. Hegel, *Elements of the Philosophy of Right*.

8. Jürgen Habermas, *Strukturwandel der Öffentlichkeit: Untersuchungen zu einer Kategorie der bürgerlichen Gesellschaft* (Darmstadt: Luchterhand, 1962); English: *The Structural Transformation of the Public Sphere*, trans. Thomas Burger and Frederick Lawrence (Cambridge, Mass.: MIT Press, 1989).

9. Cf. Franz Böhm in his preface to *Gruppenexperiment*, the published results of a study undertaken by the Institute for Social Research exploring ideologies of various population groups in postwar Germany:

What is it then that produces the shock when reading the present investigation?
I would like to think that it is a double aspect.
First of all the overly clear perception that alongside the so-called "public opinion," which expresses itself in elections, referenda, public speeches, news-

paper articles, radio broadcasts, the platforms of political parties and groups, parliamentary discussions, political meetings, there is also a *non-public opinion*, whose contents can diverge very considerably from the contents of the actual public opinion, whose statements however circulate alongside the statements of the public opinion like the monetary units of a *second currency*— indeed they have perhaps a more fixed and stable rate than the values of actual public opinion, which we flaunt according to propriety in public, especially for the audience abroad, and of which we imagine they represent our own and only currency, as though they expressed what we really mean to say, although after all they are only formal expressions we use when we are wearing our Sunday clothes. Yes, it almost appears as though what circulates about us as public opinion represents the sum of those (mutually contradictory) opinions that we wish people would believe are our true opinions, whereas non-public opinion is about the sum of those (likewise mutually contradictory) opinions that we actually have.

Second, the likewise overly clear perception of what the non-public opinion actually looks like. So that is what many of us actually think!

In other words: the one shock results from the perception that we have *two currencies of opinion*, each encompassing a whole bundle of diverse opinions. And the other shock overcomes us when we look at the values comprising the unofficial opinion.

(Franz Böhm, "Geleitwort," in Gruppenexperiment: Ein Studienbericht, *bearbeitet von Friedrich Pollock, vol. 2 of* Frankfurter Beiträge zur Soziologie *[Frankfurt: Europäische Verlagsanstalt, 1955], here excerpted from pp. xi–xii)*

Cf. also Franz Böhm, "Das Vorurteil als Element totaler Herrschaft," in vol. 17 of *Vorträge gehalten anläßlich der Hessischen Hochschulwochen für staatswissenschaftliche Fortbildung* (Bad Homburg vor der Höhe: Verlag Dr. Max Gehlen, 1957), 149–167.

10. In Germany all universities are public institutions and all professors are state employees.

11. Heinrich von Kleist's novella *Michael Kohlhaas* (1810), in which the eponymous hero, "one of the most virtuous and also most terrifying men of his time," is led by an unredressed grievance and his sense of justice eventually to lead a rebellion against the state.

12. Reference to a collection of essays by Ulrich Sonnemann, *Das Land der unbegrenzten Zumutbarkeiten: Deutsche Reflexionen* (Hamburg: Rowohlt, 1963; Frankfurt: Syndikat Autoren- und Verlagsgesellschaft, 1985). "*Zumutbarkeit*," of juridical provenance, is the quality of something being able to be reasonably expected or presumed of someone (for instance, a higher tax bracket for a higher income). This semantic field trades on the difference between what may reasonably be presumed (*zumutbar*) and what is an unreasonable imposition (*Zumutung*). Through a series of sardonic analyses of contemporary politics and culture, Sonnemann traces the expansion of "presumability" as the cipher of Germans' unbroken obedience to authority. He defines it as:

A category, according to which the interpersonal relations in Germany are organized . . . a Something that first opens up the space for unreasonable impositions. . . . Where it dominates people, the extent of unreasonable impositions cannot be fixed precisely. Indeed the concrete measurements of what can and cannot be reasonably expected never bear their law in themselves; rather, as a true law of inertia, they always follow only the unconscious contingency of the given power relations at the time, these one puts up with like calves put up with the feed trough and the slaughterhouse, and thus these presumabilities [*Zumutbarkeiten*], these purely ontic though still preferably metaphysically disguised traffic rules of the German event [a swipe at Heidegger], are admittedly also with good reason, in the most desperate fashion, *unlimited*: in the absence of anything that is not already based on them and hence whose dimensions are determined by them, what can set them a limit? The presumable is thus above all something expandable; indeed, as a characteristically customary *substitution* for that positive publicity of intra- and interpersonal relations, based on respect and self-respect and upon which in turn the life and the history of free people and their societies are based, the presumable is from the very beginning a negative definition of the perpetually self-renewing fundamental relation in which the German stands to his fellow human beings, and indeed, as will be shown, *to himself.*   (15–16)

13. The "*Spiegel* affair" refers to events in 1962 surrounding the weekly magazine *Der Spiegel* and the conservative minister of defense (and potential chancellor candidate) Franz Josef Strauss. An article drew on leaked classified NATO documents in describing the probable aftermath (ten to fifteen million dead) of a Soviet nuclear attack and an allied counterattack in Germany. The article further documented Germany's defenses as being only "conditionally prepared" and publicized a major disagreement about strategy among the allied powers, Strauss wanting to equip the German army with tactical nuclear weapons and the Americans emphasizing conventional forces. In order to find evidence of the military leak, Strauss bypassed the constitution and ordered an illegal search of *Der Spiegel*'s offices and the arrest of its editor Rudolf Augstein and the article's author Conrad Ahlers on charges of treason. Protests and demonstrations erupted as the entire West German media condemned the antidemocratic shutdown of a free press and likened it to Nazi practices. This in turn led to a party split in the governing coalition; several ministers and eventually Strauss himself were forced to resign.

14. Franz Leonard Schlüter was named by the regional coalition government to the post of minister of culture in Lower Saxony in May 1955. Schlüter, a frustrated patriot (judged by the Nazis unfit for military service because of his Jewish mother) who had failed his doctoral exams and been under investigation for improper conduct as head of the criminal police in Göttingen after the war, had been a vociferous member of the nationalist "German Party of the Right" (Deutsche Rechtspartei) before joining the right wing of liberal Free Democrat Party (FDP) in 1951. At that time he also founded a Göttingen publishing house that printed several works by former Nazi ideologues and functionaries as well as by professors who were forbidden to lecture by denazification strictures. In protest to Schlüter's appointment, the rector of Göttingen university, Prof. Dr. Emil Woermann, and the entire university senate resigned. The Göttingen Student Union, broadly supported by the professors, initiated large-scale student strikes and demonstrations. On 9 June 1955, fifteen days

after assuming the post of minister of culture, Schlüter submitted his resignation and a month later resigned also from the FDP leadership. On the third anniversary of his "fall," Schlüter's publishing house brought out under an anonymous author a three-hundred page book (*Die große Hetze: Der niedersächsische Ministersturz, Ein Tatsachenbericht zum Fall Schlüter* [Göttingen: Göttinger Verlagsanstalt, 1958]) recounting in detail the compromised writings published during the Nazi regime by Woermann and other prominent Göttingen professors.

15. Cf. Lessing's text "The Reviewer Need Not be Able to Do Better That With Which he Finds Fault"; "Der Rezensent braucht nicht besser machen zu können, was er tadelt" in Gotthold Ephraim Lessing, *Sämtliche Schriften,* ed. Karl Lachmann and Franz Muncker (Leipzig: Göschen'sche Verlagshandlung, 1900), 15:62–65.

16. See Gottfried Keller, *Der Grüne Heinrich*, Erste Fassung, ed. Thomas Böning and Gerhard Kaiser, vol. 2 of *Sämtliche Werke* (Frankfurt: Deutscher Klassiker Verlag, 1985):

There is a saying that one must know not just how to tear down but also how to build up, which is used everywhere by good-natured and superficial people when a probing, searching activity or discipline uncomfortably blocks their way. This saying is appropriate where one refuses or negates what one has not personally experienced or thought through; otherwise it is utter nonsense, for one does not always tear down in order to build up again; on the contrary, one pulls down actually deliberately in order to free up some space for the light and fresh air of the world that take their places on their own wherever an obstruction has been removed. When one faces things and deals honestly with them and oneself, there isn't anything negative; rather everything is positive, to use this gingerbread expression, and true philosophy knows no other nihilism than the sin against spirit, that is, insisting on self-righteous nonsense for a selfish or vain purpose. *(679–680)*

17. Cf. Karl Kraus act 1, scene 25, and act 4, scene 29, of *Letzte Tage der Menschheit*; English: *The Last Days of Mankind,* trans. Alexander Gode and Sue Ellen Wright (New York, 1974). Cf. Erich Kästner's short essay, "Eine kleine Sonntagspredigt" [A small Sunday sermon: On the sense and nature of satire] (1947) defending and in part explaining satire in language Adorno would approve of:

[The satirist] is tormented by the need to call things by their rightful name. His method is: exaggerated presentation of negative facts with more or less artistic means for a more or less non-artistic end. And moreover only with regard to man and his organizations, from monogamy to international government. . . .
He hardly understands why people get angry at him. He of course wants people to get angry at *themselves!* He wants them to be ashamed of themselves. To be more clever. More rational. For he believes, at least in his happier moments, that Socrates and all the subsequent moralists and enlightenment thinkers could be right: namely, that man can improve through reasoned insight.
("Eine kleine Sonntagspredigt," in Gesammelte Schriften für Erwachsene *[Zurich: Atrium Verlag, 1969], 7:117–120, here p. 119)*

In the article he quotes in part a poem he wrote years earlier, addressed to queru-lous readers: "And Where is the Positive, Mr. Kästner?" The poem, "Und wo bleibt das Positive, Herr Kästner?" is originally from the collection *Ein man gibt Auskunft* (1930), now in *Gesammelte Schriften für Erwachsene*, 1:218–219.

18. The "destructive instinct" [*Destruktionstrieb*] together with the "aggressive instinct" [*Aggressionstrieb*] are expressions used by the later Freud to define more clearly the biological and psychological dimensions of the "death instinct" (which he introduced in the speculative *Beyond the Pleasure Principle* in 1920) such as it is directed at the external world. See Freud, *The Ego and the Id* (1923) in vol. 19 of *The Standard Edition of the Complete Psychological Works of Sigmund Freud*, trans. James Strachey (London: Hogarth Press,1975).

19. Presumably a reference to Spinoza's proposition "*omnis determinatio est negatio*" (*Epistula* 59) refracted through Hegel's theory of the "speculative proposi-tion." Hegel claimed that Spinoza's proposition, while "of infinite importance," resulted in mere abstract juxtaposition of determination and negation, whereas real-ity contains the negation as potential and hence implies a subsumption [*Aufhebung*] of the determination and its negation at the level of a reflected category. In this way "determinate negation" [*bestimmte Negation*] drives thought and being forward to their ultimate, fully mediated identity. Cf. G. W. F. Hegel, *Wissenschaft der Logik I* and *II*, *Werke* (Frankfurt: Suhrkamp, 1970), 5:121–122; 6:195–198. English: Hegel, *Science of Logic*, trans. A. V. Miller (New York: Humanities Press, 1969), 111–114 and 536–540 respectively.

Resignation

1. Radio version: "In Marx the doctrine of the unity of theory and praxis was inspired by the possibility of action, which even at that time was not actualized but yet was felt to exist."

2. Allusion to Marx's letter to Arnold Ruge, part of the public correspondence between them and Bakunin and Feuerbach, published in the *Deutsch-Französische Jahrbücher* (1844): "If we have no business with the construction of the future or with organizing it for all time there can still be no doubt about the task confronting us at present: I mean the *ruthless critique of everything existing*, ruthless in that it will shrink neither from its own discoveries nor from conflict with the powers that be" (Marx, *Early Writings*, trans. R. Livingstone and G. Benton [London: Penguin Books, 1992], 207).

3. Cf. the first joint publication by Marx and Engels, a satirical polemic against Bruno Bauer and the Young Hegelians: *Die Heilige Familie, oder Kritik der kritis-chen Kritik* (1845); English: *The Holy Family: A Critique of Critical Criticism*, in vol. 4 of *The Collected Works of Karl Marx and Friedrich Engels*, ed. Y. Dakhina and T. Chikileva (New York: International Publishers, 1975).

4. Cf. Jürgen Habermas, "Die Scheinrevolution und ihre Kinder: Sechs Thesen über Taktik, Ziele, und Situationsanalysen der oppositionellen Jugend," *Frankfurter Rundschau*, June 5, 1968, p. 8. In English, cf. Habermas, *Toward a Rational Society: Student Protest, Science, and Politics*, trans. Jeremy Shapiro (Boston: Beacon Press, 1971).

5. Cf. act 3, scene 1, of Schiller's *Wilhelm Tell* (1804):

A man with eyesight clear and sense alert,
Who trusts in God and his own supple strength,
Will find some way to slip the noose of danger.
Mountain-born was never scared of mountains.
(*Having finished his work he puts the tools away.*)
There now! That gate should serve another twelvemonth.
An axe in the house will save a joiner's labor.
(*Reaches for his hat.*)
        (*Johann Christoph Friedrich von Schiller*, Wilhelm Tell, *trans. and ed.*
William F. Mainland [Chicago: University of Chicago Press, 1972], 64–65 [ll.
        ⟨   *1508–1513])*

6. "Instinctual aim" [*Triebziel*] in Freud refers to the activity a sexual drive tends toward in order to release an inner biological or psychological tension. Whereas Freud developed the idea in terms of various stages of infant sexuality closely bound to specific organic sources of instinctual aims in *Drei Abhandlungen zur Sexualtheorie* (1905), in the later *Triebe und Triebschicksale* (1915) he considers more sublimated cases in which the aim can be modified through the influence of object-choice, anaclisis, substitution by the instincts of self-preservation, etc. In *Vorlesungen zur Einführung in die Psychoanalyse* Freud came to see regression [*Regression*] as operative when the libido reverts to an earlier stage in the child's psychosexual development or, as presumably Adorno here implies, to a more primitive, less differentiated form of psychosexual organization, which Freud also often called "fixation."

A relatively constant concept in Freud's economical model of the psyche, the "pleasure principle" [*Lustprinzip*] denotes the strategy of directing psychological activities toward the goal of obtaining pleasure and avoiding its opposite. Several problems arise, such as the pleasure afforded from maintaining a constant tension of psychic energy (the "constancy principle") versus the tendency toward a complete dissipation of energy (the "death drive") and that of the complicity between the pleasure principle and the reality principle for the sake of guaranteeing satisfactions at the expense of the pleasure principle's fundamental (utopian) role in fantasy, dream, and wish-fulfillment, to which Adorno apparently is referring. Cf. Freud, *Jenseits des Lustprinzips* (1920); English: *Beyond the Pleasure Principle*, in *The Standard Edition of the Complete Psychological Works of Sigmund Freud*, trans. James Strachey (London: Hogarth Press, 1973), 18:7–64.

Appendix 1: Discussion of Professor Adorno's Lecture "The Meaning of Working Through the Past"

1. Cf. §143 of G. W. F. Hegel, *Enzyklopädie der philosophischen Wissenschaften I, Werke* (Frankfurt: Suhrkamp, 1970), 8:281–284. English: *The Encyclopedia Logic: Part I the Encyclopedia of Philosophical Sciences, with the Zusätze*, trans. T. F. Geraets, W. A. Suchting, and H. S. Harris (Indianapolis: Hackett, 1991).

2. Eugen Kogon, *Der SS-Staat: Das System der deutschen Konzentrationslager* (Frankfurt: Europäische Verlagsanstalt, 1946); reprinted by various publishers. Eng-

lish: Eugen Kogon, *The Theory and Practice of Hell: The German Concentration Camps and the System Behind them*, trans. Heinz Norden (New York: Berkley, 1950).

3. Adorno refers to the German idiom *ein gebranntes Kind scheut das Feuer* (literally, "a burned child shuns fire"), functionally but not affectively equivalent to the English "once bitten twice shy."

Appendix 2: Introduction to the Lecture "The Meaning of Working Through the Past"

1. Cf. *Gruppenexperiment: Ein Studienbericht*, ed. Friedrich Pollock, vol. 2 of *Frankfurter Beiträge zur Soziologie*, ed. Theodor W. Adorno and Walter Dirks (Frankfurt: Europäische Verlagsanstalt, 1955).

Index